Cross–cultural Management

KW-106-451

ST. HELENS & KNOWSLEY
HEALTH

~~Cowley Hill Lane, ST. HELENS WA10 2AP~~

This book is due for return on or before the last date shown below.

– 2 JAN 2008		

Don Gresswell Ltd., London, N21. Cat. No. 1207

Books in the series

Cross-cultural Management
Terence Jackson

Managing Business Ethics
John Drummond and Bill Bain

Marketing Strategy
Dale Littler and Dominic Wilson

Mission and Business Philosophy
Andrew Campbell and Kiran Tawadey

New Thinking in Organizational Behaviour
Haridimos Tsoukas

Strategic Information Management
R. D. Galliers and B. S. H. Baker

Strategic Issues in Finance
Keith Ward

Strategic Synergy
Andrew Campbell and Kathleen Sommers Luchs

Cross-cultural Management

Edited by Terence Jackson

Butterworth-Heinemann Ltd
Linacre House, Jordan Hill, Oxford OX2 8DP

℞ A member of the Reed Elsevier plc group

OXFORD   LONDON   BOSTON
MUNICH   NEW DELHI   SINGAPORE   SYDNEY
TOKYO   TORONTO   WELLINGTON

First published 1995

© Terence Jackson 1995

All rights reserved. No part of this publication
may be reproduced in any material form (including
photocopying or storing in any medium by electronic
means and whether or not transiently or incidentally
to some other use of this publication) without the
written permission of the copyright holder except
in accordance with the provisions of the Copyright,
Designs and Patents Act 1988 or under the terms of a
licence issued by the Copyright Licensing Agency Ltd,
90 Tottenham Court Road, London, England W1P 9HE.
Applications for the copyright holder's written permission
to reproduce any part of this publication should be addressed
to the publishers.

British Library Cataloguing in Publication Data
Jackson, Terence
  Cross-cultural Management
  I. Title
  658.049

ISBN 0 7506 1933 3

Typeset by Datix International Limited, Bungay, Suffolk
Printed and bound in Great Britain by Clays, St Ives plc

To the memory of my friend David Ward

Contents

Preface

It is becoming increasingly difficult to view management as a parochial occupation, based in one country, with no contact with the wider international community. Even though many managers may not leave the country in order to do business, they often are in contact by telephone to their foreign headquarters, or speaking to overseas suppliers. Even though they might not have to speak a foreign language in order to be understood, they will need to understand the limits of speaking, for example, international English: the difference between what is implied by the speaker and what is inferred by the hearer.

Increasingly, however, people working in business and management are directly in contact with other cultures. Increasingly, they are in face-to-face contact with foreign managers, colleagues or partners. Through international mergers and acquisitions, joint ventures, and through expatriate assignments, managers are having to make adjustments. They may even have to rethink completely their methods of working, and even rethink the nature of the organization within which they work. Management styles, for example, may differ substantially from one European country to another. What might motivate staff in one country may demotivate staff in another.

The problem is that things are not quite as simple as the last statements regarding motivation and management styles. This is because we have national cultural differences which may be sociologically stated in terms of what most people may be like. We also have company cultural differences. IBM may be quite different from DEC working in the same industry (but we also may have industry and professional cultural differences). We have individual psychological differences (personality, for example). But then this is only the start of our difficulties. How do we conceptualize personality, for example, and is this conceptualization appropriate in another national culture? Is the idea of extroversion–introversion (well known in Anglo-American society) appropriate to Japanese culture?

While the current text may not answer all these questions, it certainly raises them. It gives some answers, but above all it tries to put the questions into the international and inter-cultural context. It provides approaches, theories and models. It even offers some empirical data, but with a word of warning: the purpose is not to try to establish national stereotypes, but to try to provide approaches which may be helpful in discerning cultural differences and similarities, and useful in managing across cultures generally.

The aim of this book, therefore, is to provide a good selection of different contributions on cross-cultural behaviour in order to help students of management understand the problems, implications and applications of managing across cultures. Management students are either existing or future practitioners. Readings are therefore included in this volume because of their utility: they have an application to the practice of management.

The book is divided into five parts. Part One is concerned with methodology. This highlights the historical context of the study of management with its origins in the United States, and the move towards internationalism. It looks at the centrality of the study of values in the international context, and provides a basis for understanding national cultural differences. However, the problems of cross-cultural studies are also dealt with in the introduction to Part One, and this provides a starting point for the consideration of the material in this book.

Part Two is about the management of cultural differences, focusing on the concept of organizations, on motivation (including the meaning of work to employees working in different national cultures), on management styles where the long established (western) dichotomy of relationship versus task oriented management is challenged in the international context. Finally, Part Two looks at the important area of managerial values in the context of international business, and touches on a consideration of business ethics.

Part Three then moves on to the issue of cross-cultural interactions. It looks at cross-cultural communication, raising the problems between implication and inference in a cross-cultural interaction. International negotiation is then considered, first within the framework of national culture/company culture/individual character, and then by drawing lessons from Chinese negotiators.

Part Four looks at the process of cultural adaption or acculturation, focusing first on international mergers and acquisitions, and then on expatriation. The bringing together of two cultures is becoming quite a usual experience. The problems of successful adaption or merging of cultures is discussed. Particularly in the case of expatriate assignments, where there is a high failure rate, the implications for successful cultural adaption are looked at.

Finally, Part Five focuses on management learning in the international context. This is examined cross-culturally, and then applications of learning styles to cross-cultural orientation programmes are discussed. This is concluded by looking at management learning in the context of the new Europe.

Terence Jackson

Part One

Methodology

The study of management behaviour across cultures is problematic. While this book is not specifically about methodologies in international management research, it is necessary for the reader of this text to be aware of certain issues which may have a bearing on their understanding of the work reported in the rest of this book. We therefore begin with a look at some of these problems of studying behaviour across cultures, and then provide examples of some of the methodologies employed. Such examples are not restricted to this section alone, as the work reported throughout this text provides numerous examples of different types of methodology.

The problem of parochialism

Management, as an academic subject, is essentially North American in origin, and in many of its assumptions. This alone leads us to consider the problem of ethnocentrism in understanding behaviour across cultures. In the first article Boyacigiller and Adler (1991) take a softer line, providing a critique of what they call American 'parochialism'. They provide the historical context of the problem of parochialism in academic management. They argue that the post-war dominance of the US economy has provided the pre-eminent position of US management theory rather than this theory being pre-eminent *per se*. The assumed universality of North American theory should be questioned in the light of value orientations which do not prevail in other economic areas of the world. Such orientations are:

- *Free will* versus *Determinism* (Kluckholm and Strodbeck, 1961)
- *Individualism* versus *Collectivism* (Hofstede, 1980)
- *Low context* versus *High context* communication (Hall, 1959)

The North American orientations are typified by the first in each of the above dimensions (i.e. free will, individualism and low context communication). These authors make recommendations regarding the future study of management which sets the basis for clearly distinguishing theory which is locally (nationally) applicable, and that which has a universal application. This article also provides a broad-based literature review and is an excellent starting point for considering management behaviour across national cultures.

Values: a central issue in cross-cultural studies

Theories which have gained prominence over the last few decades have concentrated on the sociological study of value orientations in different national cultures, such as those cited above. The prominent theories in this area have been those of Hall (1959, 1960), Hofstede (1980, 1991) and more recently Trompenaar (1993), and the reader is encouraged to refer to these landmark texts. These studies have sought to establish broad classifications of value orientations, such as those in the frequently quoted work of Hofstede (1980) (see also Chapter Five in the current text). These are as follows:

- *Power distance*: the extent to which inequalities among people are seen as normal, running from equal relations being highly valued (low power distance) to inequalities being accepted as normal (high power distance).
- *Uncertainty avoidance*: a preference for structured situations including work rules and regulations (high uncertainty avoidance) to a value placed on unstructured situations and being comfortable with ambiguity and flexibility (low uncertainty avoidance).
- *Individualism*: a tendency to act as individuals (individualism), versus acting as part of a collective or social group (collectivism).
- *Masculinity*: values placed on 'hard' aspects such as assertiveness and competition, and the differences between male and female (masculinity), versus valuing the 'soft' or 'feminine' values of personal relations and caring for others, while playing down the differences between male and female (femininity).

These dimensions have proved useful for a generation of management practicioners and theorists in the West, though based on statistical aggregates they can only provide clues to individual behaviour, rather than prescribing what we might expect when we interact with an individual from a different country.

The centrality of values in the understanding of differences between cultures is fundamental, and the means by which we may investigate values are an essential part of the armoury of cross-cultural researchers. Davis and Rasool (1988) in the second reading, explore a methodology for looking at individual values in different cultures. They discuss the use of a Personal Value Questionnaire (from the work of England, 1975) to focus on values of individuals from different national cultures in order to predict behaviour of those individuals. Dimensions consist of three primary orientations, and a fourth 'mixed' category, as follows:

- *Pragmatic*: behaviour is best predicted by those concepts considered important and successful.
- *Moralistic*: behaviour is best predicted by those concepts considered important and right.
- *Affective*: behaviour is best predicted by those concepts considered important and pleasant.

This study is fairly limited in its scope, but provides the basis of a methodology for cross-cultural research. However, there are problems of relying on an instrument designed in the context of one national culture and used in another. Lonner (1990), for example, points to some of these problems of measuring psychological attributes across cultures including the following, which should be borne in mind when considering using questionnaire methods across cultures.

1 *Familiarity of psychological testing to the cultural group concerned.* Western cultures are fairly familiar with such forms of testing but not so other cultures. Also with self-report questionnaires, some cultures are more conducive to accurate self-report and assessment than other cultures.

2 *The psychological constructs used may not be universally valid.* For example concepts of intelligence, and such well accepted personality concepts in English-speaking countries as extroversion and introversion, may not have relevance or meaning outside these societies.

3 *The basis of comparison may not be equivalent across cultures*, and comparisons may be difficult at the level of social norms. For example, contrast the 'politeness', of asking as many questions as possible of the person's family, as opposed to the 'politeness' of being non-intrusive in a social encounter. Problems may also occur at the level of linguistic translation, for example, in the meaning of 'leader', 'skills' and 'learning', which may not have direct equivalents in other European languages.

4 *Verbal test stimuli may not be appropriate*, or at best give rise to the problems in (3) above. It is assumed that tests purged of verbal stimuli may travel better between cultures, but even non-verbal stimuli are fraught with difficulty as prior experience is known to strongly influence perception. The classic case of this is the

Stanford-Binet Intelligence Scale of 1960 which asked children in the United States to distinguish between pictures of faces and asked the question, 'Which is the prettiest?' with the correct answer being the Nordic Anglo Saxon type rather than the Mexican–southern European or Black type (see Karier, 1971).

Constructing models of cross-cultural behaviour

Models are used in the social sciences in order to simplify reality and thus be better able to understand it. However, while research and knowledge cannot progress other than through developing such conceptual models, they are by necessity restricting in that data is forced into the strictures of these models. That is accepted as a limitation, but may be a serious distortion factor in cross-cultural studies where a model developed in one culture is used to try to understand behaviour in another culture. Perhaps this is inevitable, as research (as indced management practice) is always embedded in one culture, making the objective of cross-cultural research the understanding of one culture by another culture. Thus the early social and cultural anthropologists of Western Europe and the United States went out to investigate African, Polynesian and indigenous American societies, not for the benefit of those 'primitive' societies, but for the benefit of the developed societies from which the anthropologists came.

A distinction long made in social anthropology is that of *emics* and *etics* (from Pike, 1954) in theories or models of cultural reality. The emic viewpoint is that from within the culture, assuming non-universality for this viewpoint, and the etic view is that from outside the culture looking in, often a first approach at looking at an 'alien' culture, and attempting to apply certain supposed universals to that culture. Thus Segall, Dasen, Berry and Poortinga (1990) suggest an approach to cross-cultural research which employs these concepts, using the following steps:

1 Begin research in your own culture (emic, culture A).
2 Transport to the other culture (imposed etic).
3 Discover the other culture (emic, culture B).
4 Compare the two cultures (emic A compared with emic B).
5.1 Comparison is not possible (there is no overlap between emic A and emic B).
5.2 Comparison is possible (there is overlap between emic A and emic B, giving rise to derived etic).

We must of course, be careful of imposing our own cultural assumptions on other cultures, but in order to understand other cultures we must employ the standpoint of our own culture. The next article in this section, by Rieger and Wong-Rieger (1988) looks at model building in cross-cultural research. This paper argues for the use of multiple methods when studying something as complex as cultures. It also argues that rather than taking a theory or hypotheses to an organizational study, there should be more emphasis on hypotheses development through an inductive process. So, while an initial model is used in this study simply to classify countries and the data gathered, the real job of model construction is to be derived from the data itself. The result is a three-dimensional model based on authority distance, power, and risk orientation.

Focusing on individuals not cultures

Information we have about cultures derived from questionnaire research is statistical, that is based not on what one individual in a national culture might be like, but on what most people may be like (within the confines of the dimensions used and the sample surveyed). A simple descriptive framework used by Guy and Mattock (1991) refers to a consideration of *culture*, *company* and *character*, in cross-cultural encounters. This is further developed in Jackson (1993a). These are regarded as 'constants' in the information needed in order to understand the individual with whom you are interacting, as follows:

- *Culture*: the cultural background and upbringing of the foreign colleague will affect the way they make decisions.
- *Company*: a consideration of the organizational or profesional culture is essential for understanding how this differs from yours, and how you might bridge the gap.
- *Character*: the foreign colleague is an individual with individual characteristics of values, motives and moods.

An interesting investigation of cross-cultural negotiation, using this three-tier approach is provided by Kale and Barnes (1992) in Chapter Seven. This employs the national cultural dimensions of Hofstede (1980), organizational dimensions derived from Reynolds (1986), and personality dimensions from Myers–Briggs (Myers and Myers, 1980). This is further discussed in the introduction to Part Three.

The limitations of this approach however are highlighted by Lonner's (1990) suggestions of problems within this area, and outlined above. This would include the relevance of such concepts as introversion–

extroversion in a highly collectivist society where individual orientation may not be so relevant as within a highly individualistic society. The issue, also, of statistical aggregates still exists within this type of methodology. For example, the Myers–Briggs Type Indicator focuses on commonalities of personality, using four dimensions, which provides 16 different types of personality by employing a combination of these dimensions. Across a whole world population, these 16 types do not allow for a great deal of individual difference. At best we can say that it provides clues about the process and orientation towards decision making and interaction. However, the content of individuals' attitudinal and value structures, and the concepts and constructs they use in their perceptions of their world, are largely ignored in favour of establishing broad commonalities.

There is a dearth of research in the area of specific content identification in the cross-cultural arena, and none has been included in this section on methodology. A fruitful area for further research in cross-cultural differences can be found within Personal Construct Psychology (from Kelly, 1955). The current author has begun tentative work in this area, and such an approach has been included in Chapter Five under the title 'Ethics and the art of intuitive management' (Jackson, 1993b), to which the reader is referred.

References

Boyacigiller, N. A. and Adler N. J. (1991) 'The parochial dinosaur: organizational science in the global context', *Academy of Management Review*, Vol. 16, No. 2, 262–90.

Davis, H. J. and Rasool, S. A. (1988) 'Values research and managerial behaviour: implications for devising culturally consistent managerial styles', *Management International Review*, Vol. 28, No. 3, 11–19.

England, G. W. (1975) *The Manager and His Values*, Cambridge, Mass.: Ballinger Publ. Co.

Guy, V. and Mattock, J. (1991) *The New International Manager*, London: Kogan Page.

Hall, E. T. (1959) *The Silent Language*, New York: Doubleday.

Hall, E. T. (1960) 'The silent language in overseas business' *Harvard Business Review*, May–June.

Hofstede, G. (1980) *Cultures Consequences: International Differences In Work-related Values*, Houston: Gulf.

Hofstede, G. (1991) *Cultures and Organizations: Software of the Mind*, London: McGraw-Hill.

Jackson T. (1993a) *Organizational Behaviour in International Management*, Oxford: Butterworth-Heinemann.

Jackson (1993b) 'Ethics and the art of intuitive management', *European Management Journal*, EAP 20th Anniversary edition, 57–65.

Kale, S. H. and Barnes J. W. (1992) 'Understanding the domain of cross-national buyer–seller interactions', *Journal of International Business Studies*, First Quarter, 101–32.

Karier, C. J. (1971), 'Testing for order and control in the corporate liberal state', *Educational Theory*, 22, 2, 154–80.

Kelly, G. A. (1955) *The Psychology of Personal Constructs, Vols 1 and 2*, New York: Norton.

Kluckholn, F. R. and Strodbeck, F. L. (1961) *Variations in value orientations*, Evanston, IL: Row Peterson.

Lonner, W. J. (1990) 'An overview of cross-cultural testing and assessment' in Brislin, R. W. (ed.) *Applied Cross-cultural Psychology*, Newbury Park, CA: Sage.

Myers, I. B. and Myers, P. B. (1980) *Gifts Differing*, Palo Alto, CA: Consulting Psychologists Press.

Pike, K. L. (1954) 'Emic and Etic standpoints for the description of behaviour', in K. L. Pike, *Language in Relation to a Unified Theory of the Structure of Behaviour*, Pt 1, Glendale, CA: Summer Institute of Linguistics, 8–28.

Reynolds, P. D. (1986), 'Organizational culture as related to industry, position and performance: a preliminary report', *Journal of Management Studies*, Vol. 23, No. 3, 33–45.

Rieger, F. and Wong-Rieger, D. (1988) 'Model building in organizational/cross-cultural research: the need for multiple methods, indices, and cultures', *International Studies of Management and Organization*, Vol. 18, No. 3, 19–30.

Segall, M. H., Dasen, P. R., Berry, J. W. and Poortinga, Y. H. (1990), *Human Behaviour in Global Perspective: An Introduction to Cross-cultural Psychology*, New York: Pergamon.

Trompenaars, F. (1993) *Riding The Waves of Culture*, London: Nicholas Brealey.

1 Methodological considerations in studying cross-cultural management behaviour

1.1 The parochial dinosaur: organizational science in a global context

Nakiye Avdan Boyacigiller and Nancy J. Adler

> Its [culture's] influence for organizational behavior is that it operates at such a deep level that people are not aware of its influences. It results in unexamined patterns of thought that seem so natural that most theorists of social behavior fail to take them into account. As a result, many aspects of organizational theories produced in one culture may be inadequate in other cultures. (Triandis, 1983: 139)

Global business has become a reality. Macro and micro economic statistics daily etch that reality into the decision patterns of political and corporate leaders. Yet the American academic management tradition appears to have fallen behind. Does the creation and dissemination of management knowledge now lag behind economic reality?

Many leaders of the Academy of Management have sounded the international clarion. As president, Richard Steers focused the 1987 National Academy of Management's attention on the international dimensions of management (Steers, 1987, 1989). In 1988, president Don Hellriegel presented internationalization as one of the Academy's four main challenges. Steven Kerr, 1990 president, presided over discussions to join an international federation of academies of management. Similarly, Eastern Academy of Management president Carolyn Dexter moved her region's biannual meetings overseas, arguing that the Academy can no longer remain within the conceptual or geographical borders of the United States. The Western Academy of Management followed suit by convening its unique 1990 meeting in Japan.

This article investigates the global context of management research, education, and theory development in the United States from three perspectives: contextual, quantitative, and qualitative. First, from a contextual perspective, it reviews changes in the external environment that potentially impact academic management, including inherent influences that have resulted from its being a post-World War II, American-based profession. Second, from a quantitative perspective, it reviews the publication of international articles in U.S. management journals, along with American scholars' preparation to conduct such research. Third, and perhaps most important, it reviews a selection of management theories from a qualitative perspective. Although many differences exist between domestic and global management (including myriad issues involving scale, scope, and complexity), given the limits of a single article, we focus on the cultural assumptions that underlie and often frame management research as well as the implicit universalism inherent in much of organizational science.

Parochialism is based on ignorance of others' ways. Ethnocentrism judges foreign ways as inferior to one's own. This article does not criticize American-made organizational science for being ethnocentric. It does not suggest that the main problem is that American theorists view American theories as superior to others' theories. Rather, based on the multiple observations presented, one of our primary conclusions is that of parochialism. Americans have developed theories without being sufficiently aware of non-U.S. contexts, models, research, and values. Our goal, however, is not to extend made-in-America organizational science beyond its current geographical boundaries, but rather to strengthen it by suggesting fundamental changes in how scholars can think about and create theories. The purpose of this article, therefore, is not to castigate the field, its pioneers, or its present leaders; rather, by drawing attention to the forces promulgating parochialism, it reconceptualizes the field's roots and thereby facilitates the creation of a more relevant future. Although the indictments in this article are at times strong, they are attempts to avoid relegating the American academic management tradition to the curiosity of a mid-twentieth-century fossil.

Contextual parochialism

Industrial competitiveness: the view since World War II

In critical reviews of the field, Lawrence (1987) and Pfeffer (1982) underscored the importance of appreciating social context and its influence on theory development. They indicated that the questions organizational theorists have deemed most interesting to study have been a function of managers' concerns and, thus, *a product of time*. Similarly, such scholars as Kuhn (1962), Merton (1968), and Whitley (1984), among others, suggested that the social system of scientists and the environment of scientific activity constrain knowledge production (Graham and Gronhaug, 1989). According to Merton (1968: 539):

Social organization of intellectual activity is significantly related to the character of the knowledge which develops under its auspices. . . . Increasingly, it has been assumed that the social structure does not influence science merely by focusing the attention of scientists upon certain problems for research . . . [but also in] the ways in which the cultural and social context enters into the conceptual phrasing of scientific problems.

What is the sociocultural context of academic management? Most management schools and academic management journals are American. They, along with the Academy of Management, grew up as distinctly American institutions in a particular geographical, cultural, and temporal context – that of post-World War II United States. Although the Academy of Management is over 50 years old, two of the most prestigious management journals, *Administrative Science Quarterly* and the *Academy of Management Journal*, were established in 1956 and 1958, respectively, as Whitley (1988: 47) accurately described (based on Gordon and Howell, 1959; Pierson *et al.*, 1959: Smiddy and Naum, 1954; Whitley and England, 1977):

The encouragement of systematic research into managerial problems and business behavior in the 1950s was based on the widespread belief in the United States at the time that scientific knowledge could provide the foundation for improved managerial decision making and upgrade the quality of business education.

Thus, as William Ouchi presented in his 1990 Western Academy of Management keynote address, management knowledge began to be codified during a particular period of American history. To understand the strengths and limitations of that knowledge base, it is incumbent to understand both its particular historical context as well as the current economic situation.

The United States emerged from World War II as the only major, economically developed nation with its industrial sector unscathed. Immediately following World War II, the United States accounted for 75 percent of the world's GNP (Thurow, 1988). For the next two decades, U.S. multinational corporations dominated world trade. During this period of the United States' postwar economic dominance, American researchers focused on American firms, American perspectives, and those questions most salient to American managers, rather than systematically including either non-U.S. sites or issues. In this context, it was easy for researchers – including non-U.S. researchers (Servan-Schreiber, 1968) – to assume implicitly that American theories also dominated. We could argue that the field was imprinted with a U.S. orientation (Stinchcombe, 1965). Beechler and Pucik (1989), for example, noted that the Japanese imported American managerial theories primarily during periods of U.S. economic and organizational dominance. Similarly, consulting firms, such as McKinsey and Company, grew rapidly following World War II and actively exported both the structural and process solutions they used for U.S. industry (Blackford, 1988: 124). Today, the United States produces less than one quarter (22%) of the world's GNP. Along with the United States decline in the global economy, the need to question the previously assumed universality of U.S. theories has become apparent.

Even though some academics and managers believe that American managerial know-how created U.S. economic success – and concomitantly, that Americans must now look to their management systems to regain economic superiority – Thurow (1984, 1988) contends that America was never competitive, but rather, had effortless economic superiority. Ouchi (1984) concurs, describing U.S. corporations during the postwar period as earning monopoly profits and their workers as earning monopoly wages: this was not due to the superiority of American management techniques, but rather it was primarily due to the lack of significant foreign competition. Recognizing the presence today of vigorous foreign competition, Ouchi (1984) predicts that Americans will never again earn the monopoly profits and wages that characterized the decades immediately following World War II. Both Thurow's and Ouchi's arguments suggest an attribution error: the economic success of the United States has been attributed, in part, to Americans' conception of management (a collective internal attribution) rather than to the relative lack of competition (an external attribution).

In the 1990s, American industry faces becoming just another, albeit important, region of the globe. Though corporate and academic performance are certainly not identical, perhaps the time has come for American management professors and faculties to embrace a similar fate. Moreover, perhaps the particular American heritage that facilitated the field's inception and its initial development now hinders its future contributions. To understand better these dynamics, the central institution of American academic management, the Academy of Management, is examined.

The Academy of Management: a global perspective

As mentioned, post-World War II economic conditions played a determining role in the way business approached developing, manufacturing, and marketing products and services. In 1966, Vernon proposed a simple, yet widely used, three-phase model for understanding firms' development based on the product life cycle (see also Vernon, 1971). Adding a fourth phase to capture the complexities of today's highly competitive global environment, these phases could be labeled domestic, international, multinational, and global (Adler and Ghadar, 1990). Although the expanded model outlines key aspects of the evolution of multinational enterprises, the four phases also suggest some dimensions for understanding the evolution of American academic management theory, education, and institutions during the same period. Many attributes characterize the four phases, but a few are particularly salient in helping scholars to understand their industry, that is, the creation and dissemination of management knowledge.

The model, in brief, suggests that in the first phase (domestic), firms focus on developing and producing unique new products in and for the domestic market. To a substantial extent, these firms ignore the world outside of their own borders. During the second phase (international), firms focus on marketing. They expand their markets internationally: first by exporting their domestically produced products, next by assembling the products abroad, and finally by producing these products abroad. Using a multidomestic strategy, these firms assess each foreign country separately for its market potential. Because international activities constitute a small and generally less important portion of a firm's overall operations, it commonly relegates the management of such activities to a separate international division. By the third phase (multinational), firms face a much more competitive multinational environment. They therefore emphasize price, that is, developing least-cost production systems by using factor sourcing, production, and distribution that are integrated worldwide. At the third phase, firms frequently organize their substantially larger multinational operations into highly integrated, global lines of business. With the growing importance of economies of scale and scope during this phase, standardization becomes all-important. By the fourth phase (global), firms must operate globally as top-quality, least-cost, state-of-the-art producers and distributors to survive. Strategically and structurally, they must develop flexible systems that are globally coordinated and integrated while remaining highly differentiated and nationally responsive (Bartlett, Doz and Hedlund, 1990; Bartlett and Ghoshal, 1989: Porter, 1980; Prahalad and Doz, 1987).

Where does the Academy of Management fit when viewed from the evolutionary perspective of this four-phase model? First, scholars produce and disseminate the majority of organizational science research within the United States (Phase I – domestic). Second, the scope and primary orientation of most theories is American; however, such theories are presented as if they were universally applicable. For example, researchers conduct studies on the job satisfaction of American men and yet use the results to develop and substantiate overall theories on job satisfaction. A few scholars then test these U.S. job satisfaction theories to see if they apply abroad (Slocum and Topichak, 1972). The former is a Phase I approach (producing for the home market), while the latter is a Phase 2 approach (i.e., attempting to extend the 'market' for U.S. theories abroad). Third, the dominant nationality of the Academy is American. Its leaders, journal editors, and editorial board members are not drawn from scholars worldwide, but rather are predominantly Americans. Fourth, and as most junior scholars at leading U.S. universities know, researchers must publish in top American journals. Publication in non-U.S. journals (and, to a lesser extent, U.S. journals focusing on international topics) is considered suspect, that is, suspect of being inferior (a Phase I assumption). Fifth, international research, rather than being integrated throughout the Academy, constitutes a separate – and in the past, sometimes disparaged – division. The Academy thus echoes the structural dynamics of Phase 2 firms: it too has an international division that is kept organizationally distinct from the mainstream core of the organization. Curiously, because the International Division has been labeled as a separate division, the Academy's Management History, Organization Theory, and Organization Behavior Divisions implicitly become domestic divisions posturing as 'universal divisions.' Illogical as it seems (except through Phase 2 lenses), at present, international is a subdivision of domestic. Based on these five examples, as well as many similar observations, the Academy currently appears to combine primarily aspects of domestic and international organizations, while exhibiting few multinational or global characteristics.

Given the dramatic shifts in the external economic environment, we recommend that the Academy consider new, more global structures and processes (the final section of this article lists specific recommendations). Although the precise format for 'going global' is not important, the result – moving from Phase 1 and 2 structures to those of Phases 3 and 4 – is critically important to the future relevance and potential contribution of American academic management.

Quantitative parochialism

Having briefly reviewed the global context, we can now focus directly on the issues addressed and the research produced within that context. Today, between 15 and 30 of the world's 185 countries possess most of its scientific knowledge, while representing less than one third of its population (von Alleman, 1974). If most science is practiced in fewer than 30 countries, all social science is practiced in fewer still, and all organizational science in still fewer (Roberts and Boyacigiller, 1984: 425). The vast majority of management schools are in the United States. The majority of management professors and researchers are American trained. Moreover, as previously mentioned, the vast majority of management research focuses on the United States (see Gergen, 1973, for similar trends in social psychological theory). Lawrence (1987: 2–3) cited 30 key contributions in the development of organizational science, only 5 of which were contributed by non-Americans (6 if Kurt Lewin is included). Additionally, all five of the non-U.S. researchers are European; none are from outside of the occidental tradition (see Adler, Doktor and Redding, 1986).

Academic institutions (management schools included) produced and disseminate knowledge. The following section reviews the record of American management schools in producing internationally educated managers and professors, as well as the record of those professors in producing internationally focused research.

Management schools

Several studies have recommended improving the international business education offered to U.S. college graduates in order to improve the performance of American executives working abroad (American Association of School Administrators, 1983; National Advisory Board on Education Programs, 1983; President's Commission on Industrial Competitiveness, 1985; Porter and McKibben, 1988). In 1974, the American Assembly of Collegiate Schools of Business (AACSB) changed its accreditation standards to include a worldwide dimension in the curriculum. By 1979, the AACSB approved an interpretation of that standard, saying, 'Every student should be exposed to the international dimension in the curriculum' (Nehrt, 1987). Yet, in 1984, over 20 percent of the AACSB schools' MBA programs had done nothing to internationalize their curricula (Nehrt, 1987). Moreover, at the 1989 global INTERMAN Conference, the only worldwide meeting for management school deans, only 10 deans from the more than 700 American management schools attended, fewer than the number attending from the People's Republic of China. Perhaps even more serious, only 17 percent of the doctoral students had taken an intenational course: that is, less than one doctoral student in five was prepared in any way to teach the international dimensions of their discipline (Nehrt, 1987).

Similarly, 'fewer than half of all colleges and universities now require foreign language study for the bachelor's degree, down from nearly 90% in 1966' (Bowen, 1984: 91), with most doctoral programs counting a computer language as sufficient to meet the foreign language requirement. In the most recent AACSB survey (Thanopoulos, 1986), schools were not even asked if they offered an international organizational behavior course or if they included an international dimension to their regularly required organizational behavior courses (Thanopoulos and Vernon, 1987). Even though the AACSB (1988–1989: 28) now directs business schools to 'provide for a broad education preparing the student for imaginative and responsible citizenship and leadership roles in business and society – domestic and worldwide,' there is little indication that U.S. business schools are currently able to fulfill the 'worldwide' part of their mandate. Given this pattern, it is not surprising that Kobrin (1984) found that most American managers still acquire their international expertise through business experience and not in management seminars and courses.

Management research

In a survey of 24 journals during the decade 1971 to 1980, Adler (1983) found that less than 5 percent (4.2%) of the organizational behavior articles published in top American management journals focused on cross-cultural or international issues. Of those with a cross-cultural focus, the majority were unicultural, single-country studies (1.9%). Less than 2 percent (1.4%) compared two or more cultures, and less than 1 percent (0.9%) investigated the interaction among people from different cultures, even though interaction is the essence of most international business transactions. Adler (1983) found no increase in the number or proportion of international organizational behavior articles over the decade.

Two studies replicated Adler's results and found no significant increase in the number of cross-cultural organizational behavior articles (Godkin Braye and Caunch, 1989a: Peng, Peterson and Shyi, 1990); this despite the continued commitment of such journals as the *Journal of International Business Studies*, the *Columbia Journal of World Business*, and the newer *Organization Studies, Strategic Management Journal*, and *California Management Review* to publish top-quality international management research. This is neither an impressive showing nor a particularly favorable harbinger. Godkin and his colleagues (1989b: 9) concluded that:

> While global economic interdependence has increased and accredited business schools have been required to internationalize their curricula, publication in the field of cross-cultural management seems to lag as in the late 70's. This is a regrettable, but seemingly continuing trend. The dangers inherent in remaining ignorant of our neighbors are disturbing: the ramifications of competing in ignorance more so. The bliss proverbially associated with ignorance and the arrogance accompanying it have a down side.

Why is there such a paucity of international research in organizational science? As described previously, doctoral programs fail in training researchers both to understand international issues and to develop the tools, such as foreign language skills, to conduct such research. Moreover, even if prepared, international research is more difficult to conduct than its domestic counterpart, given the complexity of the multinational environment and the higher monetary and time costs involved in multicountry studies (Adler, 1984; Wind and Perlmutter, 1973: 131). In addition, Graham and Gronhaug (1989) contrasted the lack of fit between the domestic U.S. emphasis on rigorous quantitative methods and internal validity, with the nature of international studies which, by definition, tend to be contextual and therefore demand approaches incorporating high levels of external validity (see Adler, Campbell and Laurent's (1989) description of the challenges involved in collecting valid survey data in a politically repressive environment). To ignore or to minimize external validity is to assume that theories apply irrespective of context, that is, that they apply under any political, economic, cultural, legal, or historical situation. The general acceptance of laboratory studies in American social science exemplifies this acceptance of context-free methodologies.

Unfortunately, there has been no systematic study of the international aspects of the review process to determine if international research, once produced, gets published. However, as mentioned previously, the preponderance of American journal editors, the paucity of foreign editorial board members, and the lack of recognition of foreign sources is striking. As Whitley (1984: 27–28 recognized:

> A major manifestation of the way reputational control limits the originality of contributions to collective intellectual goals is the necessity of referring to the previous work of colleagues. While this may be necessary to avoid prolix redundances in the text, it is also a way of exerting social control over novel ideas. . . . In a sense, citations are a way of ritualistically affirming group goals and norms, of demonstrating group membership and identity.

Given that few international articles have been published and that articles published in foreign journals are of suspect quality by many American editorial boards, international researchers are hard pressed to 'ritualistically affirm group membership', that is, to cite a sufficient number of relevant articles published in leading American journals to pass the test of 'building on prior research' (Graham and Gronhaug, 1989). Arndt (1985: 19) attested to the difficulties of breaking the American-based, logical empiricist mold (in marketing, although the same is certainly true for organizational science): 'In our enlightened age, the dissident . . . scientist is not burned at the stake. Instead, he or she is rather likely to suffer the slow burnout of never emerging from the journals' revision purgatories.' Graham and Gronhaug's (1989) accurate, and yet discouraging, conclusion is that research methods are driving knowledge production rather than the problems and needs of managers, policy makers, and students.

Qualitative parochialism

> The concepts of the field are seldom value-free and most could be replaced with other concepts carrying far different valuational baggage . . . if our values were otherwise, social conformity could be viewed as pro-solidarity behavior; attitude change as cognitive adaptation; and the risky shift as the courageous conversion. . . . Perhaps our best option is to maintain as much sensitivity as possible to our biases and to communicate them as openly as possible. (Gergen, 1973: 312)

Assumptions about underlying values would be unimportant if either organizational theories were based on universal values or values did not have an impact on organizational behavior (Gonzalez and MacMillan 1961). Neither supposition is tenable given the research substantiating the cultural diversity of values and the impact of such diversity on organizational behavior (e.g. England, 1975: Hofstede, 1980; Keller and Worthley, 1981; Lane and DiStefano, 1988; Laurent, 1981; Moore, 1974; Oberg, 1963). Child, 1981: 347–348) summarized diversity's impact on micro organizational behavior:

> Cultural effects will be most powerful in the process of organizations relating to authority, style, conduct, participation, and attitudes, and less powerful in formal structuring and overall strategy. However, we will require a more adequate theory of organizations which specified the points at which contingency, culture and the system of economic relationships have their main effects.

Even though values and cultural assumptions profoundly influence micro organizational behavior, they equally clearly influence macro organization theory. For example, Laurent (1983: 75–76) described his difficulty explaining matrix management to French managers:

> The idea of reporting to two bosses was so alien to these managers that mere consideration of such organizing principles was an impossible, useless exercise. What was needed first was a thorough examination and probing of the holy principle of the single chain of command and the managers' recognition that this was a strong element of their own belief system rather than a constant element in nature.

Not surprisingly, Lawrence (1987) credited European researchers (with their more sociological orientation and therefore keen interest in size, technology, structure, and contingency theory) with being the impetus behind the development of the macro side of the field.

Organizational theorists appear to be victims of an attribution error. As described by Jones and Nisbett (1971), the fundamental attribution error posits that individuals are prone to view the behavior of others as determined by their individual characteristics and motivations rather than by characteristics of the environment. Similar to other individuals, organizational theorists seem to have underestimated the extent to which their perceptions and interpretations, and consequently their building of organizational theory, are influenced by the external cultural environment. Cultural biases keep scholars from seeing the full range and diversity of organizational phenomena. For example, in reviewing contributions by leading European scholars, Hofstede (1981: 32) found remarkable differences in focus according to the particular researcher's background: 'Authors from Latin Europe, focus on power, from Central Europe, including Germany, on truth: from Eastern Europe, on efficiency; from Northern Europe, on change' (also see Hofstede and Kassem, 1976; Lammers, 1990). Laurent (1983) used British scholars' focus on structure as contrasted with their French counterparts' focus on power to exemplify the same point. Similarly, Roberts and Boyacigiller (1983), in a survey of cross-national researchers, also found national patterns in research emphasis.

Assumed universality and organizational theory

Although important, recognizing culture's profound influence on the development of theories is difficult (Triandis, 1972). If culture is invisible, one's own culture is most invisible (Hall, 1959). As Boulding (1961: 16) eloquently summarized over 25 years ago:

> The development of images is part of the culture or the subculture in which they are developed, and it depends upon all elements of that culture or subculture. Science is a subculture among subcultures. It can claim to be useful. It can claim rather more dubiously to be good. It cannot claim to give validity.

Like all nations, the United States has deeply embedded values that influence the ways in which Americans perceive and think about the world as well as the ways in which they behave within that world. Most American theories, however, have been developed and presented as if they were cultural. Yet, as Berger and Luckman (1966) argued in *The Social Construction of Reality*, acultural perception, observation, interpretation, and theory building have yet to be proven to exist.

As has been noted, most organization theories were 'made-in-the-USA' and, therefore, were influenced by the political, economic, and cultural context of the United States. Yet, few researchers have explicitly addressed the influence of American values on U.S.-based organizational science (Adler, 1986; Adler and Jelinek, 1986; Burrell and Morgan, 1979; Hofstede, 1980; Newman, 1972). Rather, most organization theories appear implicitly to assume universality (see Hofstede and Bond, 1988; Lammers and Hickson, 1979, Osigweh, 1989a,b; Smith and Peterson, 1988, for notable exceptions). Even when the applicability of these theories to other cultures is tested, researchers usually select methods that are most acceptable according to American norms, thereby rendering results that are just as culturally conditioned (see Morey and Luthans, 1984; Sekaran, 1983, for exceptions).

Though cultural values potentially have an impact on a range of micro and macro organizational phenomena, the scope of this article limits the number of examples we might cite. The following section offers examples of particularly powerful cultural influences. Because a number of models for examining value orientations are well regarded and increasingly widely used in the field, rather than limiting ourselves to one model, we have chosen examples from three: Kluckhohn and Strodbeck (1961), Hofstede (1980), and Hall (1959). The selected examples demonstrate how U.S. values regarding free will, individualism, and a low-context orientation profoundly affect how the field conceptualizes organizational behavior. The selected examples neither represent all value differences nor the complete range of their impact on organizations and management.

Free will versus determinism: orientations toward power and efficacy

A prevailing American cultural belief is that individuals can affect their immediate circumstances, are responsible for their actions, and can influence future events (Stewart, 1972). Americans generally see themselves as capable of controlling their own circumstances and, to a substantial degree, their environment:

> While recognizing the influence of both nature and nurture. Americans rarely see themselves as ultimately constrained by their biological or psychological inheritance, their childhood socialization, or even their prior experience. Instead, they see themselves as infinitely capable of self-change, as evident from the number of self-help books lining the shelves of popular American bookstores.
> (Adler and Jelinek, 1986: 82)

Similarly, the huge amount ($210 billion) spent annually in the United States on work-related training (American Society for Training and Development, 1989) reflects Americans' confidence in adult learning and, therefore, the possibility of directed change.

By contrast, many other cultures traditionally see causality as determined by factors beyond their control, factors such as God, fate, luck, government, one's social class, or history. Most fundamentalist Moslems, for example, see life as following a path preordained by the will of God (e.g., Harns and Moran, 1979: 46). Similarly, the Chinese invoke 'Joss,' a combination of luck and fate, to explain events. These more deterministic cultures generally define accountability and responsibility more diffusely than cultures that rely on free will. In deterministic cultures, people cannot assume responsibility for many events because such events are perceived as occurring outside of their control. Perhaps the essentially stable, post-World War II economic, political, social, and legal environment in the United States made it particularly easy for American managers and management theorists to emphasize free will and, thus, personal efficacy and control. For instance, because Americans have not had to contend with major changes or radical breakdown in their legal system, they generally trust the enforceability of contracts. Similarly, because coups, military or otherwise, have not altered the political dynamics of the United States, Americans can reliably predict an environmental stability that is absent in many other parts of the world.

Americans' emphasis on free will and their related belief that people can control and dominate the environment (Kluckhohn and Strodbeck, 1961) profoundly influence their view of organizational design and change (Galbraith, 1973; Miles and Snow, 1978). Most commonly today through organizational culture and leadership models and metaphors, American theorists describe organizations as malleable; that is, given the appropriate intervention, managers can change organizations to create a better alignment with the environment. Similarly, American theorists conceptualize managers as having sufficient power to influence the environment, thus ensuring the continued flow of critical resources (Pfeffer and Salancik, 1978).

By contrast, Kiggundu (1988: 182) notes that in Africa, similar to many other economically developing areas of the world, because of the asymmetrical relationship between the organization and its relevant environment, managing interdependencies with the external environment is much more problematic than it is in the United States. In such cultures, neither the organization as a whole nor the individual manager can strongly influence organizational outcomes.

External environmental determinism is not irrelevant for Americans. It simply fails to have the pronounced, irrefutable relevance that it has for many other cultures. Americans, for instance, used the oil crisis (an external factor perceived to be beyond their control) to explain the U.S. dollar's high value in 1974. Similarly today, in referring to Japanese protectionist legislation. Americans accept a limited determinism in explaining some of their difficulties in resolving the U.S. trade deficit. From the perspective of organizational science, the problem is that most theories fail to sufficiently emphasize external environmental factors in general, or to include such cultural variants as determinism in particular.

Individualism and collectivism: orientations toward motivation and commitment

> In what cultural and historical context does the greatest good involve being able to break apart from one's collective base to stand alone, self-sufficient and self-contained? In the context of an individualistic society in which individualism and self-containment is the ideal, the person who most separates self from the group is thereby seen as embodying that ideal most strongly: the person who remains wedded to a group is not our [American] esteemed ideal. (Sampson, 1977: 776)

Hofstede's (1980) research investigating dominant cultural values ranks the United States highest on individualism among his 40-country sample. When this research was extended to over 50 countries, the United States still maintained its first-place position on individualism (Hofstede, 1983). Americans define themselves using personal characteristics and achievements rather than their place within a group or collectivity. Note, for example, the U.S. selection practice of using résumés listing personal achievements rather than hiring relatives, which is pejoratively labeled as nepotism. Sampson (1977:769) summarized this issue: 'Our [American] culture emphasizes individuality, in particular a kind of individual self-sufficiency that describes an extreme of the individualistic dimension.'

Many organizational theories reflect this individualist bias. Allen, Miller, and Nath (1988) note that in countries where individualism dominates, individuals view their relationship with the organization from a calculative perspective, whereas in collectivist societies, the ties between the individual and organization have a moral component. Clearly, the concept of organizational commitment (e.g. Staw, 1980) carries very different connotations in collectivist societies than in individualistic societies. Employees who have collectivist values commit to organizations primarily due to their ties with managers, owners, co-workers (collectivism), and much less due to the job itself or the particular compensation scheme (individualistic incentives). Consonant with its individualistic orientation, the United States has the most executive search firms and one of the highest levels of managerial mobility in the world. It is therefore not surprising, and yet highly unfortunate, that American theoretical structures fail to include a full range of explanations for organizational commitment and the lack thereof (see Earley, 1989, for a notable exception).

Similarly, most American theories of motivation reflect a decidedly individualistic perspective. In a review of the motivation literature, Staw (1984: 650–651) states that 'whether the driving force is thought to be prior reinforcement, need fulfillment, or expectancies of future gain, he individual is assumed to be a rational maximizer of personal utility.' Staw (1984: 651) questions how this individual/calculative view of motivation applies across cultures, suggesting that it 'could be a fundamental omission in our motivation theories.' Equity theory provides a case in point. According to Sampson (1977: 777), social psychologists continue to search within the psychology of the individual to explain demands for personal equity, rather than within the group or collectivity for less-individualistic explanations. What would our theories of motivation look like if theorists viewed the individual as part of a tightly bound social fabric? What would they look like in a country with more than a quarter of the population unemployed (e.g., in many parts of Africa)? How would our theories explain motivation if scholars viewed jobs as critical not only for the individual's well-being but also for the well-being of the extended family? What would a motivation theory look like in countries where the government assigns people to jobs, rather than allowing individuals to exercise free choice (e.g. for workers in the People's Republic of China)?

Miller and Grush (1988: 119) argued that the popularity of expectancy theory can be explained by 'the logical appeal of its underlying assumption that the perceived consequences of actions rationally determine human behavior,' and 'that conceptual advances can be made in expectancy theory by including additional variables or by identifying the theory's limiting conditions.' Cross-culturally based research would facilitate theory development by suggesting additional variables as well as identifying such limiting conditions. The importance of *biaoxian* in evaluating Chinese workers exemplifies this point. *Biaoxian* means:

to manifest something that is an expression of a deeper, hidden quality ... the term applies to the broad and *vaguely* defined realm of behavior that is subject to leadership evaluation ... behavior that indicates underlying attitudes and orientations worthy of reward. (Walder, 1983: 60–61, emphasis added)

Incorporating this view and, in particular the vagueness of its measurement, becomes highly problematic for expectancy theory.

The extreme individualism of the U.S. culture also influences leadership theories (see Bass, 1981, for a cross-cultural review). Smith and Peterson (1988: 97) noted that 'the particular uniqueness of the USA should alert us to the possibility that the individualistic nature of much American-derived leadership theory is a facet of U.S. culture, rather than a firm base upon which to build leadership theories of universal applicability.' For example, although charismatic leadership is valued and studied today by Americans (e.g. Conger, 1989), it is disparaged by Germans.

High- and low-context cultures: orientation toward communication and understanding

A high-context communication or message is one in which most of the information is either in the physical context or internalized in the person, while very
little is in the coded, explicitly transmitted part of the message. ... A low-
context communication is just the opposite; i.e. the mass of information is vested
in the explicit code. ... Although no culture exists exclusively at one end of the
scale, some are high while others are low. (Hall, 1981/1976: 91)

In high-context cultures, the external environment, situation, and non-verbal behavior are crucial for understanding communication. By contrast, in low-context cultures, a much greater portion of the meaning in a given communication comes from the spoken word. In languages spoken in high-context cultures, such as Japanese, Arabic, and Chinese, subtlety is valued. Much of the meaning of messages is derived from the paralanguage, facial expressions, setting, and timing. Alternatively, in low-context cultures, the literal words chosen convey much more of the meaning. The relatively low-context orientation of the United States is evident in Americans' emphasis on written legal documents, whereas many other cultures put more faith in face-to-face personal agreement. In many cultures, the relationship, not the legal document, binds the agreement. Given this orientation, it is not surprising that the United States has the most lawyers per capita in the world: 279 lawyers per 100,000 population, as compared with 114 in the United Kingdom, 77 in West Germany, 29 in France, and 11 in Japan (Council on Competitiveness, 1988: 3). Americans' low-context orientation also underlies their concept of separation, for example, separation of church and state, employees' societal status from their organizational status, and managers' cultural conditioning from their expected behavior at work.

The low-context orientation of the United States (and also England) may explain the minimal emphasis organizational theory historically has placed on such contextual factors as history, social setting, culture, and government. Thus, for the future development of the field, one benefit from scholars' current interest in Japan lies in Japan's high-context culture. Japanese organizational phenomena cannot be understood without using a contextual, institutional framework. Scholars understand Japanese employees only when they understand the organizations and society in which these employees are embedded, including the network of relationships among Japanese government and business organizations (e.g. Gerlach, 1987; Lincoln and McBride, 1987; Ohmae, 1987). The contextual, historical, and institutional approaches necessary to explain Japanese organizational behavior undoubtedly are enriching the study of organizations worldwide.

How would organizational researchers incorporate massive environmental and political change into models of motivation, leadership, and organization structure? Carroll, Delacroix and Goodstein (1988: 360) note that:

> Although foundations of organizational theory lie within political sociology, current perspectives on organizations show little of this heritage. . . . Curiously, the major intellectual leap from closed to open systems models of organizations has coincided with the de facto dismissal of many of the political issues that concerned many of the early theorists such as Michels (1949), Selznick (1949), and Gouldner (1954).

At the ecological level, Carroll and his colleagues found that political variables had a significant impact, for example, on organizational founding and death rates (Carroll and Delacroix, 1982; Carroll and Huo, 1986; Delacroix and Carroll, 1983). Similarly, at the individual level, ignoring what the 1997 return of Hong Kong to the People's Republic of China means to the Chinese in Hong Kong or what the 1989 violence in Beijing means to the Chinese in the People's Republic of China relative to their work motivation and commitment trivializes any theory's explanatory power.

Together, these three cultural characteristics – free will, individualism, and low-context orientation – also explain much of the emphasis that organizational science places on managers. All three characteristics foster the view that managers have a high degree of discretion and much influence over their organizations. However, surprisingly few empirical studies have tested the actual impact of managerial actions (Lieberson and O'Connor, 1972; Thomas, 1988). Despite the spirited debate in some quarters over the influence of managerial behavior on organizational outcomes (Aldrich, McKelvey and Ulrich, 1984; Child, 1972), much of organizational science is based on the assumption that managerial behavior makes a difference. The blatancy of this assumption belies the existence of deeply held cultural values.

Important theories exist embodying cultural values other than those discussed above; one example is institutional theory. However, the current interest in institutional theories of organization (DiMaggio and Powell, 1983; Meyer and Rowan, 1977; Meyer and Scott, 1983; Scott, 1987; Zucker, 1988) does not mitigate the fact that since Selznick's classic 1949 work, organizational science has reflected primarily the American cultural values of rationality and free will (see Stinchcombe, 1965, for a notable exception). Some believe that today's emphasis on institutional and ecological perspectives (e.g. Carroll, 1987; Hannan and Freeman, 1989; Zucker, 1988) is, in part, a reaction to Americans' previous overreliance on rational and ahistorical models of organizational behavior. Even though nonrational views of organization have been published, the 'rational view steadily gained the upper hand' (Ouchi and Wilkins, 1985: 465). Ouchi and Wilkins (1985), among others, attribute the dominance of rational approaches to the increased emphasis on explicit, quantitative, and computer-aided analysis in the U.S. social sciences. Pfeffer (1982) suggested that forceful cultural values have led us to be more open to certain approaches than others.

Recommendations for a more internationally relevant organizational science

This review focuses on academic management from three perspectives – contextual, quantitative, and qualitative. From all three perspectives, we render the same verdict: inappropriate parochialism. The current body of knowledge and processes for creating that knowledge are bounded and limiting. They lack sufficient breadth and depth to explain the very phenomena that we purport to study. Organizational science has become trapped, that is, trapped within geographical, cultural, temporal, and conceptual parochialism.

Organizational science is in a state of reflection that requires theorists to review the history of the field and critique existing work (e.g. Pinder and Moore, 1979; Van de Ven and Joyce, 1981). Like a weed patch, some theories have been allowed to run rampant due to overgeneralization: They need to be cleared. Overemphasizing particular views of organizational phenomena has caused other perspectives to be underemphasized. As Pfeffer (1982: 1) observed:

> The domain of organization theory is coming to resemble more of a weed patch than a well-tended garden. . . . It is often difficult to discern in what direction knowledge of organizations is progressing – or if, indeed, it is progressing at all.

To date, the development of cross-cultural organizational behavior has helped little to weed the garden because most cross-cultural studies have been unicultural or comparative, designed simply to extend U.S.-developed theories abroad (Adler, 1983; Negandhi, 1975). Rarely has the field focused on the theories themselves.

As described next and summarized in Table 1, we make 13 recommendations for creating a more globally relevant organizational science. Recommendations are made both to individual researchers and to the Academy of Management.

Recommendations: reflection

For organizational science to continue to develop, we recommend that scholars explicitly address cultural assumptions. Through this reflection, scholars will develop an appreciation of the cultural conditioning of organization theories. Thus, they will become more cognizant of how American values underlie much of organization theory and, consequently, render it constrained. Examining the cultural roots and assumptions is a necessary, but not sufficient, condition for beginning to uncover neglected, overemphasized, and overgeneralized aspects of organizational theory.

Recommendations: action steps for individual scholars

Miner (1980: 8) identified seven characteristics that a good theory should exhibit. Of the seven, one is particularly relevant:

> There should be a clear delineation of the domain the theory covers. The boundaries of application should be specified so that the theory is not utilized fruitlessly in situations for which it was never intended. This has been an often neglected aspect of theory building in the social sciences generally (Dubin, 1973), including the field of organizational behavior.

To develop a more robust organizational science, we recommend that scholars clearly state the cultural and geographical domain of their theories. By not indicating the domain, scholars inappropriately promulgate a universalistic view of organizational theory.

We support Hofstede's (1980) recommendation that researchers indicate the national and cultural characteristics of their sample so that readers can recognize the potential limitations. For example, Gersick's (1988: 34; 1989) exemplary research shows that 'groups use temporal milestones to pace their work and that . . . reaching those milestones pushes groups into transitions.' Given the variance in how different cultures view time (Hall, 1959; Kluckholn and Strodbeck, 1961), one must ask to what extent Gersick's findings are a cultural artifact. Clearly Gersick should continue her research. However, replications should be conducted in cultures with very different time orientations. At present, a clarification such as 'given the deep-seated differences in how cultures view time, these findings should be viewed with caution outside the United States' would add to her work's contribution to the literature.

We recommend researching cultures and management systems outside of the United States. Especially recommended is research, such as the recent 22-country study (based in the People's Republic of China) of Hofstede and Bond (1988), using non-U.S. settings to frame both the theoretical and methodological approach. Cross-national research forces scholars to question the adequacy of their domestically derived models, thereby encouraging them to create theoretical and methodological approaches not predicated solely on single-culture (especially American) assumptions. Through this process, single-nation, researchers can learn much from their cross-national colleagues (e.g. Child and Kieser 1979; Hamilton and Biggart, 1988; Tannen-baum, Kavcic, Rosner, Vianello and Wieser, 1974).

In addition, we recommend that scholars study foreign organizations on their own terms (idiographic research). By developing thick descriptions of other cultures (Geertz, 1973) and their management systems, scholars in-crease the types of organizational forms and environmental contexts with which they are familiar (e.g. Child and Kieser, 1979; Hamilton and Biggart, 1988). Tannenbaum and his colleagues (1974), for example, devoted a full chapter to describing the political, economic, and institutional settings of the countries they studied. Although single-nation studies may not immediately evidence such a need, McKelvey (1982), among others (Roberts, Hulin and Rosseau, 1978), urged scholars to avoid overgeneralization by describing their research settings in greater detail. This approach increases researchers' understanding of the uniqueness of U.S. organizational forms (Roberts and Boyacigiller, 1984), thus allowing them to view most previously accepted models as context specific (Clark, Kim and Freeman, 1989).

We recommend multinational and multicultural research teams to facilitate the recognition of cultural biases in theory development (Evans, 1975). To develop such collaborative relationships, we recommend that scholars take sabbaticals in foreign countries. Spending time abroad not only enhances cross-cultural understanding, but it also deepens cultural self-awareness and, thus, increases recognition of cultural biases in the theories developed. Clark (Clark *et al.*, 1989: 217) provided a provocative example of the value of foreign sabbaticals in describing his initial concern for the relevance of organizational science in Brazil:

> In particular, expectancy theory, equity theory and goal theories appear not to be predictive of successful performance in Brazilian colleges and universities. . . . Similarly, contingency theories of organizational design, including prescriptions for loose/tight coupling, seem to be contradicted by Brazilian institutional practices. . . . Finally, prescriptions resulting from distributive justice theories are also contradicted by the centralized, yet political and seemingly arbitrary functioning of the governance structure.

Although Clark concluded that basic organizational theories may still apply,

Table 1   Recommendations for a more internationally relevant organizational science

Recommendations	Significance
Reflection	
Explicitly address the influence of cultural values on how we conceptualize organization phenomena and construct organization theories.	Helps scholars uncover neglected, overemphasized, and overgeneralized aspects of theories.
Examine the extent to which the organizational sciences reflect U.S. cultural values.	Increases scholars understanding of American culture and its impact on their perceptions, thoughts and scholarship.
Action steps for individual researchers	
State the cultural and geographical domain of theories and research, as well as indicate other locales in which it applies.	Minimizes implicit universalism.
Indicate the national and cultural characteristics of research samples.	Assists readers of the research to recognize potential limitations.
Research management systems outside of the United States.	Creates new theoretical and methodological approaches not predicated on American assumptions.
Study non-U.S. management systems on their own terms (idiographic research); develop thick descriptions of organizational phenomena and the contexts in which they are embedded.	Increases the organizational forms and contexts with which scholars are familiar, as well as increasing their understanding of the uniqueness of U.S. organizational forms.
Create more multinational and multicultural research teams.	Facilitates recognition of cultural biases in theory development.
Use non-U.S. settings to frame theoretical and methodological approaches.	Expands domain of organizational theories.
Take sabbaticals in foreign countries.	Increases scholars understanding of foreign cultures and their own cultures, including providing personal thick descriptions of the foreign sabbatical culture.
Organizational changes	
Journal editors, reviewers, and scholars should question one another regarding their cultural assumptions and research domains.	Rewarding careful exposition of the geographical and cultural domain will check implicit universalism.
Expand editorial boards to include global representation and expertise.	Increases the perspectives represented, both substantively and symbolically.

Table 1 (continued)

Recommendations	Significance
Consider forming 'global lines of business,' strategic alliances, and networks among academic organizations worldwide.	Facilitates internationalization and, thus, contributes to future relevance.
Select leaders of academic management organizations from multiple nations.	Increases perspectives and knowledge bases represented, thus facilitating frame-breaking change.

given key modifications, it is clear that his Brazilian sabbatical had a great impact on his acceptance of received wisdom.

Recommendations: organizational changes

The starting point must be with each individual scholar, but solitary intro-spection probably is not most effective. Rather, we recommend that schol-ars, journal editors, and reviewers from a range of countries question one another regarding their cultural assumptions. The following questions should be incorporated into the review process: What is the cultural and geographical domain of this study, and to what extent do the findings apply in other settings? Unless the review process rewards careful exposition of the cultural and geographical domain, implicit universalism will continue.

Given the rate and extent of globalization (Miller, 1988), organizational science appears to be facing a period of frame-breaking change (Tushman, Newman and Romanelli, 1986). If this is true, incremental efforts at internationalization will be insufficient to meet increasing demands for more relevant organizational research. Rather, more fundamental change is required. Management's elite journals, despite well-intentioned efforts, still do not reflect this globalization. Tushman and his colleagues (1986: 42) found that in only 6 out of 40 cases did current CEOs initiate and implement frame-breaking changes: New leaders were essential to achieve such transformational changes. Thus, we recommend that editorial boards be expanded to include global representation (scholars from a wide range of countries) as well as global process (scholars experienced in researching topics outside of their home countries).

During this period of frame-breaking change (and chaos) the field must accept that leading journals and conferences will refer to many authors, theories, and publications that are as yet unknown and unevaluated by the American research community. At times, mistakes will be made: quality will be mixed, and scholars will wish that they had not wasted their own or their colleagues' time. However, a more inclusive editorial strategy will infuse the field with new ideas, theories, and authors, thus increasing the chance that frame-breaking advances will be made.

We recommend that academic organizations, such as the Academy of Management, consider forming 'global lines of business' (functional divisions with a worldwide orientation), transnational strategic alliances, and networks with professional organizations worldwide (e.g. the German Gesellshaft Fuer Betriebswirtshaft and the Japanese Association of Business Administration). We strongly support the Academy's membership in the newly formed International Federation of Scholarly Associations of Management. In addition, we recommend that academic organizations select their leaders from multiple nations, thus facilitating globalization efforts of a frame-breaking nature and enhancing the field's future relevance and potential contribution. The Academy of Management has made important decisions designed to move it from an excellent domestic organization to an equally excellent global organization. These decisions include creating the International Programs Committee for the entire Academy (rather than limiting it to the International Division); holding regional meetings abroad; discussing the formation of international alliances; supporting workshops on internationalizing the organizational behavior, policy, and strategy curricula; and convening special all-Academy showcase sessions on global issues presented by scholars from several countries.

Conclusion

To really understand a culture and to ascertain more completely the group's values and overt behavior, it is imperative to delve into the underlying assumptions, which are typically unconscious, but which actually determine how group members perceive, think, and feel. . . . [A]s a value leads to a behavior, and as that behavior begins to solve the problem which prompted it in the first place, the value gradually is transformed into an underlying assumption about how things really are. As the assumption is increasingly taken for granted, *it drops out of awareness*. (Schein, 1984: 446, emphasis added)

The task before us is a difficult one; for what we are asking of ourselves and our colleagues is to focus on what has, for most of us, dropped out of awareness. Yet, the cost of not progressing toward an organizational science that is more internationally relevant is very high. Not only is it unfair to constituents outside of the United States, but it also falls short of the mandate to educate and to inform managers inside the United States who are facing an increasingly multicultural and international workplace.

As the field begins to follow these recommendations, we hope that major organizational science journals will typically include articles in each of the following categories and label them as such:

1 *Universally applicable theories*: theories that can apply in widely different cultural milieux.
2 *Regiocentric theories*: theories that can apply in a range of cultures sharing certain common characteristics, for example, theories applicable in contiguous geographic areas (e.g., Asia, Latin America, or the Slavic countries) or under similar levels of economic development.
3 *Intercultural theories*: theories that explain the interaction among peoples of different cultures.
4 *Intracultural theories*: theories that describe specific cultures (e.g., American, Japanese, Indian).

If these recommendations are followed, theories applicable only to the United States will be subsidiary to a wider body of universal theories applicable globally. Domestic research will become a subsidiary of more broadly based research. The era of international research being relegated to a subsidiary of domestic research will be over.

References

Adler, N. J. 1983. Cross-cultural management research: The ostrich and the trend. *Academy of Management Review*, 8: 226–232.

Adler, N. J. 1984. Understanding the ways of understanding: Cross-cultural management methodology reviewed. In R. N. Farmer (Ed.). *Advances in international comparative management*, vol. 1: 31–67. Greenwich, CT: JAI Press.

Adler, N. J. 1986. *International dimensions of organizational behavior*. Boston: Kent Publishing.

Adler, N. J., Campbell, N. and Laurent, A. 1989. In search of appropriate methodology: Outside the People's Republic of China, looking in. *Journal of International Business Studies*, 20(1): 61–74.

Adler, N. J., Doktor, R. and Redding, S. G. 1986. From the Atlantic to the Pacific century: Cross-cultural management reviewed. *Journal of Management*, 12(2): 295–318.

Adler, N. J. and Ghadar, F. 1990. International strategy from the perspective of people and culture: The North American context. In A. Rugman (Ed.), *Research in global strategic management: International business research for the twenty-first century*, vol. 1: 179–205. Greenwich, CT: JAI Press.

Adler, N. J. and Jelinek, M. 1986. Is 'organization culture' culture bound? *Human Resource Management*, 25(1): 73–90.

Aldrich, H., McKelvey, B. and Ulrich, D. 1984. Design strategy from the population perspective. *Journal of Management*, 10(1): 67–86.

Allen, D. B., Miller, E. D. and Nath. R. 1988. North America. In R. Nath (Ed.), *Comparative management*: 23–54. Cambridge, MA: Ballinger.

American Assembly of Collegiate Schools of Business, 1988–1989. *Accreditation Council Policies. Procedures & Standards*. St. Louis. MO: American Assembly of Collegiate Schools of Business.

American Association of School Administrators, 3–12. 1983. *The excellence report: Using it to improve your schools*. Arlington. VA: American Association of School

32 *Cross-cultural Management*

Administrators, 3–12. (Contains the report to the President 1982. *A nation at risk: The imperative for educational reform.*)

American Society for Training and Development, 1989. *Training in America: Learning to work for the twenty-first century*. Alexandria. VA: American Society for Training and Development.

Arndt, J. 1985. On making marketing science more scientific: Roles of orientations, paradigms, metaphors, and puzzle solving. *Journal of Marketing*, 49(3): 11–23.

Bartlett, C. A. and Ghoshal, S. 1989. *Managing across borders: The transnational solution*. Boston: Harvard Business School Press.

Bartlett, C. A., Doz, Y. and Hedlund, G. 1990. *Managing the global firm*. London: Routledge & Kegan Paul.

Bass, B. M. 1981. Leadership in different cultures. In B. M. Bass (Ed.), *Stogdill's handbook of leadership*. 552–549. New York: Free Press.

Beechler, S. L. and Pucik, V. 1989. The diffusion of American organizational theory in postwar Japan. In C. A. B. Osigweh (Ed.), *Organizational science abroad: Constraints and perspective*: 119–134. New York: Plenum Press.

Berger, L. and Luckman, T. 1966. *The social construction of reality*. Garden City, NY: Doubleday.

Blackford, M. G. 1988. *The rise of modern business in Great Britain, the United States and Japan*. Chapel Hill: The University of North Carolina Press.

Boulding, K. E. 1961. *The image*. Ann Arbor: University of Michigan Press/Ann Arbor Paperbacks.

Bowen, E. 1984. Powerful pitch for the humanities. *Time*, December 10: 91.

Burrell, G. and Morgan, G. 1979. *Sociological paradigms and organizational analysis*. London: Heinemann.

Carroll, G. R. 1987. *Ecological models of organisations*. Cambridge, MA: Ballinger.

Carroll, G. R. and Delacroix, J. 1982. Organizational mortality in the newspaper industries of Argentina and Ireland: An ecological approach. *Administrative Science Quarterly*, 27: 189–198.

Carroll, G. R., Delacroix, J. and Goodstein, J. 1988. The political environments of organizations: An ecological view. In R. M. Staw & L. L. Cummings (Eds.), *Research in organization behavior*, vol 10: 359–392. Greenwich, CT: JAI Press.

Carroll, G. R. and Huo, Y. P. 1986. Organizational task and institutional environments in ecological perspective: Findings from the local newspaper industry. *American Journal of Sociology*, 91: 838–873.

Child, J. 1972. Organization structure, environment and performance. The role of strategic choice. *Sociology*, 6: 2–22.

Child, J. 1981. Culture contingency and capitalism in the cross-national study of organizations. In B. M. Staw and L. L. Cummings (Eds.), *Research in organizational behavior*, vol 3: 303–356. Greenwich, CT: JAI Press.

Child, J. and Kieser, A. 1979. Organization and managerial roles in British and West German companies: An examination of the culture-free thesis. In C. J. Lammers and D. J. Hickson (Eds.), *Organizations alike and unlike*: 251–271. London: Routledge & Kegan Paul.

Clark, K. S., Kim, M. V. and Freeman, S. J. 1989. Contradictions between Brazilian and U.S. organizations: Implications for organizational theory. In C. A. B. Osigweh (Ed.), *Organizational science abroad: Constraints and perspectives*: 203–226. New York: Plenum Press.

Conger, J. A. 1989. *The charismatic leader*. San Francisco: Jossey-Bass.

Council on Competitiveness. 1988. Charting competitiveness. *Challenges*, 1(5): 3.

Delacroix, J. and Carroll, G. R. 1983. Organizational foundings: An ecological study of the newspaper industries of Argentina and Ireland. *Administrative Science Quarterly*, 28: 274–291.

DiMaggio, P. J. and Powell, W. W. 1983. The iron cage revisited: Institutional isomorphism and collective rationality in organizational fields. *American Sociological Review*, 48: 147–160.

Dubin, R. 1973. *Theory building*. New York: Free Press.

Earley, P. C. 1989. Social loafing and collectivism: A comparison of the United States and the People's Republic of China. *Administrative Science Quarterly*, 34: 565–581.

England, G. W. 1975. *The manager and his values: An international perspective*. Cambridge, MA: Ballinger.

Evans, W. M. 1975. Measuring the impact of culture on organizations. *International Studies of Management & Organization*, 5(1): 91–113.

Galbraith, J. 1973. *Designing complex organizations*. Reading, MA: Addison-Wesley.

Geertz, C. 1973. *The interpretation of cultures*. New York: Basic Books.

Gergen, K. J. 1973. Social psychology as history. *Journal of Personality and Social Psychology*, 26: 309–320.

Gerlach, M. 1987. Business alliances and the strategy of the Japanese firm. *California Management Review*, 30(1): 126–142.

Gersick, C. J. G. 1988. Time and transition in work teams: Toward a new model of group development. *Academy of Management Journal*, 31: 9–41.

Gersick, C. J. G. 1989. Marking time: Predictable transitions in task groups. *Academy of Management Journal*, 32: 274–309.

Godkin, L., Braye, C. E. and Caunch, C. L. 1989a. U.S. based cross-cultural management research in the eighties. *Journal of Business and Economic Perspectives*, 15(2): 37–45.

Godlan, L., Braye, C. E. and Caunch, C. L. 1989b. *U.S. based cross-cultural management research in the eighties*. Working paper, Lamar University, Beaumont, TX.

Gonzalez, R. F. and McMillan, C., Jr., 1961. The universality of American management philosophy. *Academy of Management Journal*, 41: 33–41.

Graham, J. L. and Gronhaug, K. 1989. Ned Hall didn't get a haircut: or why we haven't learned much about international marketing in the last 25 years. *Journal of Higher Education*, 60(2): 152–157.

Hall, E. T. 1959. *The silent language*. New York: Doubleday.

Hall, E. T. 1981/1976. *Beyond culture*. New York: Doubleday.

Hamilton, G. G. and Biggart, N. W. 1988. Market, culture and authority: A comparative analysis of management organization in the Far East. *American Journal of Sociology*, 94(supplement): 52–94.

Hannan, M. T. and Freeman, J. 1989. *Organizational ecology*. Cambridge, MA: Harvard University Press.

Harns, P. and Moran, R. T. 1979. *Managing cultural differences*. Houston: Gulf.

Hofstede, G. 1980. *Culture's consequences: International differences in work-related values*. Beverly Hills, CA: Sage.

Hofstede, G. 1981. Culture and organizations. *International Studies of Management and Organizations*, 10(4): 15–41.

Hofstede, G. 1983. Dimensions of national cultures in fifty countries and three regions. In J. B. Deregowski, S. Dziurawiec and R. C. Annis (Eds.), *Explanations in cross-cultural psychology*: 335–355. Lisse, Netherlands: Swets and Zeitlinger.

Hofstede, G., and Bond, M. H. 1988. The Confucius connection: From cultural roots to economic growth. *Organisational Dynamics*, 16(4): 4–21.

Hofstede, G. and Kassem, M. S. 1976. *European contributions to organizations theory*. Assen. Netherlands: Von Gorcum.

Inzerilli, G. 1981. Preface: Some conceptual issues in the study of the relationships between organizations and societies. *International Studies of Management and Organization*, 10(4): 3–14.

Jones, E. E. and Nisbett, R. E. 1971. *The actor and the observer: Divergent perceptions of the causes of behavior.* Morristown, NJ: General Learning Press.

Kelley, L. and Worthley, R. 1981. The role of culture in comparative management: A cross-cultural perspective. *Academy of Management Journal*, 25: 164–173.

Kiggundu, M. 1988. Africa. In R. Nath (Ed.), *Comparative management:* 169–244. Cambridge, MA: Ballinger.

Kluckholn, F. R. and Strodbeck, F. L. 1961. *Variations in value orientations.* Evanston, IL: Row, Peterson.

Kobrin, S. J. 1984. *International expertise in American business: How to learn to play with the kids on the street.* New York: Institute of International Education.

Kuhn, T. S. 1962. *The structure of the scientific revolutions.* Chicago: University of Chicago Press.

Lammers, C. J. 1980. Sociology of organizations around the globe: Similarities and differences between American, British, French, German and Dutch brands. *Organization Studies*, 11: 179–205.

Lammers, C. J. and Hickson, D. J. (Eds.). 1979. *Organizations alike and unlike: International studies in the sociology of organization.* London: Routledge & Kegan Paul.

Lane, H. and DiStefano, J. 1988. *International management behavior.* Scarborough, Ontario: Nelson, Canada.

Laurent, A. 1981. Matrix organizations and Latin cultures. *International Studies of Management and Organization*, 10(4): 101–114.

Laurent, A. 1983. The cultural diversity of western conceptions of management: *International Studies of Management and Organization*, 13(1–2): 75–96.

Lawrence, P. R. 1987. Historical development of organizational behavior. In J. W. Lorsch (Ed.), *Handbook of organizational behavior*: Englewood Cliffs. NJ: Prentice-Hall.

Leberson, S. and O'Connor, J. F. 1972. Leadership and organizational performance: A study of large corporations. *American Sociological Review*, 37: 117–130.

Lincoln, J. R. and McBride, K. 1987. Japanese industrial organization in comparative perspective. *Annual Review of Sociology*, 13: 289–335.

McKelvey, W. 1982. *Organizational systematics: Taxonomy, evolution, classification.* Berkeley: University of California Press.

Merton, R. K. 1968. *Social theory and social structure.* New York: Free Press.

Meyer, J. W. and Rowan, B. 1977. Institutionalized organizations: Formal structure as myth and ceremony. *American Journal of Sociology*, 83: 340–363.

Meyer, J. W. and Scott, W. R. 1983. *Organizational environments: Ritual and rationality.* Beverly Hills, CA: Sage.

Miles, R. E. and Snow, C. C. 1978. *Organizational strategy, structure and process.* New York: McGraw-Hill.

Miller, E. L. 1988. *International management: A field in transition, what will it take to reach maturity.* Paper presented at the Research for Relevance in International Management Conference, University of Windsor, Ontario.

Miller, L. E. and Grush, J. E. 1988. Improving predictions in expectancy theory: Effects of personality, expectancies and norms. *Academy of Management Journal*, 31: 107–122.

Miner, J. B. 1980. *Theories of organizational behavior*, Hinsdale, IL: Dryden Press.

Moore, R. 1974. The cross-cultural study of organizational behavior. *Human Organization*, 33: 37–45.

Morey, N. and Luthans, F. 1984. An emic perspective and ethnoscience methods for organizational research. *Academy of Management Review*, 9: 27–36.

National Advisory Board of International Education Programs, 1983. *Critical needs in international education: Recommendations for action.* Washington, DC: National Advisory Board on International Education Programs, December.

Negandhi, A. R. 1975. Comparative management and organization theory: A marriage needed. *Academy of Management Journal*, 18: 334–344.

Nehrt, L. C. 1987. The international studies of the curriculum. *Journal of International Business Studies*, 18(1): 83–90.

Newman, W. H. 1972. Cultural assumptions underlying U.S. management concepts. In J. L. Massie and S. Laytje (Eds.), *Management in an international context*: 327–352. New York: Harper & Row.

Oberg, W. 1963. Cross-cultural perspectives on management principles. *Academy of Management Journal*, 6: 129–143.

Ohmae, K. 1987. *Beyond national borders. Reflections on Japan and the world.* Homewood, IL: Dow Jones-Irwin.

Osigweh, C. A. B. 1989a. *Organizational science abroad: Constraints and perspectives.* New York: Plenum.

Osigweh, C. A. B. 1989b. The myth of universality in transnational organizational science. In Osigweh, C. A. B. (Ed.), *Organizational science abroad: Constraints and perspectives*: 3–26. New York: Plenum.

Ouchi, W. 1984. *The M-form society.* Reading, MA: Addison-Wesley.

Ouchi, W. G. and Wilkins, A. L. 1985. Organizational culture. *Annual Review of Sociology*, 11: 457–483.

Peng, T. K., Peterson, M. F., & Shyi, Y. P. 1990. Quantitative methods in cross-national management research: Trends and equivalence issues. *Journal of Organizational Behavior*: in press.

Pfeffer, J. 1982. *Organizations and organization theory.* Boston: Pitman.

Pfeffer, J. and Saidncik, G. R. 1978. *The external control of organizations.* New York: Harper & Row.

Pinder, C. and Moore, L. F. (Eds.). 1979. *Middle range theory and the study of organizations.* Leiden, Netherlands: Martinus Nijhoff.

Porter, M. E. 1980. *Competitive strategy: Techniques for analyzing industries and competitors.* New York: Free Press.

Porter, L. W. and McKibben, L. E. 1988. *Management education and development: Drift or thrust into the 21st century.* New York: McGraw-Hill.

Prahalad, C. K. and Doz, Y. L. 1987. *The multinational mission.* New York: Free Press.

President's Commission on Industrial Competitiveness, 1985. *Global competition: The new reality* (vol. 1). Washington, DC: U.S. Government Printing Office, January.

Roberts, K. H. and Boyacigiller, N. A. 1983. A survey of cross-national organizational researchers: Their views and opinions. *Organization Studies*, 4: 375–386.

Roberts, K. H. and Boyacigiller, N. A. 1984. Cross-national organizational research: The grasp of the blind men. In B. M. Staw and L. L. Cummings (Eds.), *Research in organizational behavior*, vol. 6: 423–475. Greenwich, CT: JAI Press.

Roberts, K. H., Hulin, C. L. and Rousseau, D. M. 1978. *Developing an interdisciplinary science of organizations.* San Francisco: Jossey-Bass.

Sampson, E. E. 1977. Psychology and the American ideal. *Journal of Personality and Social Psychology*, 35: 767–782.

Schein, E. H. 1984. Coming to a new awareness of organizational culture. *Sloan Management Review*, 25: 3–16.

Scott, W. R. 1987. The adolescence of institutional theory. *Administrative Science Quarterly*, 32: 493–511.

Sekaran, U. 1983. Are U.S. organizational concepts and measures transferable to another culture? An empirical investigation. *Academy of Management Journal*, 2: 409–417.

Selznick, P. 1949. *TVA and the grass roots*. Berkeley, CA: University of California Press.

Servan-Schreiber, J. J. 1968. *The American challenge*. (R. Steel, trans.). New York: Athenum.

Slocum, J. W. and Topichak, P. M. 1972. Do cultural differences affect job satisfaction? *Journal of Applied Psychology*, 56: 177–178.

Smith, P. B. and Peterson, M. F. 1988. *Leadership, organizations and culture*. Beverly Hills, CA: Sage.

Staw, B. M. 1980. Rationality and justification in organizational life. In B. M. Staw and L. L. Cummings (Eds.), *Research in organizational behavior*, vol. 2: 45–80. Greenwich, CT: JAI Press.

Staw, B. M. 1984. Organizational behavior: A review and reformulation of the field's outcome variables. *Annual Review of Psychology*, 35: 627–666.

Steers, R. M. 1987. The international challenge to management education. *Academy of Management Newsletter*, 17(4): 2–4.

Steers, R. M. 1989. Organizational sciences in a global environment: Future directions. In C. A. B. Osigweh (Ed.), *Organizational science abroad: Constraints and perspectives:* 293–304. New York: Plenum Press.

Stewart, E. C. 1972. *American cultural patterns: A cross-cultural perspective*. Chicago: Intercultural Press.

Stinchcombe, A. L. 1965. Social structure and organizations. In J. G. March (Ed.), *Handbook of organizations:* 142–193. Chicago: Rand McNally.

Tannenbaum, A. S., Kavcic, B., Rosner, M., Vianello, M. and Wieser, G. 1974. *Hierarchy in organizations*. San Francisco: Jossey-Bass.

Thanopoulos, J. (with the assistance of J. W. Leonard). 1986. *International business curricula: A global survey*. Cleveland, OH: Academy of International Business.

Thanopoulos, J. and Vernon, I. R. 1987. International business education in the AACSB schools. *Journal of International Business Studies*. 18(1): 91–98.

Thomas, A. B. 1988. Does leadership make a difference to organizations' performance? *Administrative Science Quarterly*, 33: 388–400.

Thurow, L. 1984. Revitalizing American industry: Managing in a competitive world economy. *California Management Review*, 27(1): 9–41.

Thurow, L. 1988. *Keynote address*. Presented at the annual meeting of the Western Academy of Management, Big Sky, MT.

Triandis, H. C. 1972. *The analysis of subjective culture*. New York: Wiley.

Triandis, H. C. 1983. Dimensions of cultural variations as parameters of organizational theories. *International Studies of Management and Organization*. 12(4): 139–169.

Tushman, M. L., Newman, W. H. and Romanelli, E. 1986. Managing the unsteady pace of organizational evolution. *California Management Review*, 29(1): 29–44.

Van de Ven, A. H. and Joyce, W. F. (Eds.). 1981. *Perspectives on organization design and behavior*. New York: John Wiley.

Vernon, R. 1966. International investment and international trade in the product cycle. *Quarterly Journal of Economics*, 80: 190–207.

Vernon, R. 1971. *Sovereignty at bay: The multinational spread of U.S. enterprises*. New York: Basic Books.

von Alleman, H. 1974. International contacts of university staff members: Some problems in the internationality of science. *International Social Science Journal*, 26, 445–457. (Note: von Alleman cites 120 countries but today there are 185 according to *The Statesman's Yearbook 1989–90* edited by John Paxton. London, England: Macmillan Press, 1989.)

Walder, A. 1983. Organized dependency and cultures of authority in Chinese industry. *Journal of Asian Studies*. 43(1): 51–76.

Whitley, R. 1984. *The intellectual and social organization of the sciences*. Oxford: Clarendon Press.

Whitley, R. 1988. The management sciences and managerial skills. *Organization Studies*, 9: 47–68.

Wind, Y. and Perlmutter, H. V. 1973. On the identification of frontier issues in multinational marketing. *Columbia Journal of World Business*, 12(4): 131–139.

Zucker, L. 1988. *Institutional patterns and organizations: Culture and environment*. Cambridge, MA: Ballinger.

Reproduced from Boyacigiller, N. A. and Adler, N. J. (1991). The parochial dinosaur: organizational science in a global context. *Academy of Management Review*, **16** (2), 262–90, by permission of *Academy of Management Review*.

1.2 Values research and managerial behavior: implications for devising culturally consistent managerial styles

Herbert J. Davis and S. Anvaar Rasool

Introduction

Interest in human values dates back many years (Lewin, 1935; Allport, 1937; Murray, 1938: Hull, 1943; Bruner and Goodman, 1947: Postman, Bruner and McGinnies, 1948: and Kluckhohn and Strodtbeck, 1961). Only during the past twenty-five years or so, however, have management researchers begun to recognize the importance of personal values in understanding managerial behavior. Guth and Tagiuri (1965) gave impetus to this area of inquiry with their early scholarly article that illustrated ways in which personal values influence corporate strategy choices.

This contribution has resulted in a literature that is replete with a preponderance of evidence suggesting a positive relationship between a manager's personal values and his decision-making (Udy, 1959; McMurry, 1963; Shartle, Brumbeck and Rizzo, 1964: Tagiuri, 1965; Haire, Ghiselli and Porter, 1966; Senger, 1970; Sikula, 1971; Jacox, 1972; Manley, 1972; Farris, 1973; England and Lee, 1974; Pezeshkpur, 1975; and Hughes, Rao and Alker, 1976).

Differing values of managers have also been considered as a factor in organizational conflict. This has particularly been the case with multinational firms operating in and across diverse cultures where, unavoidably, there is considerable incongruity between the values of host country workers and their expatriate managers. The literature on cross-cultural management of multinational firms cites a number of instances where this incongruity has caused expatriate managers to be both perplexed and sometimes paranoid about the outcome of imposing their traditional or home-country management styles upon indigenous personnel. (Gellerman, 1967; Pezeshkpur, 1975: and Badar, Gray and Kedia, 1982.)

The implication of such conflicts for a successful management-system is obvious: managers must factor in differences between their own environment and the one in which they must operate before they impose any value, let alone their own, on their foreign subordinates. Knowledge of value systems, then, might aid us in devising internally consistent management styles for effective 'transcultural' management practice.

The issue of culture

Culture-induced differences have long fascinated researchers, ecclesiastics, travelers, and traders. Cultural anthropologists have developed a rich set of insights into primitive tribal ways and a perspective against which observers of administrative behavior can examine modern beliefs and practices. In addition, few cross-cultural management topics have generated more interest than human values, beliefs, and attitudes and their impact on the motivational process and resulting behavior.

One of the earliest definitions of culture was presented by Tylor in 1871. Tylor defined culture as 'the complete whole which includes knowledge, belief, art, morals, laws, customs,. and any other capabilities or habits acquired by man as a member of society' (1871, p. 1). It is important to note that Tylor himself, while developing this definition, acknowledged that the concept of culture has even greater dimensions than the definition would suggest. Sekaran expands on this when she points out that one of the criticisms of cross-cultural research is the failure to operationalize the concept 'culture.' She also indicates that while research has yet to clarify and conceptualize the concept of 'culture,' the belief exists that culture has an impact on organizations because cultural norms, values, and roles are embedded in the way that organizations develop, organizational structures emerge, and informal and formal patterns of behavior occur (1983, p. 67).

The nature of values, attitudes and behavior

Value definitions, which at times differ in only minor aspects, are generally consistent in their global meanings. Athos and Coffey (1968, p. 100) have stated that 'By "values" we mean ideas about what is desirable.' Guth and Tagiuri (1965, p. 125) also suggest that values are desirable end states. Kluckhohn *et al.* (1962, p. 369) define values as a conception of the desirable: 'A value is a conception, explicit or implicit . . . of the desirable which influences the selection from available modes, means, and ends of action.' Building from this idea, Rokeach (1968, p. 124) defines values as 'abstract ideals, positive or negative, not tied to any specific object or situation, representing a person's beliefs about modes of conduct and ideal terminal modes . . .' Values thus are global beliefs that 'transcendentally guide actions and judgments across specific objects and situations' (1968, p. 160). Conner and Becker conclude that 'values may be thought of as global beliefs about desirable end-states underlying attitudinal and behavioral processes' (1975, p. 551).

Attitudes, on the other hand, relate to specific objects and specific situations. According to Theodorson and Theodorson 'An attitude is an orientation toward certain objects (including persons – others and oneself) or situations . . . An attitude results from the application of a general value to concrete objects or situations' (1969, p. 19). In fact, Katz and Stotland indicate that one of the functions of attitudes, being object-specific, is to allow expression of more global underlying values (1959). Behavior, therefore, can be viewed as the overt manifestation of attitudes and values (Conner and Becker, 1975, p. 551). In fact, according to Cambell, attitudes have been defined by some in terms of the probability of the occurrence of a specified behavior in a specified situation (1950).

Theory and methodology of value measurement

Of the various methodologies designed to measure values, England's theory and methodology of value measurement is considered the most useful as an aid in devising appropriate management styles. England's methodology utilizes a Personal Value Questionnaire (PVQ). The Personal Value Questionnaire distinguishes values that are behaviorally-relevant from the potential values held by an individual. It is in this sense that the methodology is indicative of managerial behavior and, therefore, is useful in devising a managerial style applicable across different cultures.

The England methodology represents a major advance relative to attempts at value-measurement by such writers as Harbison and Myers (1959). Haire, Ghiselli and Porter (1966) and various other studies that used only the Allport–Vernon–Lindzey questionnaire for their research (Tagiuri, 1965; Guth and Tagiuri, 1965; and Senger, 1970). The values that these studies measured were not reliable in terms of being behaviorally relevant and, consequently, could not be used for developing an appropriate management style.

The ability of England's methodology to more closely approximate behaviorally-relevant values and thus generate the kind of management style required for effective leadership stems from the way managers' values are measured. By first classifying managers on the basis of their evaluations of the 66 concepts in the PVQ into one of four primary orientation groups (pragmatic, moralistic, affective, and mixed) and then categorizing the 66 concepts into operative, intended, and adopted values, behaviorally-relevant values can be identified.

The criterion used for identifying behaviorally-relevant values is that concepts must be considered important and must fit one of the four primary orientations of the manager. Therefore, a pragmatic manager's behavior is best predicted by those concepts considered important and successful; for a moralistically-oriented manager, behavior is best predicted by those concepts considered important and right; and for an affect-oriented individual, behavior is best predicted by those concepts considered important and pleasant. These values are known as operative values, and have the highest probability of being translated from the intended state into actual behavior.

Whereas operative values are likely to be the most influential, intended values are those concepts that an individual regards as being of high importance, but do not appear to fit his organizational experience because they are socio-culturally induced. For a pragmatic individual, intended values are those concepts rated by him/her to be of 'high importance' and 'pleasant or right'. Intended values may imply a conflict between what one has come to believe and what one sees functioning or rewarded in his/her organizational environment. Adopted values are those that fit the primary value orientation of an individual, but are not regarded as highly important. Such values seem situationally induced. While these values are borne out by an individual's organizational experience, they are, at the same time, difficult to internalize. (See England, 1975, for a detailed discussion.)

The key, therefore, that makes this methodology for assessing behaviorally-relevant values superior to previous studies is that it does not make behavioral inferences directly from a manager's primary value orientation. Primary value orientation classification is only a means to determine those concepts that are behaviorally-relevant for a manager. It is only when individuals have different value profiles (i.e. different concepts comprise operative value sets) that we should expect behavioral differences. Thus, two individuals having different primary value orientations need not be expected to behave differently. By the same logic, individuals with identical primary value orientations need not be expected to behave similarly. The crucial point is the extent to which compared individuals have different value profiles. The value profile allows interpretation of an individual's responses to the 66 concepts in the PVQ in value terms, i.e. those which have behavioral implications.

The usefulness of this methodology results from the ability of the methodology to relate values to behavior in systematic ways. In order to test the theoretical soundness of this method, a behavioral measures questionnaire was developed to provide a measure of self-reported behavior of managers when confronted with typical problem situations. This behavior simulation effort was used only with managers in Australia and India (England, Dhingra and Agarwal, 1974). The questionnaire consisted of five incidents, each representing a situation that a manager may encounter in the performance of his job. The incidents were developed to cover a problem dealing with budgeting, two problems dealing with morally questionable procedures for obtaining R & D funds, a problem dealing with selection of an assistant, and a problem dealing with delegation of authority. Managers were asked to read each incident carefully and then to indicate the action they would take by checking the appropriate statement from a list of suggested actions. (Predictions based on rational or logical expectations generated from value responses to specific concepts in the PVQ were made about behavior.) Nineteen of 25 predictions for Indian, and 18 of 25 predictions for Australian managers were supported by the responses. These results strongly attest to the relationship between managerial values measured by the PVQ and managerial behavior.

A later study was conducted by Munson and Posner (1980) to test the validity of England's PVQ and the Rokeach Values Survey (RVS), another widely used instrument for assessing personal values. This study was designed to evaluate the ability to differentiate employees and to differentiate employees with higher levels of self-perceived success. Each of the two instruments passed the validity test by correctly classifying employees into management or non-management positions as well as by distinguishing employees with high self-perceived success from those with lower self-perceived success. The fact that England's Personal Value Questionnaire is a reliable and valid tool for assessing behaviorally-relevant personal values has made it a very powerful tool for organizational research not only in one culture but across several cultures. By providing researchers with sophisticated yet readily applicable techniques, the PVQ enables researchers to generate managers' value profiles (concepts which are of higher behavioral relevance from among the 66 concepts) from different cultures. This, in turn, provides a deeper insight into management values across different cultures. Knowledge of values could help in dealing with several types of problems that might arise among managers. One example may be laying off redundant workers. Managers with dominant pragmatic values are likely to arrive at very different solutions than those with highly moralistic values. Situations like these, amplified by incongruity in managerial values, can lead to serious conflict if they are not tempered with an appropriate management style.

Comparison of managers' values

England and his associates (1974) used this conceptual framework to study personal value systems of managers from Japan, the United States, South Korea, India, and Australia. In this ambitious study that used stratifying variables such as size of organization in terms of number of employees, managerial level within the organization, and organizational function of the manager, England *et al.* investigated the responses to the PVQ of 2,556 respondents as follows: United States (997), Japan (374), South Korea (211), Australia (351) and India (623). The average managerial incumbency was 15 years and the average age of the samples was 45. Based upon the findings of this landmark study, both the primary orientations and value profiles of managers from across the five countries was considered.

Primary orientation

Major differences in primary orientations existed in the orientation of the sample groups across the five countries. Japanese managers demonstrated the most practical orientation, followed by managers from the United States and Korea. Indian and Australian managers, in contrast, were the least pragmatically-oriented. In other words, the number of concepts from the PVQ's 66 concepts that Indian and Australian managers rated important and successful were the least important and successful compared to other managers.

In terms of moralistic orientation, great variability existed among the managers sampled. Indian and Australian managers were the most moralistically-oriented, followed by managers from the United States. Japanese and South Korean managers had relatively low moralistic orientations. When considering the national samples from an indigenous perspective, 57% of American managers were found to have a pragmatic orientation and only 30% had a moralistic orientation – i.e. when they viewed the concept as important they also viewed it as right. On the other hand, only 40% of Australian managers demonstrated a pragmatic orientation, with an equal percentage being moralistic. Indian managers demonstrated an even lower degree of pragmatic orientation, with 34% pragmatically-oriented and a much higher 44% being moralistically-oriented. When examining the scores of Japanese managers England's study indicates a reversal in trend with 67% of these managers classified as pragmatic and only 10% moralistic. Fifty-three percent of Korean managers were classified as pragmatic and 9% moralistic. In summary, Japanese and Indian managers were identified as most dissimilar in terms of their primary orientations. Indian and Australian managers were identified as most similar.

Value profile differences

The value profile of a manager is simply the listing of those concepts that for him her are operative values, intended values, adopted values or weak values. In other words, it is a convenient method of distinguishing concepts of more behavioral significance. The behavioral relevance of concepts from each of the five groups – Organizational Goals. Personal Goals, Groups of People and Institutions, Ideas Associated with People, and Ideas about

General Topics – presents a framework with which to consider differences for the managers across the five countries studied.

The major differences among the five countries demonstrates that Japanese managers attached greater relevance to organizational goals, specifically to high productivity, organizational growth, profit maximization, organizational stability, and industry leadership. This implies that goals of organization are more internalized in the value structure of Japanese managers and would be expected to influence their behavior to a greater extent than is the case in other countries. Similarly, American managers have internalized organizational goals to a relatively high degree, particularly with regard to efficiency, productivity, and profit, and, to a lesser extent, growth, industry leadership, and stability.

The second difference among the five countries is the lower relevance placed on organizational goals by Korean managers, specifically organizational efficiency, industry leadership, and employee welfare. This implies a low level of internalization of organizational goals in the value structure of Korean managers, with the accompanying lowered behavioral impact. The goal of organizational growth is highly valued by Korean managers, relative to managers in other countries, and represents their strong desire for continued industrial development of Korea.

The third difference among the five countries is the low relevance of organizational goals (organizational growth and profit maximization) demonstrated by Australian managers. The goals of efficiency and productivity, however, are internalized to a considerable extent. Still, Australian managers do not seem to have internalized many of the goals of the organization to a marked degree and their behavior is not very responsive to organizational goal considerations.

Finally, Indian managers differ by placing a relatively high value on organizational stability and low value on profit maximization, high productivity and organizational efficiency are given high priority by Indian managers.

Among personal goals, the major difference among the five countries is the high relevance attached to them by Indian managers, specifically in terms of job satisfaction, security, individuality, dignity, prestige, and power. This suggests that personal goals play an important part in the value structure of Indian managers. Job satisfaction, security, and individuality would seem to represent intrinsically desirable personal goals while dignity, prestige, and power seem to represent status goals. These are what Indian managers strive to attain and appear to be a key to the motivational structure underlying Indian management behavior.

The second observation about personal goals is that U.S. and Australian managers generally attach less relevance to them than is the case with managers in other countries. This is particularly true for creativity, success, and autonomy for Australian managers, and autonomy and security for American managers. Finally, the nature of personal goals sought by Japanese managers gives greater value to achievement, creativity, and autonomy.

As for groups of people and institutions, the most striking observation is that groups of people play a much more significant part in the value system of American managers. Specifically, American managers place relatively high relevance on customers, owners, stockholders, employees, and co-workers. Indian managers, on the other hand, place relatively low relevance on managers, employees, and subordinates. Whereas American managers view large numbers of employee groups with which they interact as relevant reference groups. Indian managers view them as threatening to their career development. The same observation was found by other researchers (Haire, 1966; Negandhi and Prasad, 1971). This low relevance of other groups among Indian managers may be a function of the high level of social stratification that exists in India and the competition for egoistic gratification among Indians. Japanese managers value technical employees highly while South Koreans are similar to Indians in attaching low relevance to groups of people.

With regard to ideas associated with people, Australian managers place relatively high importance on honor, loyalty, trust, tolerance, and compassion. This is consistent with their humanistic orientation. Similarly, Indian managers score relatively high on the concepts of obedience, loyalty, and trust, suggesting an organizational compliance orientation. Both Indian and Australian managers reject the notion of aggressiveness as being behaviorally-relevant. This result is compatible with the humanistic orientation suggested for Australian managers and the organizational compliance orientation suggested for Indian managers. American managers, on the other hand, view trust, loyalty, honor, employee welfare, individuality, and dignity as important because they are socio-culturally induced but not of much behavioral significance because they are not organizationally enforced. In other words, these are intended values for American managers and not of much behavioral relevance. Ability, ambition, skill, and competence are valued more highly by American managers. Japanese managers score very low on the concepts of loyalty, honor, trust, tolerance, and obedience. This suggests a very low level of humanistic and organizational compliance orientation. Both Japanese and South Korean managers place relatively high value on the concept of aggressiveness.

Finally, in terms of ideas about general topics. American managers value change relatively highly and caution to a lower degree. This suggests an active or dynamic orientation. Japanese managers, however, value caution to a relatively high degree implying a cautious style of behavior. South Korean managers value caution, force, and compromise relatively highly and risk and change to a relatively low degree. For Australian managers, change, competition, risk, and aggressiveness are values that are organizationally enforced but not of much behavioral relevance because Australians find them difficult to internalize.

Discussion and implications

While these findings by England and his associates are indeed interesting, a critical point is the extent to which these value differences impact the kind of management style necessary for effective leadership, either in each of the countries under investigation, or cross-culturally. If the success of the much publicized Theory Z in Japan indicates anything, it is the potential value of developing a management system internally consistent with societal norms and expectations. The Theory Z approach to management simply suggests that involved workers are the key to increased productivity (Ouchi, 1981). Involved workers in large Japanese organizations are the result of an internally consistent set of norms, practices, and behaviors grounded in trust and interpersonal intimacy.

Theory Z has also been successful in Japan because it is internally consistent with Japan's managerial values of high productivity, organizational stability, achievement, and creativity, and a high level of homogeneity of values (England, 1983). The message, therefore, is that managing and leading managers of different value orientations, successfully, must relate to the different norms and expectations of the managers involved. An extension of this idea lies in the degree to which the two primary orientation systems of England differ with regard to the subjectivity or objectivity contained in their evaluative framework. In other words, if ethical standards of moralistic managers are highly objective, because they view things in terms of 'right' or 'wrong', and the 'success' standards of pragmatic managers are highly objective, a corollary to this may be that ethical mores are more firmly ingrained in the individual's personality than success standards, and that this causes moralistic managers to be more resistant to change than pragmatic managers. Following this reasoning organizations might find it easier to modify the behavior patterns of pragmatic rather than moralistic managers. Managing moralistic managers would require an individualistic program of behavior modification in which moral and philosophical justification is urged.

Managing pragmatic managers, on the other hand, would be more successful if practical arguments and approaches are used, and will be more successful if practical arguments and approaches are used, with emphasis on whether or not a particular act or decision is likely to be successful. The notion of expected outcomes of actions, also, would seem more useful for motivating pragmatic managers, while moralistic managers would be more motivated by the expected behavioral outcomes of actions. Moreover, motivating pragmatic managers through external rewards and controls would seem more appropriate, whereas moralists would feel more comfortable in a management system that rewards internal stimulation and develops their reasoning ability. Finally, pragmatic managers would be more successfully motivated if they were constantly challenged and forced to deal with change. Moralistic managers would feel, on the contrary, more at ease in a relatively static environment.

England (1975) has provided us with additional insight into this issue by indicating that businesses tend to reward managers who are pragmatic, dynamic, and achievement oriented. He further indicates that this type of manager prefers an active role in interaction with other individuals in achieving organizational goals. These are managers who are willing to take risks in achieving their goals. At the same time less successful managers tend to demonstrate passivity in their values and favor protected environments in which they might enjoy extended seniority and security in organizational position.

This value–success relationship was found in four of the five countries investigated by England (1975). This finding occurred in spite of the value diversity in each country. Therefore, the values of more successful managers in India are similar to those of successful managers in other countries. These managers depart from the model Indian pattern to such a considerable extent because they tend to favor pragmatic, dynamic, achievement-oriented values. Similar characteristics regarding successful managers have been cited or considered by other researchers (Patton, 1965; Hinrichs, 1967; Wollowich and McNamara, 1969; Kashefi-Zihajh, 1970; Cambell, Dunnette, Lawler and Weick, 1970; Bass and Klauss, 1973; Bass, Burger and Doktor, 1974; and Kraut, 1975).

The most important implication of all this is that businesses and organizations operating or intending to operate cross-culturally must recognize both the existence of and the complexity of this dilemma. Businesses and organizations operating in countries like India and Australia, for example, where moralistic values exist, must formulate management systems that relate effectively to these values in order to be successful in their pursuits.

References

Athos, Anthony G. and Robert E. Coffey: *Behavior in Organizations: A Multidimensional View.* Prentice-Hall, Englewood Cliffs, New Jersey, 1968.

Allport, G. W.: *Personality: A Psychological Interpretation.* Henry Holt, New York, 1937.

Badar, Hamed A., Edmund R. Gray and Ben L. Kedia: 'Personal Values and Managerial Decision Making: Evidence from Two Cultures.' *Management International Review.* Vol. 22, No. 3, 1982, pp. 65–73.

Bass, B. M. and R. Klauss: *Norms on Exercise Compensation for Accelerated, Normal, and Decelerated Managers from Seventeen Countries as of April, 1973.* (Technical Report 70, Management Research Center, University of Rochester, 1973).

Bass, B. M., P. Burger and R. Doktor: *What IRGOM Exercises Tell Us About*

Managerial Advancement in Different Countries. (IRGOM Technique Report 74–5, State University of New York at Binghamton, 1974).

Bruner, J. S. and C. C. Goodman: 'Value and Needs as Organizing Factors in Perception.' *Journal of Abnormal and Social Psychology*, Vol. XLII, 1947, pp. 33–44.

Campbell, Donald T.: 'The Indirect Assessment of Social Attitudes.' *Psychological Bulletin*, Vol. 47, 1950, pp. 15–38.

Campbell, J. P., M. D. Dunnette, E. E. Lawler and K. E. Weick: *Managerial Behavior, Performance and Effectiveness*, McGraw Hill, New York, 1970.

Conner, Patrick E. and Boris W. Becker: 'Values and the Organization: Suggestions for Research.' *Academy of Management Journal*, Vol. 18, No. 3, 1975, pp. 550–561.

England, George W., O. P. Dhingra and N. C. Agarwal: *The Manager and the Man.* Graduate School of Business Administration, Kent State University, Kent, Ohio, 1974.

England, George W.: *The Manager and His Values: An International Perspective.* Ballinger Publishing Company, Cambridge, Mass, 1975.

England, George W. and R. Lee: 'Relationship Between Managerial Values and Managerial Success in the U.S., Japan, India and Australia.' *Journal of Applied Psychology*, Vol. 59, No. 4, 1974, pp. 411–419.

England, George W.: 'Japanese and American Management: Theory Z and Beyond.' *Journal of International Business* (Fall 1983), pp. 131–141.

Farris, Martin T.: 'Purchasing Reciprocity and Antitrust.' *Journal of Purchasing* (Feb. 1973), pp. 15–27.

Gellerman, Saul W.: 'Passivity, Paranoia and Pakikisama.' *Columbia Journal of World Business* (Sept.–Oct. 1967), p. 59–66.

Guth, William D. and Renato Tagiuri: 'Personal Values and Corporate Strategy.' *Harvard Business Review* (Sept.–Oct. 1965), pp. 123–132.

Haire, M., E. Ghiselli and L. W. Porter: *Managerial Thinking: An International Study.* John Wiley, New York, 1966.

Harbison, F. and C. Myers: *Management in the Industrial World – An International Analysis.* McGraw-Hill, New York, 1959.

Hinrichs, J. R.: 'Comparison of Real Life Assessments of Management Potential with Situational Exercises, Paper and Pencil Ability Tests and Personal Inventories.' *Journal of Applied Psychology*, Vol. 53, 1967, p. 425–432.

Hughes, G., V. R. Rao and H. A. Alker: 'The Influence of Values, Information and Decision Orders on a Public Policy Decision.' Journal of Applied Social Psychology (April–June 1976), pp. 145–158.

Hull, C. L.: *Principles of Behavior*, Appleton Century, New York, 1943.

Jacox, Gordon Lee: 'Managerial Values and Organizational Goals.' Unpublished Ph.D. Dissertation, University of Utah, 1972.

Kashefi-Zihajh, M.: 'An Empirical Investigation of the Relationship Between Value Systems and Organizational Effectiveness.' Unpublished Ph.D. Dissertation, Michigan State University, 1970.

Katz, Daniel and Ezra Stotland: 'A Preliminary Statement to a Theory of Attitude Structure and Change,' in S. Koch (Ed.). *Psychology: A Study of Science*, McGraw-Hill, New York, 1959, pp. 423–475.

Kluckhohn, Clyde, *et al.*: 'Values and Value-Orientations in the Theory of Action,' in Talcott Parsons and Edward A. Shils (Eds.), *Toward a General Theory of Action*. Harper and Row, New York, 1962, pp. 388–433.

Kluckhohn, Clyde and F. L. Strodtbeck: *Variation in Value Orientations.* Row, Peterson and Company, Evanston, Illinois, 1961; and Greenwood Press, Westport, Conn. 1973.

Kraut, Allen I.: 'Some Recent Advances in Cross-National Management Research.' *Academy of Management Journal*, Vol. 18, No. 2, 1975, pp. 538–549.

Lewin, Kurt: *A Dynamic Theory of Personality*. McGraw Hill, New York, 1935.

Manley, T. R.: 'Personal Value Systems of Managers and the Operative Goals of Organization: An In-Depth Analysis of One Firm.' Unpublished Ph.D. Dissertation, Rensselaer Polytechnic Institute, Troy, NY, 1972.

McMurray, Robert N.: 'Conflicts in Human Values,' *Harvard Business Review* (May–June 1963), pp. 130–142.

Murray, H. A.: *Explorations in Personality*. Oxford University Press, New York, 1938.

Munson, J. Michael and Barry Z. Posner: 'Concurrent Validation of Two Value Inventories in Predicting Job Classification and Success for Organizational Personnel.' *Journal of Applied Psychology*, Vol. 65, No. 5, 1980, pp. 536–542.

Negandhi, A. R. and S. B. Prasad: *Comparative Management*. Appleton Century Crafts, New York, 1971.

Ouchi, W.: *Theory Z*. Addison-Wesley, Reading, Mass., 1981.

Patton, A.: 'Deterioration in Top Executive Pay.' *Harvard Business Review* (Nov.–Dec. 1965), pp. 106–118.

Pezeshkpur, C.: 'The Effects of Personal Value Structure on Decision-Making: A Study of Relationship Between Values and Decisions of University Business Administration Students.' Unpublished Ph.D. Dissertation, Louisiana State University, 1975.

Postman, J., J. S. Bruner and E. McGinnes: 'Personal Values as Selective Factors in Perception,' *Journal of Abnormal and Social Psychology*, Vol. 43, No. 2 (April 1948), pp. 142–154.

Rokeach, Milton: *Beliefs, Attitudes and Values*. Jossey-Bass, San Francisco, 1968.

Sekaran, Uma: 'Methodological and Theoretical Issues and Advances in Cross-Cultural Research,' *Journal of International Business Studies*. Vol. 14, No. 2 (Fall, 1983), pp. 61–73.

Senger, John: 'The Religious Manager,' *Academy of Management Journal* (June 1970), pp. 179–186.

Shartle, C., G. Brumbeck and J. Rizzo: 'An Approach to Dimensions of Values', *Journal of Psychology*, Vol. 57, 1964, pp. 101–111.

Sikula, A. F.: 'Values and Value Systems: Relationship to Personal Goals,' *Personnel Journal* (April 1971), pp. 310–312.

Tagiuri, Renato: 'Value Orientations and the Relationship of Managers and Scientists,' *Administrative Science Quarterly* (June 1965), pp. 39–51.

Tylor, Edward B.: *Primitive Culture*, I. John Murray, London, 1871.

Theodorson, George A. and Achilles G. Theodorson: *A Modern Dictionary of Sociology*. Cromwell, New York, 1969.

Udy, S. H.: *Organizations of Work*. HRAF Press, New Haven, 1959.

Wollowich, H. B. and W. J. McNamara: 'Relationship of the Components of an Assessment Centre to Management Success,' *Journal of Applied Psychology*, Vol. 53, 1969, pp. 348–352.

Reproduced from Davis, H. J. and Rasool, S. A. (1988). Values research and managerial behavior: implications for devising culturally consistent managerial styles. *Management International Review*, **28** (3), 11–20, by permission of *Management International Review*.

1.3 Model building in organizational/cross-cultural research: the need for multiple methods, indices and cultures

Fritz Rieger and Durhane Wong-Rieger

We shall here use two studies to illustrate the merits of various research methodologies in cross-cultural management. These studies were part of a larger research project whose primary goal was to develop a model relating societal culture, organizational strategy, and organizational performance. Study 1 consisted of field research on nine international airlines representing five different types of societal culture.[1] The primary data-collection methods were unobtrusive observations and interviews with key personnel. Study 2 was essentially archival research, using the published statistics and performance records of a sample of 32 international airlines, 8 of which were also included in the field study.[2]

The overriding objectives in terms of building a model were to ensure that it was grounded in reality and that it was generally applicable across a variety of societies. The rationale for adopting a multimethod approach was to attempt to achieve convergence through a process of triangulation. In this way it would be possible to compensate partly for the limitations and biases inherent in any one form of inquiry by using a method that did not share those same limitations and biases. Similarly, the purpose in using archival data was to have access to a larger sample; this would address the lack of generalizability of findings revealed in field research, which necessarily involves a smaller number of participants.

There is a particularly critical need for multiple methods when studying phenomena as complex as organizations or cultures. According to Weick, organizational behavior is best captured and examined through 'multiple hypotheses, multiple theoretical degrees of freedom, multiple indicators, and multiple methods' [1; 2, pp. 188–93]. Similarly, when comparing cultures, researchers have argued for more than one methodological approach in order to increase the general validity of theories and models [3,4]. As noted by Brislin [5, p. 400], each method has its own biases; however, if several methods with nonoverlapping biases are employed and they all lead to the same conclusions, one has increased confidence in the robustness of the model under investigation.

Another essential aspect of building organizational and/or cross-cultural models is to start with theories that are grounded in reality, that is, with data gathered in real organizational settings [6]. According to Rothwell [7], the state of knowledge about organizational behavior is still limited. There has been a tendency to engage in 'armchair theorizing', to generate hypotheses on the basis of 'sketchy' and 'fortuitous' observations, and to reach 'premature parsimony' in theory-building. To rectify this situation, greater emphasis should be placed on induction instead of deduction, on developing rather than testing hypotheses, and on gathering a broad range of information in a few settings rather than highly specific data from many subjects.

Although field methods increase external validity and the ability to produce useful and usable findings, they have limitations, which affect primarily internal validity and the ability to generalize beyond the sample. In terms of the field research reported here, these limitations included interference from extraneous or confounding environmental factors; nonmanipulation of many independent variables; lack of precise, standardized, dependent measures; nonrandomized sampling in terms of both the selection of participants and their assignment to groups; and small sample size, which reduces representativeness.

The first two problems, lack of environmental and independent-variable control, mostly affect the ability to detect true relationships and make causal inferences – that is, internal validity. This was addressed partially by focusing on a single setting, the international airline industry, for field testing. The key advantage in limiting scope in an inductive research program is that one reduces random 'noise' and makes 'pattern detection' more evident [6]. The disadvantage, however, is loss of generalizability to other areas.

The lack of precision in measurements was dealt with partly by using multiple sources of data. Two principal methods were unobtrusive measures of verbal and nonverbal behavior and self-report interview data. To the degree that the information provided by the two sources converged, that is, yielded a similar conclusion, it could reasonably be considered 'true'. In addition, the findings from Study 2 served as a check on the field measures.

Finally, Bochner [8, p. 330] has argued that when participants are not randomly assigned, as is the case in cross-cultural studies in which the variable used to assign subjects to treatment levels is based on cultural grouping, multiple corroboration of methods and indices is essential. The following excerpts from the two studies serve to illustrate these principles.

Study 1: Field research

The field research was conducted with a sample of nine international airlines from nine countries, chosen to represent five theoretically derived cultural configurations. The goals of the research were to confirm these groupings; to determine differences among the airlines in their organizational structure, behavior patterns, and strategic decision-making; and to derive relationships between organizational measures and cultural indices. Thus, the project was primarily an inductive study that attempted to build a model relating cultural groupings to organizational patterns of behavior.

An initial cultural model was proposed as a guide for classifying countries and gathering data. The intent was not to substantiate the model, but to use it as a frame of reference. The actual model was to be derived from the field data; however, the initial one provided an orienting framework that could be used to categorize the sample and to suggest dimensions and variables that should be examined in the field settings. It also suggested relationships between culture and organizational measures.

A review of the literature[3] suggested four cultural dimensions that potentially differentiated among most known societies:

> *Power* refers to the ability of leaders to effect decisions and to control choices in the organization. To the degree that executives exercise unilateral control, their power is high.
>
> *Authority distance* refers to the degree of separation between the superior and the subordinate in the hierarchical structure. Authority distance affects the flow of information to key decision-makers and the centralization of decision-making activities.
>
> *Group orientation* refers to the use of small groups to accomplish social or organizational goals. Group orientation affects the informal circulation of information and the support of group members for their leader, especially in interactions with other groups.
>
> *Cognitive orientation* refers to the way information is processed by the key decision-makers. It is characterized as either intuitive, that is, based on executive judgments of timely, qualitative information, or analytic, that is, characterized by linear and systematic analysis of quantitative information.

Two other cultural dimensions, fatalism and risk orientation, have been included by some researchers as additional cultural dimensions. Because they seem to have their primary impact at the individual decision-making level, they were not included in the original model. As noted in the following discussion, however, risk orientation, which is defined as the proclivity of the leader to make bold, high-stakes decisions, did emerge in these studies as an important differentiating variable.

A fundamental principle underlying this research is that organizations are not random collections of characteristics, but form coherent configurations. From a functional perspective, organizations are inherently driven toward

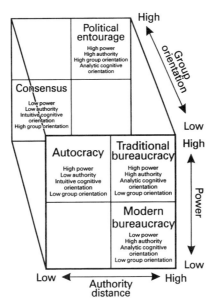

Figure 1 *Cultural configuration framework*

configuration in order to achieve internal consistency, to operate synergisti-
cally in their processes, and to exist in harmony with their surrounding
economic, political, and cultural realities [12]. This paradigm implies that the
number of viable configurations will be limited. In this case, although the 4
dimensions gave rise to 16 possible combinations, only 5 configurations were
needed to account for the various organizational types reviewed in the
literature (Figure 1). These were defined as follows:

Modern bureaucracies (MBs) are typically low along the dimensions of power
and group orientation, but high on authority distance and analytic cognitive
orientation. They are typified by Germanic societies such as those of Germany
and Austria and other societies in northern Europe and North America.

Traditional bureaucracies (TBs) are similarly low in group orientation and
highly analytic in cognitive orientation, but are differentiated from MBs by high
authority and power distances. Representatives include countries with
Romance-language origins, such as Italy and Spain.

Political entourages (PEs) are like TBs except that they exhibit high group
orientation. They are found in certain West African and Asian countries such as
Nigeria and Thailand.

Asian autocracies (AUTs) differ along several indices, with low authority
distance, high power, low group orientation, and highly intuitive, as opposed to
analytic, cognitive orientation. This combination is found in certain Asian
countries such as Singapore, Indonesia, and the Philippines.

The consensus configuration (CON) was based on descriptions of large Japanese
organizations [13–15] and was characterized by low authority distance, low power,

very high group orientation, and moderately intuitive (holistic) cognitive orientation.

The model suggested that organizations within the same cultural grouping should show similar structures and processes and that there should be clear differences among cultural groupings. The first task in the field research, then, was to examine organizational indices of authority, power, group orientation, and cognitive orientation to determine whether the predicted similarities and differences were obtained. The nine airlines chosen to represent four of the five cultural groups were: Lufthansa (Germany), Alitalia (Italy), PIA (Pakistan), VARIG (Brazil), Thai International (Thailand), SIA (Singapore), Garuda (Indonesia), PAL (the Philippines), and Air Canada (Canada). The researchers visited each of the headquarters offices, were able to fly on eight of the airlines, and consulted company documents and published airline-industry materials.

A primary source of information was unobtrusive field observations. These are defined as naturally occurring, nonreactive measures of persons and environment. They included overt behaviors of employees and contextual indices such as office arrangement and size of the work group. Unobtrusive measures are important because they are not contaminated by self-report biases (see Proshansky [16, p. 109]). The other form of relatively nonbiased field data consisted of written documents, both proprietary and public.

These were complemented, then, by information obtained in interviews with key personnel. In contrast to unobtrusive measures, interviewing is a highly obtrusive form of data collection; it is defined as conversation for the purpose of obtaining specific information. With certain types of respondents, it is more useful than written questionnaires [17, p. 94], particularly where language differences exist. The respondent has an opportunity to seek clarification of questions and to explain his or her responses. In addition, the rapport established between the interviewer and the interviewee increases the likelihood of obtaining responses. Interviews also produce several other types of important information. Verbal, unobtrusive data are revealed in the subsequent analysis of the content (topics) and process (who initiated a topic, responded, offered support, etc.) of the interview sessions. At the same time, nonverbal, obtrusive measures may be obtained – e.g. indices of the behavior of the interviewee, the amount of eye contact, the length of the meeting, the amount of hesitancy, and the withholding of information.

The problems and limitations associated with the interview method are the opposite of those inherent in unobtrusive measures – e.g. a high potential for response bias and a lack of anonymity that increases the potential for deception, acquiescence, and biased presentation of self. Moreover, the experimenter also introduces bias by asking leading questions and providing nonverbal cues concerning desired and desirable responses. All these factors serve to decrease validity.

As discussed previously, the process followed here was one of mutual corroboration; tentative conclusions drawn from one source were checked against those from another. For example, observations that Thai employees worked in small groups and had close personal relationships were confirmed by interviews with their managers and by company documents outlining their training programs and objectives. According to Webb and co-workers [18], if multiple indices that are based on the same underlying dimension but have different imprecise components all lead to the same conclusion, then that conclusion tends to be substantiated. Thus, through a process of triangulation, we could be reasonably confident in concluding that operations at Thai International did indeed reflect a high group orientation.

A final form of data gathered in the field consisted of case studies about strategic decisions made by each of the airlines. These were obtained primarily from interviews and company documents. They served the purpose of providing a more general perspective about the airlines, and this was then checked against the profile generated by the more specific indices.

As a result of the discrepancies between the model and the field-study findings, three major, but related, changes in the framework were made: the political entourage was abandoned: a new configuration, the implicitly structured organization (IMP), was added; and risk orientation supplanted group orientation in the model (Figure 2). According to the original framework, high group orientation should have distinguished the political entourages from the traditional bureaucracies; however, the two highly group-oriented airlines. Varig and Thai International, exhibited few of the characteristics expected of the political entourage. The only other type that depended on high group orientation was the consensus configuration. Since the principal consensus configuration country (Japan) was not studied in either research project, it is only tentatively included in the revised cultural framework.

In the case of the implicitly structured configuration, risk orientation was observed to be a more important dimension than originally proposed. The IMPs, which were based partly on Hofstede's [9] description, were expected to exhibit high risk orientations and consequent greater reliance on intuitive judgment than the modern bureaucracies. According to Hofstede, the IMPs would include the predominantly anglophone countries, the Netherlands, and the Scandinavian countries.

The airline representing the IMPs in the field sample, Air Canada, operated much like Lufthansa, which had been classified as a modern bureaucracy. According to the initial model, the only differentiating feature was risk orientation; MBs displayed low risk orientation whereas the IMPs were thought to be relatively high on this dimension. In fact, the IMP airline also displayed only moderately higher risk orientation than the modern bureaucracy. Because of the limited sample size, it was important to check the generality of this finding in a larger sample and, specifically, to determine whether there were three or four distinct cultural groupings.

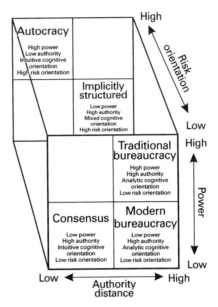

Figure 2   *Revised cultural configuration framework, recognizing the importance of risk orientation and replacement of the group orientation dimension*

Study 2: Correlational research

The second study was in the form of correlational research.[4] The purpose here was partly inductive, that is, to contribute to building the cultural model; however, a more specific focus was to test whether the model and relationships derived from the field research were substantiated when a larger sample and other indices were used. In this respect, it tended to involve deductive hypothesis-testing, especially with regard to the airlines' operational strategies and performance.

A sample of 32 airlines was selected, and data were obtained from the published statistics of the International Civil Aviation Organization (ICAO) for the years ending 1974 and 1978. This period was chosen because it paralleled an important industry cycle discussed by respondents in Study 1.

Because of the archival nature of the data, the variables used were surrogates for the constructs of interest. For example, the proportions of persons employed in various functional specialities were used as indicators of the functional emphasis (strategy) of each company. Similarly, administrative ratios indicated the degree of bureaucratization. Other relationships included measures of strategy (pricing, level of service, types of aircraft, degree of diversification) and performance (productivity, profitability, growth). Structure was hypothesized to be related primarily to power, authority distance, and group orientation: strategy was expected to be related to cognitive orientation and authority distance.

The airlines were categorized according to five cultural groupings on the basis of the four final dimensions revealed in Study 1, using data abstracted from Hofstede's [9] 40-nation survey. Thus, as discussed previously, the correlational research could serve to corroborate and extend the generality of findings from Study 1. However, this method also introduced its own biases and limitations. In general, results from correlational research may be misleading because of the influence of spurious, intervening or moderating variables. Since independent variables are not manipulated, it is not possible to rule out reverse or reciprocal causal relations. Moreover, when there are intervening variables, the results may inaccurately suggest a direct relationship between the independent and the dependent variables, when the true relationship exists with a third intervening variable that is not measured. For example, if an airline such as Thai International had an inegalitarian distribution of salaries, this might suggest relatively high individual competitiveness and hence low group orientation; but if salary differentials were pegged to industry-wide standards for job classifications, not to individual achievement, they would not necessarily lead to competition or disrupt group harmony. In the research reported here, however, the true causal variable, salary standards, was not measured.

Another problem common to the type of correlational research conducted here is information bias. The data are often obtained from secondhand sources, either public or private, and are not 'scientifically pure.' Because records were not made for the purpose of the research at hand, they are biased by selective deposit (what was stored) and selective survival (what was retained). In this case, however, the correlational data were examined in conjunction with the firsthand information obtained in the field, thus compensating in part for such biases.

In general, the overall field relationships were indeed substantiated. Cultural indices of power and authority distance were reflected in measures of deployment of personnel and salary differentials, high authority/high power countries showing greater differences among occupational groups. Moreover, the data tended to confirm the field observations of similarities between the MBs and the IMPs, and greater differences among all other groupings. In other respects as well, the IMPs functioned like the MBs. More importantly, in terms of the findings of Study 1, they did not pursue aggressive passenger or growth strategies, as was predicted by the original model, but, as suggested by the Air Canada field data, had low risk orientation, like the modern bureaucracies. Specifically, ticketing strategies and load factors indicated low risk orientation for the MB, IMP, and TB groups. The growths in assets and passengers were also lowest for both the MB and IMP groups, but highest among the AUT, high-risk-orientation group. Finally, diversification in terms of revenue-producing acquisitions appeared to be very low among the MBs, in contrast to the IMPs, which were second only to the high-risk-orientation AUTs.

Conclusions

Overall, there appeared to be considerable consistency in the conclusions derived from two studies using different methodological approaches and measures. Thus, although each approach separately could be considered to have biases and limitations, together each tended to compensate for the other's deficiencies and jointly lent confidence to the validity of the findings, which were necessarily based on relatively small organizational samples.

This account has shown how a modest research program addressed methodological problems that are very common in international research. Its implied message, whether the researcher's primary strategy is quantitative or qualitative, is to incorporate some of the other strategy's methods in the research program.

For the researcher conducting a quantitative survey, this means including at least one field method in the program. The most convenient choice for survey researchers is to include in-depth interviews of key personnel on a broad range of related topics during the pilot testing of the survey instrument. But why stop there? Once the researcher has overcome all the obstacles to entry into an organization, it would seem economical to include a short program of unobtrusive observation and the collection of historic archival materials.

For the field researcher conducting a qualitative study, the message differs somewhat. Field researchers can, however, search for limited quantitative data bases and exploit the ones that are known. For example, there is a vast amount of untapped, publicly available data related to airline management in the sources cited here. Other sources of archival data include reports published by intergovernmental organizations, such as the United Nations and the OECD, and articles in the various industry presses, especially those related to capital-intensive and financial-services industries. The reliability of such data must be carefully evaluated, but we suspect that data useful for corroborating fieldwork is often overlooked. As an illustration, we were aware of the ICAO data base throughout the period of our field research, but a full year passed before it occurred to us to use it for the statistical analysis presented here.

In summary, the message to be drawn from these examples is that the use of multiple research methods and alternative sources of data in a research program can effectively aid in understanding and corroborating the initial findings of exploratory research.

Notes

1 F. Rieger (1987) 'The Influence of National Culture on Organizational Structure. Process and Strategic Decision Making: A Study of International Airlines.' Unpublished Ph. D. dissertation. Montreal: McGill University.
2 F. Rieger and D. Wong-Rieger (1985) 'Towards a Contingency Model of Strategy and Performance: Cross-national Comparisons of Airline Strategies under Stable and Dynamic Conditions.' Paper presented at the Fifth Annual Strategic Management Society Conference, Barcelona, Spain.
3 See Rieger (note 1) for a thorough review. Important influences on the development of the four dimensions were Hofstede [9]. Mintzberg [10], and Redding [11].
4 Rieger and Wong-Rieger (1985) *Op. cit.*

References

1 Webb, E., and Weick, K. (1979) 'Unobtrusive Measures in Organization Theory: A Reminder.' *Administrative Science Quarterly. 24*, 650–59.
2 Weick, K. (1979) *The Social Psychology of Organizing.* Reading. MA: Addison-Wesley.
3 Campbell, D. T. (1968) 'Quasi-experimental Design.' In D. L. Sills (Ed.), *International Encyclopedia of the Social Sciences.* New York: Macmillan. Vol. 5. pp. 259–63.
4 Campbell, D. T., and Fiske, D. W. (1959) 'Convergent and Discriminant Validation by the Multitrait-Multimethod Matrix.' *Psychological Bulletin. 56*, 178–93.
5 Brislin, R. W. (1980) 'Translation and Content Analysis of Oral and Written Material.' In H. Triandis and J. W. Berry (Eds.), *Handbook of Cross-cultural Psychology.* Vol. 2, *Methodology.* Boston: Allyn and Bacon, pp. 389–444.
6 Glaser, B. G., and Strauss, A. L. (1967) *The Discovery of Grounded Theory: Strategies for Qualitative Research.* Hawthorne. New York: Aldine.
7 Rothwell, A. (1980) 'Research in Progress – is Grounded Theory What Management Needs?' *Journal of European Industrial Training, 4*, xi–xiii.
8 Bochner, S. (1980) 'Unobtrusive Methods in Cross-cultural Experimentation.' In H. Triandis and J. W. Berry (Eds.), *Handbook of Cross-cultural Psychology.* Vol. 2. *Methodology.* Boston: Allyn and Bacon, Pp. 319–87.
9 Hofstede, G. (1980) *Culture's Consequences: International Differences in Work-related Values.* Beverly Hills, CA: Sage.
10 Mintzberg, H. (1973) 'Strategy Making in Three Modes.' *California Management Review, 16[2]*, 44–53.
11 Redding, S. G. (1980) 'Cognition as an Aspect of Culture and Its Relation to Management Processes: An Exploratory View of the Chinese Case.' *Journal of Management Studies, 17*, 127–48.
12 Miller, D., and Mintzberg, H. (1983) 'The Case for Configuration.' In G. Morgan (Ed.). *Beyond Method: Strategies for Social Research.* Beverly Hills, CA: Sage. pp. 57–73.
13 Abegglen, J. (1968) *The Japanese Factory: Aspects of Its Social Organization.* New York: The Free Press.
14 Yoshino, M. (1968) *Japan's Managerial System.* Cambridge, MA: M.I.T. Press.

15 Rohlen, T. (1974) *For Harmony and Strength: Japanese White Collar Organization in Anthropological Perspective* Berkeley, CA: University of California Press.
16 Proshansky, H. M. (1981) 'Uses and Abuses of Theory in Applied Research.' *Applied Social Psychology Annual.* Beverly Hills, CA: Sage. Vol. 2, pp. 97–136.
17 Fisher, R. J. (1982) *Social Psychology: An Applied Approach.* New York: St. Martin's Press.
18 Webb, E., Campbell, D., Schwartz, R., and Sechrest, L. (1966) *Unobtrusive Measures: Nonreactive Research in the Social Sciences.* Chicago: Rand McNally.

Reproduced from Rieger, F. and Wong-Rieger, D. (1988). Model building in organizational/cross-cultural research: the need for multiple methods, indices and cultures. *International Studies of Management and Organizations,* **XVIII** (3), 19–30, by permission of *International Studies of Management and Organizations.*

Part Two
Managing cultural differences

Are organizations, and the ways in which they are managed, becoming similar? With an increase in the globalization of business and the increasing importance of 'transnational' organizations, is one management style applicable in any country within which the international manager chooses to work? This part of the text looks at differences and similarities in various aspects of management: how the organization is perceived, the management of motivation, management styles, and managerial values in the international context.

Organizations and cultural convergence

'Mind set' is an important aspect of the evolution of transnational organizations, as the focus is not simply on organizational structures and systems, but on how managers think and operate in the international setting. Hence van Dijck (1990), in the first reading, outlines the main tendencies towards 'transnationalization' as:

- an increase in cross-border operations
- increase international personnel mobility
- more intra-European competition between companies
- a growing need for companies to balance local and international strategies
- having to manage diversity
- changing multinational organizational structures
- possibilities of a real 'social Europe' for personnel.

He discusses the trend towards cultural convergence at the deeper level of value orientation, such as in decreasing religious emphasis, a commitment to the democratic process, work as an important value in itself, and the drive towards quality of life. However, contrasted to this is the apparent social and cultural diversity of Western Europe, particularly on the organizational 'surface' of economic and social life. This is particularly apparent in management styles, organizational forms and human resource practices.

From this tendency towards transnationalism, in the way depicted by van Dijck (1990), we can begin to understand the requirements for managers working in this context. He identifies a profile of European management which may be distinct from that of Japanese and American management (this aspect is revisited in Chapter Ten of the current text. The profile he lists as comprising such elements as managing diversity, sharing across borders missions and strategies within the transnational organization, while promoting cross-cultural communication and learning, and having a greater mobility of human resources to encourage this learning.

The second reading in Chapter Two (Vertinsky, Tse, Wehrung and Lee, 1990) looks for evidence that organizational design and management are subject to globalization leading to convergence of management practices. They compare organizations in the People's Republic of China, Hong Kong and Canada, concluding that there are significant differences in orientation towards participation, formal structure and internal competition and risk; but no differences in strategic adaptiveness, democratic organization and centralization. Similarly, when focusing on desirable attributes of managers within these organizations, there are similar requirements for general management skills across the three countries. However, there are differences in the views towards experimentation and innovation, and in 'traditional Chinese values' such as ascribed status, intuition and loyalty to the organization.

The conclusions drawn are that while there is evidence to suggest convergence, barriers created against outside influences (such as in the People's Republic of China) inhibit these convergence processes. But, rather than the results of this research being against convergence, it does suggest that this process is occurring in the world through greater globalization.

Differences in motivation

Theories of motivation can be conveniently divided into process theories (for example attribution theory: Kelley, 1967; Rotter, 1966; and expectancy theory: Porter and Lawler, 1968; Campbell and Pritchard, 1976) and content theories (for example, Maslow, 1954; Hertzberg *et al.* 1959; McClelland (1987). The assertion is made by Jackson (1993) elsewhere that process theories can travel across cultures as they simply provide the 'how' of motivation. Thus attribution theory focuses on people's perceptions of how an outcome was achieved, which will influence future performance and motivation towards particular actions; and expectancy theory focuses on how desirable an outcome is in terms of its attractiveness and the perceived effort needed to achieve the outcome, and the likelihood of the outcome following the action taken. Content theories try to answer the question, 'What outcomes are attractive to the individual and why?' Thus they provide us with a content which may or may not be appropriate in one particular culture, and a methodology which has been employed in cross-cultural research in order to discover what the differences may be between an indigenous employee working in a multinational company's subsidiary in Spain and one working in Germany.

Most studies of this nature are fairly small scale, but provide us with useful information about such differences, and how, as managers, we may act to recognize and stimulate different types of needs and motives in different cultural settings. Even if we cannot draw conclusive results from published studies, we can perhaps use some of the methods to gain valuable insights into local situations as we move into a new cultural setting. It is with this view that the first reading has been offered, in Chapter Three, as a starting point for understanding cultural differences in motivation.

Alpanda and Carter (1991) provide details of a study undertaken in a major multinational pharmaceuticals company in eight different countries. The results reveal that the most important motivator for the professional and front-line supervisors surveyed in all countries is the need to control and influence others. However, the second and third ranked motivators show differences between countries which provide important clues about how managers and organizations should attempt to meet these needs. Hence for the Japanese sample, the second ranked motivator is the need to be recognized for their achievements and the third is to belong to a social group. The authors suggest that the use of action planning in Japanese management may satisfy the need to control (through the action plan) and fulfil the need to be recognized as a result of achievement of a publicly declared goal. The work carried out in a group setting may also fulfil the need to belong. For the European respondents, economic security was ranked second after the need to control, suggesting that they may be highly motivated if they are provided with a decision-making authority and monetary rewards attached to successful task performance.

A more extensive study was carried out by the Meaning of Work (MOW) project which collected data from nearly 15,000 respondents in eight countries in the early 1980s. England's (1986) article, the second reading in Chapter three, uses this data to focus on three major economic players, Germany, USA and Japan, in order to contrast differences in the centrality of work and its implications on constraints on management action. The main findings reported show work is very central in the life of Japanese workers, and relatively low for German employees. Furthermore, economic motivators are far more important for German workers than they are for Japanese workers who place importance on 'expressive' work goals, such as autonomy and interesting work. US workers are at a mid-distance on these two indicators. This has implications for management action which is expressed in terms of the constraint on action by England (1986) who also considers other indicators of the way employees in different cultures may be motivated. The MOW study still represents an important contribution to knowledge in that it provides an extensive overview of different cultural attitudes and values.

Differences in management styles

The extent to which styles of management are comparable between national cultures has been debated in the literature, with the apparent American management 'imperialism' of consultants and multinational companies who seek to introduce Western ideas of participative management, employee empowerment, and Management By Objectives, for example, into other countries without due consideration for the nature of indigenous management styles. Convergence theory seems to support such efforts. For example, Kerr *et al.* (1976) suggest that as societies develop towards economic parity with Western societies, so their management styles will converge with those of the West. These theories have perhaps been assumed by Western practitioners in developing countries (but see Jaeger and Kanungo, 1990), and are being taken up in Eastern European countries as they move towards free market economies.

The antithesis of this argument is that managerial style is related to national culture, and such writers as Hofstede (1980) have been warning that Western management theories and practices may not work well in other cultures, and that we should therefore consider the nature of the host culture and its relationship to management style. However, this argument is not clear cut. For example, can a highly autocratic style of management in one country be supported by advocates of participative management in an industrialized country (see for example, Sashkin, 1986, who argues that participative management is an ethical issue)?

The article by Evans, Hau and Sculli (1989), the first reading in Chapter Four, looks at this debate and examines the way cultural values appear to influence managerial styles.

A distinction has long been made in Anglo-American literature between 'task' or performance behaviour (with a concentration on getting the job done, and on directive communication) and 'maintenance' behaviour (with a concentration on building relations, and on two-way communication) (Morse and Reimer, 1956; Fiedler, 1967; Tannenbaum and Schmitt, 1973; Hersey and Blanchard, 1977; Blake and Mouton, 1985), a theory which is still prevalent today and used extensively in management development programmes. The second reading (Smith, Misumi, Tayeb, Peterson and Bond, 1989) questions the application of these dimensions across different cultures. Their research, presented in the following pages, found that what constituted these two leadership styles actually differs from one culture to another, to the point that a finer distinction betwen these two dimensions is made in the USA and the UK, and the distinctions start to blur in Chinese and Japanese management behaviour. Perhaps this is not too surprising with a theory with Anglo-American origins!

A major question we should therefore ask, particularly regarding the management of motivation and of styles of management, is, can we transport Western theories (or Anglo-American theories) to other cultures? Are they relevant to the particular cultures with which we are working?

Values and working ethically in international business

The centrality of cultural values in the study of cross-cultural management has been discussed in Part One. In Chapter Five Hofstede (1994) outlines the updated value dimensions from his recent book *Cultures and Organizations: Software of the Mind* (1991), while Lachman, Nedd and Hinings (1994) point out that it is necessary not only to identify value orientations, but also to discover the centrality of these values within a particular culture. However, they are not specific on methods for doing so. In the contribution by Jackson (1993) the implications of different values for ethically doing business across cultures is discussed. A method, based on personal construct psychology (Kelly, 1955) is also proposed which identifies superordinate values together with subordinate values in a hierarchy of values structure which may meet the requirement of Lachman and associates (1994) in discovering the centrality of particular values for specific cultural groups.

References

Alpanda, G. G. and Carter, K. D. (1991) 'Strategic multinational intra-company differences in employee motivation', *Journal of Managerial Psychology*, Vol. 6, No. 2, 25–32.

Blake, R. R. and Mouton, J. S. (1985) *The Managerial Grid III*, Houston, Tx: Gulf.

Campbell, J. P. and Pritchard, R. D. (1976) 'Motivational theory in industrial and organizational psychology', in Dunnette, M. D. (ed.), *Handbook of Industrial and Organizational Psychology*, Chicago: Rand McNally.

van Dijck, J. J. J. (1990) 'Transnational Management in an evolving European context', *European Management Journal*, Vol. 8, No. 4, 474–9.

England, G. W. (1986) 'National work meanings and patterns – constraints on managerial action', *European Management Journal*, Vol. 4, No. 3, 176–84.

Evans, W. A., Hau, K. C. and Sculli, D. (1989) 'A cross-cultural comparison of managerial styles', *Journal of Management Development*, Vol. 8, No. 3, 5–13.

Fiedler, F. (1967) *A Theory of Leadership Effectiveness*, New York: McGraw-Hill.

Hersey, P. and Blanchard, K. (1977) *Management of Organizational Behaviour: Utilizing Human Resources*, Englewood Cliffs, New Jersey: Prentice-Hall.

Herzberg, F., Mausner, B. and Snyderman, B. (1959) *The Motivation to Work*, New York: Wiley

Hofstede, G. (1980) 'Motivation, leadership and organization: Do American theories apply abroad?' *Organizational Dynamics*, Summer, 42–63.

Hofstede, G. (1991) *Cultures and Organizations: Software of the Mind*, London: McGraw-Hill.

Hofstede, G, (1994) 'The business of international business is culture', *International Business Review*, Vol. 3, No. 1, 1–14.

Jackson, T. (1993) 'Ethics and the art of intuitive management', *European Management Journal*, EAP 20th Anniversary edition, 57–65.

Jackson, T. (1993) *Organizational Behaviour in International Management*, Oxford: Butterworth-Heinemann.

Jaeger, A. M. and Kanungo, R. N. (eds) (1990) *Management In Developing Countries*, London: Routledge.

Kelly, G. (1955) *The Psychology of Personal Constructs, Vol. 1 and 2*, New York: Norton.

Kelley, H. H. (1967) 'Attribution theory in social psychology', *Nebraska Symposium on Motivation*, 15, 192–238.

Kerr, C, Dunlop, J. T., Harbison, F. H. and Myers, C. A. (1976) *Industrialism and Industrial Man*, Cambridge Mass.: Harvard University Press.

Lachman, R., Nedd, A. and Hinings, B. (1994) 'Analysing cross-national management and organizations: a theoretical framework', *Management Science*, Vol. 40, No. 1, January 1994, 40–55

Maslow, A. H. (1954) *Motivation and Personality*, New York: Harper and Row.

McClelland, D. (1987) *Human Motivation*, Cambridge: Cambridge University Press

Morse, N. C. and Reimer, E. (1956) 'The experimental change of a major organizational variable', *Journal of Abnormal and Social Psychology*, Vol. 52, 120–9.

Porter, L. W. and Lawler, E. E. (1968), *Managerial Attitudes and Performance*, Illinois: Dorsey Press.

Rotter, J. B. (1966) 'Generalized expectancies for internal versus external control of reinforcement', *Psychological Monographs*, 80, 1, whole No. 609.

Sashkin, M. (1986) 'Participative management remains an ethical imperative', *Organizational Dynamics*, Vol. 14, No. 4, 62–75.

Smith, P. B., Misumi, J., Tayeb, M., Peterson, M. and Bond, M. (1989), 'On the generality of leadership style measures across cultures', *Journal of Occupational Psychology*, Vol. 62, 97–109.

Tannenbaum, R. and Schmitt, W. H. (1973) 'How to choose a leadership pattern', *Harvard Business Review*, 1973, May-June.

Vertinsky, I., Tse, D. K., Wehrung, D. A. and Lee K-H (1990) 'Organizational design and management norms: a comparative study of managers' perceptions in the People's Republic of China, Hong Kong, and Canada', *Journal of Management*, Vol. 16, No. 4, 853–67.

2 Organizations

2.1 Transnational management in an evolving European context

Jules J. J. van Dijck

The year '1992' is symbolically and factually a mile-stone in transforming business and social life in Europe. I like to term the intent and the outcome of the many border-crossing processes: 'transnationalization' of business. The accelerating process of internationalization in economic and socio-political life in Europe will stimulate comparison, confrontation and critical reflection on so-called 'national' ideas, preferences and patterns in management. Many academic comparative studies on management styles, organizational patterns, industrial relations are showing us that institutional factors on the macro-level still reinforce 'national identities'. Important factors are the educational system (patterns of recruitment and socialization in management), collective labour relations, the business-government relationship (Maurice *et al.*, 1982). The consciousness of the strengths and weaknesses of these 'national' patterns and styles is definitely increasing. Applying Anglo-Saxon ideas and approaches on management behaviour in large French firms, Michel Crozier (1989) sketches an interesting option for organizational renewal that might enable French firms to adapt more successfully to the complex international environment. What is going on is a cross-national, cross-cultural learning process. It may offer for managers and their firms a tremendous potential for renewal. It will eventually lead to a competitive European model set against American and Japanese models which are still so dominating management science.

Transnationalization: increasing evidence

- A considerable increase in cross-border operations, investment and strategies of firms and corporations in Europe.
- International mobility and personnel flows of young graduates, professionals and managers are expected in the 90s. This raises the need for business education objectives and systems that are based on trans-European ideas and realities.

- There will be more competition between firms and businesses in Europe than between countries.
- Within both 'young' and mature MNCs there is a growing need for an effective balancing of international business strategies on the one side (R&D, human resources, logistics, rationalisation of the manufacturing system), and strong local/regional (national) demands on the other. Strong local demands and consequently an increasing awareness of diversity in international management relate in particular to quality, customer service and social responsiveness, i.e. the development of employment.
- In international management both the dilemmas and challenges of the 'management of diversity' are becoming evident (Prahalad and Doz, 1987). Rational and strategic utilisation of all kinds of resources across borders (capital, information, knowledge, people) on the one hand, and the necessity of differentiating between areas (countries, regions) in terms of political, market and socio-cultural approaches on the other, have their impact on management thinking. A new paradigm may be the search for 'transnational solutions' in the realm of organisation, business–government relationships, human resources and culture (Bartlett and Ghoshal, 1989).
- The organizational structure of the larger MNCs is changing. MNCs are trying to move beyond a 'static' matrix of product strategies (conceived and directed in the divisions of headquarters in the home country) and local production and sales operations in 'national' organizations in the various host countries. MNCs are building up 'transnational' networks and procedures for strategic decision making, product development and coordination. Internationalization and transnationalization in the functional realms of R&D, human resource management, logistics, are becoming very important. All this means that many professionals and managers from different countries are getting involved, through taskforces, project groups, conferences, etc., in international activity and learning.
- Lastly, there is a real chance of a 'Social Europe' as far as worker rights (information and consultation), personnel mobility, and legal and socio-political aspects of business are concerned. The dynamics of international business development in Europe will determine to a large extent the European employment structure.

In search of European 'excellence'

The creation of effective trans-European business organizations requires new managerial approaches and systems (Thurley and Wirdenius, 1989).

Managerial reforms will create '*élan*' and will receive support only if they are rooted in the values and behaviour of a European way of life. Set against American and Japanese styles, managerial reform in European countries will have to cope with the following issues and challenges:

- increasing effectiveness: productivity, quality and flexibility;
- translating better and faster science and technology into improved and/or new products;
- integrating through 'organic' work systems R&D, production and marketing (Burns and Stalker, 1961). This means that the management of professionals and the management of innovation should receive a high priority;
- managing and developing human resources along lines and principles of self-development, in a context of a rather widespread attitude to work and life that is called 'individualization';
- organizing 'intrapreneurship' through international business networking;
- developing social strategies for a transnational approach of education, employment and worker rights.

Following this line of reasoning, the concept or meta-strategy of *Trans*nationalization seems to be quite different from the classic approach of *Multi*nationalization.

A key element is the search for transnational solutions given the problems and opportunities related to the management of diversity. In the model presented below (Figure 1) 'management of diversity' is a very central viewpoint. Strategic, organizational, administrative and social (and human resources) choices are all very much related. Orientations and attitudes of top management constitute a decisive independent factor. A consistent transnational pattern in these various choices might emerge in the forthcoming years in many large European businesses. This pattern has once been coined 'geocentric' (Perlmutter, 1984; Perlmutter and Heenan, 1979).

The main characteristics of the transnational pattern or ideal-type are: more attention to international processes than to structures; a dominance of horizontal international networking over classic headquarter-subsidiary relations in terms of financial control mechanisms; a shift from formal mechanisms for control and coordination (hierarchy, accounting systems) to more subtle and informal mechanisms in which cross-cultural communication and learning are basic; emphasis on the building of corporate commitment and identity across many borders; the sharing of visions, values and style does ask for an internationalization of human resource policies as a key factor for transnational success. Summarizing all this, one could say that a transnational configuration of strategy, structure, processes and human resources depends highly on 'investment' and intervention in the field of transnational organization development.

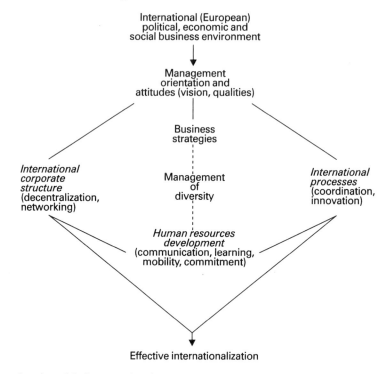

Figure 1   *A model of transnational management*

Values and culture in Europe: convergence

As has been said before, the creation of a transnational European model of management should be rooted in the values and behaviour of a European way of life. Values are ideas of desirable states shared by collectivities or majorities within a group. Values orient human activities in a broad range of life fields. In the 70s and 80s, several comparative studies on values and value orientations have been done in Europe. It is possible to give here a brief synopsis (Strümpel, 1989).

The main conclusion is that a convergence is emerging on the deeper level of value orientations. The main elements in this emerging pattern are the following:

- *The decreasing value of religion as a source of moral obligation*
  There is currently an increasing participation of individuals, groups and organizations in the discussion and reformulation of moral regulations, together with a widespread process of democratization of norms and values impacting on economic, social and political

life. This process of modernization (secularization) has proceeded further in northern European countries (with a higher level of economic and technological development).

- *Democratic political systems* Western societies have developed a fairly stable attitude towards their democratic political systems. New elements like direct forms of participation by individuals and groups, and even 'unconventional' political action of groups, have been incorporated (Inglehart, 1976, 1989).
- *The increasing value of multiple social relations* There are many more relevant social relations outside work and the family: partners, friends, voluntary associations, etc. Quasi-family private lifestyles are important: they provide for emotional support and social learning. This change is more manifest in countries like Denmark, Holland and West Germany than in so-called 'traditional' countries like Italy, Spain and Ireland.
- *Work as strong a value as leisure* The educational explosion and the changing technological and organizational character of work are being reflected in an advance of intrinsic values in work ('work gives the feeling of accomplishment', etc.). Work and leisure seem to become complementary values. Several equally acceptable meanings of work can all form the basis of a strong motivation: traditional, instrumental, social and 'post-material' meanings. This pluralism of work related values is characteristic for European countries.
- *Towards a general achievement orientation* (Hondrich, 1989) The orientation to work and leisure is becoming more inner directed. The act of accomplishment may become a value in itself. The reward is: self-development. This orientation is individualistic. Accomplishment can too be given a collective meaning. There is a general upgrading of both self-reliance and responsibility for other people. The increasing value of self-development presupposes equality of chances for more and more people. It means that distributive norms and social justice are becoming increasingly important in European societies.
- *Quality of life: a new religion?* Values like 'peace', 'human rights', 'protection of the natural environment', 'fighting poverty' indicate a deeper reorientation in Western attitudes to the world. It might have in Europe the significance of a new moral dimension in economic and social life.

Social and organizational patterns in Europe: divergence

There is still an apparent social and cultural diversity in Western Europe. Not so much on the deeper level of value orientations but on the organizational and institutional 'surface' of economic and social life. There is a diversity in management styles, organizational forms and practices, human resource policies, entrepreneurial behaviour and industrial relations systems. Different approaches of government's role *vis-à-vis* business illustrate too the diversity which exists in Europe. Recent comparative studies enable us to speak in concluding terms about organizational and managerial diversity in Western Europe (Hofstede and Bollinger, 1987; d'Iribarne, 1989; Laurent, 1985; Maurice *et al.*, 1982, 1984).

As one travels from the northern (Sweden, Denmark, United Kingdom) to the southern countries (Belgium, France, Italy, Spain), the cultural needs in work, organization and society are substantially different. For example, a low tolerance for uncertainties in life and work and a liking for hierarchies explains why bureaucracy in firms and societies is so well developed and even cherished in countries like France, Italy and Spain. Again the cultures and patterns in society of the southern countries, especially Italy, Spain and Portugal reflect less the individual than northern countries like the UK, the Netherlands, Germany and Denmark, the former group being more community oriented. In some, a strong attachment to work and career is socially prestigious and in others there is a tendency to distinguish between the roles of men and women. However, in northern countries like Sweden. Denmark and the Netherlands, caring for others and having a pretty and clean environment are considered more important than work and careers.

A further comparison between 'western' countries (USA, UK, the Netherlands, Germany and Australia) leads to the conclusion that individualism is present everywhere. The same is not true of the desire to avoid uncertainty and to develop bureaucracy. The latter is stronger in Germany and Australia where huge bureaucratic corporate structures are still dominant.

In European management one has to become aware of and able to distinguish between the 'culture clusters': the Anglo cluster (US, UK and the Netherlands in some respects), the Nordic cluster (Sweden, Denmark and Norway), the Germanic cluster (Germany and Australia) and the Latin cluster (France, Belgium, Italy and Spain).

Institutional characteristics, in particular the educational system and management–labour relations, affect the views of managers (and of young graduates too?) of what good management should be about. From country to country different 'images of organization' are apparently still dominating (Morgan, 1986). In Latin European countries (France, Belgium, Spain) there is also a strong propensity to bureaucratization and a view on organizations as authority systems in which managers have a strong internal and external power orientation. Management is seen both as a political and as an 'elite' role in business organizations. In northern European countries, a more specialized and limited concept of management prevails: managers are strategic leaders and 'organizers' within the corporation. In southern European countries managers are seen as also having a public role in the larger society. They seem to form a clear 'business elite'.

Thinking in terms of the rather popularized system analysis of the McKinsey Consulting Group one could say that the 'hard' components – strategy formal structure, control and information systems – do have a rather universal organizational meaning and applicability. The 'soft' components – patterns of leadership, human resource practices, organizational values, processes of communication and cooperation – are, on the contrary, culturally specific. These factors may explain the differences in success when comparing Dutch with French companies, British with German, and so on. Organizational renewal – project organization, the use of taskforces, networking between functional areas, etc. – seem to have better chances in the Netherlands or Sweden than in France or Italy.

A profile of European management

The main elements of a European approach in international management are the following:

- 'Reading' and interpreting the complex and diversified social, cultural and political European business environment.
- Discussing and sharing across borders mission and strategies within the multinational firm.
- Structuring the international firm along lines of decentralization to business units, horizontal coordination and 'networking' (task groups, meetings, conferences, etc.). Organizing the international staff to manage entrepreneurial and innovative projects.
- Building a transnational corporate identity based on economic and social values by promoting cross-cultural communication, exchange and learning.
- Accepting the fact that there are various interest groups within and outside the company. Managerial legitimacy can only be created if the objectives of the transnational firm attract the support of various local and 'national' stakeholders.
- International mobility of human resources. Many professionals and managers should follow a European career path. One of the aims here is cross-cultural learning and flexibility.

Management development in Europe

The ambitious view of a European model of management raises questions about educational systems in Europe built as they are on national assumptions and divergent ideologies. There are questions too about lifelong learning in view of the demography of the European workforce (on the average 10–20 years older than their Asian competitors). An individual not only will have several jobs but may also have several careers in his lifetime. It is important to have all possible age groups in continuous employment and learning. Learning should take place alongside work. Present attitudes to education will have to change as far as vocational and management training are concerned.

A European style in management education should develop in a climate of increasing individualization. This is a crucial concept in modern human resource thinking (Beer *et al*., 1984; Fombrun *et al*., 1986; van Dijck, 1989; Dowling, 1990). It is up to individuals themselves to upgrade and update their 'human capital', i.e. competence and education, to meet the new demands of the working environment.

The Report of the European Round Table, *European Competence and Education*, has catalogued industry's opinions on education (ERT, Feb. 1989). Main issues regarding education in northern countries have to do with: communication skills, holistic thinking, business initiative, and 'broad' education. In Latin European countries there is a need for flexibility and management science. In English countries communication skills and strategic thinking are emphasized.

The main idea is that 'European excellence' not only depends on cognitive knowledge but also on attitudes and organizational culture or managerial style. Graduates should be equipped with the ability to think holistically (not only analytically) and have the capability to communicate and take initiative; they should be aware of the complex 'European' and global environment. Their education should be broad, including a sense of culture (ERT, 1989, p. 22).

Where stands the young generation of managers in Europe?

In order to discover some answers to the career orientations and opinions on managerial qualities of the upcoming generation of 'Euro-managers', a joint research of MSL International and Tilburg University was undertaken on the occasion of the second Euro-managers Conference (Brussels, Dec. 1989). Data were obtained from 1935 graduates. The sample contained 91% from EEC countries. The average age of the participants was 25 years.

If one word was to be used to describe this group it would be 'mobility'. Most of them are seeking to work abroad within 3 years. More than half of them intend to spend a major part of their career working transnationally. Irrespective of the size of the company and location, there is an overwhelming preference for the fully fledged multinational, i.e. transnational company where competence outweighs nationality and where both the headquarters and the subsidiaries are staffed by mixed nationalities. The political stability of the host country was a major factor. Surprisingly, the question of children and native identity was not within the top five reasons for refusing or ending an international position. Within this group, management, dedication, lifestyle and challenge emerge as the most important career values. When asked what qualities were important for success as managers, interpersonal skills and conceptual effectiveness came top of the list of attributes and were appreciated more than achievement and operational effectiveness.

Conclusions

It is obvious from the foregoing that human resource management will have to play a strategic and critical role in the process of internationalization and transnationalization of economic and social life in Europe. The same holds for transnational organization development which is the other side of the same coin.

References

Bartlett, P. and Ghoshal (1989) *Managing across Borders*.

Beer, M. *et al.* (1984) *Managing Human Assets*, Harvard.

Crozier, M. (1989) *L'Enterprise à l'Ecoute*, Paris: Interedictions.

van Dijck, J. J. J. (1989) *Ondernemen met Mensen*. Deventer: Kluwer.

Dowling, P. *et al.* (1990) *Human Resource Management*, Boston, Mass: Kent. (PWS-Publ. Comp.).

Fombrun, Ch. *et al.* (1986) *Strategic Human Resource Management*.

Hofstede, G. and Bollinger, D. (1987) *Les Différences Culturelles dans le management*, Paris: Editions d'Organisation.

Inglehart, R. (1989) *The Culture Shift*, Princeton.

d'Iribarne, Ph. (1989) *La Logique de l'Honneur*, Paris: du Seuil.

Laurent, A. (1985) 'The Cultural Diversity of Western Conceptions of Management', in: *Managing in Different Cultures*, P. Joynt and M. Warner (eds), Oslo.

Maurice, M. *et al.* (1982) *Politique d'education et organisation industrielle en France et en Allemagne*, Paris: PUF.

Morgan, G. (1986) *Images of Organization*, London: Sage

Prahalad, C. K. and Doz, Yves L. (1987) *The Multinational Mission*, New York: Free Press.

Strumpel, B. (ed.) (1989) *Industrial Societies after the 1970s*, Berlin: de Gruyter.

Thurley, K. and Wirdenius, H. (1989) *Towards European Management*, London: Pitman.

Reproduced from van Dijck, J. (1990). Transnational management in an evolving European context. *European Management Review*, **8** (4), 474–9, by permission of *European Management Review*.

2.2 Organizational design and management norms: a Comparative Study of managers' perceptions in the People's Republic of China, Hong Kong and Canada

Ilan Vertinsky, David K. Tse, Donald A. Wehrung and Kam-hon Lee

Introduction

'Is the diversity of behavior in organizations across cultures increasing, decreasing, or remaining the same? Trying to resolve what is commonly labeled the convergence/divergence dichotomy, scholars ask whether organizations world-wide are becoming more similar (convergence) or are maintaining their culturally based dissimilarity (divergence)' (Adler, Doktor and Redding. 1986: 300). The evidence is mixed (e.g. see Hickson, Hinning, Mc Millan and Schwitter, 1974; Negandhi, 1985; and Tse Lee Vertinsky and Wehrung, 1988 versus Hofstede, 1980: Laurent, 1983; Lincoln and Hamada. 1981). Child (1981) examined a variety of cross cultural studies and observed that those studies dealing with macro-level variables found few differences that were attributed to culture, whereas those studies focusing upon micro-variables found many significant differences. Thus it is possible that organizational structure and technologies converge, whereas behaviors and attitudes of individuals within organizations diverge.

Asking people to provide descriptions of ideal organizations (i.e norms rather than descriptions of actual situations) may provide insight into the direction of change in a society (e.g. O'Brien and Dowling, 1980). Although forms of organization and management may superficially converge, it is the basic values that are likely to fill these formal molds with behavioral content. In the long run, 'People build organizations according to their values and societies are composed of institutions and organizations that reflect dominant values within their culture' (Hofstede, 1984: 81).

The main question addressed in this article is whether norms for organizational design and management are subject to a process of globalization.

Globalization is the convergence process through which cross-cultural and national differences are reduced.

In this study we compare norms of executives from three different environments: Canada, Hong Kong, and the People's Republic of China (PRC). The PRC represents a non-market business environment with tight regulatory constraints and a closed culture with a low level of interaction with other cultures. Hong Kong is a cosmopolitan city with an open, highly competitive market economy, a low level of regulation, and a single dominant ethnic culture. Canada is a multicultural Western society with an open, competitive economy and an elaborate system of government regulation.

The three distinct national environments: possible influences upon patterns of organizational design

'Theoretical' arguments that support the hypothesis of globalization are typically based upon the convention that some normative systems of organizational design and management are universally superior. Thus, through a process of evolutionary selection and learning, these systems provide a focus for convergence in all national environments.

In contrast, those who suggest that diversity in normative systems is increasing or remaining the same, argue that normative systems are molded by differences in political and regulatory environments and differences in ethnic culture. Thus, values in a particular task environment are a reflection of dominant values within the broader environment. In this section we highlight some of the major factors in each of the three selected national environments that could influence the evolution of normative systems of organizational design and management.

The political and regulatory environment of the PRC

The PRC is a planned economy with tight social and economic controls (e.g. Tung, 1981). Economic organization and management are central to the system. A specific detailed policy line on organizational reform was consolidated in the Decision Document of the Third Plenary Session of the Twelfth Central Committee of the Communist Party of China on October 20, 1984. This document specified changes in the managerial decision-making structure and was reinforced by a system of management education, incentives, and management renewal (Henley and Nyaw, 1986).

Initially, the PRC adopted a Stalinist system of industrial management modified by the special Chinese revolutionary traditions of the Yan'an era (Andors, 1977: Brugger, 1976). The main characteristics of this system included a high degree of centralization with clear, detailed plans and standard operating procedures for their implementation. Risk aversion and adherence to formal rules dominated. Within the enterprise a pluralistic structure was adopted. This structure consisted of the Director, the Enterprise Party Committee, the Workers' Congress, and the Trade Union Committee. Though the balance of power among the four institutions shifted over time, a tradition of limited participation of workers as part of the formal structure has remained (see also Shenkar and Ronen, 1987).

Since 1978, a process of experimentation with organizational reform has led to several important modifications of the economic system. As part of these changes, the reforms introduced a new motivational system officially promulgated by the State Council in 1984 as the 'responsibility system'. The basic principles of the system were a combination of 'responsibility, authority and benefit' or 'simply a performance-oriented organization.' The new imperative is to 'calculate [profit] prior to action' rather than 'action before calculation' (Henley and Nyaw, 1986). Rationalization of management techniques with a strong emphasis on the introduction of means-ends analysis characterized the normative basis of these reforms.

At the enterprise level, these changes were accompanied by a move from participatory management in the Yan'an tradition (i.e. pluralistic decision making with tight state control over information and agenda: e.g. Lindsay and Dempsey, 1983) to a new structure of collective leadership and democratic management by workers under the direct leadership of the factory director. According to the Decision Document of 1984, 'modern enterprises have a minute division of labour, a high degree of continuity in production, strict technological requirements and complex relations of cooperation. It is therefore necessary to establish a unified, authoritative and highly efficient system to direct production and conduct operations and management. This calls for a system of the managing director assuming full responsibility.' This document also prescribes that 'enterprises must specify in explicit terms the requirements for each work post and the duties of each worker and staff member and must establish various forms of the economic responsibility system with contracted jobs as the main content so as to invigorate the urban enterprises, raise the sense of responsibility of workers and staff members and bring into full play their initiative, enthusiasm and creativity.' The system as a whole, though somewhat more flexible at the plant level, still retains a high degree of centralization and control.

The 1984 reform thus modified the mechanism for worker participation norms in the design of business organizations, introduced the values of teleological structures (i.e., means-ends orientation), emphasized formality of authority structures, and promoted the value of adaptiveness and flexibility within a rigid structure. In terms of leadership, the reforms emphasized values of innovation and experimentation. The importance of general managerial skills such as interpersonal and rational decision-making skills was also upgraded. The reforms, however, did not involve a basic change in the totalitarian nature of the government or the intensive use of both incentives and coercion to ensure implementation of government policies. Recent events in the PRC have demonstrated that one should not confuse economic modernization with a process of political reform. Indeed, while suppressing democratic aspirations, the PRC government is continuing its efforts to implement managerial reform. In attempting to protect its political system, however, the government is likely to insulate its people from uncontrolled foreign influences and increase its selectivity in recruiting candidates for management positions and international contacts.

The political and regulatory environment of Hong Kong

To understand the regulatory system in Hong Kong, one must consider its geographic and economic position and its colonial history. The territory of Hong Kong was acquired by Britain in three stages during the 19th century. For the past four decades the PRC has reasserted its claims for sovereignty over the entire territory, a claim that was accepted by Britain after prolonged negotiations. The proposed new Basic Law of Hong Kong promises to provide a large measure of autonomy to the colony and preserve its economic system. Indeed, it is the benefit that the PRC has derived from using Hong Kong as its continuing major channel to the outside world that has offered the Crown colony a certain measure of security and stability in the past and some promise for economic autonomy in the future.

Its position as one of the major ports of the world and its dependence on exports of goods and services has ensured an open economy with a regulatory structure that is geared to maintain its competitive advantage. The preeminence of international trade and finance has fostered the evolution of a flexible 'light touch' regulatory system. The main thrust of government policy, even in the sensitive financial sector, has been described as positive non-intervention: that is, a mix of light regulations designed to ensure stable growth for the economy while maintaining a reputation for order sufficient to attract foreign investors and foreign trade activities. Crises threatening stability have been met by periodic reform, the implementation of which ensures maximum flexibility and coordination with business interests (Lee and Vertinsky, 1987/8). The regulatory stand of this colonial regime has been cited by Friedman and Friedman (1980) as probably the best, if not the only, current example of a minimalistic non-interventionist government. (See also Lee, 1982.)

The political and regulatory environment of Canada

Canada represents a blend between an interventionist state and a market economy. The federal structure and the size and divergence of its regional economies combine to give government a significant role in shaping the economy. Indeed, it is argued that Canada represents the triumph of political will over enduring, contrary economic forces (e.g. see Stanbury, 1987: Royal Commission, 1985). The importance of its trade and cultural links with the United States and its position as an open economy have helped to define the role of the Canadian government system as one where economic adjustments are often heavily assisted by government spending and taxation powers and by an elaborate system of regulation based on consultation with business organizations. Although the macro-economic regulatory system is wide in scope. Canada's market position (strengthened recently by the Free Trade Agreement with the U.S.) has constrained government interventions with respect to the structure and management of private sector organizations.

Implications of Chinese ethnic culture for organizational design and management

According to most scholars, the prime distinction between Chinese and Western cultures appears to be the collective orientation of the former and the individualistic orientation of the latter (e.g. see Chan. 1986; Ch'ien, 1973; Yin, 1976). A collective orientation implies an emphasis on relationships, harmony, order, and discipline. These Confucian values support a formal and clearly specified organizational structure, unambiguous authority relationships, low internal competition, harmony in management/labor relationships, and centralized authority vested at the top. In terms of leadership. Chinese values would place greater weight upon ascribed rather than achieved status and upon diffused rather than specific status. In addition, Chinese values would focus upon the formal authority and the interpersonal abilities of the manager.

Implications of culture for organizational design and management in Canada[1]

Canada is a multi-cultural society. It is strongly influenced by its neighbor – the U.S. The dominant value system is one with an individualistic democratic orientation that encourages diversity. The influence of U.S. business culture is marked and is especially reflected in the training and acculturation of business executives. The general norms prescribed by the extant theories of organizational design generally favor flexible, adaptive organizational structures and a motivational system based on merit, competition, and risk taking. Recent developments in the normative theory of organizational design associated with the shift to knowledge- and service-based industries also see some merit in employee participation in decision making and the development of an informed labor force. Prescribed key attributes of a good manager are general analytical skills and interpersonal competence.

Research design

One problem in comparing beliefs or attitudes toward organizational design is the difficulty of identifying relevant dimensions. Laurent (1983) attempted to provide mental maps of organizations for several Western European countries and the U.S. His findings yielded four dimensions: (a) political systems, (b) authority systems, (c) role-formalization systems, and (d) hierarchical systems. The first dimension was related to internal and external power relations. The second dimension reflected the attitudes of managers with respect to the degree of authority that a position in the hierarchy confers, the degree to which authority is accepted, and the degree to which a manager must serve as a negotiator. The third dimension reflected the perceived relative importance of formally and precisely defining and specifying the functions and roles of organization members. The last dimension reflected attitudes toward the function and role of a formal hierarchy and structure.

Hofstede (1980, 1984) studied employees of a large multinational corporation in 67 countries using 32 value statements concerning organizational attributes. Statistical analysis yielded four underlying value dimensions along which the countries could be positioned. These were: (a) individualism versus collectivism, (b) large versus small power distance, (c) strong versus weak

---

[1] It is important to note that our study focused upon the population of English-speaking Canadians in Western Canada. This population is highly mobile and enjoys a high degree of cultural diversity. The study of French-speaking executives from Quebec could yield different results.

uncertainty avoidance and (d) masculinity versus femininity. The first value dimension relates to a preference for a loosely knit versus tightly knit social framework. The second dimension relates to preferences for and acceptance of a hierarchy. The third dimension reflects the degree to which the members of a society feel uncomfortable with uncertainty and ambiguity. The last dimension concerns preferences in a society for achievement, assertiveness and material success versus a preference for relationships, caring, and quality of life.

Other scholars have postulated important organizational design and management style dimensions for cross-national studies but have not tested these empirically (e.g. see Negandhi, 1985, and the review by Ronen and Shenkar, 1985). Because our study focused upon norms of organizational design and management, we have distilled from the literature on cultural differences those attributes that have been linked to the characteristics of these two dimensions. We have added to this list items that the participants in the pilot studies proposed as essential attributes missing from our original list. The 21 attributes of organizational design represent dominant alternatives in the literature concerning structure, relationships between members and organization climate, and communication and decision processes. The 24 attributes of management style reflect different approaches to human relations, decision making and communication styles, personal attributes, and perceived status. In each category attitudes and desirable skills associated with the different approaches were generated. The instrument provided respondents with an opportunity to add important missing attributes in both sets, but no additional attributes were identified by the respondents.

In contrast to the approach taken by Laurent (1983), we have focused upon salient attributes rather than the rationale for endorsing a particular attribute. This was done to simplify the statements presented for subject evaluation and reduce the impact that cognitive styles may play in judging the desirability of an attribute. The focus upon teleological relationships in the Laurent instrument may cause some difficulty for Oriental respondents (e.g. see Redding 1980: Maruyama. 1984: Adler, Doktor and Redding, 1986: Adler, Campbell and Laurent, 1989). In contrast to Hofstede (1980, 1984), our study focused only on description of the 'ideal' rather than mixing normative judgments and judgments of truth statements.

This study surveyed executives from three societies (PRC, Hong Kong and Canada) using two different sets of Likert-like importance scales. One set of scales examined organizational design norms including scales on worker participation, formal structure, strategic adaptiveness, internal competition, and risk taking. The other set of scales focused on the desired attributes of a good manager, including scales of general managerial skills, experimentation and innovation, and dimensions targeted at traditional Chinese values. Each set of scales was derived to represent dimensions previously identified in the literature as discussed earlier. Likert-type scales were chosen over other more cumbersome ranking procedures because they were better suited to investigate cultural differences and had been found reliable in previous studies (e.g. Munson and McIntyre, 1979).

The questionnaire was translated into simplified Chinese characters by a doctoral student from the PRC who was studying management at a Western university. The translated questionnaire was reviewed by a panel consisting of another PRC doctoral student and two of the authors whose mother tongue is Chinese. The Chinese version was used in pretests conducted in the PRC as well as in the main study, and the English version was used in Hong Kong and in Canada. Three pretests were conducted with: (a) 45 PRC teachers of management. (b) 16 Master of Business students in a Canadian university, and (c) 20 Chinese-Canadian executives. Following the pretests several ambiguous items were modified.

The sample used in this study consisted of 155 executives. Fifty working executives from the PRC who participated in a management training program composed the PRC sample. They were selected from different provinces and cities according to criteria set by the PRC First Ministry of Machine Building. The Ministry set quotas for different geographic regions according to their relative importance as industrial centres. The sample thus represented a broad cross-section of manufacturing operations in the PRC. Forty-five working executives from Hong Kong who participated in an executive program formed the Hong Kong sample. They came from a variety of industries. The Canadian sample of 60 executives was pooled from two sources. The sample consisted of 34 executives attending an evening business program at a West Coast Canadian university and 26 executives who were identified as past participants of an executive program and agreed to participate in the study. Aside from differences in sex, age, and amount of work experience, the two Canadian samples showed no significant differences in responses. In particular, a MANCOVA using the two sets of factor scores as dependent variables and the two Canadian subject groups as independent variable, with sex and work experience as covariates, showed that differences in the two groups were insignificant.

Eighty-five percent of the Canadian subjects were mid-level executives or senior professionals. This group constituted 74% of the Hong Kong sample and 80% of the PRC sample. Ninety percent of the Canadian sample had a university degree compared to 100% for those from Hong Kong and 62% for the PRC executives.

Findings

The 21 attributes of organizations and the 24 attributes of management were analyzed separately with the three national samples pooled. The variance–covariance matrix from each set of scales was first tested using the Kaiser test. The scores ranged well above 0.80, suggesting the data for each set of scales had appropriate variance-covariance for factor analysis. Each set of scales was subjected to factor analysis with varimax rotation to derive orthogonal factors. The factors were chosen based on their eigenvalues and the scree test results. The factor scores were then analyzed by ANOVA with nationality as the independent variable.

Norms of a good organization

The 21 attributes of organization were factor-analyzed with the three national samples pooled. Based on the scree test results, six factors with eigenvalues greater than one were obtained. They explained almost 100% of the variance associated with norms of a good organization. The first factor related to interpersonal processes viewing the organization as a collective with emphasis upon consultation and participation. The second factor related to the degree of formality in operating procedures, authority structure, and evaluation and control systems. The third factor defined technical characteristics of organization associated with strategic management. These included adaptiveness, flexibility, and efficiency. The fourth factor related to democratic values in the organization. The fifth factor described internal competition and risk taking, and the sixth factor related to the degree of centralization of authority. Factor loadings for each of the attributes are given in Table 1. The factors obtained were clean with no cross-factor loading exceeding 0.25, a conservative standard.

Significant differences in factor scores among the three samples of executives were found for factors 1, 2 and 5. Results of the ANOVA and the simultaneous Tukey tests for these factors are given in Table 2.

PRC executives scored highest on factor 1, which reflected norms of worker participation in decision making. Participation has consistently been a feature of PRC business organizations since the Yan'an era. Even recent attempts to centralize decision making within the business enterprise prescribe the maintenance of formal participation of workers in the planning process as well as the retention of some worker authority over the appointment and retention of the manager. Participation norms are in contradiction to traditional Chinese values that emphasize the authority of the hierarchy and show participation as a threat to 'face saving' norms (Moore, 1967). Indeed the significant difference in scores among the three groups of executives on this norm was between PRC and Hong Kong executives. The latter group of executives saw less value in participation than the other groups. The mean score for Canadian executives was between the two extremes.

PRC and Hong Kong executives considered having a formal structure more important than the Canadians. In the PRC, the combination of a bureaucratic institutional structure, aversion to conflict, and the need for

Table 1   Factor analysis of organizational design norms[a]

Factor 1 (Participation) explained 52% of the variance
  1 Consults employees about important decisions (0.79)
  2 Has harmony among its members (management/labor) (0.62)
  3 Has employees who are well informed about decisions (0.53)
  4 Is responsive to employees' needs (0.42)
  5 Makes decisions after bargaining/negotiating among managers of different units (0.35)
Factor 2 (Formal Organization) explained 15.4% of the variance
  1 Has clear and formal rules of action (0.78)
  2 Has well specified lines of authority (0.66)
  3 Has employees who are evaluated and controlled well (0.51)
Factor 3 (Strategic Adaptiveness) explained 10.4% of the variance
  1 Is adaptive to change (0.65)
  2 Is efficient (0.52)
  3 Is flexible (0.49)
  4 Has high degree of trust among its members (0.49)
  5 Has strong leadership (0.45)
  6 Is run by family members (− 0.34)
Factor 4 (Democratic Organization) explained 9.6% of the variance
  1 Encourages diversity of opinions (0.59)
  2 Tolerates occasional failures (0.59)
  3 Values a hightly educated workforce (0.51)
  4 Seeks consensus on key decisions (0.28)
Factor 5 (Internal Competition and Risk Taking) explained 6.7% of the variance
  1 Has high degree of internal competition for promotion (0.78)
  2 Encourages risk taking (0.49)
Factor 6 (Centralization) explained 5.6% of the variance
  1 Has centralized authority (0.70)

---

[a] The table lists the items whose factor loadings were greater than 0.25. The factor loading pattern was clean: none of the cross factor loadings exceeded 0.25.

'face saving' fosters demand for a clear formal structure of authority and unambiguous standard operating procedures. In Hong Kong, Chinese values have a similar impact upon norms of organizational design. This finding contradicts Redding (1982), who postulated a Chinese business organization characterized by ambiguous formal structure (but see Birnbaum and Wong, 1985).

Factor 3 reflected values of adaptive organization. No significant differences were found across the nationality groups. The technical environment of business enterprises appears to demand adaptiveness, efficiency and flexibility. These require strong leadership and a climate of trust. Thus these norms of organization appear to be universal. Similarly, no significant differences between the three groups of executives were found in mean scores for factor 4, which reflected democratic values of organization. The mean score of PRC executives was highest on this factor (but only 'nearly' significantly higher than their counterparts in Canada and Hong Kong). This was consistent with

Table 2 Organizational design norms: summary of ANOVA[a] results

Factor	Mean Factor Score			F-Score	Tukey's Multiple Group Test (p < .05)
	China (PRC)	Hong Kong (HK)	Canada (CND)		
	(n = 43)	(n = 45)	(n = 56)		
1 Participation	0.34	− 0.25	− 0.06	5.53**	PRC > HK
2 Formal Structure	0.40	0.31	− 0.56	24.65**	PRC > CND HK > CND
3 Strategic Adaptiveness	0.09	− 0.16	0.06	1.28	n.s.
4 Democratic Organization	0.19	− 0.07	− 0.09	1.88	n.s.
5 Internal Competition and Risk Taking	− 0.47	0.02	0.35	13.13**	CND > PRC HK > PRC
6 Centralization	0.11	− 0.08	− 0.02	0.69	n.s.

[a] One-way analysis of variance. The factor score for each subject was the dependent variable and the country grouping was the independent variable.
*$p < .05$ **$p < .01$.

the norms of participation held firmly by these executives (see factor 1). One must, however, recognize that the Chinese tolerance and encouragement of diverse opinions is embedded within a system that tightly controls the agenda for discussion (what Perrow, 1977, termed 'third order controls').

Factor 5 reflected norms of internal competition and risk taking. The results indicated that the Chinese generally shun internal competition and individual risk taking initiatives. This tendency was more pronounced in the responses of the executives from the PRC than the responses of those from Hong Kong. In the PRC, the political and regulatory systems reinforce traditional Chinese values of collective responsibility.

No significant differences among the three groups of executives were found with regard to attitudes toward centralization (factor 6).

Norms of good management

The 24 attributes of management were factor-analyzed with the three national samples pooled. By means of a scree test. three orthogonal factors with eigenvalues greater than one were identified in the inventory of attributes describing 'good managers'. The three factors explained almost 100% of the variance. Table 3 provides factor loadings. One factor of general management skills emerged from the analysis. This factor combined decision making and interpersonal skills. The second factor reflected the values of experimentation

Table 3   Factor analysis of managers' desirable attributes[a]

Factor 1 (General Managerial skills) explained 67.6% of the variance
   1 Is careful with resources (0.69)
   2 Supervises employees well (0.67)
   3 Is skilful at resolving conflicts (0.64)
   4 Communicates well (0.64)
   5 Delegates responsibilities and authority (0.63)
   6 Listens and consults before making decisions (0.61)
   7 Does not get discouraged by failures (0.59)
   8 Is consistent (0.56)
   9 Carefully analyses decisions (0.55)
  10 Has high integrity (0.53)
  11 Is compassionate with employees (0.48)
  12 Is ready for experimentation (0.48)
  13 Is cautious (0.43)
  14 Is decisive (0.41)
Factor 2 (Experimentation and Innovation) explained 20.4% of the variance
   1 Takes calculated risks (0.66)
   2 Is innovative (0.59)
   3 Follows tradition (-0.39)
Factor 3 (Traditional Chinese Values) explained 12% of the variance
   1 Is esteemed by community (0.79)
   2 Makes decisions quickly on basis of intuition (0.51)
   3 Is a successful person (0.48)
   4 Is loyal to the company (0.40)

---

[a] This table lists the items whose factor loadings were greater than 0.25. The factor loading pattern was clean: none of the cross factor loadings exceeded 0.25.

and innovation. The third factor reflected the values of ascribed status. intuition. and loyalty to the company (i.e. the traditional values of Chinese management). Again the factors obtained were clean, with all cross-factor loadings below the conservative standard of 0.25. Significant differences in factor scores among the three samples of executives were found for factors 2 and 3. Results of the ANOVA and the simultaneous Tukey tests for these factors are given in Table 4.

No significant differences were found in the mean scores of factor 1 among the three nationality groups (Table 4, factor 1). It appears that there is a global view as to general attributes of good management. These attributes combine analytical decision making skills with interpersonal skills.

Significant differences were found for the remaining two factors between the PRC and non-PRC executives (Table 4, factors 2 and 3). No significant differences in attitude were found between the Canadian and Hong Kong executives. The executives from the PRC viewed propensities for experimentation and innovations as more valuable attributes of a good manager than their counterparts in Hong Kong and Canada, reflecting the influence of

Table 4 Managers' desirable attributes: summary of ANOVA[a] results

Factor	Mean Factor Score			F-Score	Tukey's Multiple Group Test (p < ·5)
	China (PRC)	Hong Kong (HK)	Canada (CND)		
	(n = 39)	(n = 43)	(n = 59)		
1 General Managerial Skills	− 0.12	0.18	− 0.06	1.20	n.s.
2 Experimentation and Innovation	0.47	− 0.16	− 0.21	9.84**	PRC > CND PRC > HK
3 Traditional Chinese Values (ascribed status, intuition, and loyalty to organization)	0.69	− 0.36	− 0.22	23.53**	PRC > CND PRC > HK

[a] One way analysis of variance. The factor score for each subject was the dependent variable and the country grouping was the independent variable.
*$p < .05$. **$p < .01$.

modernization-oriented reforms. The attributes reflecting 'traditional values of Chinese management', namely ascribed status and loyalty to the company, were stronger in the PRC than in Hong Kong surprisingly the mean score for the Hong Kong Sample was lower than for the Canadian Sample, but not significantly lower. The process of globalization must have taken its course to erode some of the traditional values in the open, competitive economy of Hong Kong.

Discussion and conclusions

The study found some significant differences in norms of organizational design and management among the three national samples of executives. It also found a core of norms that appears to be accepted more universally.

In order to determine whether a globalization process is taking place in the norms of organizational design and management, it is not sufficient simply to point to significant differences across national environments and reject the hypothesis. One must consider the dynamic nature of the process. Proponents of globalization could argue that convergence is likely to be more rapid in a national environment where cross-national diffusion of innovations and processes of learning are unencumbered by barriers. Such barriers may include (a) physical barriers (e.g., constraints on movements of executives into and out of the country, blocking of T.V. and radio transmissions, prohibition of importation of written materials): (b) linguistic and cultural barriers (e.g. lack of access to research findings published in foreign languages or misinterpretation of culture-bound uses of a language); and (c) economic barriers (e.g. lack of resources to acquire information or access it and or high transaction and processing costs associated with the use of foreign information). Thus, if a globalization process is in effect, one would expect convergence to occur more rapidly in Hong Kong than in the PRC. An examination of the ANOVA results concerning organizational design generally confirms the globalization hypothesis. No significant differences were found in norms of strategic adaptiveness and efficiency and endorsement of within-plant democratic values. (As we have noted, in the PRC diversity of opinion is encouraged only within a very tightly controlled agenda and task environment.) Similarly, no significant differences were found in attitudes toward centralization. An examination of the pattern of norms concerning formal structure and internal competition and individual risk taking, where significant differences across the national environments were found, revealed that results for Hong Kong were consistent with the globalization hypothesis: that is, the mean for Hong Kong executives was in the interval between the means of the PRC and Canadian samples.

Examination of the norms associated with participation found, however, that the mean for the Canadian sample was between the means of the Hong Kong and the PRC samples. This surprising pattern of cross-cultural differences may be attributed to differences in the task environment and the regulatory system that molds it. Hong Kong markets are characterized by high volatility. Success in business depends on rapid decision making. Participation reduces the speed and decisiveness of decision making. Thus in this case, the influence of the task environment might combine with traditional Chinese cultural values to shun participation as a valuable attribute of organizational design. In contrast, the Canadian environment to business is more stable and predictable. The mode of doing business requires patient negotiations with government, unions, and other stakeholders in the corporation. The premium for rapid decision making is lower than in Hong Kong, whereas the costs of employee alienation may be forbidding. Participation may provide net benefits in such an environment. In the PRC the dominant ideology and the regulatory environment require participation and response to employees' needs. Bargaining and negotiation are the dominant modes of relationship with the external world. Participation is an essential feature of such a system. Thus it appears that the differences in norms with respect to participation reflect local adaptations to differences in regulatory environments and fundamental economic structures rather than the manifestation of broader cultural values.

An examination of cross-national differences of the desirable attributes of managers revealed a similar pattern of convergence: a common core of norms of good management and differences reflecting adaptations to national economic and regulatory environments. There were no significant cross-national differences with respect to norms associated with general managerial skills. Cross-national differences were found with respect to the values of experimentation and innovation. PRC executives placed a higher value upon experimentation and innovation than the other excutives, possibly responding to incentive structures introduced in the PRC in recent reforms to promote innovation. The reforms also involved an intensive effort of indoctrination emphasizing experimentation and innovation.

Significant differences were also found in what we have identified as management norms that reflect traditional Chinese values. Ascribed status and loyalty as bases for identification of a good manager reflect values antithetical to the needs of an organization operating in competitive markets. These traditional values, however, are compatible with the attributes of a manager operating within a complex bureaucracy. Not surprisingly, the traditional Chinese values were preserved in the PRC but not in Hong Kong. Indeed the acceptance of these values in Hong Kong was lower than in Canada. The higher degree of market competition in Hong Kong relative to Canada may provide an explanation for this fact.

To conclude, our findings do not reject the globalization hypothesis, but indicate that the convergence process depends to a large extent on trends characterizing the global economy. Deregulation and the opening of domestic markets are likely to result in convergence. Only a few of our findings with respect to cross-cultural differences show a resistance to convergence that can be attributed to broad cultural values. One important such dimension concerns the value of formal structure. In large organizations, Chinese executives value an organizational design that has clear formal rules of action, well-specified lines of authority, and a high degree of control over employees. These design attributes are likely to reduce problems of 'loss of face', contain conflict, and reduce ambiguity – problem dimensions that are fundamental to Chinese culture. The managerial implications of this finding are perhaps the most important in this study because they contradict the accepted stereotype of a Chinese organization. Indeed, in the small and medium Chinese organizations, where relationships between members are well defined and culturally coded, no need for formal systems exists. Disciplined and unambiguous relationships will emerge through socialization processes without the need to resort to clear formal standard operating procedures, formal role descriptions, and a clear authority structure. In contrast, the modern large multinational business organization cannot rely on culturally determined codes of behaviour, relationships and expectations, so it must clearly and unambiguously specify the formal structure of the organization.

In a decade where foreign direct investment accounts for a significant and increasing share of all investment and the dominance of North American foreign direct investment is diminishing, sensitive appreciation of local differences in norms concerning organizational design and management is required. This paper has demonstrated that such local differences are significant in some dimensions. Even though the balance of evidence supports the contention that there is a process of convergence in organizational design and management norms, it shows that accommodation to some important cultural values that are resistant to change is necessary. Our findings of a universal agreement about some norms concerning basic attributes of management and organizational design imply that there is a role for a universal organization theory, at least in dealing with business organizations. This role may increase through processes of globalization in the broader political, regulatory and economic environments (e.g., liberalization of markets and democratization) or require the development of a contingent theory of organization to reflect differences in regulatory, political, and economic structures.

References

Adler, N. J., Campbell, N. and Laurent, A. 1989. In search of appropriate methodology: From outside the People's Republic of China looking in. *Journal of International Business Studies*. 20(1): 61–74.

Adler, N. J., Doktor R. and Redding, S. G. 1986. From the Atlantic to the Pacific century: Cross-cultural management reviewed. *Journal of Management*. 12(2): 295–318.

Andors, S. 1977. *China's industrial revolution: Politics, planning and management, 1949 to present*. New York: Pantheon Books.

Bhagat, R. S. and McQuaid, S. J. 1982. Role of subjective culture in organizations. A review and directions for future research. *Journal of Applied Psychology Monograph* 67(5): 653.

Birnbaum, P. H. and Wong, G. Y. Y. 1985. Organizational structure of multinational banks in Hong Kong from a culture-free perspective. *Administrative Science Quarterly*. June 30(2): 262–277.

Brugger, W. 1976. *Democracy and organization in Chinese industrial enterprise, 1948–1953*. Cambridge: Cambridge University Press.

Ch'ien, M. 1973. On the systems of academic knowledge. In P. Shen (Ed.), *Higher education and university students*: 15–32. Hong Kong: University Press.

Chan, W. T. 1986. *Chu Hsi and neo-Confucianism*. Honolulu: University of Hawaii Press.

Child, J. D. 1981. Culture, contingency and capitalism in the cross-national study of organizations. In L. L. Cummings and B. M. Shaw (Eds.), *Research in Organization Behaviour*: 303–356. Greenwhich. CT: JAI Publishers.

England, G. and Lee, R. 1979. The relationship between managerial values and managerial success in the United States, Japan, India, and Australia. *Journal of Applied Psychology*: 59(4): 411–419.

Friedman, M. and Friedman, R. 1980. *Free to choose*. Harmondsworth: Penguin Books.

Hall, E. T. 1977. *Beyond culture*. Garden City, NY: Anchor Books.

Hannerz, U. 1969. *Soulside: Inquiries into ghetto culture and community*. New York: Columbia University Press.

Henley, J. S. and Nyaw, M. K. 1986. Introducing market forces into managerial decision-making in Chinese industrial enterprises. *Journal of Management Studies.* November: 635–656.

Hickson, D. J., Hinning, C. R., McMillan, C. J. M. and Schwitter, T. P. 1974. The culture-free context of organization structure: A tri-national comparison. *Sociology.* 8: 59–80.

Hofstede, G. 1980. *Culture's consequences: International differences in work-related values.* Beverly Hills. CA: Sage Publications.

Hofstede, G. 1984. Cultural dimensions in management and planning. *Asia Pacific Journal of Management.* January: 81–99.

Kelley, L., Whatley, A. and Worthley, R. 1988. Assessing the effects of culture on managerial attitudes: A three culture test. *Journal of International Business Studies.* 19(2): 17–31.

Kelley, L. and Worthley, R. 1981. The role of culture in comparative management: A cross-cultural perspective. *Academy of Management Journal.* 24(1): 164–173.

Laurent, A. 1983. The cultural diversity of western conceptions of management. *Studies of Management and Organization,* 13(1–2): 75–96.

Lee, K. H. 1982. Development of Hong Kong's place in international trade. *The World Economy* 5(2): 187–200.

Lee, K. H. and Vertinsky, I. 1987/8. Strategic adjustment of international financial centers (IFCs) in small economies: A comparative study of Hong Kong and Singapore *Journal of Business Administration,* 17(1): 153–172.

Lincoln, J. R. and Hamada. M. 1981. Cultural orientations and individual reactions to organizations: A study of employees of Japanese-owned firms. *Administrative Science Quarterly,* 26: 93–115.

Lindsay, C. P. and Dempsey, B. L. 1983. Ten painfully learned lessons about working in China: The insights of two American behavioral scientists. *The Journal of Applied Behavioral Science,* 10(3): 265–276.

Maruyama. M. 1984. Alternative concepts of management: Insights from Asia and Africa. *Asia Pacific Journal of Management,* 1(1): 100–11.

Moore, C. A. 1967. *The Chinese mind: Essentials of Chinese philosophy and culture.* Honolulu: University of Hawaii Press.

Munson, J. M. and McIntyre, S. H. 1979. Developing practical procedures for the measurement of personal values in cross-cultural marketing. *Journal of Marketing Research,* 16(February): 48–52.

Negandhi, A. R. 1983. Cross-cultural management research: Trend and future directions. *Journal of International Business Studies,* Fall: 1–28.

Negandhi, A. R. 1985. Management in the third world. In P. Joynt and M. Warner (Eds.), *Managing in different cultures: 69–97.* Oslo: Universitetsforlaget av Oslo.

O'Brien, G. E. and Dowling, P. 1980. The effects of congruency between perceived and desired job attitudes upon job satisfaction. *Journal of Occupational Psychology,* 53: 91–100.

Perrow, C. 1977. The bureaucratic paradox: The efficient organization centralizes in order to decentralize. *Organizational Dynamics.* 5: 3–14.

Redding, S. G. 1980. Cognition as an aspect of culture and its relation to management processes: An exploratory view of the Chinese case. *Journal of Management Studies.* 17(2): 127–48.

Redding, S. G. 1982. Cultural effects on the marketing process in southeast Asia. *Journal of Market Research Society,* 24(2): 98–114.

Ronen, S., & Shenkar. O. 1985. Clustering countries on attitudinal dimensions: A review and synthesis. *Academy of Management* 10: 436–454.

Royal Commission on the Economic Union and Development Prospects for Canada. 1985. *Report* (3 volumes). Toronto: University of Toronto Press.

Rugman, A. 1989. *International business in Canada*. Scarborough. Ontario: Prentice-Hall.

Shenkar, O., & Ronen, S. 1987. Structure and importance of work goals among managers in the People's Republic of China. *Academy of Management Journal*. 30(3): 564–576.

Stanbury, W. T. 1987. Direct regulation and its reform: A Canadian perspective. *Brigham Young University Law Review*, 1987(2): 467–539.

Swidler, A. 1986. Culture in action: Symbols and strategies. *American Sociological Review* 51(April): 273–286.

Tse, D. K., Lee, K. H. Vertinsky, I and Wehrung, D. A. 1988. Does culture matter? A cross-cultural comparison of executive choice, decisiveness and risk adjustment in international marketing. *Journal of Marketing*. 52(October): 81–95.

Tung, R. I. 1981. Patterns of motivation in Chinese industrial enterprises. *Academy of Management Review* 6(3): 481–489.

Yin, H. K. 1976. *The future of Chinese culture*. Hong Kong: The Arts Book Store.

Reproduced from Vertinsky, I., Tse, D. K., Wehrung, D. A. and Lee, K-H. (1990). Organizational design and management norms: a comparative study of managers' perceptions in the People's Republic of China, Hong Kong, and Canada. *Journal of Management*, **16** (4), 853–67, by permission of *Jounal of Management*.

3 Motivation

3.1 Strategic multinational intra-company differences in employee motivation

G. G. Alpander and K. D. Carter

Productivity through motivation

Keeping employees motivated in order to accomplish organisational objectives is a difficult task, yet both initial and ongoing motivation are critical to succeed in today's business world. Worker alienation carries some steep price tags: underproduction, poor quality, sabotage, turnover, absenteeism, and alcoholism.

Work motivation is generally defined as a series of energising forces that originate from both within and beyond an individual's self. These forces initiate work-related behaviour and determine the nature, direction, intensity and the duration of the individual's behaviour [1]. Researchers have attempted to explain motivation to work through two basic types of motivational theory: content theories and process theories. Content theories are concerned with 'what' energises behaviour while process theories focus on 'how' behaviour is energised. This study concentrates on the 'what' aspect of the motivation theory.

Content theories assert that needs determine an individual's behaviour [2–5]. Individuals have a multitude of needs in varying degrees of intensity. These needs or activators create a state of disequilibrium within the person. The individual develops an urge to fulfil the need or needs he/she is experiencing. Consequently, the individual begins to search the environment for potentially satisfying goals, which once attained will lead to the reduction of the disequilibrium or the fulfilment of his/her needs [6]. In a work situation, motivation is explained by the degree to which employee needs can be satisfied on the job [7, 8]. Motivation levels can be weak or strong, vary between individuals under different circumstances, and can be related to multiple needs [9].

This brief description of the motivation process implies that human needs are the primary determinant of work-related behaviours [10, 11]. Most organisational efforts to improve employee motivation concentrate on providing opportunities for the individual to receive intrinsic and extrinsic satisfaction from his/her work [11].

This article assumes that managers can affect performance by influencing employee motivation through work-related outcomes. Work motivation can be attributed to the nature of individual needs and to the distribution by managers of work-related outcomes perceived by employees as both valid and relevant. In other words, managers influence motivation both by making use of individual differences in employee needs and by providing rewards and punishments that are consistent with those needs. As Michael MacCoby [12] notes, in his practical essays on employee work motivation, getting to know one's workers and finding ways for them to participate in enhancing their jobs are a manager's main tasks in motivating employees. Tailoring motivational tactics to natural needs is the key to getting employees to use their judgement as well as their skills.

Managers face basically two categories of problem as they attempt to implement these principles of motivation. The first problem concerns the assessment of the pattern and the intensity of a particular employee's needs. The second deals with the types and amounts of available rewards and punishments [13]. Solutions to this set of problems involve company policies as well as action by individual managers.

The conceptual framework used in this study implies that in order to motivate employees, managers and organisations must determine what kinds of outcome or reward are valued by their employees [14]. Therefore, the first step in instituting an effective motivational system is a study of the need patterns of employees. Although it is very difficult to *change* what people want, it is fairly easy to *find out* what they want. Effective managers and organisations emphasise diagnosis of needs, not changing the individuals themselves [15].

What do employees want?

Maslow's Need Hierarchy Theory [5] proposes that each individual has a set of needs arranged in a developmental hierarchy. Maslow assumes that people have a need to grow and develop and, as basic survival needs are met, the person becomes increasingly concerned with higher-level needs such as belongingness, esteem, and self-actualisation. While attempts to develop research support for Maslow's assertions have been generally unsuccessful, the theory was used in the construction of this diagnostic instrument because of its widespread popularity among managers.

Theorists Atkinson [12] and McClelland [10, 16] state that there are three basic motives which are relevant to the work situation: the need for self-actualisation, the need for affiliation, and the need for power. Although all people possess these needs or motives, individual differences occur in the relative strengths of these factors. Further, the trigger for a particular motive is usually activated by the situation in which the person is involved. Atkinson and McClelland use this theory to increase job performance by adjusting conditions to activate the achievement motive.

Another pertinent content theory is Herzberg's Two-factor Theory [11] which proposes that two dimensions describe motivation: extrinsic job conditions ('hygiene factors') and intrinsic factors ('motivators'). According to Herzberg, the hygiene factors (such as wages and working conditions) do not actually motivate employees, but their presence reduces dissatisfaction among employees. On the other hand the intrinsic factors or motivators do contribute to employee satisfaction and motivation.

Based on the works of Herzberg, Maslow and McClelland, five categories of need that may motivate employees have been identified: the needs for economic security, control, recognition, self-worth, and belongingness. To determine the intensity of each of the five need categories we used Kafka's Self-discovery Checklist [17] which asks each participant to identify the extent to which the ten statements for each of the five need categories on the checklist fit their own description of themselves. The following is a brief description of the self-discovery checklist.

The need for economic security. This need is defined as the need a person has to feel secure by making and saving money. The following two items exemplify the statements used to determine the intensity of this need: 'I am interested in financial or material rewards'; and 'I enjoy setting financial or material goals for my future economic security'.

The need for control. This need is defined as the need an employee has to influence a situation or another individual's thinking, attitudes or behaviour. The following two items exemplify the statements used to determine the intensity of this need: 'I like to make my own decisions'; and 'I seek out positions of authority'.

The need for recognition. This need is defined as the need a person has for attention, high visibility, and to be noticed by others. The following two items exemplify the statements used to determine the intensity of this need: 'I welcome assignments that provide a lot of recognition'; and 'I display symbols of my success so people will notice them'.

The need for personal self-worth. This need is defined as the need a person has for reassurance that one is appreciated for one's contributions. The following two items exemplify the statements used to determine the intensity of this need: 'I strive to meet the needs of my family'; and 'I want to feel that what I am doing is making a contribution to others'.

The need to belong. This need is defined as the need of an employee to be accepted as a member of the group with which he/she identifies. The following two items exemplify the statements used to determine the intensity of this need: 'I avoid behaviour that would set me apart from my group'; and 'I desire sociability and harmonious relationships within my group'.

Table 1 Professional and first-line supervisors in each subsidiary

Subsidiary	Total population		Respondent population	
	A	B	A	B
Belgium	75	15	17	5
Spain	80	10	19	3
Germany	68	7	20	2
Italy	85	11	18	4
Venezuela	50	9	16	6
Mexico	90	17	18	4
Colombia	70	8	19	3
Japan	77	7	20	2
Total	595	84	147	29

A = professionals; B = first-line supervisors.

Methodology

The Kafka 50-item self-discovery checklist [17] identifying five major human needs was administered to a volunteer group of professionals and supervisors from eight foreign subsidiaries of a major multinational pharmaceutical company. Ten items were used to get a measurement of each of the needs for economic security, control, recognition, self-worth, and belongingness. The participants were asked to identify the extent to which each statement on the checklist fitted their own description of themselves. A Likert scale with a range from 1 ('to a very little extent') to 5 ('to a very great extent') was used.

The questionnaire, accompanied by a covering letter, signed by the researcher and the general manager of the subsidiary, was distributed by the company's local human resources development manager to 22 professionals and/or first-line supervisors from eight countries. All the respondents were host country nationals and had volunteered to participate in this study. The respondents were assured of their anonymity. The total pool of professional and first-line supervisory personnel was 679. Of this population, 176 volunteered to become involved in the project resulting in a 25 per cent (+ / −) participation rate (see Table 1). The percentage of volunteers out of the total population pool within each type of employee group and within each country ranged from a low of 20.5 per cent in Mexico to a high of 37.2 per cent in Venezuela.

Due to the relatively small size of the sample from each country no attempt was made to differentiate the responses of the supervisors from those of the professionals. The 22 participants from each country are, therefore, treated as a single group. One final caveat is that because our sample was drawn from only one company caution must be exercised in generalising to the population at large.

In an effort to address the national culture rather than the multinational company culture, the questionnaire items were not work-specific (reflecting the company's culture) but asked about life in general (reflecting the societal values for each individual). The 50-item checklist was translated into Spanish by a bilingual individual and translated back into English by another bilingual individual as a check on the content/meaning accuracy of the original translation. The Spanish version was used in Colombia, Mexico, Spain and Venezuela. The English version was administered in Belgium, Germany, Italy and Japan.

The rank order pattern of needs

The overall mean need intensity for respondents within each country was calculated and the results arranged in rank order (see Table 2).

In each of the eight countries the need to control stands out. Furthermore, there were no meaningful differences in the relative importance of the needs among the employees in the eight subsidiaries of this multinational company. Also, no significant relationship was found when correlations were calculated by sex, age, size of the subsidiary, and the participants' length of service with the company. Although there are vast cultural, economic and political differences among the eight countries, our data suggest that the most dominant need in each case is the need to control. Does it follow that what fulfils an employee's need to control in one country will do so in another country? Will a simple strategy that works in one country also work in the subsidiaries of a company located in other countries? The answer lies in studying not necessarily the most dominant need but also the formation of country-specific needs patterns. Our study has identified several unique patterns (see Figures 1–4) suggesting some interesting alignments of people from quite distinctly different cultures. The strategies and action plans that follow in this article, designed to contribute to need satisfaction through work behaviours that are effective and appropriate both from the company's and employee's perspectives, were developed by a panel of local human-resource managers from the participating countries.

The European pattern

The employees from Belgium, Germany, Italy and Spain (see Figure 1) all displayed similar priorities in their needs hierarchies. Employees in Belgium

Table 2   Rank order needs by country

	Most important				Least important
	1	2	3	4	5
Belgium	C	E	B	S	R
Spain	C	E	B	S	R
Germany	C	E	R	B	S
Italy	C	E	R	B	S
Venezuela	C	E	B	R	S
Mexico	C	B	S	E	R
Colombia	C	B	S	E	R
Japan	C	R	B	E	S

Key: C = Need to control; S = Self-worth; B = Belongingness; R = Recognition; E = Need for economic security.

and Spain have identical needs patterns headed by control and followed by economic security, belongingness, self-worth and recognition. Workers from Germany also exhibit similar dominant needs but have a stronger need for recognition and a weaker need for self-worth activities than the Belgian and Spanish respondents. The panel of organisational development specialists recommends that the employees with this needs pattern will be highly motivated if the work environment provides them with decision-making authority and monetary rewards attached to successful task performance.

Economic rewards, if linked adequately to performance, could be powerful motivators for workers in these countries. Steeply increasing financial rewards for greater accomplishment may yield significant results in these countries where such rewards symbolise not only economic security but also control and recognition. The review of compensation systems may be a worthwhile exercise for senior management. An audit of any compensation system should focus on incentives, salary differentials between wage levels, and the size of wage increases at promotion. After the employees' control and economic security needs have been satisfactorily established, the manager should focus on ways to develop an environment that is both supportive and respectful of the worker. Of the European group, Italian employees seem to have the strongest need for recognition. These workers value highly the perquisites and symbols that come with a job well done. Again the key is to differentiate accurately between levels of performance. Monetary rewards should not be the only means of documenting success for Italian personnel.

Of further interest is the German employees' views of the relationship of needs, one to another. When German respondents indicated a high need for control, they generally displayed a very low need for both belongingness and

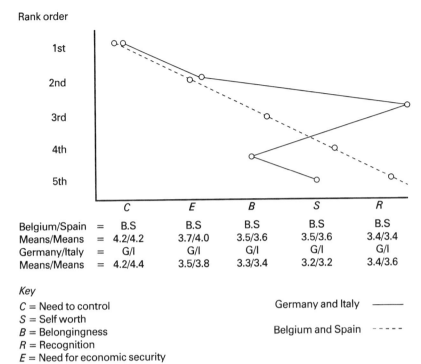

Rank order

	C	E	B	S	R
Belgium/Spain =	B.S	B.S	B.S	B.S	B.S
Means/Means =	4.2/4.2	3.7/4.0	3.5/3.6	3.5/3.6	3.4/3.4
Germany/Italy =	G/I	G/I	G/I	G/I	G/I
Means/Means =	4.2/4.4	3.5/3.8	3.3/3.4	3.2/3.2	3.4/3.6

Key

C = Need to control   Germany and Italy ———
S = Self worth
B = Belongingness   Belgium and Spain - - - -
R = Recognition
E = Need for economic security

Figure 1   *The European group needs: rank order patterns denoted by respondents*

self-worth. In other words, the employees who exhibit a dominant need for control do not perceive belongingness and self-worth needs as important. The reverse relationship is also true. Those high on belongingness and self-worth are low on their need for control.

A dominant need is an important motivator. The dominant need has to be either fulfilled or its dominance is somehow reduced. In either case, employee behaviour is influenced by the dominant need. The unique needs pattern in the German subsidiary suggests the possibility of using an innovative strategy in dealing with the need for control. Instead of attempting to provide an organisational environment, whereby the individual fulfils this need, managers might concentrate on reducing the dominance of the need to control. This relationship suggests that if the need for belongingness increases, a corresponding decrease in the need for control may follow. The question then becomes how to increase the perceived importance of the need for belonginess thus reducing the dominance of the need for control.

Need for belongingness can be stimulated by creating an organisational environment requiring teamwork whereby individual effectiveness depends on the co-operation and acceptance received by other members of the work group [18]. The more task performance becomes contingent on effective

Rank order

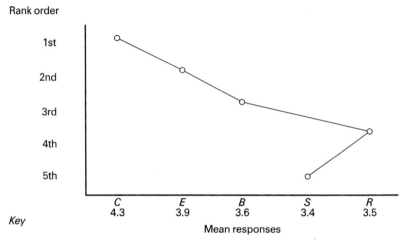

Key

C = Need to control
S = Self worth
B = Belongingness
R = Recognition
E = Need for economic security

Figure 2   *The Venezuelan group needs: rank order patterns denoted by respondents*

interaction with others at an equal level, the greater is the need for belonging-ness. Dependence on others in task fulfilment is the key issue. If tasks are structured in such a way that a reciprocal relationship between individuals becomes a necessity then mutually dependent work groups may be created [19].

The Venezuelans

The Venezuelan respondents represent a needs rank order pattern that is more similar to that of the Europeans than that of the other Latin American respondents (see Figure 2). The Venezuelan worker shows a high need for control and economic security and, like the Belgian and Spanish, holds the need for belonging and recognition in high regard but has less interest in self-worth. It is likely that meeting the need for recognition may substantially satisfy the Venezuelan need for self-worth. Providing concrete positive feedback on how well the individual is doing can be extremely motivational. If the situation allows the individual to control his/her own actions, recognition of the successful completion of such tasks will be an excellent incentive.

Opportunities to give presentations and to receive recognition for good work will be well accepted by such individuals. Situations in which the

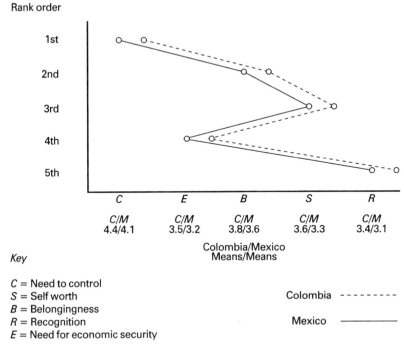

Rank order

Key

C = Need to control
S = Self worth
B = Belongingness
R = Recognition
E = Need for economic security

Colombia - - - - - - - -
Mexico ——————

Figure 3 *The Latin American group needs: rank order patterns denoted by respondents*

employee takes personal responsibility for finding solutions to problems will be regarded as highly motivating [16]. These individuals will welcome specific projects in addition to their jobs if such projects allow them to exercise control and get recognition for personal accomplishments.

The Latin American pattern

This group (see Figure 3) includes employees working in Mexico and Colombia. Unlike the people in Europe, these workers list belonging as their second most important need. Although living conditions in these countries are poor, the need for economic security is relegated to fourth place behind belongingness and self-worth. In group meetings they make efforts to establish friendly relationships, often agreeing or giving emotional support. Jobs which offer opportunities for friendly interactions are sought. It is important for these individuals to maintain good relationships with their peers and subordinates.

The managers working with these individuals need to provide an added amount of mutual respect and support in helping the employees feel that they are part of the company culture. Strategies enabling fulfilment of the need to control at the expense of satisfying the need to belong may be initially effective but may eventually lead to an environment conducive to psychological failure for the employee [20].

Employee-centred supervision and acceptance by others are important organisational factors. Acceptance by others helps these employees to fulfil their need for self-worth thereby increasing their self-respect.

Attempts to fulfil the need for self-esteem are carefully gauged against their need for belongingness. For these individuals control of others will most likely be handled very carefully. They will seek fulfilment of their dominant need through their peers and work groups [21]. Motivational rewards should be tasks that impact on the welfare of the work group. Having the opportunity to make a positive difference and be liked by others increases perceptions of self-worth and is also a means of fulfilling their need for control.

The Japanese pattern

As is so often the case in our examination of the Japanese business environment, these employees express a unique needs preference list – unlike the other groups. The Japanese workers appear to favour both the need for control and the need for belonging (see Figure 4). Small rewards, which reinforce self-concept and self-worth while enhancing one's control over the work environment, will provide great motivation for these individuals. Such things as public recognition of their contributions, certificates of appreciation, assignment to team leader status, may be potential motivators. If the demands of the work group are congruent with their individual self-concept, these individuals will be effective employees. Small task forces or work teams operating independently and with relative autonomy will lead to effective results if the necessary co-ordination and integration is accomplished by higher management.

A strong and positive relationship among all need groups may also explain why the Japanese employees seem to be highly motivated. Managerial action plans contributing to needs satisfaction in one category seem to influence satisfaction of another group of needs. The Japanese employee's need to influence a situation may be fulfilled, for instance, by action plans contributing to the satisfaction of the need for recognition. In other words, acknowledging the personal contributions of an employee working in a group setting not only helps to fulfil the need for recognition but also the need to belong and control.

An effective strategy for Japanese managers may be to provide their

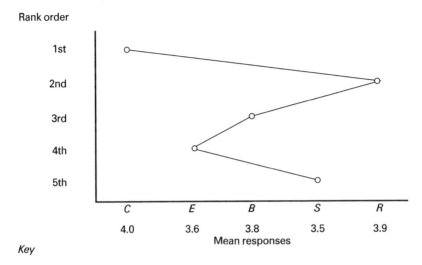

Rank order

Key

C = Need to control
S = Self worth
B = Belongingness
R = Recognition
E = Need for economic security

Figure 4 *The Japanese group needs: rank order patterns denoted by respondents*

employees with ways and means to fulfil their need for recognition by allowing involvement in attention-getting projects, providing group awards for accomplishments, and praising the group as well as the individual for personal accomplishments.

Being respected, maintaining the *status quo*, and striving to do the right things, are all important for employees with a strong need for self-worth. Also equally important is the need to feel like part of the company's 'family' [22]. Because of these characteristics, employees with relatively strong needs for personal self-worth and recognition will attempt to put forth their best work efforts if their accomplishments are recognised within the confines of this family atmosphere. Perhaps that is why quality circles, employee participation in decision making, and decision making by consensus are so successful in Japanese companies.

Conditions that seem to foster greater employee motivation in Japan centre on the development of commitment and loyalty, and recognition of personal achievements without disturbing the harmonious work-group relationships. Because of Japanese workforce characteristics, an effective management system may be based on such things as reliance on promotions from within, focusing on work groups in task accomplishment and fostering feelings of loyalty and commitment between the individual and the company [22].

Lacking a distinguishable dominant need, the Japanese worker is not obsessed with a single motivator. In contrast, employees with a strong dominant need may be unmotivated at the workplace if they do not perceive the organisation as fulfilling that particular need. In addition, it is generally easier for managers to provide ways of satisfying needs with medium intensity rather than fulfilling strong-intensity needs.

Conclusions

In all eight countries surveyed, the need to control is identified as the most dominant need. Strategies to create a motivational environment must take into consideration the strong need to control that most employees exhibit.

Research on motivating managerial styles focuses on such concepts as participatory management, Theory Y, Theory Z, and the Japanese system of management [23]. The common link among these theories is the empowerment of the employee. This is accomplished through delegation of authority and responsibility, employee involvement in the decision-making process, and most importantly by creating an environment in which the need for control is addressed [24].

If most employees have a high need to control, satisfaction of this dominant need becomes very difficult within the confines of the organisational structure. Often an employee's fulfilment of the need to control may be at the expense of another employee.

Successful companies highlighted by Peters and Waterman [15] have one thing in common, a management that is dedicated to the motivation of its human resources. These companies stress strategies by management which empower employees and give them control of their work and their work environment.

Empowering employees is not an easy task. Indeed, it may be the most difficult change to bring about in an organisation. Furthermore, not all management strategies which provide greater employee control are well accepted and successful. For instance, Japan's industrial success in the late 1970s and early 1980s is attributed to its management system [25]. The so-called Japanese management system, through its quality circles and teamwork concepts, seems to be a highly motivational system which many US and Western countries are attempting to imitate. Controversy and frustrations abound; many state that the Japanese system is unique to Japan and will not work elsewhere [26].

Although vast cultural, economic and political differences exist among the countries surveyed, our data suggest the most dominant need in each case is the need to control. However, a deeper examination of the employee rank-order patterns suggests the employer cannot assume that attending to the control need alone will maintain or improve productivity in a variety of cultural settings. In developing an effective strategy, management should not only study the needs profiles but also investigate how the various culturally biased needs hierarchies interact. This study identifies several major culturally-specific needs patterns that are linked to employee motivation. In some instances motivation can be stimulated through rather simplistic approaches, such as a pat on the back, while in other cultures, short of making an employee president, nothing may work. This information should help the executives of a multinational company to understand why the workers in the Japanese subsidiary, who have the same amount of control over their work and work environment as the workers in the European subsidiary, seem to be more motivated to do a good job. These findings suggest that management methods that work well in one country, such as the Japanese management system, may not be easily transferable to other cultures without first taking into account the needs of the employees.

References

1 Locke, E. A., Shaw, K. N., Saari, L. M. and Latham, G. P., 'Goal Setting and Task Performance: 1969–1980', *Psychological Bulletin*, Vol. 90, 1981, pp. 125–52.
2 Atkinson, J. W., *An Introduction to Motivation*, Van Nostrand, Princeton, New Jersey, 1964.
3 Coffer, C. N. and Appley, M. H., *Motivation: Theory & Research*, John Wiley and Sons, New York, 1964.
4 Murray, H., *Explorations in Personality*, Oxford University Press, New York, 1938.
5 Maslow, A. H., *Toward a Psychology of Being*, Van Nostrand Reinhold, New York, 1968.
6 Szilagyi, A. D. and Wallace, M. J., *Organizational Behavior and Performance*, Scott, Foresman and Company, Glenview, Illinois, 1987.
7 Argyris, C., *Personality and Organization*, Harper & Row, New York, 1957.
8 McGregor, D. M., *The Human Side of Enterprise*, McGraw-Hill, New York, 1960.
9 Alderfer, C. P., *Existence, Relatedness and Growth*, The Free Press, New York, 1972.
10 McClelland, D. C., 'Achievement Motivation Can Be Developed', *Harvard Business Review*, Vol. 43, 1965, pp. 6–24, 178.
11 Herzberg, F., *Work and the Nature of Man*, World Publishing Co., Cleveland, Ohio, 1966.
12 MacCoby, M., *Why Work: Leading the New Generation*, Simon and Schuster, New York, 1988.
13 Pinder, C. C., *Work Motivation: Theory, Issues, and Applications*, Scott, Foresman and Company, Glenview, Illinois, 1984.
14 Vroom, V., *Work and Motivation*, John Wiley and Sons, New York, 1964.
15 Peters, T. J., and Waterman, R. H. Jr, *In Search of Excellence*, Warner Books, New York, 1982.

16 McClelland, D. C. and Winter, D. G., *Motivating Economic Achievement*, Free Press, New York, 1969.
17 Kafka, V. W., *Patterns in Human Needs*, Effective Learning Systems, Moraga, California, 1986.
18 Durbin, R. (Ed.), *Handbook of Work, Organization and Society*, Rand McNally, Chicago, Illinois, 1975.
19 Galbraith, J. W., *Designing Complex Organizations*, Addison-Wesley, Reading, Massachusetts, 1973.
20 Wolf, M. G., 'Need Gratification Theory: A Theoretical Formulation of Job Satisfaction/Dissatisfaction and Job Motivation', *Journal of Applied Psychology*, Vol. 54, 1970, pp. 87–94.
21 Bacharach, S. B. and Lawler, E. J., *Power and Politics in Organizations*, Jossey-Bass, San Francisco, California, 1980.
22 Hatvany, N. and Pucik, V., 'An Integrated Management System: Lessons from the Japanese Experience', *Academy of Management Review*, Vol. 6 No. 3, 1981, pp. 469–81.
23 Ouchi, W. G., *Theory Z: How American Business Can Meet the Japanese Challenge*, Addison-Wesley, Reading, Massachusetts, 1981.
24 Dunphy, D., 'Convergence/Divergence: A Temporal Review of the Japanese Enterprise and Its Management', *Academy of Management Review*, Vol. 12 No. 3, 1987, pp. 445–59.
25 Sethi, P. S., Namiki, N. and Swanson, C. L., 'The Decline of the Japanese System of Management', *California Management Review*, Vol. 26 No. 4, 1984, pp. 35–46.
26 Modic, S. J., 'Myths about Japanese Management', *Industry Week*, 5 October 1987, p. 49.

Reproduced from Alpander, G. G. and Carter, K. D. (1991). Strategic multinational intra-company differences in employee motivation. *Journal of Managerial Psychology*, **6** (2), 25–32, by permission of *Journal of Managerial Psychology*.

3.2 National work meanings and patterns – constraints on management action

George W. England

The importance of working

There is widespread recognition that the activity of working and the outcomes flowing from working are of fundamental significance to most individuals. In Japan, Germany and the United States (as in most industrialized societies), employed people spend approximately one third of their waking hours in the activities which are known as working. Additionally, the time one spends in training and preparation for work, seeking work and planning for a changed work situation suggest that work related activities constitute a major use of time in the adult life. Connected to this time-use feature is the fact that a majority of individuals in these societies derive the major part of their economic well-being from income and fringe benefits generated by their work activities.

Working, and outcomes from working, also provide non-economic benefits to individuals. Were this not the case, it would seem impossible to explain why 65 to 95 per cent of individuals in national labour force samples in a variety of countries (including Japan, Germany and the USA) state that they would continue to work even if they had enough money to live comfortably for the rest of their life without working [1–3]. This stated preference for working even when financial necessity is presumed not to be a major consideration is undoubtedly related to the broader social value or significance individuals attach to working as demonstrated in various studies.

Working activities and situations also have the potential to generate negative consequences and outcomes for individuals and this factor must affect work meanings. Working can be experienced as boring, dull or unchallenging at one end of the spectrum or as excessively overloaded at the other; it can result in frustration, dissatisfaction, stress or inadequate person–job fit; and may have a bad effect on both mental and physical health. Cooper and Payne have recently summarized much of this relevant literature [4, 5].

The general significance to individuals of working also is indicated by fifty years of research concerning the impact of unemployment and retirement on people who have been productive and active during their lives, contained in numerous studies. If the non-working person cannot find some other meaningful set of activities in which to become involved, the effects of inactivity, idleness and work outcome loss often are very demoralizing and dehabilitating. Studs Terkel [6] presents dramatic testimony to the identity loss suffered by an unemployed forty-five year old construction worker:

> Right now I can't really describe myself because . . . I'm unemployed . . . So, you see, I can't say who I am right now . . . I guess a man's something else besides his work, isn't he? But what? I just don't know.

Working, then, would seem to be of general significance to the individual because it occupies a great deal of time, because it generates economic and socio-psychological benefits *and* costs, and because it is so interrelated with other important life areas such as family, leisure, religion and community.

If working is important and significant for individuals, it seems logical that the collective view of work and working in national labour forces would be a major element with which management and managers must contend. While such a view is often assumed or implicitly accepted, it is seldom examined in sufficient scope or depth and with adequate data.

The MOW study

This paper uses a portion of the data base from a comprehensive Meaning of Working (MOW) study jointly designed and conducted by behavioural scientists from advanced industrial and technological nations. This study was reported in the scientific literature in 1981 [7]. The primary data collection from nearly 15,000 respondents in eight countries took place in 1982–83 and international comparative results are published in the book, *The Meaning of Working: All International Perspective* [3].

The MOW project suggested that the meaning of working should be defined and assessed in terms of three major components:

- The degree of general importance and value attributed to the role of working in one's life (Work Centrality).
- Normative beliefs and expectations concerning specified rights and duties attached to working (Societal Norms about Working).
- Work goals and values sought and preferred by individuals in their working lives (Work Goals).

The general purpose of this paper is to examine national data on work centrality, societal norms about working and work goals which suggest potential constraints upon management action in the utilization of human resources within organizations. It should be clearly understood that while work meanings, and patterns of work meanings, may function as constraints upon management action, they also may function to enlarge management's potential for action. While this paper focuses upon potential constraints to management actions, we should not forget that this is only one side of the story. The Federal Republic of Germany, Japan and the USA were the countries selected for inclusion in the present analysis because they are important industrial and technological nations and because they will represent the range of national diversity on work centrality, societal norms about working and work goals found in the eight country study.

The samples

Table 1 describes the composition of the samples (representative samples of the employed labour force in each country) which are utilized to assess the work meanings in the three countries. As noted in Table 1, there are some differences between the three samples in most characteristics. These, however, largely reflect actual labour force composition differences as opposed to sampling biases. A total of 5,506 respondents were interviewed in 1982–83 in the three countries and it is their responses which provide the basic data presented in this paper.

Work centrality

Work centrality was assessed by the use of two component measures which were combined into a composite Work Centrality Index. The first component was a 7-point scaled response (from 'one of the least important things in my life' to 'one of the most important things in my life') to the question, 'How important and significant is working in your total life?'

Work centrality component II utilized the allocation of 100 points to five major life roles (leisure, community, work, religion and family). The more points assigned to a given role (out of 100), the more important that role is to the individual. Obviously, for purposes of studying work centrality, one focuses attention on work results as compared to other life roles.

Figure 1 shows the combination of the two component measures of work centrality into a single Work Centrality Index which ranges from the lowest possible score of 2 to the highest possible score of 10 for any individual. The differences between adjacent country pairs are significantly different (in a statistical sense) and one can observe the magnitude of country differences

Table 1   Description of German, Japanese and USA national samples. Each country interviewed a representative sample of the working labor force in their country. Sample sizes were: Germany = 1278; Japan = 3226; USA = 1002

		Germany	*Japan*	*USA*
Sex	% male	65	66	54
Age	% 16–19	6	2	3
	20–29	23	18	30
	30–39	21	27	31
	40–49	25	29	18
	50–59	18	16	13
	60 +	7	8	5
	Mean age	39	41	37
Highest level of education	% Primary	17	2	5
	Secondary	65	57	35
	Some College	8	14	30
	Univ. Degree	10	27	30
Organizational role	%Non-Supervisory	–	65	56
	Supervisory	–	9	22
	Managerial	–	26	22
Number of hours worked/week		40	49	43
Net income/month		DM1735	Y340 000	$1394

in Table 2. It can be seen that country differences in the Work Centrality Index are largest at the extremes (very low centrality and very high centrality) which are the areas where one would expect the greatest impact on management action. Obviously, the most striking comparative finding concerns the large difference in work centrality between Japan and the other two countries. Work is more important and significant in the lives of the Japanese labour force than it is in the lives of Germans or Americans.

When one inquires about potential effects those national levels and distributions of work centrality may have upon management of human resources in organizations, two points need to be made. First, work centrality deals with the life of an individual human being as the focal unit for study and the relative importance of working in one's life at a given point in time as the content of concern. No specified *a priori* set of reasons is assumed as to why working should be important in one's life or in what way it is important. Working may be important to one individual primarily because of what is received from working, to another primarily because of what he or she invests in the process of working or because of some combination of these two rationales. Our concept of work centrality remains neutral to differing

Table 2 Percentage frequency distribution of work centrality scores

	Very low centrality (2, 3 or 4)	*Moderately low centrality (5 or 6)*	*Moderately high centrality (7 or 8)*	*Very high centrality (9 or 10)*
Germany (N = 1276)	14%	32%	36%	18%
USA (N = 996)	10	31	39	20
Japan (N = 3144)	5	20	32	43

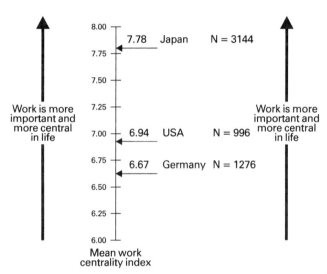

Figure 1 *Work centrality index (mean score) for each country. The method chosen for combining the two component measures of work centrality for each individual was a simple addition after each component was transformed to the ordinal position of work on a scale of 1 to 5. Complete details are presented in MOW International Research Team, 1986, Chapter 5.*

rationales for work importance as do our measurement procedures. Thus any deductions one makes solely from work centrality to influences on human resource issues within organizations must be based on a generalized notion of work importance and not upon any assumed rationales of why work is important.

Secondly, we do know that there is a statistically significant moderate positive relationship between work centrality and average number of hours

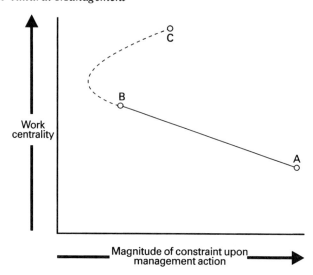

Figure 2   *Hypothesized relationship between work centrality and magnitude of con-straint upon management action*

per week spent at work (an objective indicator of involvement with working) and between work centrality and non-financial commitment to working (would continue to work even if one's financial situation did not require it) within each of the three national labour forces. The magnitude of these relationships in the three national samples is as follows:

	Work Centrality Index Correlated With:	
	Average no. hours worked/week	Work continuation (Lottery Question)
Germany	.21	.22
Japan	.21	.12
USA	.15	.20

All correlations are significant at .001 level

These relationships are also very general as they are found when samples are divided into age groups, occupational groups and sex groups.

The hypothesized relationship between work centrality and the general level of constraint upon management action is as shown in Figure 2. A general linear form of the relationship is depicted in the solid line A–B. The higher the level of work centrality (i.e. the more important work is as a life role) in a country's labour force, the lower is the magnitude or degree of general constraint upon management action. We do recognize conceptually, however, that at some point work could become so important as a life role, that this high degree of centrality itself could function to constrain manage-ment action possibilities. This possibility is depicted by the broken segment

B–C and would probably only pertain to some proportion of individuals in a given labour force who had an extremely high level of work centrality. The general conclusion, then, is that Japan faces considerably less constraint upon management action potential than either Germany or the USA solely as a function of work centrality level distributions. A realistic estimate of these constraint differences is difficult to formulate in any precise terms, but if our logic is basically correct, the difference seems highly likely to be practically important [8]

Societal norms about working

Figure 3 shows that the three countries exhibit different degrees of balance between work entitlements (or rights) and work obligations (or duties). Plotted in Figure 3 are the mean country scores (G = Germany, J = Japan, US = USA) for two selected entitlement items and two obligation items. These items are general in nature and represent two pairs of conceptually matched entitlement-obligation expressions. For example, the first entitlement or rights statement identifies the level of agreement with the normative view that, 'A job should be provided to every individual who desires to work.' The conceptually matched obligation or duties statement is, 'It is the duty of every able-bodied citizen to contribute to society by working.' The respondents utilized a four point scale (strongly disagree, disagree, agree, strongly agree, scored 1, 2, 3, 4 respectively) to show the extent of their agreement with each item. While these results could be viewed from many value perspectives, for the present purpose it seems most relevant that the German sample has work norms that are least balanced and that the direction of the imbalance is toward an entitlement or rights orientation. Japan shows very little imbalance while the USA is moderately imbalanced toward an obligation or duties orientation (these same general conclusions for the three countries are reached when data from all eight countries are examined on all work norm items).

Given the content domains of the two types of work norms, we would suggest that the greater the imbalance toward an entitlement or rights orientation, the greater may be the level of general constraint upon management action. Thus, based on work norm results alone, we would conclude that the labour force in Germany presents a higher level of general constraint upon management action than is the case in Japan and the USA. Again, the magnitude of the reported differences and their generality across subsamples suggest that the practical significance of these differences is apt to be nontrivial.

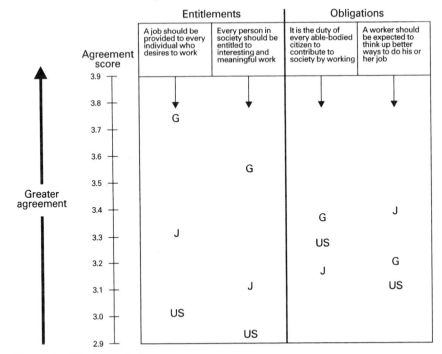

Figure 3   *Work norm balance*

Work goals

Table 3 provides data on the relative importance of eleven work goals as reported by the national samples in the three countries. The respondents were given the following directions: 'What about the nature of your working life? How important to you is it that your work life contains the following? Please rank the items from 11 = the most important to you to 1 = the least important to you.

While one can make a number of interesting observations from the data in Table 3 about both similarities and differences on specific work goals among the three countries, it seems relevant for present purposes to focus upon general and systematic differences on work goal dimension. 'Good pay' and 'good job security' were found through factor analyses to belong to a general economic work goal dimension in each of the three countries. 'A lot of autonomy (you decide how to do your work)', 'interesting work (work that you really like)' and 'a good match between your job requirements and your abilities and experience' were similarly found to belong to a general expressive work goal dimension. Figure 4 portrays a general and systematic difference between the three countries concerning the relative importance of

Table 3 Mean ranks and intra-country importance ranks of work goals (national samples)

Work Goals	Countries					
	Germany (N = 1248)		Japan (N = 2897)		USA (N = 988)	
Interesting work	7.26	3	7.38	2	7.41	1
Good pay	7.73	1	6.56	5	6.82	2
Good interpersonal relations	6.43	4	6.39	6	6.08	7
Good job security	7.57	2	6.71	4	6.30	3
A good match between you and your job	6.09	5	7.83	1	6.19	4
A lot of autonomy	5.66	8	6.89	3	5.79	8
Opportunity to learn	4.97	9	6.26	7	6.16	5
A lot of variety	5.71	6	5.05	9	6.10	6
Convenient work hours	5.71	6	5.46	8	5.25	9
Good physical working conditions	4.39	11	4.18	10	4.84	11
Good opportunity for upgrading or promotion	4.48	10	3.33	11	5.08	10

economic and expressive work goal dimensions. For Germany, the pattern is for economic work goals to be relatively more important than they are in the other two countries. Additionally in Germany, economic work goals are more important than expressive work goals. The pattern is just reversed in Japan where expressive work goals are relatively more important than they are in the other two countries. Additionally in Japan, expressive work goals are more important than economic work goals. For the USA, there is little difference in the importance of the two types of work goals.

When one considers the potential effects these national work goal levels and patterns may have upon management action within organizations, it becomes clear that we are now focused upon content areas of constraints as

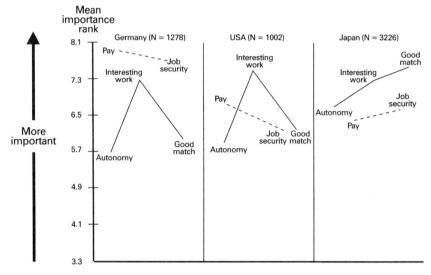

Figure 4 *Importance of economic and expressive work goals in three national labor forces*

opposed to the previous more abstract notion of general constraints. More generally, we have shifted emphasis from hypotheses about quantitative but general constraint influences to one concerned with hypotheses about qualitatively different constraint influences. The general conclusion, then, is that Germany faces considerably more constraints (as compared to Japan or the USA) upon classes or types of management action which would be counter to the primacy of economic over expressive work goals. Japan, however, would seem to face considerably more constraints (as compared to Germany and the USA) upon types of management action which would be counter to the primacy of expressive over economic work goals. For the USA, the two work goal dimensions are about equally important and at present one logically can only suggest that the two types of content oriented constraints would be similar in magnitude of influence.

Work meaning patterns

The previous expectations about constraint possibilities were generated by considering each major work meaning variable independently. It is clear, however, that the totality of meaning assigned to working by a person may be quite incomplete when we only examine single dimensions in isolation. Realistically, the major work meaning variables do not operate independently within the individual; rather, they form some pattern. The

Table 4 Mean T-scores on work meaning variables on clusters

Cluster	Work centrality index	Expressive index	Economic index	Entitlement orientation	Obligation orientation	Cluster percentages
A	39.6[a]	48.2	48.7	51.5	47.8	28.2%
B	55.6	54.3	51.2	45.0	49.4	28.4
C	55.3	57.1	38.5	50.3	51.2	19.7
D	51.2	41.1	59.7	54.1	52.4	23.7

[a] Scores which are used in identifying the work meaning pattern in each cluster are underlined.

development of work meaning patterns moves toward this more holistic view.

Work meaning patterns were developed using the three work meaning variables previously discussed so that individuals within a cluster or pattern were maximally similar to each other while different patterns or clusters were maximally different from each other. The specific method used was Ward's hierarchical clustering method [9, 10]. After determining that the optimum number of clusters was four; data on cluster stability, within cluster homogeneity and across cluster heterogeneity were examined to interpret the clusters. All scores on variables (or work meanings) were expressed as standardized T-scores with a mean of 50 and a standard deviation of 10.

Table 4 shows the mean T-scores on the five work meaning variables which were used for clustering on each of the four clusters. Cluster A is essentially a group of individuals who are characterized by having low work centrality and near average scores on the other variables. In constraint terms, they exhibit a high level of generalized constraint where constraint content is neutral or not known. They are the only cluster or group of individuals where hypothesized level of constraint operates without an accompanying content focus. Cluster B is a group of individuals with high work centrality, low entitlement orientation and relatively high expressive values. The high work centrality and low entitlement orientation both indicate low generalized constraint levels while the high expressive index suggests a content focus on expressive concerns. Cluster C represents high work centrality (low constraint) and a substantial primacy of expressive concerns over economic concerns. Cluster D has relatively high entitlement orientation (moderate constraint) and a substantial primacy of economic concerns over expressive concerns.

To use these cluster work meaning patterns in further considering the issue of constraint possibilities in Germany, Japan and the USA, one needs to know what proportion of the labour force in each country is most closely

Table 5 Work meaning cluster composition of German, Japanese and American labor force samples

Work meaning cluster	Germany (%)	USA (%)	Japan (%)	Total (%)
A	33.5	30.3	20.8	28.2
B	18.7	29.6	36.9	28.4
C	11.9	20.2	26.9	19.7
D	35.9	19.9	15.3	23.7

identified with each of the four clusters. Table 5 presents this information. Table 5 reveals that Japan and Germany represent the high and the low composition percentages on each cluster while the USA is in the middle in terms of percentage composition. Additionally there is indication that Cluster A primarily portrays a composition difference between Japan and the two other countries while Clusters B, C and D primarily portray composition differences between Germany and the other two countries. The data in Tables 4 and 5 combined with notions on types of constraints to management action discussed earlier suggest that we have identified four constraint-content situations within the three countries. First, we have a very low constraint situation where there is some preference for expressive over economic work goals or values as identified in Cluster B. Secondly, we have a low constraint situation which centers on a primacy of expressive over economic preferences (Cluster C). Cluster D represents a moderate constraint situation where there is a primacy of economic values over expressive values. Finally, we have a very high constraint situation which is neutral to expressive and economic preferences (Cluster A). Figure 5 combines all of this information in a constraint level-content matrix for the three countries.

The constraint level-content matrix shown in Figure 5 reinforces earlier conclusions and allows one to extend them. Based on meaning of working patterns, we believe that nearly two-thirds of the German labour force are in categories which imply high or moderate levels of constraint upon management actions. The comparable proportions are about one-half for the USA and about one third for Japan. These large differences in constraint levels should have practical consequences for management action. Work meaning data also suggest major country differences in the nature or content of constraints whatever their level. Managers of the Japanese labour force face constraints which reflect concern with expressive work issues of a greater extent than with economic work issues. The situation in the German labour force is for economic concerns to predominate over expressive concerns. The US situation is between that of the other two countries but it parallels that of the Japanese to a greater extent than it does that of the Germans.

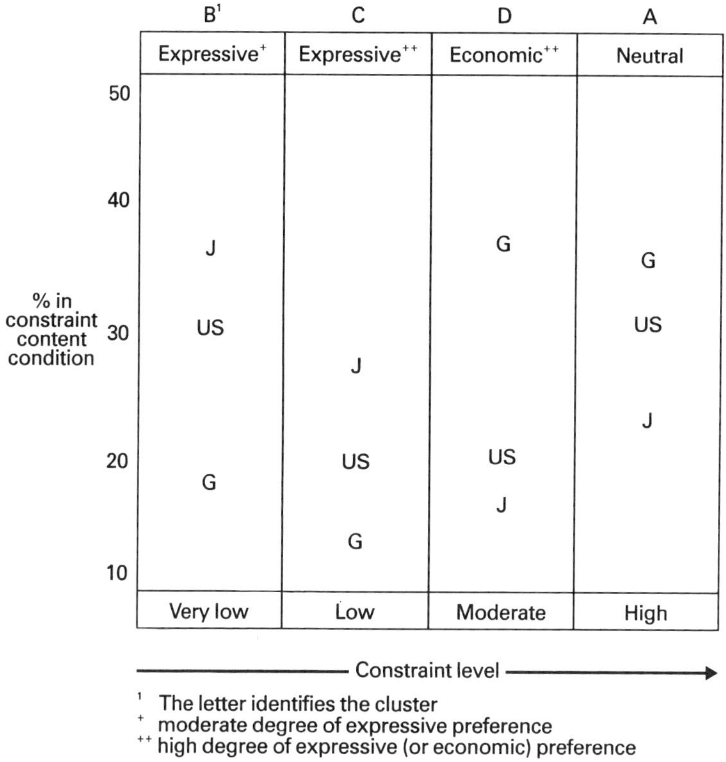

	B[1]	C	D	A
	Expressive[+]	Expressive[++]	Economic[++]	Neutral
50				
40	J		G	G
% in constraint content condition 30	US	J		US
				J
20	G	US	US J	
		G		
10				
	Very low	Low	Moderate	High

Constraint level ⟶

[1] The letter identifies the cluster
[+] moderate degree of expressive preference
[++] high degree of expressive (or economic) preference

Figure 5 *Constraint level content matrix in three countries*

In sum, there is a lot of evidence which suggests that work meanings and work meaning patterns are a source of national differences in both the type and level of constraints faced by organizational managers.

References

1 Vecchio, R. P. (1980). The function and meaning of work and the job: Morse and Weiss (1955) revisited. *Academy of Management Journal*, 23, 361–67.
2 Warr, P. B. (1982). A national study of non-financial employment commitment. *Journal of Occupational Psychology*, 55, 297–312.
3 MOW International Research Team. (1986). *The meaning of working: An international perspective*. London–New York: Academic Press.
4 Cooper, C. L. and Payne R. (1980). *Stress at work*. New York: John Wiley and Sons.
5 Cooper, C. L. and Payne R. (1980). *Current concerns in occupational stress*. New York: John Wiley and Sons.

6 Terkel, S. (1972). *Working* New York: Pantheon.
7 MOW International Research Team. (1981). 'The Meaning of Working.' In G. Dlugos and K. Weiermair (Eds.), *Management under differing value systems: Political, social and economical perspectives in a changing world.* Berlin–New York: Walter De Gruyter & Co., 565–630.
8 England, G. W. (1986). Work centrality in Japan and the USA. *Journal of Cross-Cultural Psychology* (in press).
9 Ward, J. (1963). Hierarchical grouping to optimize an objective function. *Journal of the American Statistical Association*, 58: 236–44.
10 Wishart, D. (1982). *Supplement, CLUSTAIN User manual, Third edition.* Program Library Unit, Edinburgh University.

Reproduced from England, G. W. (1986). National work meanings and patterns – constraints on management action. *European Management Journal*, **4** (3), 176–84, by permission *European Management Journal*.

4 Management styles

4.1 A cross-cultural comparison of managerial styles

W. A. Evans, K. C. Hau and D. Sculli

A review of the literature on the cross cultural aspects of management style reveals two main themes. One asserts that the management style adopted in a particular society is determined by the level of technology or the general state of development of that society. It is argued that as the society develops, the management style will inevitably converge towards the style adopted in the developed Western countries [1]. The other main theme asserts that the particular culture of a society is a dominant factor in managerial style, and management will retain its own unique cultural identity even as the society develops.

Many authors have shown how cultural factors influence behaviour in organisations and have indicated the importance of cultural differences in managerial development [2, 3, 4]. Hofstede [3], in particular, has challenged 'management experts' who attempt to introduce 'good management practice' into an organisation to examine carefully the managerial techniques and models they wish to introduce, in terms of the culture of the country in which the organisation operates. He has pointed out that managerial models developed in one culture may not easily translate to another because of the different traditions and values of the management and workforce.

The principal objective of this article is to examine how cultural values appear to influence managerial styles with particular emphasis on managerial communication. We will first discuss apparent differences between 'Western' and 'Asian' cultures. Specifically, we will contrast Hong Kong, Japan, China and the USA, which differ not only in cultural values but also in their degree of industrialisation. The effect of cultural values on the managerial style adopted in the society will then be examined. Managerial practices in companies in Hong Kong that are run by both local Chinese and by Western management will be discussed, and compared with the 'American' and 'Japanese' style of management. The influence of the level of technology on management style, with particular reference to changes that have taken place in the management of Hong Kong enterprises as they have developed, will also be discussed. Finally, we will comment on the apparent validity of the two themes mentioned above, that is, the relative importance of cultural values and the level of industrialisation in the society.

Differences in cultural values

In very general terms, cross-cultural studies are concerned with differences in factors such as educational background, beliefs, art, morals, customs, laws, economic and political frameworks, etc. Indeed, there is no reason why the complex whole of 'culture' should not also include history, economics and politics. While individual comparisons between these factors may not prove significant, the combined effect can become significant. It is important to understand, of course, that any cultural analysis is, in essence, relative, and it is therefore inappropriate to infer that any one culture is 'the best'.

With any complex system, a conceptual framework is required to facilitate the presentation and the relative ordering of ideas and understandings. If it is to be of value, a conceptual framework should have an optimum number of dimensions; too many dimensions will increase the complexity of the framework, leading the user to only one possible conclusion; too few dimensions will tend to make the framework trivial and of limited use as an aid to understanding. It is uncommon to find conceptual frameworks with more than eight or less than four dimensions. The other main characteristic of a useful conceptual framework is that the dimensions should, as far as possible, be 'orthogonal'. This term, borrowed from mathematics, implies that an idea or quantity can possess the characteristic described by any one of the dimensions without the need to possess the characteristic of any of the other dimensions.

A number of authors have proposed conceptual frameworks for evaluating cultural differences. Hofstede [3], for example, has used a four-dimension framework to examine the dominant value patterns in over 50 countries around the world. Kluckholm [5] used a value-orientation approach to identify five common or universal problem areas that are faced by most societies. These values give a sense of order, stability and predictability to a culture. We have used the five dimensions of Kluckholm's conceptual framework – human nature, time, family relationships the relationship between man and nature and the supernatural, and activity – to investigate differences in cultural values and the implications for managerial style and managerial development.

Human nature

All societies appear to have a predominant perception of human nature. At one end of the spectrum are societies which regard man's nature as basically good; bad or evil behaviour is explained in terms of pressures imposed on the individual by society. At the opposite end of the spectrum are societies which hold that man is naturally bad, and, in consequence, it is the function of the society to control and impose norms on the individual to ensure socially acceptable behaviour. In practice, most societies would lie between these two extreme positions, with western societies being closer to the perception 'that man is inherently good' than their Asian counterparts. Historical Chinese writings refer to the two concepts of human nature, i.e. that a man is either born good or bad. However, the theme emphasised in writings by Confucius, perhaps the most influential Chinese philosopher, often dwells on the nicety of the 'golden mean', which lies between the good and bad theories. This middle doctrine had gained widespread acceptance by both the Chinese and Japanese people.

Time

The way in which time is perceived is another important value orientation that exhibits differences between societies. Westerners tend to see time as an unending continuum that can be subdivided into precise units which form part of an interlocking logical system. Asians do not appear to take time as seriously, and are not used to precise scheduling and punctuality. Indeed, Hofstede [3] has suggested that in the Indonesian, Javanese tradition, time is perceived as circular rather than linear.

The time concept, or the awareness of time, is also, of course, dependent on the level of industrialisation, with a rural society being very much tied to nature's cycles and less aware of the short-term significance of time. In Western-influenced Hong Kong, the majority of Chinese people are, in fact, punctual and will act according to precise schedules if there are sufficient incentives. However, a section of the population, particularly the more traditional, older generation, still do not pay much attention to the importance of time. The Japanese are very punctual, and adhere to very precise and structured schedules. But their work habits and meetings often show disregard for time, suggesting that their concept of time is closer to the Chinese than to the Westerners.

Family relationships

The importance of family relationships is often used as a cultural discriminator. Hofstede [3], for example, described societies on a continuum of individualism versus collectivism, with Western soceites falling near the individualism end and most Asian societies near the collectivism end. The results of economic improvements in many Western nations have manifested themselves in a greater independence of the individual. This is evidenced by smaller families, high divorce rates, and the early departure of children from families. Chinese families are usually large, and close relatives often live together under the same roof. The children, particularly sons, usually look after their parents and grandparents when they are too old to work. The head of the family is expected to look after the children and help relatives in times of urgent need. The management of finance, whether it be that of the family or a small family business, is usually the undisputed job of the head of the family. He will, in turn, groom his heir, usually the son, to take over the job in due course. The head of the family also shows his authority by making practically all family decisions, sometimes even those concerning his children's private matters. The rules and obligations in the family hierarchy will be monitored by all family members and close relatives, and pressure will be applied on individuals to ensure conformity.

State intervention has always been minimal throughout China's history, except for taxation, education and military services, where the state must obviously impinge on the family [6]. The state authorities of modern Communist China have tried to impose their own social ideology on families and individuals, but even after 40 years of communist rule, traditional Confucian mores are still dominant in family and social relationships.

Even in western-influenced Hong Kong, most locals have traditional family links similar to those in mainland China. However, the younger generation in Hong Kong has gradually moved out of the control of their parents and grandparents. Economic improvements have made housing more affordable, and changed work and leisure habits have reduced the time that is spent with relatives. Nevertheless, the influence of relatives and clan relationships still exist. The general lack of social services for the elderly in Hong Kong means that the young still look after their aged relatives.

The Japanese family orientation is generally similar to that of the traditional Chinese, though state intervention appears to be stronger. Respect and compliance towards family elders remains an important cultural trait. They still look with suspicion on strangers, but presumably because of the confidence they have gained through their recent economic predominance, there is more individualism and they are now more willing to express opinions which may conflict with the societal norms.

The relationship between man and nature and the supernatural

On the value orientation of human nature and the supernatural, many Asian cultures emphasise the individual's duties towards his family and community. The Chinese, for example, set up 'lofty models' of desirable behaviour and then exhort their citizens to attain them. Both China and Japan are historically well unified by culture and language, and even physical features. The people identify closely with their country, and patriotism for its 'own sake' is particularly strong [7].

Equality and individual rights are emphasised in many Western nations, and are often protected by constitutions. Their original objective was to further human welfare and to liberate the country from old colonial invaders. These rights are now seen as being right for their own sake. The Chinese Confucian, doctrine is centred on loyalty, harmony, families and hard work. The original concern of Confucius was to stabilise the country's political and economic conditions, and to assert the authority of the ruler. Some Asian countries still regard such a doctrine as useful in the attainment of economic and socialist objectives [8, 9]. In Hong Kong, such values are evident in behaviour relating to family and business matters [10]. The Japanese regard the doctrine useful in the sense of business stability, and the integration of the individual and organisation with government. The Oriental emphasis on social harmony has created the concept of 'face' which is a subtle sensitivity to one's pride. Hence to 'have face' implies that one has pride and respect, while to 'lose face' implies the opposite [11].

Activity

Westerners are generally considered to be more aggressive in everyday life than Asians. They are more inclined to engage in open and often conflicting discussion. They seem to be able to divide issues, and can strongly disagree on certain issues while still maintaining friendly relationships. They place more emphasis on individual rights and achievements, and are better able to tolerate odd and creative people. Asians tend to be more passive and defensive; they will often strive for social harmony, even at the expense of efficiency, and a public show of disagreement must be avoided. This is exemplified by a well-known Japanese saying that 'nails that stick out will be hammered down'. In Japanese society, one must be humble and tolerant, and refrain from open confrontations which may hurt another's pride. The notion of 'saving face' is an important feature in their social relationships. Emphasis is placed on the individual's obligations to the group or society, harmony with the world at large, and the community's 'well-being'.

Such concepts are characteristic of a 'parochial culture' [12]. They can be seen at work in many spheres of life in Asian countries. Examples include the selection of Japanese political leaders by internal consultation and compromise, the persistence of one-party politics in Communist China, and even the apparent lack of understanding of simple political choices proposed in a recent Government consultative document in Hong Kong.

The influence of culture on managerial styles

To manage is, in a general sense, to direct the work of others. Managerial effectiveness will thus depend on the manager's ability to communicate their wishes to subordinates, and the subordinates' commitment to carrying out the appointed tasks in a manner that conforms with the managers' wishes or in a way that produces the result they desire. All this is obviously a function of the general nature of the relationship between managers and subordinates. Differences in this relationship are evident if we compare management styles in different societies. Many of the differences can be related to the cultural value orientations discussed earlier.

How 'human nature' is perceived clearly influences the degree of flexibility exhibited in managerial communication. The two extreme value orientations towards human nature proposed by Kluckhohn [5] have, in fact, been formulated into managerial theory in the form of 'theory X' and 'theory Y' [13]. Theory X has a negative view of human nature and assumes that man requires external control. Theory Y assumes that man is self-directed and responsible. The manager/subordinate relationship is generally more flexible in the typical Western enterprise than it is in an Asian one, suggesting that the Western perception favours 'theory Y', whereas the Asian perception is closer to 'theory X'. The Western manager may readily accept an alternative approach that can also produce the desired results, while his/her Asian counterpart may insist that the task be performed strictly according to his/her own wishes. This difference may reflect cultural differences in that there is less trust between individuals in the Asian enterprise.

The value orientation of the society towards time is reflected in differences in managerial styles in Western and oriental enterprises. In the West, workers 'sell' their time to the company for wages and do not owe any allegiance to the company in their own time. Workers in Asian companies, however, have a more general, long-term relationship with their employers; their accountability for end results is stressed, but not within the same strict time frame [14].

Some of the major differences between Western and Oriental management styles can be explained in terms of the paternalistic value orientation in Asian culture; respect and obedience towards one's parent is extended to include obeying one's boss. Small firms in Hong Kong are often run on what is termed 'family lines'. Here, many of the employees are family members, and those that are not have been appointed on recommendations via family connections. Communication within the company parallels that within the family, with the manager taking on the role of a father figure. The workers are expected to carry out the paternal instructions exactly as specified. Decisions within the 'family company' can be made promptly and can be implemented with minimal opposition.

Japanese companies, even the large corporations, also foster family-type relationships, in that personnel see themselves as becoming part of the 'clan' on joining the company. Staff and workers are bonded to the company by many indirect benefits, which can include loans for home purchases, company holiday packages, transport to and from the workplace, etc. The fact that the length of service is an important promotion and remuneration factor also tends to cement workers to one company. Japanese society has also been described as regimented, placing high value on loyalty, reliability, punctuality, etc. And these are also the qualities that a company tends to value highly when assessing its staff. Such characteristics have led many authors to describe Japanese management as consultative paternalism [15].

Man's relationship to nature and the supernatural is perceived as being much more subordinate in Asian cultures, and this is reflected in some aspects of managerial style. The concept of 'luck' plays an important role in Oriental culture. 'Luck' is a belief that much of a company's fortunes are determined by luck rather than good management. The reason for this appears to be an acceptance that much of a company's success appears to come from harmonious social relationships, but it cannot be described as an exact function of that social relationship. Hence the term 'luck' is used to explain why the inexact relationship produced a successful result. Top management must thus spend a considerable time building social relationships and on ceremonial engagements. A large part of a manager's daily work on operational decision making must therefore be delegated to subordinates. This is why most operational decisions of Asian companies are in the hands of middle management, and why middle management plays such a significant role.

In the West, man is perceived to be much more in control of his own destiny. One consequence of this is that management in Western companies is more overtly aggressive than that in the typical Asian-managed company. The decision-making process is often a 'conflict' situation, where individuals, often of different levels of seniority, will argue over a particular issue until a decision is reached. In the Asian company, decisions are reached in a more passive way, with the views of those individuals with greater seniority being given greater weight.

Quality Control Circles (QCC) is a managerial technique which has achieved widespread success in Japan, credited with improving productivity, quality and better relationships between management and workers. In fact, QCC was originally an American development introduced to Japan after the Second

World War. QCC involves the creation of small groups of five to twelve workers. These groups hold regular meetings in which they discuss and make suggestions on such matters as quality control, safety, working conditions and procedures. Meetings are held after work and overtime wages are paid to the group members. The workers are recruited on a voluntary basis.

An investigation undertaken in Hong Kong in 1983 revealed that QCC was not as successful in at least one local watch-making factory as had been reported in Japan. The reason for the lack of success was due in part to differences in values of the management and the workforce.

The company concerned was Japanese owned and largely Japanese managed. The introduction of QCC was initially treated with enthusiasm by the workers, but the technique had 'died out' in the company after a short time. The workers claimed that they were not rewarded sufficiently when their suggestions led to improvements; they were 'doing the job of the management and not getting paid for it'. There was also a complaint that Japanese management personnel were always present at meetings and tended to suppress any discussions which were critical of management.

It is interesting that the Hong Kong workers appear to be expressing values more usually associated with Western culture, while the Japanese management's behaviour more closely follows typical 'Asian' values. The workers view their relationship with management as largely economic and appear to resent the paternalistic attitude of management. The management expect the workers' loyalty, but wish to avoid any criticism that might lead to loss of face.

The attitude of the Hong Kong workers suggests that a Western management style would have been more effective in this case. The Hong Kong worker is obviously not a typical product of the Confucian tradition: he has clearly adopted some Western attitudes towards work. The social environment in Hong Kong has clearly led to some convergence between East and West. Management style should take into account both culture and the level of industrialisation.

The influence of industrialisation on management styles

The level of industrialisation obviously influences the management style in a society. This can be seen in the changes that have taken place in Hong Kong as it has developed. The major industry has for many years been textiles. This industry was introduced by Shanghainese who came to the territory in 1949 following the communist takeover in mainland China. The industry was based very much on 'family-style' Confucian principles. Textile manufacturing is a stable industry, requiring some managerial adaptation to changes initiated from outside, but not requiring much innovation. It is typical of the 'mechanistic' organisation [16]. The management style most appropriate to such an industry is the typical 'Asian' style described earlier.

As Hong Kong has developed, it has moved into the production of more high technology light manufactured goods, consumer electronics, etc. Such industries fall into the category of 'organismic' organisations described by Burns and Stalker [16]. They must, of necessity, be internally innovative and able to adjust to rapid technological changes. The 'Western style' management is most appropriate to the organismic organisation.

The management styles adopted in Hong Kong industries appear to conform to the general categories described above, but some cultural differences remain. Even in the high-tech industries, elements of Confucianism prevail. Compared with Western counterparts, there appear to be strong work ethics, self-discipline, an acceptance of hierarchy, obedience and respect towards the 'company'. Perhaps the difference between the 'Western' and 'Asian' styles can best be appreciated by observing the way in which Asian culture limits the communication of conflict and disagreements.

Conclusions

The general conclusion appears to be that the management style is a function of the level of industrialisation, but is tempered by cultural characteristics. Industrial development produces wealth and changes life styles. Individuals become less dependent on the family, and this, in turn, leads to a general self-assertion of workers. There is thus a convergence of social environments which, to some extent, must influence culture. However, this should not be interpreted to mean that Asian culture is changing by rejecting its Confucian basis. Rather, the convergence that is evident can be perceived as a rationalisation of Confucianism. Cultural beliefs are evolving, rather than being abandoned.

The implementation of management development activities, or the evaluation of existing activities, in different cultures must be undertaken with an understanding of the underlying traditions and values of that culture. This means that the 'management expert' must have knowledge of the cultural value systems of the workforce, and the management, if these are different. In Hong Kong, it is possible to have a Japanese management, with a Cantonese workforce, operating within a social structure very much based on that of the United Kingdom. As the example described in the boxed section shows, the implementation of a managerial technique may not succeed if it is based on assumptions valid in one 'culture' but not in another.

Clearly, management development must be adapted to the requirements of local culture and managerial style. This will be a major challenge for Western organisations working in Asia. It will be a particular development need for executives who are being moved from one country to another, even within Asia itself. In the next few years, we will see major changes in the way organisations develop their managers to cope with the challenge and variety of different cultures.

References

1 Kerr, C., Dunlop, J. T., Harbison, F. H. and Myers, C. A., *Industrialism and Industrial Man*, Harvard University Press, Cambridge, Mass., 1976.

2 Ratiu, I., 'Introduction', Special Issue on Management Development and Culture, *Journal of Management Development*, Vol 6 No 3, 1987.

3 Hofstede, G., 'Motivation, Leadership and Organization: Do American Theories Apply Abroad?', *Organizational Dynamics*, Summer Issue, Amacom, New York, 1980.

4 Hofstede, G., 'The Applicability of McGregor's Theories in South East Asia', *Journal of Management Development*, Vol 6 No 3, 1987.

5 Kluckhohn, F. and Strodtbeck, F. *Variations in value orientations*, Row, Peterson, Evanston, IL.

6 Hamilton, G. G. and Biggart, N. W., 'Market Culture and Authority: A Comparative Analysis of Management and Organization in the Far East', working paper 85–04, Department of Sociology, University of California, 1985.

7 Pye, L. W., *Asian Power and Politics*, Harvard University Press, Cambridge, Mass, 1985.

8 Redding, S. G., and Tam, S., 'Networks and Molecular Organisations: An Exploratory View of Chinese Firms in Hong Kong', in Mun, K. C. and Chan, S. T. (Eds.), Proceedings of the Inaugural Meeting of the Southeast Asian Region Academy of International Business, Chinese University of Hong Kong, 1985.

9 Evans, W. A. and Sculli, D., 'A Comparison of Managerial Traits in Hong Kong and the USA', *Journal of Occupational Psychology*, Vol 54, 1981, pp. 183–6.

10 Wong, S. L., 'Modernisation and Chinese Culture in Hong Kong', *Chinese Quarterly*, June 1986.

11 Lockett, M., 'Culture and the Problems of Chinese Management', Oxford Institute of Information Management, Templeton College, Oxford, 1987.

12 King, Y. C., 'Political Culture of Kwun Tong: A Chinese Community in Hong Kong', *Southeast Asian Journal of Social Sciences*, Vol 5 Nos 1–2, 1977.

13 McGregor, D., *The Human Side of Enterprise*, McGraw-Hill, New York, 1960.

14 Redding, S. G., 'Cognition as an Aspect of Culture and its Relation to Management Processes: An Exploratory View of the Chinese Case', *Journal of Management Studies*, May 1980.

15 Kast, F. E. and Rosenzweig, J. E., *Organization and Management: A Systems and Contingency Approach*, 3rd ed., McGraw-Hill, New York, 1979.

16 Burns, T. and Stalker, G. M., *The Management of Innovation*, 2nd ed., Tavistock, London, 1968.

Reproduced from Evans, W. A., Hall, K. C. and Salli, D. (1989). A cross-cultural comparison of managerial styles. *Journal of Management Development*, **8** (3), 5–13, by permission of *Journal of Management Development*.

4.2 On the generality of leadership style measures across cultures

Peter B. Smith, Jyuji Misumi, Monir Tayeb, Mark Peterson and Michael Bond

Research into styles of leadership has been dominated for several decades by a series of distinctions among different types of leader. While such distinctions clearly date back to the studies by Lewin, Lippitt and White (1939), the most enduring typology has been that provided by the Ohio State University researchers (Fleishman, 1953) with their distinction between consideration and initiating structure. Contemporary thinking has moved rather sharply away from the oversimple notion that a global measure of leader style could by itself account for any substantial amount of the variance in subordinate performance, and the Ohio State measures have been shown to be defective in a variety of ways (Schriesheim and Kerr, 1974). Nonetheless, leader style continues to figure largely in the various conceptualizations of person – situation interaction which are seen as providing a more adequate model of the influence processes surrounding leaders. For instance, the leader may select that style which facilitates the subordinate's path towards a goal (House, 1971), the style appropriate to a particular decision (Vroom and Yetton, 1973), or the style congruent with a particular attribution about a subordinate's behaviour (Green and Mitchell, 1979). Alternatively, the leader may be seen by subordinates as embodying a certain style because of prior success (Phillips and Lord, 1981), or as using differing styles in relation to the varying members of a role set (Smith and Peterson, 1988).

The attractiveness of the concept of leader style clearly lies in the possibility of labelling and objectifying an otherwise confusing diversity of behaviours. Such precision would be particularly attractive if it permitted us to make generalizations about leader behaviours within differing organizations or even different cultural contexts. This paper takes the position that in order to understand a given leadership style it must be examined both in terms of general structure and of specific expression (Misumi, 1985; Misumi and Peterson, 1985). In other words, there may well be certain underlying universal structures to the way a leader's behaviour is interpreted, which are 'general' or inherent in the nature of leader–subordinate relationships. However, the skilful leader will need to express these general structures in a variable manner, which is affected by numerous factors in the specific environment. If this could be established, then one could anticipate that, while general measures of leader style might yield uniform relations with criterion measures in a wide variety of settings, more specific analysis would show that the nature of the relationships obtained in each setting was comprehensible only in terms of the interpretive framework extant within that setting at that time. Thus general findings would be both 'true', but also only meaningful in a given setting in the light of other much more specific information.

In testing these propositions it is important to bear in mind that no measure can be devised which is entirely general or entirely specific, since the formulation of all measures is influenced to some degree both by widely shared notions about the nature of leadership and by cultural and linguistic conventions obtaining in the settings where a measure is formulated. However, it is intended to demonstrate that some measures have a more general emphasis while others are more culturally specific.

The scientific paradigm in fashion in psychology until recent times has ensured that the various widely used measures of leader style were construed with the aim of being applicable to as wide a range of settings as possible in order to enhance their external validity. Consequently, questionnaire items were selected which were worded in a vague and general manner, which now appears methodologically weak. For instance, typical items from the Ohio State research were: 'Is your supervisor friendly and approachable?' and 'Does your supervisor talk about how much should be done?' Such items are clearly general in emphasis. The first does not touch upon questions such as how the supervisor in a particular setting would signal friendliness or approachability. It could well prove that in one setting the supervisor's physical presence for a high proportion of the day would indicate his or her approachability, while in others the crucial signal could be willingness to be interrupted, amount of smiling, or out-of-hours contact. The second Ohio State item fails to address the question of how frequently the supervisor talks about how much should be done, or by whom. Furthermore, there are a dozen possible ways in which a supervisor might talk about how much should be done.

Difficulties in conceptualizing the possible divergence between general style and the skill of expressing it in a manner appropriate to the context increase still further if samples are taken from organizations within a wide range of national cultures. For instance, in individualist cultures a supervisor might show consideration by respecting subordinates' autonomy; in collectivist cultures considerate supervision would entail a much higher rate of interaction and a reduced conception of privacy or personal space.

This study examines responses to a measure of leader style which comes closer to the general type, namely a version of Misumi's PM questionnaire, which has been developed and extensively validated in Japan over the past 30 years. Responses to this questionnaire are compared with answers to much more specific measures of leader actions gathered from subordinates in a variety of organizations in four national cultures. The assumption is made that specific leader actions achieve their impact because they are interpreted in terms of particular leader styles by subordinates and others. Consequently, both the general and specific measures in this study are based upon the questionnaire responses of subordinates. Other sources of data which were also collected are not presented, as these form part of a larger project concerned with the effectiveness of Japanese leadership styles in Western organizations (Peterson, Smith & Tayeb, 1987; Smith, 1984). Three main hypotheses were tested in this study and reported here:

- *Hypothesis 1   The factor structure of general measures of leader style would show high similarity across national cultures.*
- *Hypothesis 2   The factor structure of specific measures would vary between national cultures.*
- *Hypothesis 3   Specific measures would show different relations to general measures across national cultures and the pattern of these differences would be explicable in terms of the leadership values espoused within each national culture.*

The data for this study were collected from shopfloor work teams and their immediate supervisors. At this level employees' attitudes to team work and their behaviour as group members are of crucial importance. We selected Britain, the United States, Hong Kong and Japan as the settings for the study since these countries represent two pairs of cultures whose values about leadership are characterized by individualism and collectivism, respectively (Hofstede, 1980).

Method

A questionnaire entitled 'Leaders and groups' was constructed with two components. The first section comprised 20 items taken from Misumi's PM questionnaire (Misumi and Peterson, 1985). Then of these items referred to his P (Performance) scale and the other 10 to his M (Maintenance) scale. The second comprised 36 items specially created for the purpose, each of which referred to a specific behaviour by the supervisor or their subordinates. All of the above items were re-phrased, where necessary, as questions rather than statements, and the person referred to in them was described as 'the superior'. Five response categories were provided for each item. For 20 of the 56 items these categories were always/usually/sometimes/rarely/never,

Table 1   Sources of data

Country	Ownership	Number of respondents	Average age	Female (%)
Britain	British	201	32.3	77.8
Britain	Japanese	79	36.0	79.0
Japan	Japanese	138	24.0	89.9
Japan	Japanese	394	36.2	28.7
USA	Japanese	197	34.3	77.2
Hong Kong	US	168	n.a.	n.a.

while for the remainder a variety of more precise terms was used, specifying hours, days or whatever metric was appropriate to the item. The instructions at the head of the questionnaire made it clear that it referred to the behaviour of one's immediate supervisor or manager. The text of the specific questions is given later in Table 3, in which it can be seen that they do not necessarily comprise what might be thought of as leadership acts. They describe a variety of specific events and actions, the meaning of which could only be construed from a knowledge of their context.

Data were obtained during 1984–87 from shopfloor work teams employed within a series of closely similar electronics assembly plants. Details of the sample are given in Table 1. In Britain, two plants were studied, both of whom were manufacturing the same electronics consumer product. In Japan, two plants were also studied. These were owned by the same two Japanese firms whose plants in Britain and USA were included in the sample and were manufacturing the same products. In Hong Kong, a US-owned electronics assembly plant was surveyed. Demographic data were not obtained at this site, but respondents were once again predominantly young and middle-aged women.

The data were collected in a manner which guaranteed confidentiality of response. Respondents in Britain and the United States completed the same version of the questionnaire. Hong Kong and Japanese respondents completed Cantonese and Japanese versions, whose translation accuracy had been checked by back-translation. The 1177 sets of data were analysed at the level of individual responses, rather than at the level of the teams to which the respondents belonged.

Results

The universality of the general measure of leader style was tested by separate factor analyses for the data set from each country. Table 2 shows

Table 2 Factor loadings for general items

	Factor 1				Factor 2			
	B	*H*	*A*	*J*	*B*	*H*	*A*	*J*
Items with high loadings on factor 1 in all countries								
Does your superior try to understand your viewpoint? (M2)	77	75	77	77	30			
When a problem arises in your workplace, does your superior ask your opinion about how to solve it? (M3)	58	58	50	57				
Does your superior treat you fairly? (M4)	77	72	77	80				
Can you talk easily with your superior regarding your work? (M5)	78	74	70	74				
Is your superior concerned about your personal problems? (M6)	68	59	76	73				
Do you think your superior trusts you? (M7)	71	52	74	72				
Is your superior concerned about your future career success? (M8)	63	56	75	68				
Does your superior generally support you? (M10)	78	73	78	71				
When you do your job well does your superior give you recognition? (M9)	72	57	66	67	31	40		
Items with some loading on both factors								
When you ask your superior to improve the facilities needed for your work, does he try to do so? (M1)	69	62	54	63			44	40
Is your working time ever wasted because of inadequate planning and organization on the part of your superior? (P9)	52	40	48	41			54	

Table 2   *Continued*

How knowledgeable is your superior about the machinery or equipment for which you are responsible? (P4)	51	40		33	37		45	37
Does your superior let you know about plans and tasks for your day-to-day work? (P1)	36	42			60	32	68	42
Items with high loadings on factor 2 in all countries								
Does your superior urge you to complete work within a specified time? (P7)					84	70	54	66
To what extent does your superior give you instructions and orders? (P2)					64	59	62	75
Is your superior strict about observing regulations? (P8)					50	38	54	62
Does your superior try to make you work to your maximum capacity? (P10)		48			69	58	60	53
How precisely does your superior work out plans for goal achievement each month? (P6)	42	40	39	40	56	46	65	55
When your superior gives you assignments, does he or she clear deadlines for completing the work? (P3)				40	71	74	47	59
Does your superior require you to report on the progress of your work? (P5)				32	51	74	32	60
Eigenvalue	7.85	6.50	6.26	7.04	2.19	1.89	2.51	2.11
Percentage variance explained	39.2	33.3	31.3	35.2	11.0	9.4	12.6	10.6

Note: B = United Kingdom; H = Hong Kong; A = United States; J = Japan. P = Performance; M = Maintenance. Only factor loadings > 0.30 are shown.

Table 3 Numbers of cosines of a given value between factor axes for general and specific behaviours by country pairs

Country pair	Comparison of diagonals				Comparison of non-diagonals			
	>0.99	>0.97	>0.90	<0.90	>0.99	>0.97	>0.90	<0.90
General behaviours (Two-factor solution)								
Britain–Hong Kong	2							2
Britain–America		2						2
Britain–Japan	2							2
Hong Kong–America			2					2
Hong Kong–Japan	2							2
America–Japan	2							2
Specific behaviours (10-factor solution)								
Britain–Hong Kong			1	9				90
Britain–America			1	9				90
Britain–Japan		1		9				90
Hong Kong–America			1	9				90
Hong Kong–Japan		1		9				90
America–Japan			1	9				90

the outcome of these analyses, using varimax rotations and extracting two factors in each instance. The variance accounted for by the two factors within each national culture was moderately similar, which lends some support to the stability of these factors. Actual variance explained was 50.2 per cent in the British sample, 42.7 per cent in the Hong Kong sample, 43.8 per cent in the US sample and 45.8 per cent in the Japanese sample. The two-factor solution was selected since this was the number of general leadership functions specified by Misumi's theory. The table shows a clear M or Maintenance factor within each country's data. The M factor loads equally strongly on the original Japanese M items in all four countries. Thus there is substantial evidence for the generality of this factor.

The structure of the second factor is a little less clear. The P items do cluster together, but several of those which focus on planning by the leader also show some loading on the first factor. This has also been found in Japanese studies (Misumi and Peterson, 1985). The evidence for the generality of the P factor is nonetheless substantial. Tests of the generality of these factor structures were made through computation of the cosines between the unrotated factor axes for each of the pairs of samples, using the Fortran program RELATE (Veldman, 1967). The results are shown in the top half of Table 3, which separates the cosines for comparisons of diagonals, where one would expect a factor match, from non-diagonals where one would not. It can be seen that all diagonal factor axis pairs had cosines in excess of 0.9 and most were in excess of 0.99. Equally high cosines are obtained where three-factor solutions are used, which permit the differentiation of planning and pressure factors, but the two-factor solution is preferred for reasons of parsimony and to maintain consistency with Misumi's earlier work using the PM questionnaire.

The second hypothesis proposed that specific behaviours would vary across cultures. A simple comparison of mean scores on each variable would not suffice to test this hypothesis, since any differences found between cultures could equally well be attributed to slightly differing connotations of the different language versions of the questionnaire. What is required is evidence that the behaviours which the questionnaire investigates cluster in a different manner *within* each cultural setting. While such evidence does not entirely overcome the problem of differential language usage, it does reduce its potency.

Further factor analyses were made of responses to the 36 specific behaviours for each country's data. Since these items were not selected on the basis of any unified conceptual scheme, but rather on the basis of choosing behaviours likely to vary between cultures, there was no reason to expect that behaviours would load on any particular factor. Consequently, it was no surprise that 10–12 factors with eigenvalues greater than 1.0 were obtained in each country's data set. Cosine values for the factor axes derived from 10-factor unrotated solutions are reported in the lower part of Table 3. The table shows evidence of generality of factors only for the first factor extracted, and even this one was weaker than that found for the general items. The two halves of Table 3 should be compared with some care. Since a larger number of factors was extracted for the specific items than for the general items, the specific factors are likely to be less well determined. Indeed, the fact that the specific items were constructed to reflect varying behaviours enhances this possibility. However, it can be seen that none of the off-diagonal cosines exceeded 0.90, which argues against the possibility that general factors were present but emerged in differing sequences in the analyses from different countries. As a further check on the presence of general factors within the specific items, unrotated two-factor solutions were also extracted from each country's specific items. These showed cosine values in excess of 0.90 for comparisons between all pairs of countries. Hypothesis 2 is therefore not wholly supported. It appears that some at least of the specific behavioural items do cluster together in a manner which is similar across cultures. However, many of the remaining specific behaviours do not load on either of the first two factors.

The testing of hypothesis 3 provides the main focus of this paper. The data reported in Table 2 indicated the presence of two reliable general factors. Accordingly, hypothesis 3 was tested in relation to the scores on M and P assigned to supervisors by respondents in the four countries. On the basis of Table 1, the M score was taken as the mean of items M3–M10, while P was the mean of items P2, P3, P6, P7, P8 and P10. Within the present data, reliability of M was 0.88 (UK), 0.84 (Hong Kong), 0.87 (US) and 0.88 (Japan). For P it was 0.76 (UK), 0.72 (Hong Kong), 0.66 (US) and 0.74 (Japan). The product moment correlations obtained between M and P were 0.51 (Hong Kong), 0.42 (Japan), 0.48 (UK), but only 0.24 in the US sample. Reasons for this will become apparent when testing hypothesis 3 below.

Table 4 reports those correlations between the general and specific measures which proved to be significant at $P < 0.001$ in each country.[1] It can be seen that of the 36 specific behaviours, significant correlations with M were found for only eight behaviours, and with P for only four behaviours. Many of the other behaviours did correlate significantly with P or M, but only in some of the countries, rather than all of them. The chosen method of data analysis proposes that the element of interest is the difference found between the correlations with each specific behaviour in each of the countries. The significance of differences found between correlations for each of the possible pairings of countries was computed through the use of z transformations. Table 5 shows which of the differences were significant at $P < 0.01$, and 36 significantly different pairs of correlations with M and 42 pairs with P are indicated.

Discussion

The results indicate that a few of the specific behaviours sampled are construed as representative of one or other general measure of leadership style in all four countries. For instance, in all the organizations sampled a high M supervisor was seen as one who is told about a team member's personal difficulties and responds sympathetically. The high M supervisor also spends time discussing subordinates' careers and plans, and is more likely to accept suggestions for work improvements. The specific behaviours associated with being a high P supervisor in all the countries sampled include talking about progress in relation to a work schedule, sharing information and being within sight. Some of these behaviours were seen as representative of both M and P. However, even on some of the specific behaviours which show a high correlation with M or P in all countries, there are significant differences in the strength of the correlations found in different countries. The finding that there are certain specific behaviours which are related to P or to M in all countries is consistent with the results obtained when hypothesis 2 was tested. The specific items mentioned above are the same ones that were found to factor together in a similar manner in all countries.

---

[1] Response categories for specific behaviours which were categorical were pooled to enable use of correlations.

Table 4   Specific behaviours which correlate with M or P styles in all countries

		B	H	A	J
Behaviours correlating significantly with both M and P					
B8 When your superior learns that a member is experiencing personal difficulties, does your superior . . . discuss the matter sypathetically with the person concerned?	M:	60	54	61	53
	P:	25	32	26	31
B12 On average how often does your superior talk about progress in relation to a work schedule?	M:	31	30	25	18
	P:	41	35	24	27
B30 How much of the information available to your superior concerning the organization's plans and performance is shared with the group?	M:	56	33	36	37
	P:	27	25	22	31
Behaviours correlating with M only					
B7 When members experience personal difficulties, do they tell their superior about them?		43	52	41	56
B10 When your superior learns that a member is experiencing personal difficulties does your superior arrange for other members to help with the person's workload?		51	46	31	42
B18 When group members make suggestions for improvements, what does your superior usually do?		62	47	47	33
B21 How often do you spend time with your superior discussing your career and plans?		44	32	29	35
B27 What does your superior do when he or she believes that there is a substantial problem in the group's work procedures?		55	34	34	31
Behaviours correlating with P only					
B19 For what proportion of the day are you within sight of your superior?		28	20	28	17

Note: B = United Kingdom; H = Hong Kong; A = USA; J = Japan. All correlations are significant at $P > 0.001$. Decimal points omitted.

For the great majority of items a significant difference is found between the correlations from one or more pairs of countries. Furthermore, it can be argued that the differences found are of more interest than the commonalities, since if supervisors in an electronics plant in a particular country are to carry through a supervisory role effectively, they need to provide not just some of the required behaviours but all of those seen as most important in that setting. The results will therefore be discussed for each country in turn.

The British supervisors who are high on M are seen as more task-centred and more consultative than are the high M supervisors from other countries. They are more likely to be judged high on M if they demonstrate or use equipment, explain new tasks, consult widely about necessary changes, hope for suggestions about work improvements and respond positively when they come. High P supervisors at the British sites are more likely to show disapproval of latecomers and to evaluate the work of the group as a whole.

Table 5 Differences in correlations between M and P styles and specific behaviours

		BH	BA	BJ	HA	HJ	AJ
B1	Would your superior show disaproval of a member who regularly arrived late for work by a certain amount of time?	M: P: + −	+ −	+ −		+ −		+ −
B3	How many hours per week is your superior usually at work compared to official work hours?	M: P:					− +	
B4	How does your superior dress while at work, compared to others in the group?	M: P:				− +		+ −
B5	Where does your superior usually eat lunch?	M: P:		− +				
B9	When your superior learns that a member is experiencing personal difficulties, does your superior . . . discuss the matter in the person's absence with other members?	M: − + P: − +		− + − +	+ − + −		− + − +
B10	(stem as B9) . . . arrange for other members to help the person's workload?	M: P:		+ −				− +
B11	On average, how often does your superior . . . check with members concerning the quality of their work?	M: P:		+ −		+ −		− +
B13	(stem as B11) . . . demonstrate or use any of the equipment used by the group?	M: P:		+ −	+ −		+ −	
B14	(stem as B11) . . . instruct you on how to increase your job skill?	M: P:		+ − + −				− + − +
B15	(stem as B11) . . . send you written notes or memos instead of speaking to you in person?	M: P: − +			+ − + −		− + − +
B16	(stem as B11) . . . explain to you how to carry out a new task?	M: + − P:		+ − + −			
B17	About how many suggestions for work improvements would your superior hope that you would make each month?	M: + − P:		+ −	+ −		
B18	When group members make suggestions for improvements, what does your superior usually do?	M: P:		+ −			
B20	How often do you spend time with your superior . . . socially?	M: P:		+ −		+ − + −	+ −	
B21	(stem as B20) . . . discussing your career and plans?	M: P:				+ −		
B22	(stem as B20) . . . talking about immediate work problems?	M: P: − +		+ −		+ − + −	+ −	− +
B23	Does your superior's evaluation depend more on your own work or on that of the group as a whole?	M: P:		+ −			

Table 5   *Continued*

		BH	BA	BJ	HA	HJ	AJ
B25 How often do you work more hours than those for which you are paid?	M:						
	P:		– +		+ –	+ –	
B26 On average, how often does your superior meet the group for social or recreational purposes outside working hours?	M:				+ –		– +
	P:				+ –		– +
B27 What does your superior do when he or she believes that there is a substantial problem in the group's work procedures?	M:	+ –		+ –	+ –		
	P:			+ –			
B29 How do you address your superior?	M:				+ –		
	P:						
B30 How much of the information available to your superior concerning the organization's plans and performance is shared with the group?	M:	+ –		+ –	+ –		
	P:						
B31 How often does this group as a whole have meetings with your superior?	M:						
	P:			+ –		+ –	
B32 How many hours do you usually spend discussing work problems with three or more people from your workgroup at the same time?	M:						
	P:		– +		+ –		
B33 How frequently do you communicate with members of other workgroups in the organization on the same level as yourself?	M:						
	P:		– +		+ –	+ –	
B34 How does your superior react when you communicate with members of other workgroups?	M:				– +		
	P:	+ –			+ –		

Note: For each behaviour, the first row refers to correlations with mean M; the second row refers to correlations with mean P. B = United Kingdom; H = Hong Kong; A = USA; J = Japan.
Only correlations which are significantly different at $P < 0.01$ are indicated; + – means that the correlation was higher in the first named country; – + that it was higher in the second named country.

The US supervisors judged high on M were those seen as showing most of the core consultative and participative behaviours also found in the British supervisors, but not task-centred behaviours. Distinctively M supervisor behaviours in the US sample are *not* showing disapproval of latecomers to work, *not* sending written memos, *not* meeting socially outside work and *not* being so likely to talk about immediate work problems. The high P supervisors in the US sample show core task behaviours, dress like their subordinates, are addressed formally by them and do not meet them socially. Thus the specific behaviours distinguishing American P and M leadership in the plants studied are more sharply differentiated than are the British P and M. In British culture, consideration can be expressed by talking about the task, whereas the American data indicate a different pattern.

Since the Chinese and Japanese data are both drawn from cultures thought of as collective, we might expect rather larger differences than those found within the Western data. The Hong Kong M supervisor's distinctive behaviours include discussing a subordinate's personal difficulties with others in their absence, spending time together socially both at work and after hours, and talking about work problems. The P supervisor also engages in all of these behaviours, but in addition discusses careers and plans, has more frequent meetings with subordinates and encourages communication with other workgroups. In the plants studied the Chinese, like the British, thus make a less clear distinction between M and P than do the Americans. However, in their case M is best exemplified by the tactfulness employed in resolving personal difficulties in an indirect manner, while P is shown by encouragement of cooperative work behaviours. These findings accord well with other studies of Chinese cultural patterns (Bond and Hwang, 1986).

The Japanese data are of particular interest since the P and M measures are of Japanese origin. The data indicate that the most distinctive M supervisor behaviours are speaking about a subordinate's personal difficulties with others in their absence rather than face-to-face, teaching new job skills, talking about work problems and sending written notes. In addition several behaviours are seen as less linked to high M behaviour than in some of the other samples. These include not demonstrating or using equipment, and neither seeking suggestions for work improvements nor accepting them when they come. Distinctive high P supervisor behaviours are meeting socially after hours, arranging help with the workload of someone with personal difficulties and checking work quality. Like high M supervisors they also score high on teaching new job skills and discussing difficulties in the person's absence.

At first reading the Japanese findings provide the greatest surprises of this study. Some of the behaviours reported as uncharacteristic of high M supervisors are among those widely reported as most characteristic of Japanese management styles (Smith, 1984). However, it must be borne in mind that the present findings are based on a correlational analysis. Behaviours which are uniformly shown both by supervisors who are seen as high M *and* low M show little or no correlation with M. Thus the present findings should be read as stating that these behaviours were no more distinctive of high M Japanese supervisors than of low M ones, at least within the organizations sampled.

The findings of this study have lent support to Misumi's distinction between general and specific aspects of behaviour, as expressed in hypothesis 3. It appears that transcultural dimensions of leader style can indeed be identified, but that the skill of executing each style effectively varies by cultural setting, as has been found in earlier studies (Tayeb, 1988). Some caution is needed before assuming that the differences found within our sample of electronics firms would necessarily obtain within other samples from the same range of countries. However, it is noteworthy that data from samples of management trainees from the USA, Britain and Hong Kong, which are not included in this paper, showed patterns which are broadly similar to those found within the electronics plant samples.

It is perhaps no coincidence that the clearest delineation of P and M behaviours was found within the US sample, since that is the country where the Ohio State styles were first conceptualized. The correlations reported earlier between mean M and mean P are also consistent with the view that the US is distinctive in separating out what pertains to the task and what has to do with interpersonal relations. In the other settings we either find that task behaviours can also connote consideration, or that considerate behaviours are used to facilitate task issues. Such cross-cultural differences may provide insight into earlier US findings. For instance, the Ohio State Researchers found some ambiguity as to whether their 'initiating structure' factor comprised items focused upon the supervisor's pressuring subordinates for production or upon the supervisor's planning of future work. The findings reported here indicate that, within the Western data, behaviours which pressure subordinates are a much stronger element in P than they are in the Eastern data. Conversely, planning and goal facilitation are much stronger in the Eastern conception of P, and P and M are therefore closer together. This contrast fits in rather well with Hofstede's (1980) finding of individualist leadership values in Western countries and collectivist values in China and Japan. Where individualist values prevail a leader's options may be expected to include the option of exerting direct pressure towards a goal. Where collectivist values prevail, leadership is more likely to emphasize reciprocal influence processes.

The mode of data analysis employed within this study indicates one way in which we may transcend the debate within cross-cultural psychology as to the relative advantages of emic and etic studies (Lonner, 1980). Our intra-cultural correlations provide a series of related emic studies in a format where they may then be validly compared in an etic manner. The further potential of this method remains to be explored.

Acknowledgements

This research was made possible by grants from the Economic and Social Research Council for a study entitled 'Leadership processes in Japanese and Western organizations' and from one of the participating organizations.

We are grateful to Chic Kanagawa, Emiko Misumi, Fumiyasu Seki and

Toshio Sugiman for assistance in data collection, to David Hitchin for statistical assistance and to Viviane Robinson for comments on earlier drafts.

References

Bond, M. H. and Hwang, K. K. (1986). The social psychology of Chinese people. In M. H. Bond (Ed.), *The Psychology of the Chinese People*. Hong Kong: Oxford University Press.
Fleishman, E. A. (1953). The description of supervisory behaviour. *Personnel Psychology*, **37**, 1–6.
Green, S. G. and Mitchell, T. R. (1979). Attributional processes of leaders in leader–member interactions. *Organizational Behaviour and Human Performance*, **23**, 429–458.
Hoftstede, G. (1980). *Culture's Consequences*. Beverly Hills, CA: Sage.
House, R. J. (1971). A path–goal theory of leader effectiveness. *Administrative Science Quarterly*, **16**, 321–338.
Lewin, K., Lippitt, R. and White, R. (1939). Patterns of aggressive behaviour in experimentally created 'social climates'. *Journal of Social Psychology*, **10**, 271–299.
Lonner, W. J. (1980). The search for psychological universals. In H. C. Triandis and W. W. Lambert (Eds), *Handbook of Cross-cultural Psychology*, vol. 1. Boston, MA: Allyn & Bacon.
Misumi, J. (1985). The behavioural science of leadership: An interdisciplinary Japanese research program. Ann Arbor, MI: University of Michigan Press.
Misumi, J. and Peterson, M. F. (1985). The Performance–Maintenance (PM) theory of leadership: Review of a Japanese research program. *Administrative Science Quarterly*, **30**, 198–223.
Peterson, M. F., Smith, P. B. and Tayeb, M. H. (1987). Development and use of English versions of Japanese PM leadership measures in electronics piants. Proceedings of the Annual Meeting of the Southern Management Association, New Orleans, November.
Phillips, J. S. and Lord, R. G. (1981). Causal attributions and perceptions of leadership. *Organizational Behaviour and Human Performance*. **28**, 143–163.
Schriesheim, C. A. and Kerr, S. (1974). Psychometric properties of the Ohio State leadership scales. *Psychological Bulletin*, **81**, 756–765.
Smith, P. B. (1984). The effectiveness of Japanese styles of management. *Journal of Occupational Psychology*, **57**, 121–136.
Smith, P. B. and Peterson, M. F. (1988). *Leadership, Organizations and Culture*. London: Sage.
Tayeb, M. H. (1988). *Organizations and National Culture: A Comparative Analysis*. London: Sage.
Veldman, D. J. (1967). *Fortran Programming for the Behavioural Sciences*. New York: Holt, Rinehart & Winston.
Vroom, V. and Yetton, P. W. (1973). *Leadership and Decision-making*. Pittsburgh, PA: University of Pittsburgh Press.

Reproduced from Smith, P. B., Misumi, J., Tayeb, M., Peterson, M. and Bond, M. (1989). On the generality of leadership style measures across cultures. *Journal of Occupational Psychology*, **62**, 97–109, by permission of *Journal of Occupational Psychology*.

Table 1 Distances according to power distance

Small power distance societies	Large power distance societies
In the family:	
Children encouraged to have a will of their own	Children educated towards obedience to parents
Parents treated as equals	Parents treated as superiors
At school:	
Student-centered education (initiative)	Teacher-centered education (order)
Learning represents impersonal 'truth'	Learning represents personal 'wisdom' from teacher (guru)
At work place:	
Hierarchy means an inequality of roles, established for convenience	Hierarchy means existential inequality
Subordinates expect to be consulted	Subordinates expect to be told what to do
Ideal boss is resourceful democrat	Ideal boss is benevolent autocrat (good father)

endorsed by the followers as much as by the leaders. Power and inequality, of course, are extremely fundamental facts of any society and anybody with some international experience will be aware that 'all societies are unequal, but some are more unequal than others'.

Table 1 lists some of the differences in the family, the school, and the work situation between small and large power distance cultures. The statements refer to extremes; actual situations may be found anywhere in between the extremes. People's behaviour in the work situation is strongly affected by their previous experiences in the family and in the school: the expectations and fears about the boss are projections of the experiences with the father – or mother – and the teachers. In order to understand superiors, colleagues and subordinates in another country we have to know something about families and schools in that country.

2 Individualism versus collectivism

Individualism on the one side versus its opposite, collectivism, is the degree to which individuals are integrated into groups. On the individualist side, we find societies in which the ties between individuals are loose: everyone is expected to look after him/herself and his/her immediate family. On the collectivist side, we find societies in which people from birth onwards are integrated into strong, cohesive in-groups, often extended families (with uncles, aunts and grandparents) which continue protecting them in exchange

Table 2 Difference according to collectivism individualism

Collectivist societies	Individualist societies
In the family:	
Education towards 'we' consciousness	Education towards 'I' consciousness
Opinions pre-determined by group	Private opinion expected
Obligations to family or in-group:	Obligations to self:
– harmony	– self-interest
– respect	– self-actualization
– shame	– guilt
At school:	
Learning is for the young only	Permanent education
Learn how to do	Learn how to learn
At the work place:	
Value standards differ for in-group and out-groups: particularism	Same value standards apply to all: universalism
Other people are seen as members of their group	Other people seen as potential resources
Relationship prevails over task	Task prevails over relationship
Moral model of employer–employee relationship	Calculative model of employer–employee relationship

for unquestioning loyalty. The word 'collectivism' in this sense has no political meaning: it refers to the group, not to the state. Again, the issue addressed by this dimension is an extremely fundamental one, regarding all societies in the world.

Table 2 lists some of the differences between collectivist and individualist cultures; most real cultures will be somewhere in between these extremes. The words 'particularism' and 'universalism' in Table 2 are common socio-logical categories (Parsons and Shils, 1951, 1977). Particularism is a way of thinking in which the standards for the way a person should be treated depend on the group of category to which this person belongs. Universalism is a way of thinking in which the standards for the way a person should be treated are the same for everybody.

3 Masculinity versus femininity

Masculinity versus its opposite, femininity, refers to the distribution of roles between the sexes which is another fundamental issue for any society to which a range of solutions are found. The IBM studies revealed that: (a) women's values differ less among societies than men's values; (b) men's

Table 3 Differences according to femininity masculinity

Feminine societies	Masculine societies
In the family:	
Stress on relationships	Stress on achievement
Solidarity	Competition
Resolution of conflicts by compromise and negotiation	Resolution of conflicts by fighting them out
At school:	
Average student is norm	Best students are norm
System rewards students' social adaptation	System rewards students' academic performance
Student's failure at school is relatively minor accident	Student's failure at school is disaster – may lead to suicide
At the work place:	
Assertiveness ridiculed	Assertiveness appreciated
Undersell yourself	Oversell yourself
Stress on life quality	Stress on careers
Intuition	Decisiveness

values from one country to another contain a dimension from very assertive and competitive and maximally different from women's values on the one side, to modest and caring and similar to women's values on the other. The assertive pole has been called 'masculine' and the modest, caring pole 'feminine'. The women in feminine countries have the same modest, caring values as the men; in the masculine countries they are somewhat assertive and competitive, but not as much as the men, so that these countries show a gap between men's values and women's values.

Table 3 lists some of the differences in the family, the school, and the work place, between the most feminine versus the most masculine cultures, in analogy to Tables 1 and 2.

4 Uncertainty avoidance

Uncertainty avoidance as a fourth dimension was found in the IBM studies and in one of the two student studies. It deals with a society's tolerance for uncertainty and ambiguity: it ultimately refers to man's search for truth. It indicates to what extent a culture programs its members to feel either uncomfortable or comfortable in unstructured situations. Unstructured situations are novel, unknown, surprising and different from usual. Uncertainty avoiding cultures try to minimize the possibility of such situations by strict laws and rules, safety and security measures, and on the philosophical and religious level by a belief in absolute truth; 'there can only be one truth and we have it'. People in uncertainty avoiding countries are also more emotional, and motivated by inner nervous energy. The opposite type, uncertainty accepting cultures, are more tolerant of opinions different from what they are used to; they try to have as few rules as possible, and on the philosophical and religious level they are relativist and allow many currents to flow side by side. People within these cultures are more phlegmatic and contemplative, and not expected by their environment to express emotions.

Table 4 lists some of the differences in the family, the school, and the workplace, between weak and strong uncertainty avoidance cultures.

5 Long term versus short term orientation

This fifth dimension was found in a study among students in 23 countries around the world, using a questionnaire designed by Chinese scholars (The Chinese Culture Connection, 1987). It can be said to deal with Virtue regardless of Truth. Values associated with long term orientation are thrift and perseverance; values associated with short term orientation are respect for tradition, fulfilling social obligations, and protecting one's 'face'. Both the positively and the negatively rated values of this dimension remind us of the teachings of Confucius (King and Bond, 1985). It was originally called 'Confucian dynamism'; however, the dimension also applies to countries without a Confucian heritage.

There has been insufficient research as yet on the implications of differences along this dimension to allow the composition of a table of differences in the family, the school and the work place similar to those for the other four dimensions (Tables 1–4).

Scores on the first four dimensions were obtained for 50 countries and three regions on the basis of the IBM study, and on the fifth dimension for 23 countries on the basis of the student data collected by Bond *et al.* All scores have been transformed to a scale from approximately 0 for the lowest scoring country to approximately 100 for the highest. Table 5 shows the scores for twelve countries. For the full list the reader is referred to Hofstede (1991).

Power distance scores tend to be high for Latin, Asian and African countries and smaller for Germanic countries. Individualism prevails in developed and Western countries, while collectivism prevails in less developed and Eastern countries; Japan takes a middle position on this dimension. Masculinity is high in Japan, in some European countries like Germany, Austria and Switzerland, and moderately high in Anglo countries; it is low

Table 4 Differences according to uncertainty avoidance

Weak uncertainty avoidance societies	*Strong uncertainty avoidance societies*
In the family:	
What is different, is ridiculous or curious	What is different, is dangerous
Ease, indolence, low stress	Higher anxiety and stress
Aggression and emotions not shown	Showing of aggression and emotions accepted
At school:	
Students comfortable with:	Students comfortable with:
– Unstructured learning situations	– Structured learning situations
– Vague objectives	– Precise objectives
– Broad assignments	– Detailed assignments
– No time tables	– Strict time tables
Teachers may say 'I don't know'	Teachers should have all the answers
At the work place:	
Dislike of rules – written or unwritten	Emotional need for rules – written or unwritten
Less formalization and standardization	More formalization and standardization

Table 5 Scores of 12 countries on five dimensions of national culture

Country	*Power distance*		*Individualism*		*Masculinity*		*Uncertainty avoidance*		*Long term orientation*	
	Index	*Rank*	*Index*	*Rank*	*Index*	*Rank*	*Index*	*Rank*	*Index*	*Rank*
Brazil	69	14	38	26–27	49	27	76	21–22	65	6
France	68	15–16	71	10–11	43	35–36	86	10–15	no	data
Germany	35	42–44	67	15	66	9–10	65	29	31	14–15
Great Britain	35	42–44	89	3	66	9–10	35	47–48	25	18–19
Hong Kong	68	15–16	25	37	57	18–19	29	49–50	96	2
India	77	10–11	48	21	56	20–21	40	45	61	7
Japan	54	33	46	22–23	95	1	92	7	80	4
The Netherlands	38	40	80	4–5	14	51	53	35	44	10
Sweden	31	47–48	71	10–11	5	53	29	49–50	33	12
Thailand	64	21–23	20	39–41	34	44	64	30	56	8
USA	40	38	91	1	62	15	46	43	29	17
Venezuela	81	5–6	12	50	73	3	76	21–22	no	data

Ranks: 1 = highest, 53 = lowest (for long term orientation, 23 = lowest).

in Nordic countries and in The Netherlands and moderately low in some Latin and Asian countries like France, Spain and Thailand. Uncertainty avoidance scores are higher in Latin countries, in Japan, and in German speaking countries, lower in Anglo, Nordic, and Chinese culture countries.

A long term orientation is mostly found in East Asian countries, in particular in China, Hong Kong, Taiwan, Japan, and South Korea.

The grouping of country scores points to some of the roots of cultural differences. These should be sought in the common history of similarly scoring countries. All Latin countries, for example, score relatively high on both power distance and uncertainty avoidance. Latin countries (those today speaking a Romance language, i.e. Spanish, Portuguese, French or Italian) have inherited at least part of their civilization from the Roman empire. The Roman empire in its days was characterized by the existence of a central authority in Rome, and a system of law applicable to citizens anywhere. This established in its citizens' minds the value complex which we still recognize today: centralization fostered large power distance and a stress on laws fostered strong uncertainty avoidance. The Chinese empire also knew centralization, but it lacked a fixed system of laws: it was governed by men rather than by laws. In the present-day countries once under Chinese rule, the mindset fostered by the empire is reflected in large power distance but medium to weak uncertainty avoidance. The Germanic part of Europe, including Great Britain, never succeeded in establishing an enduring common central authority and countries which inherited its civilizations show smaller power distance. Assumptions about historical roots of cultural differences always remain speculative but in the given examples they are quite plausible. In other cases they remain hidden in the course of history (Hofstede, 1980, pp. 127, 179, 235, 294).

The country scores on the five dimensions are statistically correlated with a multitude of other data about the countries. For example, power distance is correlated with the use of violence in domestic politics and with income inequality in a country. Individualism is correlated with national wealth (per capita gross national product) and with mobility between social classes from one generation to the next. Masculinity is correlated negatively with the share of gross national product that governments of wealthy countries spend on development assistance to the Third World. Uncertainty avoidance is associated with Roman Catholicism and with the legal obligation in developed countries for citizens to carry identity cards. Long term orientation is correlated with national economic growth during the past 25 years, showing that what led to the economic success of the East Asian economies in this period is their populations' cultural stress on the future-oriented values of thrift and perseverance.

The cultural limits of management theories

The culture of a country affects its parents and its children, teachers and students, labour union leaders and members, politicians and citizens, journalists and readers, managers and subordinates. Therefore management practices in a country are culturally dependent, and what works in one country does not necessarily work in another. However not only the managers are human and children of their culture; the management teachers, the people who wrote and still write theories and create management concepts, are also human and constrained by the cultural environment in which they grew up and which they know. Such theories and concepts cannot be applied in another country without further proof; if applicable at all, it is often only after considerable adaptation. Four examples follow.

1 Performance appraisal systems

These are recommended in the Western management literature. They assume that employees' performance will be improved if they receive direct feedback about what their superior thinks of them, which may well be the case in individualist cultures. However, in collectivist countries such direct feedback destroys the harmony which is expected to govern interpersonal relationships. It may cause irreparable damage to the employee's 'face' and ruin his or her loyalty to the organization. In such cultures, including all East Asian and Third World countries, feedback should rather be given indirectly, for example through the withdrawing of a favor, or via an intermediary person trusted by both superior and employee.

2 Management by objectives

Management by Objectives (MBO) is a management concept developed in the USA. Under a system of MBO, subordinates have to negotiate about their objectives with their superiors. The system therefore assumes a cultural environment in which issues can be settled by negotiation rather than rules, which means a medium to low power distance and a not too high uncertainty avoidance. In the German environment it had to be adapted to the more structured culture of a stronger uncertainty avoidance; it became 'Führung durch Zielvereinbarung' which is much more formal than the US model (Ferguson, 1973).

3 Strategic management

This is a concept also developed in the USA. It assumes a weak uncertainty avoidance environment, in which deviant strategic ideas are encouraged.

Although it is taught in countries with a stronger uncertainty avoidance, like Germany or France, its recommendations are rarely followed there, because in these cultures it is seen as the top managers' role to remain involved in daily operations (Horovitz, 1980).

4 Humanization of work

This is a general term for a number of approaches in different countries trying to make work more interesting and rewarding for the people who do it. In the USA, which is a masculine and individualist society, the prevailing form of humanization of work has been 'job enrichment': giving individual tasks more intrinsic content. In Sweden which is feminine and less individualist, the prevailing form has been the development of semi-autonomous work groups, in which members exchange tasks and help each other (Gohl, 1977). In Germany and German-speaking Switzerland the introduction of flexible working hours has been a very popular way of adapting the job to the worker. Flexible working hours have never become as popular in other countries; their popularity in German-speaking countries can be understood by the combination of a small power distance (acceptance of responsibility by the worker) with a relatively large uncertainty avoidance (internalization of rules).

Eastern versus Western categories of thinking

A study of students' values in 23 countries using a questionnaire designed by Chinese scholars (the Chinese Value Survey, CVS) produced partly similar, but partly different results from the two other studies (among 64 IBM subsidiaries and among students in 10 countries) which used questionnaires designed by Western (European and American, respectively) minds. The CVS study did not identify a dimension like uncertainty avoidance, which deals with the search for truth. It seems that to the Chinese minds who designed the questions the search for truth is not an essential issue, so the questions necessary to identify this dimension were not included in their questionnaire.

One of the basic differences between Eastern thinking (represented by, for example Confucianism, Buddhism, and Hinduism) and Western thinking (dominant in the Judaeo–Christian–Muslim intellectual tradition) is that in the East, a qualification does not exclude its opposite, which is an essential element of Western logic (Kapp, 1983). Thus in the East the search for truth is irrelevant, because there is no need for a single and absolute truth and the assumption that a person can possess an objective truth is absent. Instead, the Eastern instrument includes the questions necessary to detect the dimension of long versus short term orientation expressing a concern for virtue: for proper ways of living (like, practising perseverance and thrift, or respecting tradition and social obligations) which is less obvious in the West where virtue tends to be derived from truth.

These findings show that not only practices, values and theories, but even the categories available to build theories from are products of culture. This has far-reaching consequences for management training in a multicultural organization. Not only our tools, but even the categories in which we think, may be unfit for the other environment.

Organizational cultures

The use of the term 'culture' in the management literature is not limited to the national level: attributing a distinct culture to a company or organization has become extremely popular. However, organizational cultures are a phenomenon of a different order from national cultures, if only because membership of an organization is usually partial and voluntary, while the 'membership' of a nation is permanent and involuntary. Our field research to be described below showed that national cultures differ mostly at the level of basic values while organizational cultures differ mostly at the level of the more superficial practices: symbols, heroes, and rituals.

In the popular management literature, organization cultures have often been presented as a matter of values (e.g. Peters and Waterman, 1982). The confusion arises because this literature does not distinguish between the values of the founders and leaders and those of the ordinary employees. Founders and leaders create the symbols, the heroes and the rituals that constitute the daily practices of the organization's members. However, members have to adapt their personal values to the organization's needs, to a limited extent only. A work organization, as a rule, is not a 'total institution' like a prison or a mental hospital. Precisely because organizational cultures are composed of practices rather than values, they are somewhat manageable: they can be managed by changing the practices. The values of employees cannot be changed by an employer, because they were acquired when the employees were children. However, sometimes an employer can activate latent values which employees were not allowed to show earlier, like a desire for initiative and creativity, by allowing practices which before were forbidden.

Dimensions of organizational cultures

A research project similar to the IBM studies but focusing on organizational rather than national cultures was carried out by the Institute for Research on Intercultural Cooperation (IRIC) in The Netherlands. Data were collected in twenty work organizations or parts of organizations in The Netherlands and Denmark. The units studied varied from a toy manufacturing company to two municipal police corps. As mentioned above the study found large differences among units in practices (symbols, heroes, rituals) but only modest differences in values, beyond those due to such basic facts as nationality, education, gender and age group.

Six independent dimensions can be used to describe most of the variety in organizational practices. These six dimensions can be used as a framework to describe organizational cultures, but their research base in 20 units from two countries is too narrow to consider them as universally valid. For describing organizational cultures in other countries and in other types of organizations, additional dimensions may be necessary or some of the six may be less useful (see also Pümpin, 1984). The dimensions of organizational cultures found are:

1 Process-oriented versus results-oriented cultures

The former are dominated by technical and bureaucratic routines, the latter by a common concern for outcomes. This dimension was associated with the culture's degree of homogeneity: in results-oriented units, everybody perceived their practices in about the same way; in process-oriented units, there were vast differences in perception among different levels and parts of the unit. The degree of homogeneity of a culture is a measure of its 'strength': the study confirmed that strong cultures are more results-oriented than weak ones, and vice versa (Peters and Waterman, 1982).

2 Job-oriented versus employee-oriented cultures

The former assume responsibility for the employees' job performance only, and nothing more; employee-oriented cultures assume a broad responsibility for their members' well-being. At the level of individual managers, the distinction between job orientation and employee orientation has been popularized by Blake and Mouton's Managerial Grid (1964). The IRIC study shows that job versus employee orientation is part of a culture and not (only) a choice for an individual manager. A unit's position on this dimension seems to be largely the result of historical factors, like the philosophy of its founder(s) and the presence or absence in its recent history of economic crises with collective layoffs.

3 Professional versus parochial cultures

In the former, the usually highly educated members identify primarily with their profession; in the latter, the members derive their identity from the organization for which they work. Sociology has long known this dimension as local versus cosmopolitan, the contrast between an internal and an external frame of reference, first suggested by Tönnies (1887).

4 Open system versus closed system cultures

This dimension refers to the common style of internal and external communication, and to the ease with which outsiders and newcomers are admitted. This dimension is the only one of the six for which there is a systematic difference between Danish and Dutch units. It seems that organizational openness is a societal characteristic of Denmark, much more so than of The Netherlands. This shows that organizational cultures also reflect national culture differences.

5 Tightly versus loosely controlled cultures

This dimension deals with the degree of formality and punctuality within the organization; it is partly a function of the unit's technology: banks and pharmaceutical companies can be expected to show tight control, research laboratories and advertising agencies loose control; but even with the same technology, units still differ on this dimension.

6 Pragmatic versus normative cultures

The last dimension describes the prevailing way (flexible or rigid) of dealing with the environment, in particular with customers. Units selling services are likely to be found towards the pragmatic (flexible) side, units involved in the application of legal rules towards the normative (rigid) side. This dimension measures the degree of 'customer orientation', which is a highly popular topic in the management literature.

Managing organizational cultures

In spite of their relatively superficial nature organizational cultures are hard to change because they have developed into collective habits. Changing them is a top management task which cannot be delegated. Some kind of culture assessment by an independent party is usually necessary, which includes the identification of different subcultures which may need quite different approaches. The top management's major strategic choice is either to accept and optimally use the existing culture or to try to change it. If an attempt at change is made it should be preceded by a cost–benefit analysis. A particular concern is whether the manpower necessary for a culture change is available.

Turning around an organizational culture demands visible leadership which appeals to the employees' feelings as much as to their intellect. The leader or leaders should assure themselves of sufficient support from key persons at different levels in the organization. Subsequently, they can change the practices by adapting the organization's structure – its functions, departments, locations, and tasks – matching tasks with employee talents. After the structure, the controls may have to be changed, based on a decision on which aspects of the work have to be co-ordinated how and by whom at what level. At the same time it is usually necessary to change certain personnel policies related to recruitment, training and promotion. Finally, turning around a culture is not a one-shot process. It takes sustained attention from top management, persistence for several years, and usually a second culture assessment to see whether the intended changes have, indeed, been attained.

Managing culture differences in multinationals

Many multinational corporations do not only operate in different countries but also in different lines of business or at least in different product/market divisions. Different business lines and/or divisions often have different organizational cultures. Strong cross-national organizational cultures within a business line or division, by offering common practices, can bridge national differences in values among organization members. Common practices, not common values, keep multinationals together.

Structure should follow culture: the purpose of an organization structure is the co-ordination of activities. For the design of the structure of a multinational, multibusiness corporation, three questions have to be answered for each business unit (a business unit represents one business line in one country). The three questions are: (a) which of the unit's in- and outputs should be co-ordinated from elsewhere in the corporation? (b) where and at what level should the co-ordination take place? and (c) how tight or loose should the co-ordination be? In every case there is a basic choice between co-ordination along geographical lines and along business lines. The decisive factor is whether business know-how or national cultural know-how is more crucial for the success of the operation.

Matrix structures are a possible solution but they are costly, often meaning a doubling of the management ranks, and their actual functioning may raise more problems than they resolve. A single structural principle (geographic or business) is unlikely to fit for an entire corporation. Joint ventures further complicate the structuring problem. The optimal solution is nearly always a patchwork structure that in some cases follows business and in others geographical lines. This may lack beauty, but it follows the needs of markets and business unit cultures. Variety within the environment in which a corporation operates should be matched with appropriate internal variety. Optimal solutions will also change over time, so that the periodic reshufflings which any large organization undergoes, should be seen as functional.

Like all organizations, multinationals are held together by people. The best structure at a given moment depends primarily on the availability of suitable people. Two roles are particularly crucial: (a) country business unit managers who form the link between the culture of the business unit, and the corporate culture which is usually heavily affected by the nationality of origin of the corporation, and (b) 'corporate diplomats', i.e. home country or other nationals who are impregnated with the corporate culture, multilingual, from various occupational backgrounds, and experienced in living and functioning in various foreign cultures. They are essential to make multinational structures work, as liaison persons in the various head offices or as temporary managers for new ventures.

The availability of suitable people at the right moment is the main task of multinational personnel management. This means timely recruiting of future managerial talent from different nationalities, and career moves through planned transfers where these people will absorb the corporate culture. Multinational personnel departments have to find their way between uniformity and diversity in personnel policies. Too much uniformity is unwarranted because people's mental programmes are not uniform. It leads to corporate-wide policies being imposed on subsidiaries where they will not work – or only receive lip service from obedient but puzzled locals. On the other side, the assumption that everybody is different and that people in subsidiaries therefore always should know best and be allowed to go their own ways, is unwarranted too. In this case an opportunity is lost to build a corporate culture with unique features which keep the organization together and provide it with a distinctive and competitive psychological advantage.

Increasing integration of organizations across national borders demands that managers have an insight in the extent to which familiar aspects of organizational life like organization structures, leadership styles, motivation patterns, and training and development models are culturally relative and need to be reconsidered when borders are crossed. It also calls for self-insight on the part of the managers involved, who have to be able to compare their ways of thinking, feeling and acting to those of others, without immediately passing judgment. This ability to see the relativity of one's own cultural framework does not come naturally to most managers, who often got to their present position precisely because they held strong convictions. Intercultural management skills can be improved by specific training; this should focus on working rather than on living in other countries. The stress in such courses is on recognizing one's own cultural programmes and where these may differ from those of people in other countries.

References

Blake, R. R. and Mouton, J. S. (1964) *The Managerial Grid*. Gulf Publishing, Houston.

Ferguson, I. R. G. (1973) *Management By Objectives in Deutschland*. Herder and Herder, Frankfurt/Main.

Gohl, J. (Ed.) (1977) *Probleme der Humanisierungsdebatte*. Goldmann, München.

Hofstede, G. (1980) *Culture's Consequences: International Differences in Work-Related Values*. Sage Publications, Beverly Hills.

Hofstede, G. (1983) Dimensions of National Culture in Fifty Countries and Three Regions, in Deregowski, J. B., Dziurawiec, S. and Annis, R. C. (Eds), *Expiscations in Cross-Cultural Psychology*, pp. 335–355. Swets & Zeitlinger, Lisse, The Netherlands.

Hofstede, G. (1986) Cultural Differences in Teaching and Learning. *International Journal of Intercultural Relations*, Vol 10, pp. 301–320.

Hofstede, G. (1991) *Cultures and Organizations: Software of the Mind*. McGraw Hill, London.

Hofstede, G. and Bond, M. H. (1984) Hofstede's Culture Dimensions: an Independent Validation Using Rokeach's Value Survey. *Journal of Cross-Cultural Psychology*, Vol 15, pp. 417–433.

Hofstede, G. and Bond, M. H. (1988) The Confucius Connection: From Cultural Roots to Economic Growth. *Organizational Dynamics*, Vol 16, No 4, pp. 4–21.

Hofstede, G., Neuijen, B., Ohayv, D. D. and Sanders, G. (1990) Measuring Organizational Cultures. *Administrative Science Quarterly*, Vol 35, pp. 286–316.

Horovitz, J. H. (1980) *Top Management Control in Europe*. Macmillan, London.

Kapp, R. A. (Ed.) (1983) *Communicating with China*. Intercultural Press, Chicago.

King, A. Y. C. and Bond, M. H. (1985) The Confucian Paradigm of Man: a Sociological View, in Tseng, W. and Wu, D. (Eds), *Chinese Culture and Mental Health*, pp. 29–45. Columbia University Press, New York.

Parsons, T. and Shils, E. A. (1951) *Toward a General Theory of Action*. Harvard University Press, Cambridge, Massachusetts.

Peters, T. J. and Waterman, R. H. (1982) *In Search of Excellence: Lessons from America's Best-Run Companies*. Harper & Row, New York.

Pümpin, C. (1984) Unternehmenskultur, Unternehmensstrategie und Unternehmenserfolg. *GDI Impuls*, Vol 2, pp. 19–30.

The Chinese Culture Connection (1987) Chinese Values and the Search for Culture-free Dimensions of Culture. *Journal of Cross-Cultural Psychology*, Vol 18, pp. 143–164.

Tönnies, F. [1963 (1887)] *Community and Society*. Harper & Row, New York.

Reproduced from Hofstede, G. (1994). The business of international business is culture. *International Business Review*, **3** (1), 1–14, by permission of *International Business Review*.

5.2 Analyzing cross-national management and organizations: a theoretical framework

Ran Lachman, Albert Nedd and Bob Hinings

Recent literature on cross-cultural organizations and management, has considerably advanced our awareness of the complexity of the impact indigenous cultural settings may have on organizational structures and processes (Ronen 1986, Nath 1988, Shin *et al*. 1990, Miller *et al*. 1990, Martinko and Fenzeng 1990). However, more major theoretical and methodological issues still require attention. An important issue is the use of culture as an explanatory variable in the study of cross-cultural and international organizations. Frequency, cross-national studies observing differences in management or organization practices in different countries, attribute them to cultural differences (e.g. Howard *et al*. 1983, Cavusgil and Yavas 1984, Vertinsky *et al*. 1990). However, they provide neither sufficient theoretical nor empirical indications of how culture causes such differences. Consequently, relevant theories were characterized as being scarce, pre-paradigmatic, and lacking sufficient specification of the role indigenous cultures may play in the transferability of management and organizational practices (Adler 1983, Kelly and Worthley 1981, Schein 1981, Roberts and Boyacigiller 1984). It appears, therefore, that further attention ought to be devoted to key issues such as: (a) whether culture is a significant explanatory factor; (b) if so, what are the specific aspects of culture to which differences can be attributed; (c) how do these cultural elements cause the differences. A focus on these issues is important for cross-national theory building as it is for any theory development (Whetten 1989).

Recent attempts to develop theoretical frameworks have pointed at cultural values as the important elements of culture to impact organizations (Hofstede 1980). Efforts were made to identify and classify several cultural values, or patterns of values, on which different countries can be compared and contrasted in terms of commonality in values (e.g. Glenn 1981; Hofstede 1980; Triandis 1982, 1984; Ronen and Shenkar 1985). The focus on values as the relevant cultural dimensions, followed by the identification of specific values or groups of values, that are prevalent in one or a number of cultural settings, is undoubtedly an important contribution. However, we contend that theory development ought to take a further step by adding a dimension of values' centrality.

The impact cultural values have is determined by their centrality within the value system of a cultural setting more than by their prevalence in this setting. Therefore, values should be examined not only in terms of their prevalence, but also in terms of their centrality and importance within the relevant cultural setting. We argue that major problems faced by cross-cultural and international management may stem, not simply from value differences, but from incongruency between management's underlying core values and the values central to the host cultural setting. This is the focus of the paper. Proposed here is a framework that specifies the mechanisms through which culture exerts its influences, differentiates between core and periphery cultural values, and accounts for the differential impact and consequences these values have for organizations and management within and across cultural boundaries.

Specifying the effects of culture

The basic premise advocated in our proposed theoretical framework is that the social control exerted by values is the main factor in the impact of culture. The level of social control inherent in each value differs by the centrality of that value within the cultural system.

Culture is viewed here as a system of patterned meanings or the collective mental programming of a social group (Hofstede 1980). In order to appropriately articulate its effects on specific organizational structures and processes the concept of culture must be further specified. In specifying the effects of culture we propose that the focus be on the social control aspect of cultural values. Values are the bases for the choice, by a social group, of particular ends and of particular means by which these ends are to be accomplished. They determine and provide legitimacy for (or sanction) collective and individual preferences for certain states of affairs and modes of conduct over available alternatives (Kluckhohn and Strodtbeck 1961, Rokeach 1973, Schein 1985). Thus, values serve as mechanisms of social control by regulating behavior in accord with the requirements of the socio-cultural system for order and for selective, nonimpulsive behavior (Kluckhohn 1951). The value system legitimizes behavior by stipulating positive or negative sanctions for what is expected, desired, required, or forbidden behavior within a cultural setting. Cultural values have, therefore, an important role of controlling and directing social behavior, organizational behavior included.

However, not all values are equally important, or have the same impact in regulating behavior. Cultural values ought to be differentiated in terms of the impact they have in legitimizing and directing choices of modes of organizing and patterns of managerial behavior.

Centrality of values

In the cross-cultural organizational literature most of the proposed classifications of cultural values identify certain sets of values or cultural dimensions and examine the extent to which countries vary in their commitment to and expression of these values (e.g., Hofstede 1980, Ronen and Shenkar 1985). We maintain that the effect of values on organizations in a cultural setting goes beyond their mere expression. To a large extent, this effect is determined by the relative importance of a value within the given culture: the more important and central the value, the stronger will be its impact and the more consequential it will be for differences in organizational and managerial practices.

In any given culture some values are regarded as more important than others, and in different cultures the relative importance attributed to particular values may differ (Kluckhohn and Strodtbeck 1961). Shils 1961, Rokeach 1973, Allport 1961). Within a culture, values are organized in a hierarchy or a relative order of priority. This hierarchy reflects the relative importance, endurance of values in the system, and their power to control social behavior. Values higher in the hierarchy are more important, more enduring and resistant to change, are highly accepted and agreed upon, and hence are more involved in social control than those lower in the hierarchy (Rokeach 1969, 1973; Shils 1961; Schein 1985). The terms 'core' and 'periphery' may be used to represent, respectively, the relatively high and the relatively low positioning of values in the values hierarchy and the extent to which they are involved in social control. For analytical clarity, only the two ends of the continuum are contrasted here. The middle range has been omitted from the analysis.

Parsons (1964) suggests that values, as the evaluative aspect of culture, constitute the core of the stabilizing mechanisms of the social system. However, not all values are completely stable, thus allowing for continuity and change within a cultural system. The core values tend to maintain continuity in the unique and distinct characteristics of a cultural system. They maintain continuity because they tend to be more stable and resistant to change, their social control effects are more enduring, and because consensus and acceptance of core values is higher relative to that of periphery values. Periphery values are less stable or enduring because members of society may manifest different levels of attachment to them, or may even disregard them. The divergence in acceptance of periphery values and their resulting susceptibility to change make them more accommodating to social change and innovation. This perspective suggests that culture is a relatively adaptive system that can change mostly through changes in periphery values. While core values too can change, or their relative priority in the hierarchy can shift, changes impinging on periphery values are more likely to occur.

Thus, core values are the high priority values that are central to a social, cultural or an individual's value system, are important in regulating social behavior, and tend to be enduring. Periphery values refer to values of low priority, low consensus (high divergence and ambiguity), and less importance for social control. Consequently, they are relatively susceptible to change (Shils 1961).

The differential susceptibility of core and periphery values to contextual change influences can be illustrated. The Confucian value of hierarchical relations, still prevailing in China, has been described as one of the main tenets of that philosophy which underlies the Chinese cultural system (Eberhard 1971). Confucianism's emphasis on the differential hierarchical position of individuals in the social system was in conflict with the dominant egalitarian values of Maoist ideology (Liu 1964, Hsu 1981). During the Cultural Revolution this Confucian value was strongly attacked in the attempt to abolish organizational and other hierarchies. These attempts did not, however, have lasting effects on management and organizations, which have gradually returned to hierarchical systems (Laaksonen 1988). Indeed, the attempts to abolish them seem to have further strengthened the position of traditional Chinese values (Bond and Wang 1983).

However, while the value of hierarchy withstood the Maoist challenge, the Confucian value of the status of women did not. Laaksonen (1988) suggests that, under the pressure of Maoist ideology, women have been raised from their traditional subjugated status. This Confucian value was not as dominant in the overall cultural system as the value of hierarchy (Laaksonen 1988). It can be regarded as a periphery value and, therefore, was less resistant to change.

In another study the status of women relative to men was classified as a core value in four countries studied: Argentina, Chile, India, and Israel (Lachman 1983). Studying core and periphery values among factory workers it was found, however, that the values classified as core or periphery in one country were not necessarily classified in the same way in all the others. It was further found that organizational socialization influences had little or no effect on core values, but had some effect on change in employees' periphery values (Lachman 1983, 1988).

Thus, rather than searching for 'common' cultural values on which cross-cultural comparisons of managerial practices and organizational forms may be made, efforts should be directed at identifying the core values of particular cultural settings, and examining their impact on organizational practices. This does not preclude the study of values' diffusion and transferability

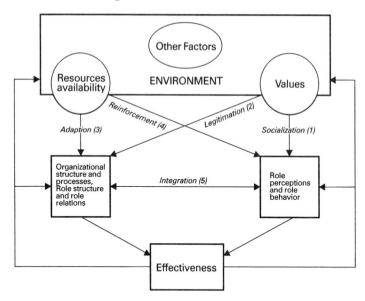

Figure 1   *A theoretical framework for cross-cultural analysis*

across countries, and the factors influencing their spread. However, it suggests that such diffusion be examined in terms of its congruence with local core/periphery values and local interpretations of the imported values.

The theoretical framework

The theoretical framework presented here describes the influences of cultural values on organizations and management, focusing on the social control functions of core and periphery cultural values. The basic arguments advocated in our framework are: (a) the general, all-inclusive construct of culture can be specified by focusing on the effects particular cultural values have in determining a range of legitimate modes of organizing and patterns of social interaction, out of which specific organizational forms and behavior are chosen; (b) a distinction ought to be made between core and periphery values in a cultural setting; (c) transferred, or contextually induced organizational adjustments that are incongruent with relevant core values of the cultural setting, will impact the effective functioning of the organization more negatively than adjustments incongruent with periphery values; (d) incongruence between the manifestations of core values at the organizational (structural) and the individual (role behavior) levels of the organization, will also impete organizational effectiveness. The processes through which cultural values influence individuals and organizations are discussed in more detail later on.

The main assertion underlying the framework is that congruence between core values governing modes of organizing in a cultural setting, and the value assumptions underlying the structure and processes of cross-national organizations operating within that setting, is of critical importance for organizational effectiveness. Another premise of the framework is that organizational adaptations to pressures and constraints posed by the environment are essential because organizations depend on their environment for necessary inputs and outputs. Many environmental dimensions such as the social, political and legal systems, the availability of resources and technology, may have important impacts on such adaptations. Undoubtedly, all these dimensions of the organization's host environment ought to be considered and incorporated into a comprehensive theory. However, since it would require a very complex framework to describe such an elaborate set of relationships, we have decided at this initial stage of theory building, to prefer parsimony and simplicity to complexity and comprehensiveness. Hence, in addition to the impact of values, the framework considers one additional dimension: the economic dimension of availability (scarcity or munificence) of resources in the organizations' environment.

There are several reasons for choosing the factor of resources out of the many relevant environmental or contextual elements affecting organizational structure and behavior. First, it has been persuasively argued in the literature that the economic aspects of any society and its cultural values are intricately bound together, and any comprehensive theory of cross-national organization and management should incorporate both (e.g. Smelser 1963, Jamieson 1982). Secondly, since economic conditions differ across nations, the conditions prevailing within a nation (or a region thereof) are of particular importance for cross-national organization theory and practice, especially when highly developed and less-developed nations are compared (Kiggundu *et al.* 1983). Finally, since cross-national management involves for the most part economic organizations and activities, the potential impact of the economic environment is of considerable importance.

Effects of cultural values

Cultural values have an important role of legitimizing the organization's existence and its modes of functioning, as well as the patterns of behavior of its members. In addition, cultural values also filter the impact of other environmental factors on the organization through their role as managerial interpretive schema (Ranson *et al.* 1980, Ford and Baucus 1987). All these effects may vary with the centrality of the relevant values, because the more central a value, the stronger its social control effects and the lower the tolerance for deviations.

Cultural values and Individual behavior

Link 1 in Figure 1 denotes that the behavior of individuals in the organization are influenced by the values, orientations, attitudes and beliefs individuals bring with them to their jobs. Acquisition of values (particularly core ones) by individuals occurs, in the main, prior to their joining work organizations. Consequently, the values held by employees are not necessarily congruent with those required by their organizations. Organizations try to minimize incongruency through selection procedures, aiming at identifying and recruiting individuals who already have at least some of the required values (Brim 1968). To further decrease incongruency, organizational socialization processes are employed to assist recruits in acquiring the required organizational values (Van Maanen and Schein 1979). The question in this regard is whether or not organizational socialization can effectively override the influence of members' previously internalized values, and change them to conform to those required by the organization. If indeed they can, the effects of previously held values on individuals' behavior in organizations becomes irrelevant.

It is well recognized that early childhood socialization plays a primary role in personality development and the acquisition of basic values. The impact of adult socialization on personal values has, however, been debated. Some scholars suggest that both early and adult socialization may be equally important in determining personal values. They argue that late socialization influences can override the influences of early socialization and change employees' values that are incongruent with the organizations' requirements (Inkeles and Smith 1974). Other studies have suggested that organizational socialization serves mainly to reinforce, rather than change, values acquired prior to joining an organization (Frese 1982, Mortimer and Lorence 1979).

Lachman (1983, 1988) tried to reconcile these different perspectives by showing that early and late socialization induce changes in different categories of values. Early socialization affects core values, and late socialization affects only periphery values. Thus, employees' periphery values may change as a result of pressures to comply with organizational requirements and managerial policies, whereas their core values will not. When organizational role requirements are incongruent with core values, employees tend to modify these role requirements. If they fail to modify them, employees may change their jobs rather than their values (Holland 1976).

Cultural values and organizational structure

At the most fundamental level, cultural legitimation may define the kinds of organizations that are allowable in a society, in terms of product or service, type of ownership and rules of competition (Child 1981, Maurice 1979). Since cultural values are embedded in the institutional arrangements of socio-political systems, they affect not only the broad nature of organizational possibilities but also the more specific structural factors such as differentiation and integration, degree of specialization, the form of hierarchies, the use of rules and procedures, and the locus of decision-making in organizations (Clark 1979, Gallie 1978, Hofstede 1980, Jamieson 1982). Thus cultural values permeate organizations by defining organizational processes, role structures, and role relations as culturally acceptable, relatively neutral, or in conflict with culturally prescribed norms and, therefore, unacceptable (link 2, Figure 1).

Cultural values also have indirect effects on structure. Managerial activities directed toward organizational adaptation are determined by processes of social cognition and social perceptions (Weick 1979, Kiesler and Sproull 1982). The cultural values held by decision makers provide interpretations of which contextual influences are critical for the organization and require a response, and which can be ignored. Thus, cultural values also affect organizational structures and processes through their influences on the selectivity of management's perceptions.

Indeed, organizations in different countries show a wide variation in structural dimensions (Lammers and Hickson 1979, McMillan *et al.* 1973). However, there has been an ongoing debate on the utility of employing cultural factors in accounting for these variations. The contrasting perspectives in the debate are the 'culture free' and 'culturalist' perspectives. Advocates of the former maintain that variations in organizational forms are due to differences in economic environments or imperatives of technology but not culture (Hickson *et al.* 1974, 1979). Proponents of the latter maintain that much of the variation is due to cultural differences (Child 1981, Child and Tayeb 1982, Jamieson 1982).

It seems, though, that this debate is misplaced. Organizations are located in milieux comprising not only their technology and economic environment but a cultural one as well (Hickson *et al.* 1974, Hofstede 1980, Jamieson 1978, Triandis 1984). Hence, the issue of cross-national variations in organizational forms is not whether variations are due to one environmental effect or another, but centers around their relative impact (Hickson and MacMillan 1981). The economic environment and the technologies employed by organizations impose constraints with respect to structural configurations. But cultural values determine range of organizational responses to such constraints; they serve to provide meaning (Ranson *et al.* 1980). In many studies the comparison of organizational adaptations has been restricted in range and incorporates only those adaptations that have already been culturally legitimized in the settings examined, or adaptations of a narrow technical nature. Consequently, these adaptations do not impinge on the cultural environment (Kiggundu *et al*. 1983). In such research, adaptations conforming to the culturally approved range, may indeed appear to be 'culture free' while in fact they are 'culture congruent', not free.

The distinction between core and periphery values may help resolve this debate about the effects of culture. Since core values resist change in the face of contextual pressures, and peripheral values are apt to yield to these pressures, configurations of organizational structures and managerial approaches that impinge on core values will be culturally bound, while those impinging on periphery values may appear to be culture-free. It is the inconsistent results of previous research, where this distinction was not made, that gave rise to this debate. This is not to say that all organizations within a culture will be the same, but that existing variability would be confined to those approved by the relevant core values.

Availability of economic resources

The framework proposes that the environmental dimension of relative scarcity of economic resources may affect organizations (link 3, Figure 1) as well as individual behavior (link 4) within given settings. Such possible effects are briefly discussed here.

Economic resources and organizational structure

Although the dimension of scarcity vs. munificence of resources has been regarded by organization theorists as an important component of the organizational environment (Katz and Kahn 1978, Pfeffer and Salancik 1978) it has not been given sufficient attention by researchers. The few studies that have examined the effects of resource munificence on organizations have indicated that choices of organizational structures and practices can vary with resource availability (Leff 1978, Robbins 1984, Staw and Szwajkowski 1975, Zussman 1983). In some developing nations, for example, a rather unique form of structuring organizational activities, the 'economic group', has been developed as a basis of capital formation, industrial organization and entrepreneurship. The 'economic group' is a multiorganizational entity comprising organizations which operate in synergy in a variety of economic sectors but share entrepreneurial, managerial and financial control. The capital and top managerial resources are mobilized from and remain within the group, which constitutes a combined economic unit. This enables the group to utilize its own resources to expand and diversify its investments, or to support organizations within it.

Leff (1978) argues that in developing nations this organizational form is a successful response to scarcity of resources. Because of conditions of market imperfections, mobilization of resources is otherwise difficult for organizations, even when resources are not really scarce. A similar organizational form that serves similar functions is the Kereitsu, which has developed in Japan as a post-war offspring of the more traditional form of Zaibatsu. One of its main characteristics is the synergy among the firms comprising it and the form of cross share holding among them (Abegglen and Stalk 1985).

Another example is the tendency of organizations in relatively munificent economic environments to develop considerable slack to buffer their operational core from environmental fluctuations, permitting a strategy concerned mainly with expansion and growth. On the other hand, in environments of relative scarcity, organizations generally have little slack and, consequently, management's main concern is organizational maintenance and survival. It is quite clear that the organizational processes and managerial approaches required by the latter organizations are very different from those required by the former (Whetten 1980, Zussman 1983).

A similar argument can be found in research on the organizational life cycle. It has been suggested that managing organizational growth is different from managing decline, particularly when organizational decline results from cutbacks (Levine 1979, Rudie-Harrigan 1980, Whetten 1980, Cameron *et al.* 1987). For example, the structure of such organizations tends to become centralized and controls are tightened. It has also been suggested that organizations with relatively abundant resources tend to use inter-organizational labor markets as sources of specialized and qualified personnel, as well as the vehicle for disposing of personnel. On the other hand, organizations faced with scarcity of resources tend to utilize their internal labor market as the source of needed personnel (Pfeffer and Cohen 1985).

Staw and Szwajkowski (1975) have shown that the congruence of organizational adaptation practices with prescribed norms is related to scarcity or munificence of resources. They studied the effect of scarcity in economic resources on the tendency of organizations to deviate from the legally prescribe range of activities in their coping attempts. The findings suggested that under conditions of scarcity, when organizations were forced to exert greater efforts to obtain needed resources, they were more likely to engage in legally questionable or clearly-proscribed activities (e.g. price fixing, franchise violations, tax evasion).

Organizational adaptation is a vehicle for absorbing the effects of economic or other contextual constraints into organizational structures and practices (link 3, Figure 1). However, organizational choices of responses to these constraints are controlled and bound by cultural legitimation. While adoption of responses incongruent with peripheral values may be possible, adoption of responses incongruent with core values may have serious consequences for the effectiveness of organizational functioning.

Economic resources and individual behavior

Scarcity of economic resources influences individual adherence to certain values, by reinforcing specific choices within the legitimized range (link 4, Figure 1). This proposition is supported by Triandis (1984). He argues, for example, that in less-developed countries under conditions of meager economic resources, the high uncertainty about the economic pay-off of work efforts reinforces the low emphasis placed there on work and work values.

A study of managers' work-goals priority in four Chinese societies (PRC, Hong-Kong, Taiwan, Singapore) suggests that observed differences in rankings of earnings and benefits as work-goals, can be explained by the different economic conditions of these culturally similar societies (Shenkar and Ronen 1990). These findings suggest that it is probable that different levels of resource scarcity may engender individual differences in value emphasis even within the same cultural setting.

Congruency and organizational effectiveness

Emphasized in the framework is the congruency between core value assumptions underlying specific organizational structures and processes, and the core values of the host cultural setting that govern and legitimize (or sanction) corresponding patterns of behavior. It is proposed that incongruencies among these elements may strongly impact organizational effectiveness. This is manifested not only at the interface of organization and culture (link 2) but also within the organization at the interface between role expectations and behaviour, on the one hand, and prescribed structures and processes on the other (link 5). We acknowledge the importance of effective organizational adaption to the economic and other context factors of its environment (link 3) which has frequently been argued by others, (e.g. Lawrence and Lorsch 1969, Pfeffer and Salancik 1978, Kiggundu *et al.* 1983). However, we contend that not every adaptation will necessarily be effective. Those adaptations which are consistent with and legitimized by core values will be more effective than adaptations incongruent with core cultural values. Similarly, if management were to engage in activities that are negatively sanctioned by local cultural (particularly core) values, culturally based resistance may impede these activities or alienate important constituencies whose support is required for the effective organizational functioning.

Also proposed by the framework are feedback effects of organizations effectiveness within as well as outside the organization. This suggests that the level of effectiveness may, in turn, influence role expectations and organizational structures and processes. Similarly, it can influence the availability of resources in the environment, or even some cultural values.

The effect of differential cultural congruency on effectiveness is illustrated in a study by Roniger (1987). It examines the organizational consequences of different cultural emphases on hierarchical relations in Brazil, Mexico and Japan. These cultural differences were found to affect the formulation of organizational patterns of mobilizing commitment to collective tasks. Roniger argues that the nature of the hierarchical trust particular to these societies resulted in divergent patterns of modernization: more effective in Japan than in the two Latin-American societies. Another example, on the level of managerial practices is Shenkar and Ronen's (1987) argument that many business negotiations conducted by Americans in China have failed because the former may have failed to accommodate for the negotiation patterns acceptable to the latter.

However, incongruencies of management activities with periphery values may be less consequential and more easily overlooked. While the Staw and Szwajkowski (1975) study did not deal directly with the effect of periphery values, such an effect can be suggested. It can be speculated that among American firms there is no strong and wide acceptance of the values governing the illegitimate activities examined in their study (e.g. price fixing, franchise violations), and the social sanctions for their violation are not very strong. Consequently, firms facing economic pressures choose to overlook, or 'bend', these values and engage in those questionable activities.

Specifying cultural effects on organizational dimensions: illustrations

By articulating the impact of cultural values on organizational structure and processes, the framework can serve as an hypotheses-generating schema (Figure 2). The relationships proposed in the framework can be translated into testable hypotheses by presenting them as a set of separate or interrelated propositions. For example, linking its parts together, the schema proposes that values (core or periphery) influence individuals through different socialisation influences (home, community, or workplace) exerted at different (early or adult) life cycle stages, and sanctioning (positively or negatively) patterns of action manifested in organizational structure and processes that correspond to resource availability (scarcity or munificence). This leads to

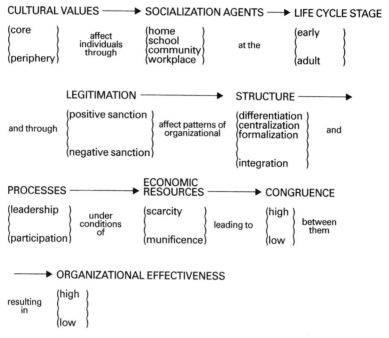

CULTURAL VALUES ⟶ SOCIALIZATION AGENTS ⟶ LIFE CYCLE STAGE

{core   }   affect   {home   }   {early   }
{   } individuals {school   }   at the   {   }
{   }   through   {community }   {   }
{periphery}   {workplace }   {adult   }

LEGITIMATION ⟶ STRUCTURE ⟶

                  {positive sanction }   {differentiation }
and through   {   } affect patterns of {centralization } and
                  {   }   organizational   {formalization   }
                  {negative sanction }   {integration   }

PROCESSES ⟶ ECONOMIC RESOURCES ⟶ CONGRUENCE

{leadership   }   under   {scarcity   }   {high }
{   } conditions   {   } leading to   {   } between
{   }   of   {   }   {   }   them
{participation }   {munificence}   {low }

⟶ ORGANIZATIONAL EFFECTIVENESS

              {high }
resulting   {   }
   in   {   }
              {low }

Figure 2 *Hypothesis generating scheme*

(high or low) congruence, which results in (high or low) organizational effectiveness. Various combinations of all or some of these propositions can be generated from the schema and tested separately, or as path models (Lachman 1988).

As an illustration, it can be proposed that organisational socialization influences will have little effect on employees' core values inculcated at their early life stage. Consequently, when these values are concerned, employees' selection and differential retention may be more effective methods for obtaining congruence with organizational values than organizational efforts to socialize employees. Further, it can be proposed that the higher the incongruency between employees' core values and those of the transplanted organization, the lower the employees' satisfaction, the higher the turnover and the more difficult it will be for the organization to recruit employees. Similarly, it can be proposed that local values adopted by employees at the adult life stage, can be changed through organizational socialization since these will constitute periphery values of these employees. Other propositions can be formulated in a similar way.

In addition, by inserting particular values into the framework, specific hypotheses regarding their impact on organizational dimensions can be derived and tested. Four values, often studied, are used for illustration:

Table 1 The effects of cultural values on organizational choices: an illustration

Cultural values	Structure	Processes	Behavioral style
Power			
High/low power	Hierarchy: differentiation high/low	Decision making: participative/ nonparticipative	Leadership: authoritarian/democratic
	Centralization: high/low	Communication: vertical/horizontal	Subordinates' compliance strategies:
		Control: tight/loose	high/low authoritarian, or coercive/permissive
		Coordination: vertical/horizontal	
Social relations			
Individualistic/ collectivistic orientation	Horizontal differentiation: specialization high/low	Rewards and incentives: individual/group emphasis	Commitment: self/group goals
	Rewards: differential high/low	Communication: specific/diffuse	Compliance strategies: calculative/moralistic
		Decision making: contentious/consensus	Climate: competitive/cooperative
Work orientation			
Work/nonwork centrality	Span of control: wide/short	Rewards and incentives: intrinsic/extrinsic	Climate: expressive/instrumental
			Commitment: internal/external
Uncertainty			
High/low avoidance	Formalization: high/low	Locus of decisions: hierarchical/diffuse	Climate: reserved/open
	Centralization: high/low		

values governing power relations, social relations, orientations to work and values pertaining to uncertainty. Table 1 summarizes several hypotheses illustrating some implications of these four values for the structure and processes of organizations, as well as for the behavioral styles of their members.

Power values are cultural values that specify appropriate forms of power relationships and authority in social organizations. They define the appropriate hierarchical arrangements and the power-compliance strategies that should be employed within organizations. Derived from these values are, for example, preferences for long as opposed to short power distances in social relations (Hofstede 1980). Thus, it can be hypothesized (link 2, Figure 1) that a cultural emphasis on high power distance will be associated with the choice of compatible patterns of structural configurations such as high hierarchical differentiation or high centralization. Similarly, it can be associated with the choice of corresponding organizational processes of nonparticipative decision making, hierarchical rather than collegial or 'clan' control and coordination. Through the effects of cultural values on individual behavior (link 1, Figure 1) it can be hypothesized that preference for high power distance will be associated with preference for an authoritarian leadership style. It can be further hypothesized that congruence between the choice of a highly centralized organizational power structure and nonparticipative decision processes, on the one hand, and the preference for a style of high distance in interpersonal relations on the other, will enhance organizational effectiveness.

Some concrete examples can be suggested as illustrations. A study by Hinings and Badran (1981) describes how the high degree of participation required by the prescribed structure of public organizations in Egypt was difficult to implement, because the indigenous cultural values emphasized social and hierarchic distance in interpersonal relationships. The outcome of this incongruency were poor internal processes and low levels of participation in the realized organizations, not the high levels required by the prescribed structure (Badran 1979, Hinings and Badran 1981).

Birnbaum and Wong (1985) suggested that in Hong Kong where the cultural emphasis was on high power distance, the structure of organizations will tend to be centralized, and local employees (Chinese) will be more satisfied working in a centralized rather than decentralized structure. This was supported by the results of their study on multinational banks in Hong Kong. However, similar hypotheses regarding satisfaction with organizational differentiation and formalization, were not supported. While Birnbaum and Wong do not use this interpretation, their findings can be explained by suggesting that the value governing hierarchical power relations is (as they do argue) core to the Chinese culture in Hong Kong, whereas those governing formalization and differentiation are not. Consequently, when a core value is concerned, value incongruency can explain employees' dissatisfaction (i.e. lower effectiveness). But when variations in practices (differentiation or formalization) among the multinational organizations were incongruent with values that were not core, work satisfaction of local employees was not affected.

Social interaction values specify the particular forms of human bonds, determining cultural preferences for particular interaction patterns and role relationships. They may range from an individualistic to a collectivistic orientation. Illustrating the effect of such values is Schein's (1981) argument that it will be difficult to implement Japanese management approaches in an American context when the core cultural values underlying these approaches differ considerably from core American values. He points to individualism as a key value of U.S. culture which emphasizes the pursuit of self-interest and the individual's responsibility for his/her actions. The Japanese place a high value on collectivity and deliberately blur individual responsibility by adopting methods, like consensus decision making, that accommodate such blurring. This consensus method is incongruent with American individualism and in many ways irrelevant to management in the U.S. (Schein 1981).

From this, it can be hypothesized that in a cultural setting where individualism is a core value (e.g. the U.S.) contentious rather than consensual methods of decision making should be employed. Local employees will be more satisfied working in organizations employing a contentious decision process than in organizations employing consensual ones. This hypothesis is corroborated by findings that in Japanese organizations operating in the U.S., Japanese employees were the most satisfied with the organizational structure, Japanese-Americans were less satisfied and non-Japanese Americans were the least satisfied (Lincoln *et al.* 1981).

The effects of the other two values can be similarly analyzed and hypotheses generated (Table 1). The value placed on work itself governs the view of work as a distinct form of social activity, and the centrality of work in life. It specifies the importance of organized work activity to individuals and the preferred methods to motivate and direct the investment of human energy in this activity. In this respect, cultural preferences may range from a strong emphasis on work as a means for achieving nonwork goals and social status (instrumental orientation), to a strong emphasis on work as a highly valued activity in itself (expressive orientation). Values pertaining to uncertainty govern the culturally preferred reaction to it, which may range from high avoidance of uncertainty to its acceptance (Hofstede 1980). However, the framework here is by no means limited to these particular values or to an examination of the possible effects of a single value at a time. The core values or combinations of values particular to any cultural, or subcultural settings can be introduced to generate testable hypotheses about their effects on organizational forms and managerial practices. In either case, the basic approach underlying the framework is that of 'cultural congruence' with core values.

Coping with incongruencies

Our argument suggests that not every incongruency in organizational adaptation with local values is dysfunctional and should be avoided. It suggests differential effects of incongruencies with core or periphery values. Advocated here is a contingency approach of 'cultural congruence' describing different incongruencies which may have different consequences for cross-cultural organizations and may require different managerial approaches or

Table 2   Contingencies of value incongruencies

Values at the low cultural level

		Core	Periphery
Values at the organizational level	Core	**Contention** — A	B — **Primacy**
		Overall strategy Coupling *Entry strategy* Joint ventures *Coping strategy* Negotiation Log-rolling Coalition formation	*Overall strategy* Forcing change *Entry strategy* Transplantation *Coping strategy* Proactive Change-oriented Innovative
	Periphery	**Submission** — C	D — **Indifference**
		Overall strategy Yielding *Entry strategy* Operating through locals Franchises Mergers *Coping strategy* Compliance Accommodation Reorientation	*Overall strategy* Ignoring differences *Entry strategy* Nonspecific *Coping strategy* Nonspecific

coping strategies. For analytical purposes the organization-culture value incongruencies can be presented as crude combinations on the core/periphery dimension. Four 'types' of incongruencies or congencies may be encountered by organizations: (a) between values core to the organizational system and values core to the cultural system; (b) between values core to the organization but peripheral to the cultural system; (c) between those peripheral to the organization but core to the culture; (d) between values peripheral to both systems. These contingencies call for different management approaches, involving different entry, and coping strategies (Table 2).

Type A: Contention

This incongruency is potentially most problematic for the effectiveness of cross national organizations and management. Here the core organizational values contest the local core ones, attempting to radically change them. This contingency has high potential for severe conflicts and frictions that may alienate important constituencies whose cooperation may be essential for the organization. This may impair effectiveness, even if radical change is eventually obtained. Some forms of value coupling are, therefore, proposed as a overall strategy. The *entry strategy* to a host setting under this contingency should account for the equally dominant local values. A joint venture with a local organization may be an entry form that allows the conjugation or loose coupling of core values from both the local and foreign parents, in a way that corresponds with the local setting. The *coping strategy* that may be advisable here is conflict avoidance. Negotiation, log-rolling, coalitions, or at times even co-optation, may be more effective than contention or confrontation as strategies for coping with the host culture. Given the incongruency in core values it can also be proposed that attempts to increase congruence between values required by the organization and those held by members (both at the top and at lower levels) will focus on human resources strategies of election rather than on organizational socialization efforts.

The examples of Confucian values in China dismissed earlier can serve as a case in point. The traditional Confucian value of obligation to kinship affiliation has maintained its centrality in the Chinese cultural system for many generations. Although the Maoist ideology officially opposed kinship affiliation it has preferred not to challenge this value, thus leaving intact a major basis of the traditional system. Moreover, kinship allegiances were utilized by the Maoist system for its own benefit (Parish and Whyte 1978). On the other hand, the traditional core value of hierarchical relations was contested by the Maoist system which also regarded this value as a core one. However, as indicated above, Maoist attempts to radically change hierarchical relations by abolishing them, have failed (Laaksonen 1988). These examples suggest that even a very powerful and culturally indigenous organization may find it more effective to accommodate core cultural values than to challenge them.

Type B: Primacy

This contingency is conducive to change and innovations introduced by the 'imported' organization. The organization can adopt a general approach of increasing congruence with its host cultural environment by pressuring for change in local peripheral values to match the core organizational ones. The *entry approach* proposed for foreign organizations in this situation is of organizational 'transplantation.' Organizational structures and processes can be transplanted across the cultural boundaries into the host setting, mostly as is. Incongruencies will then be reduced through changes in the local periphery values. Unlike the previous contingency (A), efforts to attain congruence here imply a *coping strategy* of organizationally planned and controlled change for management. Under this type of incongruency an externally induced change may even be desired and encouraged by the host country. Similarly, since organizational core and host periphery values are concerned, a strategy of transferring expatriate management into the host setting can be proposed. Through this strategy organizational core values can be maintained, possible incongruency between the values of top managers and those of the organization can be reduced, and the required change in local values can be stimulated. Lower level employees can be recruited locally and their (periphery) values changed through organizational socialization practices.

Type C: Submission

In this contingency, periphery organizational values are incongruent with local core ones. Since the incongruent values are peripheral to the organization, efforts to change local core values may not be worthwhile. Organizational compliance with, or adoption of local core values may be a more effective *coping strategy* for achieving congruence or at least accommodation. The *entry strategy* that may be appropriate under this contingency is to operate through local organizations (e.g. mergers, franchises, or purchases), to reduce possible incongruency with local core values. Similarly, hiring local human resources at all levels of the organization may be a valid strategy.

Type D: Indifference

This is perhaps the least disruptive incongruency for cross-cultural organizations. Incongruency between peripheral values may either be bridged, or left to co-exist, with relatively low costs to the organization. Consequently, no specific coping and entry strategies are proposed. Strategic choices can be made based on other considerations.

Thus, the above approach to cultural congruence strongly suggests that when moving across cultural settings, management should carefully examine the type of incongruency they may encounter, as these may require different entry and coping strategies. Much like market, resources, and feasibility surveys conducted by organizations, values' congruency with a local setting ought also be surveyed and investigated as a major organizational consideration. Some methodological issues regarding value examination are discussed in Appendix A.

Conclusions

The framework presented here attempts to articulate the impact of cultural values on the structures and processes of cross national organizations. It proposes that: (1) core and periphery cultural values exert differential social control at both the individual and organizational levels by legitimizing certain ranges of behavior and patterns of organizing; (2) individual behavior is regulated by the values inculcated through early or late socialization processes; (3) organizations are shaped through the legitimation of certain choices of organizational structure and processes; (4) particular organization choices, within the legitimized ranges, are influenced by other contextual factors, one of which is availability of economic resources that pose constraints to which organizations have to adapt; (5) these contextual factors also influence individual choices by reinforcing certain values and behaviours; (6) incongruencies in integrating these influences affect organizational effectiveness and have to be contended with.

Thus, the framework offers a theory-based approach for crossnational as well as intranational (regional) comparisons, and contributes toward the development of a much-needed paradigmatic approach to crossnational organizations. As such, this framework has both theoretical and practical contributions. The importance of the effects of cultural values on transferred organizational and management practices has been stressed by previous research. The theoretical contribution in our framework goes beyond that. It points to the social control and social sanctions that values exert on behavior, as the specific value dimension to which differences in organizational practices ought to be attributed. Hence, the focus offered here is on the differentiation between core and periphery cultural values which reflect their differential social control. The framework goes further to describe and discuss the processes and mechanisms through which these differential social control effects, embedded in core and periphery values, are exerted at the organizational and individual levels. It argues for a cultural congruence approach to cross-national organizations not in terms of similarity in specific values but in terms of value centrality at both the organizational and the cultural levels. It is this congruency that may impact organizational effectiveness. Furthermore, proposed and discussed here were contingencies under which culture may have differential impact and consequences for organizations. Another important advantage of the framework is its capacity for generating specific testable hypotheses pertaining to the effects of values particular to a cultural setting.

The proposed framework also has a contribution in offering a uniform and coherent interpretation to different studies that previously were not tied together under a single conceptual scheme. For example, the framework may help resolve the debate between the 'culture free' and 'culturalist' approaches to cross-cultural analysis. We argue that the focus in the debate should be shifted from the question of the relative impact of cultural and noncultural influences, to the 'culture congruence' perspective, and the impact of core relative to periphery cultural values in determining the range of acceptable adjustments to contextual factors. We suggest that inconsistencies in results of previous research concerning this debate may have resulted from the comparison of 'unlikes'; while some studies examined organizational adaptations all governed by values of similar susceptibility to change (e.g. all peripheral values), giving the impression of 'culture-free' adaptations, others focused on adaptations governed by values of different susceptibility to change (e.g. some governed by core and some by peripheral), thus giving rise to the 'culturalist' interpretation. The comparison of organizational adaptations governed not by similar values but by values of similar susceptibility (e.g. all core) is an important issue that needs to be carefully addressed and considered by future research. A potentially fruitful line of research is to compare not only organizations in different settings but also organizations in settings of the same core values. Also, research may benefit most by focusing on longitudinal rather than cross-sectional comparisons of such organizations. This design can help identify the factors facilitating and restraining change and innovation.

Of a more practical nature are the implications of the framework for the cross-national transferability of organizational arrangements and managerial practices. Managerial choices of structural adjustments should be in line with the relevant core values of the particular host setting and those held by its members. 'Imported' practices may fail, or be ineffectively implemented, if they are inconsistent with the core values of local settings (e.g. Schein 1981, Sethi *et al*. 1984). However, if the underlying values of an imported organizational practice are incongruent with the peripheral values of the host setting, socialization efforts exerted by the organization can be directed at reducing incongruency, and a successful transfer of this practice may be achieved. We maintain that forcing change while challenging local core values may be very difficult to accomplish. The contingency approach to cultural congruency proposed here, offers management of cross-cultural organizations a conceptual tool for analyzing and better understanding their interface with local cultural settings, and the implications this may have for effectiveness. Furthermore, considering these contingencies may be important for organizations in their choice of organizational adaptations, practices, and strategies for their operations in local settings.

The conformity to local values implied by the framework, raises some important ethical issues. These issues require theoretical and empirical attention which are beyond the scope of this paper. For example, an interesting question is to what extent should management compromise its own values to comply with those of local settings? Recent practices of multinational organizations have brought such ethical issues to the foreground. Systematic study of these issues ought to follow.

In conclusion, the congruence of a given practice with local cultural values can be an important contingency to be considered in any decision to transfer across cultural settings. Careful preliminary assessment of compatibility between local core values and those underlying organizational structures and processes may prevent costly and sometimes irreversible mistakes of implementing structures and practices that are not suited to local environments.

Appendix A

Measuring core and periphery values

The call for a close examination of core and periphery values of a cultural setting, raises the methodological issue of the identification of specific values as core or peripheral in given cultures. Although such methods require further development, few approaches can be proposed. One possible approach is qualitative methods for classifying values through analyses of contents, behaviors, or the implicit assumptions in social discourse. Such analyses can be performed by social scientists expert on a given culture (e.g. Eberhard 1971, Ouchi 1981, Pascale and Athos 1981, Schein 1981). A shortcoming of this approach is that the results obtained by different scientists may not always be consistent and it may be difficult to evaluate their validity and reliability.

Another approach is a systematic study of choice of actions or social goods within a cultural setting. For example, iterative interviewing methods can be used (Schein 1985), or individuals in a certain culture can be asked to rank values in terms of importance (Dawson *et al.* 1971, Rokeach 1973, Hofstede 1980). A high consensus or disagreement on the importance or unimportance of certain values can indicate their relative position as core or peripheral values, respectively. Lachman (1983) has shown that on the basis of consensus in ranking, a number of values previously measured by Inkeles and Smith (1974) in four countries, can be classified as core or periphery.

While each of these approaches can provide some indications as to the values' rank order, it appears that employing a multimethod approach may be a preferred way for tapping and classifying values in local settings. Since each of the above methods has its limitations, a multimethod approach is more likely to result in valid and reliable classifications than a single measure. Evidently, further research efforts are required in order to develop more adequate and reliable measures for differentiating core from periphery values in a cultural setting.

References

Abegglen, J. C. and G. Stalk, Jr., *Kaisha, The Japanese Corporation*, Basic Books, New York, 1985.

Adler, N. J., 'Cross-cultural Management Research: The Ostrich and the Trend,' *The Academy of Management Review*, 8 (1983), 226–232.

Allport, G. W., *Patterns and Growth in Personality*, Holt, Rinehart & Winston, New York, 1961.

Argyris, C., *Integrating The Individual and The Organization*, Wiley, New York, 1964.

Badran, M., *The Relationship Between Democratic Administration and Bureaucracy*, Ph.D. Thesis, University of Birmingham, England, 1979.

Birnbaum, P. H. and G. Y. Y. Wong, 'Organizational Structure of Multinational Banks in Hong Kong from a Culture-Free Perspective,' *Administrative Sci. Quarterly*, 30 (1985), 262–277.

Bond, M. H. and S. Wang, 'China: Aggressive Behavior and the Problem of Maintaining Order and Harmony,' In A. P. Goldstein and M. H. Segall (Eds.), *Aggression in Global Perspective*, Pergamon Press, New York, 1983.

Brim, O. Jr., 'Adult Socialization,' *International Encyclopedia of Social Sciences*, 14, (1968), 555–562.

Cameron, K. S., 'The Effectiveness of Ineffectiveness,' In B. M. Staw and L. L. Cummings (Eds.), *Research in Organizational Behavior*, 6, JAI Press, Greenwich, CT, 1984.

Cameron, K. S., D. A. Whetten and M. U. Kim, 'Dysfunctions of Organizational Decline,' *Academy of Management J.*, 30 (1987), 126–138.

Cavusgil, T. S. and U. Yavas, 'Transfer of Management Knowhow to Developing Countries: An Empirical Investigation,' *J. Business Research*, 12 (1984), 35–50.

Child, J. 'Culture Contingency and Capitalism in Cross-cultural Study of Organizations.' In L. Cummings and B. Staw (Eds.), *Research in Organizational Behavior*, 3 (1981), 303–356.

Child, J. and M. Tayeb, 'Theoretical Perspectives in Crossnational Organizational Research,' *International Studies of Management and Organization*, 12, 4 (1982), 23–70.

Clark, P., 'Cultural Context as a Determinant of Organizational Rationality: A Comparison of the Tobacco Industries in Britain and France,' In C. G. Lammers, and D. J. Hickson (Eds.), *Organizations Alike and Unlike*, Routledge & Kegan Paul, London; 1979.

Connolly, T., E. J. Conlon and S. J. Deutch, 'Organizational Effectiveness: A Multiple-Constituency Approach,' *Academy of Management Review*, 5 (1980), 211–217.

Dawson, J. L., M. Law, A. Leung and R. W. Whitney, 'Scaling Chinese Traditional–Modern Attitudes and the GSR Measurement of Important vs. Unimportant Chinese Concepts,' *J. Cross-Cultural Psychology*, 2 (1971), 1–29.

Downey, H. K., D. L. Hellriegel and J. W. Slocum, Jr., 'Environmental Uncertainty: The Construct and Its Application,' *Administrative Sci. Quarterly*, 20 (1975), 613–629.

Eberhard, W., *Moral and Social Values of the Chinese – Collected Essays*. Chinese Materials and Research Aids Service Center, Washington DC, 1971.

Ford, J. D. and D. A. Baucus, 'Organizational Adaptations to Performance Downturns: An Interpretation Based Perspective,' *Academy of Management Review*, 12 (1987), 366–380.

Frese, M., 'Occupational Socialization and Psychological Development,' *J. Occupational Psychology*, 55 (1982), 209–224.

Gallie, D., *In Search of the New Working Class*: Cambridge University Press, Cambridge: England, 1978.

Glenn, E., *Man and Mankind: Conflict and Communication Between Culture*, Ablex, Horwood, NJ, 1981.

Hickson, D. J., C. R. Hinings, C. J. McMillan and J. P. Schwitter, 'The Culture-Free Context of Organization Structure,' *Sociology*, 8 (1974), 59–80.

Hickson, D. J. and C. J. McMillan, *Organization and Nation*, Gower Press, London, England, 1981.

Hickson, D. J., C. J. McMillan, K. Azumi, and J. P. Schwitter, 'Grounds for Comparison of Organization Theory: Quicksands or Hard Core?' In C. J. Lammers and D. Hickson (Eds.), *Organizations Alike and Unlike*, Routledge and Kegan Paul, London, England, 1979.

Hinings, C. R. and M. Badran, 'Strategies of Administrative Control and Contextual Constraints in a Less Developed Country,' *Organization Studies*, 2 (1981), 3–22.

Hofstede, G., *Culture's Consequences*, Sage Publication Ltd., London, England, 1980.

Holland, J. L., 'Vocational Preferences,' In M. D. Dunnette (Ed.), *Handbook of Industrial and Organizational Psychology*, Rand McNally, Chicago, IL, 1976.

Howard, A., K. Shudo and M. Umeshima, 'Motivation and Values Among Japanese and American Managers,' *Personnel Psychology*, 36 (1983), 883–898.

Hsu, Francis L., *American and Chinese: Passage to Differences*, The University Press of Hawaii, Honolulu, HI, 1981.

Inkeles, A. and D. H. Smith, *Becoming Modern*, Harvard University Press, Cambridge, MA, 1974.

Jamieson, I. M., 'Some Observations on Socio-Cultural Explanations of Economic Behavior,' *Sociological Review*, 20 (1978), 777–805.

Jamieson, I. M., 'The Concept of Culture and Its Relevance for an Analysis of Business Enterprise in Different Societies,' *International Studies of Management and Organization*, 12, 4 (1982), 71–105.

Katz, D. and R. Kahn, *The Social Psychology of Organizations*, Wiley, New York, 1978.

Kelly, L. and R. Worthley, 'The Role of Culture in Comparative Management: A Cross Cultural Perspective,' *Academy of Management J.*, 24 (1981), 164–173.

Kiesler, S. and L. Sproull, 'Managerial Response to Changing Environments: Perspectives on Problem Sensing from Social Cognition,' *Administrative Sci. Quarterly*, 27 (1982), 548–570.

Kiggundu, M. N., J. J. Jorgensen and T. Hofsi, 'Administration Theory and Practice in Developing Countries: A Synthesis,' *Administrative Sci. Quarterly*, 28 (1983), 66–84.

Kluckhohn, C., 'Values and Value Orientations in the Theory of Action: An Exploration in Definition and Classifications,' In T. Parsons and E. Shils (Eds.), *Toward General Theory of Action*, Harvard University Press, Cambridge, MA, 1951.

Kluckhohn, F. R. and F. L. Strodtbeck, *Variations in Value Orientations*, Row, Peterson, New York, 1961.

Laaksonen, O., *Management in China*, Walter de Gruyter, Berlin, 1988.

Lachman, R., 'Modernity Change of Core and Periphery Values of Factory Workers,' *Human Relations*, 36, 6 (1983), 563–580.

Lachman, R., 'Factors Influencing Workers' Orientations: A Secondary Analysis of Israeli Data,' *Organization Studies*, 99 (1988), 487–510.

Lammers, C. J. and D. J. Hickson (Eds.), *Organizations Alike and Unalike*, Routledge & Kegan Paul, London, 1979.

Lawrence, P. R. and J. W. Lorsch, *Organization and Environment*, Irwin, Homewood, IL, 1969.

Leff, N. H., 'Industrial Organization and Entrepreneurship in the Developing Countries: The Economic Groups,' *Economic Development and Cultural Change*, 26 (1978), 661–675.

Levine, C. H., 'More on Cutback Management: Hard Questions for Hard Issues,' *Public Administration Review* (1979), 179–183.

Lincoln, J. R., M. Hanada, and J. Olsen, 'Cultural Orientations and Individual Reactions to Organizations: A Study of employees in Japanese Owned Firms,' *Administration Sci. Quarterly*, 28 (1981), 93–115.

Liu, Hui-chen W., 'An Analysis of Chinese Clan Rules: Confucian Theories in Action,' In A. F. Wright (Ed.), *Confucianism and Chinese Civilization*, Stanford University Press, Stanford, CA, 1964.

Martinko, M. J. and Y. Fenzeng, 'A Comparison of Leadership Theory and Practice in the People's Republic of China and the United States,' In *International Human Resource Management Review*, 1 (1990), 109–122.

Maurice, M., 'For a Study of "The Societal Effect," ' In Lammers and Hickson (Eds.), *Organizations Alike and Unlike*, Routledge and Kegan Paul, London, 1979.

McMillan, C. J., D. J. Hickson, C. R. Hinings and R. E. Schneck, 'The Structure of Work Organizations Across Societies,' *Academy of Management J.*, 16 (1973), 555–569.

Miller, Edwin L., Rosalie L. Tung, Robert W. Armstrong and Bruce W. Stening, 'A Comparison of Australian and United States Management Succession Systems,' *International Human Resource Management Review*, 1 (1990), 123–140.

Mortimer, J. T. and J. Lorence, 'Work Experience and Occupational Value Socialization: A Longitudinal Study,' *American J. of Sociology*, 84 (1979), 1361–1385.

Nath, Raghu, *Comparative Management: A Regional View*, Ballinger Publishing Company, Cambridge, MA, 1988.

Negandhi, A. R., 'Comparative Management and Organizational Theory: A Marriage Needed,' *Academy of Management J.*, 18 (1975), 337.

Nivison, D. S. and F. Wright (Eds.), *Confucianism In Action*, Stanford University Press, Stanford, CA, 1959.

Ouchi, W., *Theory Z: How American Business Can Meet the Japanese Challenge*, Addison-Wesley, Reading, MA, 1981.

Parish, W. L. and M. K. Whyte, *Village and Family in Contemporary China*, Chicago University Press, Chicago, IL, 1978.

Parsons, T., *Social Structure and Personality*, Free Press, New York, 1964.

Pascale, R. T. and A. G. Athos, *The Art of Japanese Management: Applications for American Executives*, Simon & Schuster, New York, 1981.

Peterson, K. and J. A. Dutton, 'Centrality, Extremity, Intensity,' *Social Forces*, 54 (1975), 394–414.

Pfeffer, J. and Y. Cohen, 'Determinants of Internal Labor Markets in Organizations,' *Administrative Sci. Quarterly*, 29, 4 (1985), 550–572.

Pfeffer, J. and G. R. Salancik, *The External Control of Organizations. A Resource Dependence Perspective*, Harper and Row, New York, 1978.

Price, J. L., 'The Study of Organizational Effectiveness,' *The Sociological Quarterly*, 13 (1972), 3–15.

Ranson, S., C. R. Hinings and R. Greenwood, 'The Structuring of Organizational Structures,' *Administrative Sci. Quarterly*, 25 (1980), 1–17.

Robbins, S. P., *The New Management: Managing Declining Organizations*, Paper Presented at the Western Academy of Management Annual Meeting, Vancouver, B. C., Canada, 1984.

Roberts, K. H. and N. A. Boyacigiller, 'Cross-National Organizational Research: The Grasp of the Blind Men,' In L. Cummings and B. Staw (Eds.), *Research in Organizational Behavior*, 6, JAI Press Inc., Greenwich, CT, 1984.

Rokeach, M., *Beliefs, Attitudes and Values*, Jossey-Bass, Inc., San Francisco, 1969.

Rokeach, M., *The Nature of Human Values*, The Free Press, New York, 1973.

Ronen, S., *Comparative and Multinational Management*, John Wiley & Sons, New York, 1986.

Ronen, S. and O. Shenkar, 'Clustering Countries on Attitudinal Dimensions: A Review and Synthesis,' *Academy of Management Review*, 10 (1985), 435–454.

Roniger, L., 'Coronelismo, Caciquismo, and Oyabun-Kobun Bond: Divergent Implications of Hierarchical Trust in Brazil, Mexico and Japan,' *The British J. Sociology*, 38 (1987), 310–329.

Rudie-Harrigan, K., 'Strategy Formulation in Declining Industries,' *Academy of Management Review*, 5 (1980), 599–604.

Schein, E. H., 'Does Japanese Management Style Have a Message for American Managers?' *Sloan Management Review*, 21, 1 (1981), 55–68.

Schein, E. H. *Organizational Culture and Leadership*, Jossey-Bass, San Francisco, 1985.

Sethi, S. P., N. Namiki and E. L. Saranson, *The False Promise of the Japanese Miracle*, Pitman, Boston, MA, 1984.

Shenkar, O. and S. Ronen, 'The Cultural Context of Negotiations: The Implications of Chinese Interpersonal Norms,' *J. Applied Behavioral Science*, 23 (1987), 263–275.

Shenkar, O. and S. Ronen, 'Culture, Ideology or Economy: A Comparative Exploration of Work Goal Importance Among Managers in Chinese Societies,' In S. B. Prasad (Ed.), *Advances in International Comparative Management*, 5 JAI Press, Inc., Greenwich CT, 1990.

Shils, E., 'Center and Periphery,' In M. Polany (Ed.), *The Logic of Personal Knowledge*, Routledge and Kegan Paul, London, 1961.

Shin, Y. K., R. M. Steers, G. R. Ungson and S. Nam, 'Work Environment and Management Practice in Korean Companies,' *International Human Resource Management Review*, 1 (1990), 95–108.

Smelser, N., 'Mechanisms for Change and Adjustment to Change,' in B. F. Hoselitz, and W. E. Moore (Eds.), *Industrialization and Society*, UNESCO/Moimt, Paris, 1963, 32–48.

Staw, B. M. and E. Szwajkowski, 'The Scarcity–Munificence Component of Organizational Environment and the Commission of Illegal Acts,' *Administrative Sci. Quarterly*, 20 (1975), 345–354.

Thompson, J. D., *Organizations in Action*, McGraw-Hill, New York, 1967.

Triandis, H. C., 'Dimensions of Cultural Variation as Parameters of Organizational Theories,' *International Studies of Management and Organization*, 12 (1982), 139–169.

Triandis, H. C., 'Toward a Psychological Theory of Economic Growth,' *International J. Psychology*, 19 (1984), 79–95.

Van Maanen, J. and E. H. Schein, 'Toward a Theory of Organizational Socialization,' In B. Staw (Ed.), *Research in Organizational Behavior*, 1 (1979), 209–264.

Vertinsky, I., K. Tse, D. A. Wehrung and K. Lee, 'Organizational Design and Management Norms: A Comparative Study of Managers Perception in the People's Republic of China, Hong Kong and Canada,' *J. Management*, 16 (1990), 853–867.

Weick, K. E., *The Social Psychology of Organizing*, Addison-Wesley, Reading, MA, 1979.

Whetten, D. A., 'Sources, Responses and Effects of Organizational Decline,' In J. Kimberly and R. H. Miles (Eds.), *The Organization Life Cycle: Issues in the Creation, Transformation and Decline of Organizations*, Jossey-Bass, San Francisco, 1980.

Whetten, D. A., 'What Constitutes a Theoretical Contribution?' *Academy of Management Review*, 14 (1989), 490–495.

Zussman, Y. E., 'Learning from the Japanese: Management in a Resource Scarce World,' *Organizational Dynamics* 11, 3 (Winter 1983), 68–80.

Reproduced from Lachman, R., Nedd, A. and Hinings, B. (1994). Analyzing cross-national management and organizations: a theoretical framework. *Management Science*, **40** (1), 40–55, by permission of *Management Science*.

5.3 Ethics and the art of intuitive management

Terence Jackson

The number of taught courses in Business Ethics in the United States, and more recently in Europe has increased over the last few years. A growing number of European companies are adopting the American practice of publishing codes of ethics for employees (see Langlois and Schlegelmilch, 1990 for a review). The subject is the focus of a growing literature, much of which offers particular formulae to which to adhere, or algorithms to follow, for successful ethical decisions.

But is it really possible to train managers to be ethical? Can we really make managers ethical by laying down codes of conduct within an organization? Can we guide managers to make ethical decisions by providing them with logical algorithms? These approaches may be altogether too simplistic! We examine here some of the more useful approaches but explain some of their limitations. We also show why the problems are compounded when we consider managing in an international, and inter-cultural environment. We also argue that these approaches may be inappropriate for everyday management and the cultural dilemmas which confront international managers, and why we should take a more 'intuitive' approach. We therefore suggest an approach based on Personal Construct Psychology, which helps managers focus on their underlying assumptions, in order to judge the 'survival value' of their value systems in the international environment.

Two types of decision: conceptual and intuitive

We can loosely distinguish decisions by their size: major (international) decisions; and, minor, quick, everyday decisions. The former can be reflected and pondered on for some time. This type of decision has been the subject of such approaches as decision algorithms (for example, Donaldson, 1989) or other such decision guide-lines. In this type of approach we have time to look at all the angles, and to think for some time about the consequences of our actions. We can call this approach a *conceptual* one. This type of approach can be taught in business schools, and can be guided by companies' codes of ethics: a 'logical' process can be used to try to solve ethical and cultural dilemmas to a certain extent. Let us look at a couple of examples.

An assistant manager in an international chain of hotels currently holds a position in its London hotel. She wishes to further her career by gaining international experience. A suitable position has arisen in Cairo, as manager of the company's hotel. She applies to the Director of International Operations, making a good case for why she should have this job. Although she realizes that it will be extremely difficult for a woman within this predominantly Arab culture, she believes that she can overcome the problems and make a success of the job. The Director, however, disagrees. He believes that the situation could be embarrassing for the company. No woman has ever been appointed by the company to a management position in the Middle Eastern Moslem countries, believing that the cultural problems would be too great to overcome. Many businessmen simply would not do business with her. She argues for equality of opportunity and status for women, and that she is extremely well qualified to do this job.

Such a case reflects an example of the type of dilemma an international company might have in its human resources management practices across different cultures. At least this type of decision may be guided by policy, or it may be the subject of serious deliberation and a structured decision process. We will return to this example later. Another example may be cited which is a typical dilemma posed both in practice and on many business school ethics courses.

In order to gain a major contract in a West African country, a company's Managing Director had to decide whether or not it should pay a large corporate bribe being asked for by an official in the West African company. Without the bribe it would not get the contract. The contract would enable the company to carry on operations in its home country so that it would not have to make anyone redundant. If it did not get the contract, one of its plants would have to close. The Managing Director was worried that if some of the existing customers of the company found out that it had done business by paying bribes, they might withdraw their custom. Again we will return later to this case, in order to suggest a way in which the dilemma may be solved.

Let us now look at the other type of decision: the quick, everyday decision. For this we can take examples from what Izraeli (1988) has termed 'behavioural situations'. This might include such incidents as:

- Passing blame for own errors on to an innocent co-worker, or otherwise concealing errors
- Claiming credit for someone else's work
- Giving preferential treatment for favours received or through family, tribal or in-group connections

- Calling in sick to take a day off work
- Taking extra personal time, such as longer breaks and early departures
- Doing personal business on company time
- Using the company's services (for example, telephone, photocopier or secretarial time) for personal use
- Pilfering company's supplies and materials;
- Claiming extra expenses from the company for which you are not entitled
- Divulging confidential information
- Not reporting others' violations of company policy.

We could say that for these types of behaviour, managers may not have the opportunity or inclination to ponder for some time, but to be oriented towards them in either a positive, negative or neutral way because of their prior value orientation or because of the way they see the consequences of these behaviours. These orientations or ways of dealing with everyday decisions may not be conceptualized or verbalized. They may be more *intuitive* in that the means by which the decision is made is more part of the person, rather than involving an abstract decision making process. These intuitive orientations may be quite different between different cultures, and the international manager may have to deal with a whole range of values and attitudes towards such behavioural situations, when managing an international team.

For example, a manager may be averse to providing favours to a subordinate just because he or she knows the family of the subordinate. Any form of nepotism may be frowned upon in that particular society. In another society, showing favouritism to an 'in-group' member may be a way of life, and not just accepted but expected. In another example, that of 'fiddling' company expenses, the manager may simply weigh the likelihood of being caught against not being caught: an examination of the results of his or her actions, rather than any prior value orientation or guiding principle. These two different ways of seeing ethical behaviour are summed up in what Brady (1990) terms 'formalism' and 'utilitarianism'. These two approaches provide our starting point for looking at how we might solve ethical dilemmas in international situations.

Rules or results

We have already seen that cultural 'values' are important to decision making, and particularly so when we consider decisions made which cut across national cultures. As in our example above, a Western European businessperson may do business in a West African country where corporate bribery may be the norm: this involves an interface between two sets of cultural values.

The question of what is ethical in this situation (and also, what is good business) is raised.

From an inter-cultural perspective, it may be that the value content of the decision is fundamental to an understanding of decision making. To what extent do individual managers consider (consciously) their value system when making decisions? To what degree is their value system an unconscious (or at least a non-verbalized) influence on decision making? What principles (either verbalized or conceptualized or not) are applied when decisions are made? What principle should we follow when the other culture's principles or values are different to our own?

Brady (1990) distinguishes two basic ethical principles upon which decision making may be based: rules and results. This is based on two main schools of thought in ethics: the 'formalism' of Kant (a German) and the 'utilitarianism' of Bentham (an Englishman).

Utilitarianism

The utilitarian approach is predominantly a North American one, and this is reflected in much of the management literature on ethical decision making (for example, Blanchard and Peale, 1988). Here we find the premise that ethical decision making has a pay-off. If only companies are ethical then they will be prosperous. Ethics is good for business. This stems from the principles of utilitarianism which is based on the premise of results or outcomes of a decision. We judge a decision to be ethical on the basis of its perceived outcomes. Utilitarianism in its original form was based on the precept of the greatest good for the greatest number of people. Hence, governments could make policy on the basis that its outcome would benefit the greatest number of people (even at the expense of the minority). A business example could be a decision to make a minority of people redundant from a factory, in order for the factory to be run more cost-effectively and therefore benefit the majority who would remain in their jobs.

A modern day derivative of this theory is cost–benefit analysis which looks at decisions from the point of view of their total costs, both financial and social, and total benefits. Environmental decisions involving such issues as pollution may be decided on this basis, where the costs of pollution control may be weighed up against the potential benefits to the community.

Utilitarianism tends to be a forward looking philosophy. Decisions are made on the basis of looking into the future, to look at future gains and future costs. However, there are problems in this school of thought. The first is the question of justice. It is perfectly justifiable, using these principles, to persecute a minority in the interests of the majority. Democratic systems are often based on this principle in both the national arena and the organizational arena. The example of the minority being made redundant in favour of the majority, above, illustrates the problem of 'persecution' of minorities.

There is also the question of subjective benefits, or the way people see the benefits which will accrue to them, and the possibility of 'preference manipulation': persuading people that they will enjoy more benefits from a decision than is possibly the case. So, in negotiations, a manager may 'sell' a decision to his or her opposite number by using manipulative persuasion techniques to convince the other negotiating team of the benefits available to them.

Formalism

Formalism is independent of wants and needs, and is based on 'universal' moral principles. Instead of anticipating the results of the decision, we ask the question 'Is it right?' based on certain established principles. Kant's principle is that of the 'Categorical Imperative' whereby everyone should act to ensure that similar decisions would be reached by others in similar circumstances. As such, formalism is established on the basis of a shared understanding. Everybody (at least within your organization, or within your society) understands the principles of right and wrong which you are applying. This type of decision making is backward-looking in perspective as it is based on historically formulated principles. As such it can lead to bureaucratic practice in the following of rules which govern decisions and actions, and can lead to dogmatism. It also tends to ignore individualism. However, it is on the principles of formalism that company codes of ethics are written.

It may be that individuals from different cultures have different preferences for one or the other decision principle. Adler (1991) reports research findings which suggest that Russian (former Soviet) negotiators were more likely to appeal to overriding normative principles in negotiation, than were their negotiating partners from Western Europe or the United States who tended to emphasize the benefits of a negotiated decision.

Hosmer (1987), discussing ethics in making decisions about human resources, develops a useful model of 'ethical analysis' of management decisions. This, we can see as a development on the rules and results approaches discussed above, and goes some way towards combining these two approaches to ethical decision making. This is illustrated in Figure 1.

Applications of the rules and results approach

In order to illustrate this model (Figure 1) and how we can use it to combine the two approaches of rules and results let us return to the case above of the

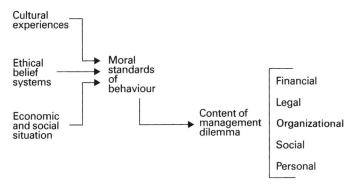

Figure 1 *Model of ethical analysis in management decisions (adapted from Hosmer, 1987)*

hotel manager wanting a position in Egypt. Let us now consider this problem by first looking at the content of the managerial dilemma: its financial, legal, organizational, social and personal aspects.

The financial content involves the benefits or costs which might accrue from deciding one way or another on whether we should appoint this female manager to a post in a predominantly Moslem society. The financial concern may, in fact, dominate the decision. What are going to be the financial gains or losses to the company if we allow this appointment? Firstly, if Moslem businessmen (local suppliers, potential customers) refuse to do business with a woman, there may be substantial losses to the company. On the face of it, this person is a good manager and would protect the financial interests of the company. In the type of culture under discussion, however, she may be powerless to use her business and management acumen to the full.

This post also represents a promotion for our female assistant manager and a possible loss in potential income if she does not get it. The offer of a comparable post would solve this individual aspect of the problem.

The legal content involves any legislation which permits or prevents this appointment. If there is no legislation specifically preventing a woman taking up such a post in the host country, there may be equal opportunities legislation in the home country whereby the woman manager could claim discrimination. However, an offer of a comparable post, and one less sensitive in another country would probably allay any such legal action.

The organizational consequences of the proposed action must also be considered. This involves the general implications for the organization. This appointment is fairly high risk, and may be detrimental to the organization in its Middle Eastern operations. The appointment could be considered insensitive to the local culture. As well as financial losses, the company may incur a loss of standing in this part of the world. This may involve losing business partners, shedding staff and other organizational consequences which could be far reaching. However, if this appointment is refused and becomes public, this may have implications for other female employees within the company in the way they see their careers and their future within the company. Talent may be lost to competitors with a more 'progressive' approach!

The social content would involve the implications for this action on the wider society. Perhaps this may result in a decreasing competitive position for the company in this particular market. It may diminish the reputation of the company in the locality, or it may have implications in the home community as a result of charges of discrimination.

The personal content is the impact it will have on the person making the decision. Will it affect the career of, in this case, the Director of International Operations? Will he lose his job, suffer a demotion or have future promotions blocked if he makes the wrong decision? The high risk decision for him is to allow the appointment, judging from the discussion above. The 'safest' decision to make would be to refuse the appointment, as it is difficult to see that this would have any implications on his future career.

It is clear that the discussion of costs and benefits above is a utilitarian one, where the results of the action are considered. It is also, on reflection, clear that not all the perceived results are based on objective data. Even when such data are available, their interpretation may be quite different from decision maker to decision maker. We could have looked at this in a very optimistic, positive way, as breaking new ground for the organization and developing more liberal approaches to doing business in Arab countries, as well as providing equal opportunities for women in this international company.

Within Hosmer's (1987) model there is a consideration of moral standards of behaviour, prior to the consideration of the dilemmas facing the decision maker. He describes these as the criteria we use to judge our behaviour and that of others. He warns that they tend to be subjective, imprecise and variable between individuals, they also may vary from one situation to another (for example, our attitude towards lying). We can, and should, trace these moral standards back to our ethical systems of belief, which we can clarify as providing guiding principles for our decision making. He identifies five such systems of belief which actually subsume our distinction between rules and results. These are summarized in Table 1.

These ethical belief systems contribute, with cultural experiences and with prevailing economic and social conditions, to moral standards of behaviour within Hosmer's (1987) model. It may be that different national cultures tend to have a preference for one of these belief systems in decision making. Also, the decision to appoint a woman to such a position in this case, if taken by a company with its home base in a Moslem country may not have posed such a dilemma, as a different set of values would have been in operation. It may also be that different prevailing economic situations would have affected the decision. Companies may be more able to make 'ethically' acceptable decisions when they are prosperous, and are big enough to support a

Table 1 Five belief systems in ethical decision making (adapted from Hosmer, 1987)

	Nature of this belief system	*Problems in this belief system*
Eternal law	Moral standards are revealed in religious teachings and represent an eternal law to which we should adhere.	The problem of multiple interpretation of this law.
Utilitarian theory	Standards are derived from the perceived outcomes of the action	It is easy to justify immoral acts by reference to benefits to majorities at the expense of a minority
Universal theory (formalism)	Standards are derived from the intent of the decision according to universal principles	There are problems in the concept of universality and who judges the morality of the principles
Distributive justice	Moral standards are based on the primacy of the single value of justice. Everyone should act towards the more equitable distribution of benefits as an essential factor in social cooperation	This is dependent on accepting that a more equitable distribution of benefits ensures social cooperation
Personal liberty	Moral standards are based on the primacy of the single principle of liberty. Everyone should act to secure greater freedom of choice, promoting market exchange and social productivity	This is dependent on accepting that a market system promotes social productivity

decision which does not have an immediate pay-off. A new company may have to cut corners and think more short-term, whereas a large established conglomerate can take a long-term view.

If systems of belief are different between different cultures (that is, incompatible) then a utilitarian approach (that is, a more pragmatic approach) may need to be used when considering ethical issues in international decision making, such as the case we have just reviewed. However, this may be too simple, as our treatment of the case shows:

- A utilitarian approach may be cultural in its formulation, perhaps reflecting a 'Western' or 'North American' culture based on pragmatism and a results-oriented and forward looking culture.
- The 'rules' (values, attitudes or moral principles) by which we approach the problem may influence our perceptions of the 'results': hence in the case above we could view the appointment as a positive challenge, or a threat to the position of the company.

It is therefore difficult to avoid the influence and implications of different value systems on our decision making in an international decision. We can use the case of corporate bribery quoted above to discuss another dilemma in doing business internationally. When we do business across cultures should we adhere to our own (national) ethical standards or conform to the standards of our 'hosts'? So, for example, is corporate bribery justifiable in cultures where this is normal practice – that is, you do not get the business if you do not do it – and should we (from countries which do not condone it) follow this practice? Let us try to provide some answers to this dilemma by looking at the issue of cultural relativism.

Cultural relativism in ethical decision making

The idea of cultural relativism in ethical decision making is common (perhaps more common in practice than in conceptualization). The idea goes something like this. All cultures are different and no culture is any better or worse than any other, they are simply different. It is therefore correct to accept a culture, and its values, for what they are, and not to be judgemental. Therefore, if the value system within one culture allows for corporate bribery, then this should be acceptable. Donaldson (1989: 16) believes this position to be untenable, suggesting that people mistakenly endorse cultural relativism, confusing it with cultural tolerance. He argues:

> If a culture disagrees with the Shiite Moslem practice of having women wear veils, yet owing to its tolerance believes nonetheless that it should refrain from forcing its views on Shiite Moslems, then tolerance counts as a *moral*, not relativist, value . . .
>
> . . . were a cultural relativist asked whether culture A's belief in tolerance is any better than B's belief that values should be forced down people's throats, the relativist would be forced to deny it. The relativist would not endorse tolerance over intolerance.

He also claims that cultural relativism requires an absence of any objective grounds for morality, such as a concept of evil and good, for example:

> . . . consider the practice of Japanese Samurai warriors in earlier centuries. A new sword would be tested by murdering a complete stranger. When the sword had been forged, the Samurai would find a stranger in the road, confront him face to face, and without warning swing the sword down in a diagonal arc. If the sword cut neatly from the side of the neck to the waist on the opposite side, it was of adequate quality. If not, it was unfit for a warrior. (Donaldson, 1989: 17).

Whilst rejecting a moral free-for-all, and the international arena as a moral 'free zone', Donaldson (1989) also does not accept the ethnocentric view of applying the moral values of one country (perhaps the United States) on another. It may therefore be difficult to establish a moral objectivity which can be applied in all countries of the world. Instead, he suggests an 'ethical

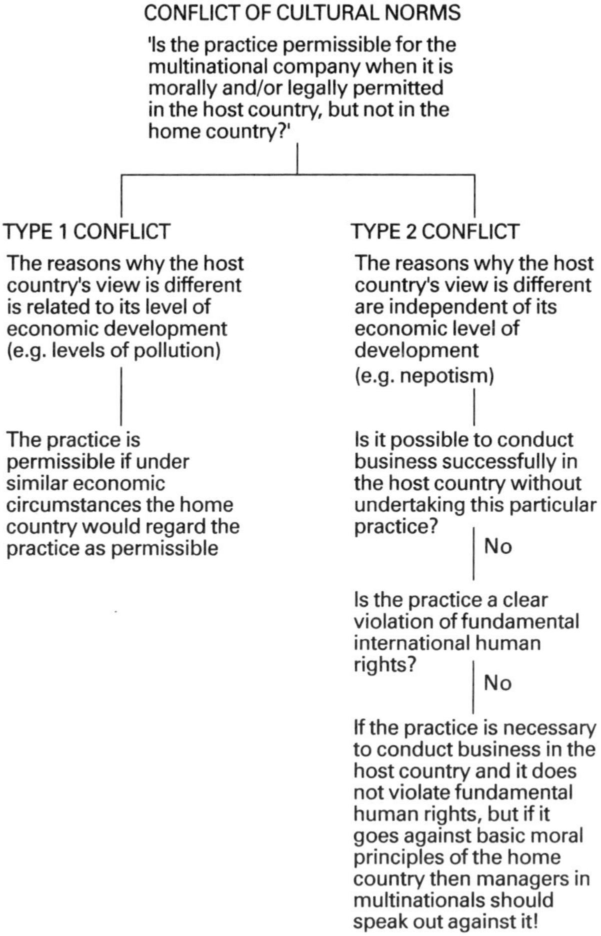

CONFLICT OF CULTURAL NORMS

'Is the practice permissible for the multinational company when it is morally and/or legally permitted in the host country, but not in the home country?'

TYPE 1 CONFLICT

The reasons why the host country's view is different is related to its level of economic development (e.g. levels of pollution)

The practice is permissible if under similar economic circumstances the home country would regard the practice as permissible

TYPE 2 CONFLICT

The reasons why the host country's view is different are independent of its economic level of development (e.g. nepotism)

Is it possible to conduct business successfully in the host country without undertaking this particular practice? No

Is the practice a clear violation of fundamental international human rights? No

If the practice is necessary to conduct business in the host country and it does not violate fundamental human rights, but if it goes against basic moral principles of the home country then managers in multinationals should speak out against it!

Figure 2 *An algorithm for international ethical decision making (adapted from Donaldson, 1989)*

algorithm' which provides a guide-line for those attempting to answer the question 'is the practice permissible for the multinational company when it is morally and/or legally permitted in the host country, but not in the home country?' We will summarize this algorithm in diagrammatic form in Figure 2.

Donaldson (1989) separates the two types of conflict (Figure 2), because practices which purely reflect the level of economic development are easier to empathize with, provided that the home country would do the same thing in similar circumstances (a current debate about the world's rainforests may fit into this type of category, where the local economy is dependent on tree felling and reflects a level of economic development, but still the developed world is telling these countries to halt the level of tree felling).

An issue such as corporate bribery may not be dependent on the level of economic development of a country, although it may be a reflection of low salaries. This is particularly the case where bribery concerns petty officials in some developing countries. It is often the case that business cannot be done without bribery, and it does not seem to contradict any fundamental international human right. However, managers from multi-national companies doing business in such a country may feel that they have to speak out against such practices. From a purely pragmatic point of view, however, this may cause embarrassment to both the company and to the host country's government.

Whilst Donaldson's (1989) algorithm does not entirely meet all the problems of cultural relativism in international decision making, it goes some way in offering managers a way of approaching ethical decision making involving what we have previously called 'major international decisions' across cultures. Continuing on this note, it may be useful to distinguish those aspects of an ethical decision which are culturally specific, and those (which individuals from some cultures) may regard as transcending cultures.

Values and ethics

Seeing a distinction between 'values' and 'ethics' may help us to clarify some of the issues which cultural relativism raises. We can refer to the view of Condon (1981), for example, that:

• Values reflect the culture
• Ethics transcend the culture.

Thus we posit an idea that ethical decision making is not culturally relative. That is, we do not have to accept the values of the host country which we do not feel are right (as is the implication of Donaldson's theory). However, this is a complex issue which may be simplified by identifying the various factors involved in ethical decision making in an international context. These seem to be:

Sources of values:

• Personal values which individuals hold which may result from:
• Group values which are held in common by, for example, a peer group
• Religious values which have different relative influences in different societies and for different groups and individuals
• Cultural values which are particular to a particular community or nation
• Fundamental human values which may be held in common by all or most countries (for example, not allowing murder).

Types of international values:

- Ethnocentric: our values are best
- Realistic cultural relativism: allowing for differences in values between one society and another (within reason).

Universal ethical values:

- Declarations of fundamental human rights by such international bodies as the United Nations
- Acceptance of universal values by power and dominance of one or many countries over others, through economic or political power in world affairs (for example, the military enforcement of the moral principle that Iraq's invasion of Kuwait was wrong).

We could probably think of other factors of international ethical decision making, but we have tried to cover here most of the relevant ones involved in decision making where the final arbiter may be an individual manager, the executive of a multinational national company or a national government. Identifying these different aspects of decision making may help us in arriving at an ethically acceptable decision.

We can conceptualize in a number of ways, those aspects of international decision making. However, in practice, how do managers actually arrive at a decision? So far we have almost exclusively dwelt on the larger international decision, where a conceptual approach is far more useful.

What about day to day decisions? What about decisions that are not made in a 'rational' way? For example, the idea of 'cognitive dissonance' suggests we manufacture rationalizations for our own behaviour, rather than being rational decision makers (Festinger, 1957, suggests that when there is a clash between our attitudes and our behaviour we reduce the internal conflicts by rationalizing our behaviour). Indeed, with a utilitarian view of ethical decision making we can justify practically any decision taken by an argument of its benefits!

Personal construct psychology and ethical decision making

The Personal Construct Psychology of Kelly (1955) suggests that we are able to do this because the way we see and organize our world is through a system of personal constructs. Some are superordinate (perhaps not to be violated) and some are subordinate and more capable of change and modification. It is through an understanding of our construct system, we now argue, that we can better understand the ethical decision making process in an inter-cultural context, and to decide whether our construct system is sustainable with a high 'survival value' in a developing international situation, or whether it is in need of change. Constructs may be easy for a person to verbalize, or may be 'pre-verbal' (rather than 'unconscious' in Freudian terms). It is quite often the pre-verbal constructs, those which cannot be easily verbalized, which are the most entrenched and important to our lives, and are often our superordinate constructs. We do not stop to think about these ways of construing the world and the decisions we make, they are just there. This, we can posit, provides the basis for an understanding of 'intuition': those decisions we make instinctively, pragmatically or by 'the seat of our pants'.

Let us consider more closely what we mean by intuition in ethical decisions by again referring to the ideas of Brady (1990) on Rules and Results.

Knowing how and knowing that

Brady (1990) discusses two forms of knowing: 'knowing how' and 'knowing that'. These categories make a distinction between the acquisition and presence of knowledge about something which can be fairly easily verbally conveyed on the one hand, and knowledge of how to do something which is often difficult to convey verbally on the other hand. Thus a manager might know that interest rates influence business growth, and that employees are more productive where goals are made clear and realistic. This is perhaps something which may be learnt at business school, for example, or read in a book. On the other hand, a manager might know how to inspire subordinates, or sell products to customers. The latter being better learnt through practice on the job, emulation of a mentor, or through a skills workshop where 'know how' can be developed in practice rather than in theory.

The way Brady (1990) relates this distinction to management ethics is as follows. Decision making in business requires the exercise of ethical judgement. This judgement is in itself based on a dichotomy of Utilitarianism and Formalism. In the traditional way that ethical thinking has been considered, this has been more by reference to what is desirable, rather than what is done in practice (*knowing that*). By introducing the dichotomy of knowing that/knowing how a further dimension can be added which helps to clarify decision making as shown in Table 2.

The question might be posed, for example, 'How do you teach compassion in a business school?' You might teach cost–benefit analysis, but it is far more difficult to convey verbally the know how of good will and empathy! 'How do you ensure that a person is reliable or consistent, by publishing a code of ethics in a company?' It is only by making apparent a manager's construct system that we can find out the intuitive basis of his or her decision making, and to understand whether the construct system is sustainable or not in the international situation.

Table 2 Ethics and the knowing that/knowing how dichotomy (adapted from Brady, 1990)

	Utilitarianism	*Formalism*
	Examples:	*Examples:*
Knowing that	Policy analysis	Legalistic
	Technical comparison	Law abiding
(at a *conceptual* level)		
Knowing how	Compassion	Comfortably principled
	Good will	Reliable
	Empathy	Consistent
(at an *intuitive* level)		

Understanding constructs

To illustrate this, we can ask pre-experience business students what they think of a manager (let us say a purchasing manager) taking a bribe from a supplier in order to buy equipment from that particular supplier. A normal reaction is that this is unethical and should not be done. If we ask the student to distinguish between a person who takes a bribe and one who does not, we would normally find a black and white distinction between 'immoral' versus 'moral'. This would be the way the student would construe this type of decision (in Kelly's terms). Let us now say the student is in the position of a purchasing manager and accepts Christmas presents from his suppliers. We could now ask him or her to distinguish between a purchasing manager who accepts gifts and one who does not. A possible construct could be 'creates a relationship with supplier' versus 'does not create a relationship'.

Let us suppose that another student is now a sales manager who is under pressure from his or her company to increase sales. The cost of not doing so, in a recession, may be the loss of his or her job. Other colleagues are offering 'inducements' to customers to increase sales and this seems to be working. Our sales manager has a mortgage to pay and a family to support, so that he or she sees little choice but to follow his or her colleagues. Again, we could ask the manager to distinguish between a sales manager who offers inducement and one that does not in the face of a recession and an insecure job. We might now get something like 'looks after family' versus 'puts integrity first'.

It is clear that either the student's perception of the world is changing or that the constructs which we describe above are 'subordinate', capable of being changed or modified, but only within the confines of a 'superordinate' construct which is far more important to the world view of our student/manager, as yet has not been verbalized.

Discovering superordinate constructs

Let us now transport our line of questioning to a petty official in a developing country (the generalization is intentional) who asks for a bribe before he will process your application for an extension of your visa. Let us ask him how he would distinguish between an official who accepts gifts and those who do not. We might hear something like 'prudent' versus 'foolish'. What we now wish to do is to understand the values behind this construct (the superordinate constructs), by a process which is technically called 'laddering' (see, for example, Stewart and Stewart, 1981) which can be reduced to a process of asking the question 'why?' in order to climb the ladder of a person's construct system in order to reach the top or the most important constructs.

So, we could ask our official, 'why is a person foolish if he doesn't accept gifts'. The reply might be 'because everybody does it and a person would not be prudent not to ask for gifts'. We could then ask, 'why would he not be prudent'. 'Because our salary reflects the fact that people give us gifts of money, it is expected' could be the reply. 'Why is it expected?' we might then ask. 'Because a responsible man has a family to keep, is responsible for relatives, and sends money home' may be the reply. And then 'Why is it important to accept this responsibility, to look after your relatives?', 'Because they will do the same for me when I get older, because that is the way it has always been?'

Asking questions beyond this point may reveal nothing further. What we have discovered in this fictitious example is that the overriding value is towards the family, and other values are subordinate to this, and may be more malleable and subject to change. The superordinate value of loyalty to one's family may be less amenable to change, and may be difficult to break down in many developing countries where, for example, nepotism may act as a brake on industrial change.

Some implications and conclusions

We have said very little here about the technicalities of personal construct psychology, but have suggested that this might be a useful approach for looking at business ethics at an intuitive level, and for exploring intercultural dilemmas which may confront international managers. The reasons for this and their implications are as follows:

1 Existing approaches to ethics focus on the 'know that' level of what can be taught or what can be prescribed, rather than at the more intuitive 'know

how' level of personal attitudes and values which are fundamental to both everyday management, and when there is a clash of values such as in an international management situation. Existing approaches therefore focus on the major international decisions which are often depicted in business school case studies, and on which we can deliberate and conceptualize. Guide-lines, algorithms, codes of ethics and specific formulae are often offered in order to help ethical decision making in these cases, and we have explored some of these.

2 Personal construct psychology is based on a principle known as 'constructive alternativism' which recognizes that there are different ways of seeing things. This is particularly useful when looking across different cultures as it recognizes the diversity of value and construct systems which may be as valid as our own. This is not another form of cultural relativism, as it looks at the 'survival value' of a construct system. In other words, it asks what are the implications for a person, a company or a society, having a particular view of life or events? Is it workable in the long term? Because we perceive 'facts' within our experience in terms of our particular construct system, it may be difficult to see people, events and processes in any different way.

3 Let us say that the female manager cited above who wanted a job in Cairo, saw the businessmen in Egypt with whom she would have to do business, in terms of 'male chauvinism', and saw all behaviour directed towards her by them in these terms, and therefore demonstrated a degree of antagonism. This would not be a very constructive approach to building relations with them if she were to get the job. She would have to ask herself why she saw these businessmen in these terms, what her fundamental values (superordinate constructs) were, and whether these can be changed to develop a more constructive view of this world.

4 Personal construct psychology provides a systematic methodology (known as the Repertory Grid) with a rich and varied literature developed over the last four decades, which we have not had the opportunity to explore in this text. This has implications for both practical management application and for research opportunities. We can mention some of these by reference to the cases cited above.

5 By using the Repertory Grid technique, a thorough ethical audit could be conducted in the company which in our example is thinking of doing business with the West African company. This would focus on the real values which are important to the various stakeholders concerned. It would aid a decision on whether to take the contract or not. This could be extended to the managers who would be involved directly in business dealings with their counterparts in the other country to understand the 'survival value' of their construct systems in this new situation.

6 In the hotel company, the Repertory Grid technique could be used as a 'selection' aid. Why does our female manager want to go to Cairo? Has

she got something to prove? What are her underlying values and reason? An in-depth Repertory Grid interview could help the company understand the viability of her 'motives' and provide an idea of her potential for success.

7 In the same way, development needs could be identified. An approach to change, through the idea of constructive alternativism, is through individuals looking for different approaches or alternatives to their present construct system. If our female manager really has a construct of 'male chauvinism' versus (say) 'new man' which is of primary importance to her, alternative ways of looking at Moslem businessmen could be explored. 'Devout' versus 'irreligious' may be a more useful construct to employ. 'Equality' versus 'inequality' may not be a relevant construct in certain countries of the world. If such a construct is seen by our female manager as fundamental, we have to ask the reason 'why?' We (and she) have to understand why it is so important, if it can be conceptualized in any other way which may be more useful to her in the new environment, and indeed if it is subordinate to a superordinate construct which may be more difficult to change, but under which she has room to change her less crucial constructs. This type of understanding will help her far more in the day to day inter-cultural situation she will be in than will any number of codes of ethics, algorithms or other formulae for ethical decision making.

8 The implications for research into ethical decision making across cultures is immense within a personal construct psychology framework. It provides an established research tool (the Repertory Grid), and provides access to an understanding of the intuitive aspects of ethical decision making. It reveals those values and attitudes that are often difficult to directly articulate.

Within this paper we have therefore provided a discussion on existing approaches to ethical decision making. These approaches have their uses for practising managers. However, we have discussed their limitations, particularly when looking at decision making across cultures and when looking at the types of everyday decisions in which practising managers may be involved. Here it is necessary to try to understand the intuitive aspects of ethical decision making. Personal construct psychology presents a promising approach with benefits to both practising managers and management researchers.

References

Adler, N. (1991) *International Dimensions of Organizational Behaviour*, Boston, Massachusetts: PWS-Kent.

Blanchard, K. and N. V. Peale (1988) *The Power of Ethical Management*, Cedar/ Heinemann.

Brady, F. N. (1990) *Ethical Management: Rules and Results*, MacMillan.

Condon, J. (1981) 'Values and ethics in communication across cultures: some notes on the North American case', in *Communication*, Volume 6, No. 2, 1981, 255–65.

Donaldson, T. (1989) *The Ethics of International Business*, New York: Oxford University Press.

Festinger (1957) *A Theory of Cognitive Dissonance*, Stanford, California: Stanford University Press.

Homer, L. T. (1987) 'Ethical analysis and human resource management' in *Human Resource Management*, Fall 1987, Vol. 26, No. 3, 313–30.

Izraeli, D. (1988) 'Ethical beliefs and behaviour among managers: a cross-cultural perspective', in *Journal of Business Ethics*, 7, 1988, 263–71.

Kelly, G. (1955) *The Psychology of Personal Constructs*, New York: Norton.

Langlois, C. C. and B. B. Schlegelmilch (1990) 'Do corporate codes of ethics reflect national character? Evidence from Europe and the United States', in *Journal of International Business Studies*, Fourth Quarter, 1990.

Stewart, V. and A. Stewart (1981) *Business Applications of Repertory Grid*, London: McGraw-Hill.

Reproduced from Jackson, T. (1993). Ethics and the art of intuitive management. *European Management Journal*, Twentieth anniversary edition, 57–65, by permission of Elsevier Science Ltd.

Part Three
Cross-cultural interactions

Communicating across cultures

Doing business across cultures involves foremost communicating with colleagues, partners (or adversaries) with different cultural backgrounds. Chapter Six begins with a review of research and assumptions in this area (Limaye and Victor, 1991), which is critical of Western (linear) models of communication, and suggests bases for further work and development in cross-cultural business communication. This contribution argues that certain issues are largely ignored in considering cross-cultural comunication, namely:

- Different cognitive frameworks
- 'Subjective' cultural factors such as high/low communication context
- Differences between monochronic and polychronic conceptions of time
- The convergent nature of technology across cultures, but the divergent nature of the meaning conveyed through technology
- Differences in management and communication models
- Additional cultural dimensions which have largely been excluded by predominant theories such as that of Hofstede (for example, respect for guests, personal loyalty, sense of duty)
- Alternative conceptions of communication effectiveness.

The model to which the above authors refer, and from which the second contribution in Chapter Six is drawn (Haworth and Savage, 1989) is that of Shannon and Weaver (1949) who have had tremendous influence on Western communication theory. Their model is simple, linear, and comprises six elements as follows:

1 Source → 2 Encoder → 3 Message →
4 Channel → 5 Decoder → 6 Receiver.

Thus, I (1) may put into words (2) my feelings that 'I love you!' (3)

and speak the words (4) in the hope that they will be suitably understood (5) by my wife (6).

Since the publication of this model, communication theorists have either developed it, or have criticized it, but it has rarely been ignored. The main criticisms of the Shannon and Weaver model have been its linearity (depicting a one-way process) and that it is devoid of content. However, its linearity keeps it simple, while its process emphasis makes it adaptable, and probably portable across cultures.

It is thus that Haworth and Savage (1989) begin with this basic model and develop it into a means of understanding an important aspect of cross-cultural communication: the differences between low-context and high-context communication (see for example Hall, 1960). This has implications for the match between the explicit versus implicit content of the message intended by the 'sender', and the level of apprehended versus inferred understanding by the receiving. In other words, the mismatch between what is inferred and what is implied within a cross-cultural message may be analysed by reference to this model.

Understanding international negotiation

The task of researching negotiation behaviour is fraught with practical difficulties, the main problem being that it is difficult to undertake extensive observer research in actual cross-cultural negotiations which are often sensitive or confidential. We can first mention three methods of gaining insight into cultural differences in negotiation style, the results of which are often cited in the literature: inspection of transcripts of international negotiations and their subsequent content analysis (Glenn, Witmeyer and Stevenson, 1984); simulation of negotiations followed by the collection of data by questionnaire (Graham, 1983); and, observation of a simulation exercise accompanied by behavioural analysis (Graham, 1985). Each of these studies has its own methodological problems, but provide some insight into specific variables to be considered in negotiations across cultures.

The first approach, taken by Glenn *et al.* (1984), considered the minutes of the Security Council of the United Nations during the 1967 Arab–Israeli war, and examined the contributions of Americans, Soviet Russians and delegates from Arab countries. Transcripts were scrutinized for differences in styles between the negotiators, defined as: factual–inductive; axiomatic–deductive; and intuitive–affective. The conclusions of this study were that American negotiators are more likely to take a factual–inductive approach, while the other negotiators were more likely to take an approach based on overriding principles, or one based on feelings and intuition. However, the foundations of the definition of what a fact is in this case may be questionable and the differing concepts of rationality from one culture to another should be taken into consideration before imposing an etic viewpoint (see the discussion on etic and emic interpretations in the introduction to Part One of the current text).

The second approach, taken by Graham (1983), involves a study which looked at the differences in negotiation style of American, Japanese and Brazilian business people, by studying their reactions through data collected by post-exercise questionnaires, following a simulated business negotiation. The study investigated the relative importance of individual characteristics, situational constraints and process measures to each national group by identifying, within these three broad factors, specific variables which may influence the outcome of negotiations. These variables were:

- Process
    - openness in giving information about self
    - use of attraction, power and credibility
    - ability to form accurate impression of the other party
- Situational
    - the difference in importance of variable in explaining the outcome for each cultural group
- Individual
    - self esteem
    - extroversion
    - experience.

Graham (1983) identified differences in the importance of a number of variables for each group. For example, for American negotiations the amount of information exchanged at the negotiation table was important to the outcome, although he commented that interpersonal attraction may impede progress towards the desired result. Brazilian negotiations were influenced more by the actions of the negotiators, particularly in the use of power and influence, and deceptiveness. For Japanese negotiations, what happened before the negotiations was important: establishing relationships and the influence of status differences.

The third approach, again taken by Graham (1985), draws on the same study discussed above. Again this looks at the negotiation simulation with American, Japanese and Brazilian business people, but using video tape material to analyse the actual negotiation. The process variables considered here, in relation to outcome, were:

- Bargaining behaviours
  - promises
  - threats
  - recommendations
  - warnings
  - issuing of rewards and punishments
  - appeals to social norms (either negative or positive)
  - commitments
  - questions
  - commands
- The number of 'nos'
- Making of first offer
- Initial concession
- Silent periods
- Conversation overlaps
- Facial gazing
- Touching.

Based on such a limited sample, it is difficult to substantiate any generalization from the studies cited above, although some appeal lies in their different methodologies. The three studies discussed are widely cited, but we would question the utility of their findings. That is, it would be inappropriate for a practising international negotiator to generalize from these findings by assuming that Japanese negotiators are like those described by Graham (1983, 1985), or that Arab negotiators are like those described by Glenn *et al.* (1984). At best, the key variables identified by these three studies may be useful in describing differences between negotiators from different cultural backgrounds.

A more useful approach to understanding differences in cross-cultural negotiation is that taken by Kale and Barnes (1992). This approach was first discussed in the present text in the introduction to Part One by reference to the three factors of *culture*, *company* and *character*, and provides the first reading in Chapter Seven.

This study investigates the cross-cultural buyer-seller relationship in a business negotiation, by looking at indices of national culture, organizational culture and individual personality factors (Kale and Barnes, 1992). They employ the dimensions of Hofstede (1980), which were outlined in the current text in the introduction to Part One (see also Chapter Five), in order to investigate cultural influences on cross-cultural interactions, then use dimensions of organizational culture derived mainly from Reynolds (1986). These are five dimensions as follows:

- External versus internal emphasis
- Task versus social focus
- Conformity versus individuality
- Safety versus risk
- 'Ad hockery' versus planning.

The personality dimensions they employ for their analysis are from the Myers-Briggs Type Indicator (Myers and Myers, 1980), which have been derived from Jung's (Jung, 1921) classification of personality types which he investigated in a number of national cultures. These dimensions are as follows:

- Extroversion versus introversion
- Sensing versus intuition
- Thinking versus feeling
- Perceiving versus judging.

The first of these dimensions is related to the way individuals relate to their social environment, the second focuses on the way information is received cognitively by the individual, the third on the way the information is processed, and the fourth on the orientation to that information and decision process; thus perceivers are likely to procrastinate on decisions until all angles have been considered, and judgers are more results-oriented and more prone to making quicker decisions based on less information and deliberation.

This contribution in the present text is not being offered as a definitive approach, but as a methodology which may have importance in the investigation and understanding of interaction between different individuals from different organizational and national environments. Kale and Barnes (1992) provide useful approaches to both management research, and for the practice of management across cultures.

Negotiation lessons from China

The second reading in Chapter Seven (Kirkbride and Tang, 1990) takes a different approach in arguing that those requisite skills and abilities in negotiation which are most commonly quoted in Western literature come quite naturally to Chinese negotiators. These are:

- Setting bargaining ranges for the negotiation process
- Seeking to establish general principles early in the negotiation

- Focusing on potential areas of agreement and seeking to expand on these
- Avoiding taking the negotiation issues in sequence
- Avoiding excessive hostility, confrontation and emotion
- Giving the other party something to take home
- Negotiating as a team.

It is perhaps by drawing on these lessons that we can better understand the process of negotiation across cultures.

References

Glenn, E. S., Witmeyer, D. and Stevenson, K. A. (1984) 'Cultural styles of persuasion', *International Journal of Intercultural Relations*, Vol. 1, 52–66.

Graham, J. L. (1983), 'Brazilian, Japanese and American negotiations', *Journal of International Business Studies*, Vol. 14, No. 1, Spring–Summer, 47–61.

Graham, J. L. (1985), 'The influence of culture on business negotiations', *Journal of International Business Studies*, Vol. 16, No. 1, Spring, 81–96.

Hall, E. T. (1960) 'The silent language in overseas business' in *Harvard Business Review*, May–June, 1960.

Haworth, D. A. and Savage, G. T. (1989) 'A channel-ratio model of intercultural communication: the trains won't sell, fix them please', *Journal of Business Communication*, Vol. 29, No. 3, 231–54.

Hofstede, G. (1980) *Cultures Consequences: International Differences In Work-related Values*, Houston: Gulf.

Jung, C. G. (1921) *Psychological Types* (Collected Works, Vol. 6, 1976), New Jersey: Princeton University Press.

Kale, S. H. and Barnes J. W. (1992) 'Understanding the domain of cross-national buyer-seller interactions', *Journal of International Business Studies*, First Quarter, 101–32.

Kirkbride, P. S. and Tang, S. F. Y. (1990) 'Negotiation: lessons from behind the Bamboo Curtain', *Journal of General Management*, Vol. 16, No. 1, Autumn, 1–13.

Limaye, M. R. and Victor, D. A. (1991) 'Cross-cultural business communication research: state of the art and hypotheses for the 1990s', *Journal of Business Communication*, Vol. 28, No. 3, 277–99.

Myers, I. B. and Myers, P. B. (1980) *Gifts Differing*, Palo Alto, CA: Consulting Psychologists Press.

Reynolds, P. D. (1986), 'Organizational culture as related to industry, position and performance: a preliminary report', *Journal of Management Studies*, 1986, Vol. 23, No. 3, 33–45.

Shannon, C. and Weaver, W. (1949) *The Mathematical Theory of Communication*, Urbana, IL: University of Illinois Press.

6 Cross-cultural communication

6.1 Cross-cultural business communication research: state of the art and hypotheses for the 1990s

Mohan R. Limaye and David A. Victor

Cross-cultural business communication has become a trendy subject of study over the last decade and a half, judging by the presentations made at academic meetings. Interest in cross-cultural business communication has resulted in a steady increase in articles published in trade and scholarly journals (Bond, Leung and Wan, 1982; 1986; Gudykunst, 1983; Maison-rouge, 1983; McCaffrey and Hafner 1985; Sanders, 1988; Ting-Toomey, 1985). Similarly, several books – largely anecdotal – have been published in the field (Axtell, 1989; Chesanow, 1985; Copeland and Griggs, 1985; Kennedy, 1985; Ricks, 1983; Snowdon, 1986; Valentine, 1988). The last decade, additionally, has seen the emergence of business guides to specific cultures, including the Arab World (Almaney and Alwan, 1982; Nydell, 1987), Brazil (Harrison, 1983), China (DeMente, 1989; Seligman, 1989; Wik, 1984), France (Carroll, 1988), Japan (Condon, 1984; DeMente, 1981; Hall and Hall, 1987; March, 1988), Korea (DeMente, 1988; Leppert, 1989), Mexico (Condon, 1985; Kras, 1988), Singapore (Leppert, 1990) and Thailand (Fieg, 1980). Based on these publications, one can predict a growing authorship and audience for materials in this discipline over the decade of the 1990s as well.

Several factors have contributed to the popularity of the subject of cross-cultural business communication in recent years. Chief among these factors is the phenomenal growth in the volume of international trade. Over the last 20 years, the total value of import–export trade for the United States has grown tremendously, surpassing $857 billion in 1990: imports: $493,652,000,000 and exports: $363,807,000,000 (*Direction of Trade Statistics Yearbook, 1990*, p. 402). International trade is equally or more important elsewhere as well, comprising more than 25 percent of all economic activity in most western European and newly industrialized countries. Indeed, a host of major multinational corporations have more than half of their sales in foreign markets rather than their home base of operations (e.g., the U.S.-based IBM, Dow Chemical, Coca-Cola and Colgate-Palmolive, the Switzerland-based Nestlé and Ciba-Geigy, the Ireland-based Jefferson Smurfit group, the Netherlands-based Philips, the Sweden-based Volvo and

Electrolux, Japan's Sony and Honda, and France's Michelin, to name just a very few in a long list).

Similarly, foreign direct investment has risen dramatically around the globe. In the United States, for example, the direct investment of foreign-based companies over the last 25 years has risen from $9 billion in 1966 to $1,786 billion, and U.S. direct investment abroad has jumped from $52 billion in 1966 to $1,120 billion in 1988 (*Statistical Abstracts, 1990*, p. 793). These figures are matched or exceeded in most of Europe, Japan, Korea, and, in terms of portfolio investments, among most of the oil-producing nations of the Middle East.

Worldwide, business organizations have discovered that intercultural communication is a subject of importance not just because they have to deal increasingly with foreigners but also because the workforce of the future within their own national borders is growing more and more diverse, ethnically and culturally. Questions of multiculturalism arise domestically within national borders as well. Most obvious of these are nations with more than one native culture represented by people in large numbers. The frequently discussed differences between French and Flemish Belgians; Francophone and Anglophone Canadians; Ibo, Hausa and Yoruba Nigerians; Chinese, Malay, and Indians in Malaysia and the 16 government-recognized cultural and linguistic groups in India are only a few of the most notable examples. Similarly, the large-scale immigration of former colonials, especially to the Netherlands and Great Britain, the tremendous influx of Soviet Jews to Israel, and classic immigration to the United States and Canada have created domestic multicultural work environments in these countries.

More difficult to handle than those immigrating with the intention of becoming new citizens, however, are what the Germans have called the gastarbeiter or guest worker. These guest workers are foreign nationals living and working for long-term indefinite or even permanent periods in a host country with a higher standard of living. Attitudes toward these workers have run the gamut from acceptance and accommodation to political movements for their expulsion. Most notable among the accommodationist policies are those in Sweden whose roughly 1,100,000 guest workers (in a population of only 8,330,000 Swedes) receive the right to vote and hold local office. Indeed, since 1973, Swedish employers have been required by law to give their guest workers 240 hours of paid leave of absence to attend free Swedish lessons. At the other extreme, Switzerland's proposed 'overforeignization' national referendum was only narrowly defeated. Its guest worker population lives at standards well below the Swiss norm. Similarly, the rise in France of the extreme right wing racist platform of Jean-Marie LePen who won fully 15 percent of the 1988 French vote is based in part on a platform of tougher immigration and strong sentiment against guest workers in France where 7 percent of the population consists of immigrants. In between these two extremes are the double standards meted out to the noncitizen workforce of the United States with its 1989 immigration Control and Reform Act and of Germany whose hostile sentiments against Turks and other gastarbeiter led to street demonstrations and small-scale urban riots in the mid-1980s. In the Gulf Arab states, the native citizenry is actually a marked minority relative to the numbers of guest workers. For example, by the 1980s fully 80 percent of the workers in Qatar and pre-invasion Kuwait were guest workers.

The end result of all of these cases – direct immigration, national multicultural divisions, or guest worker relations – is similar: employers are increasingly facing the need for cross-cultural business communication even in their own domestic workplace. In short, the manager or executive does not have to engage in international business to need to know the principles of international business communication.

In this article we will (a) define the scope of cross-cultural business communication, (b) discuss the traditional paradigm, (c) review the literature in the field, (d) discuss the limitations of the work done so far, (e) delineate the issues involved and point out the research gaps in intercultural communication, and (f) pose research questions most in need of answers (as hypotheses to be tested).

Definition and scope

The term *cross-cultural business communication* merits explanation. First, it should be recognized that the word culture is too elusive to define precisely. The fact that Kroeber and Kluckhohn (1952) list more than a hundred definitions of culture only accentuates the debate surrounding the concept of culture. A precise, totally agreed-upon definition of culture seems at the moment neither possible nor necessary for the purposes of this article. Generally speaking, culture could be said to refer to the way people understand reality or the world around them. For our purposes, we might agree on the definition of Simcha Ronen (1986, p. 17) who writes that culture 'represents a shared way of being, evaluating, and doing that is passed from one generation to the next.' We could also add to this Geert Hofstede's frequently cited definition (1980, p.25) that 'the essence of culture is the collective programming of the mind.'

In this paper, no attempt is made to distinguish between the terms 'cross-cultural' and 'intercultural'. While distinctions exist, the terms have frequently been used synonymously in the literature. Similarly, in the literature on international business communication, writers have often linked culture to country or nation though this imprecision does not materially affect the review below of the scholarly literature on this subject. Since a successful manager is above all an effective communicator, the literature review also includes relevant work on comparative or cross-cultural management as partially falling within the purview of intercultural business communication.

Traditional paradigm

Both management and communication theories, during the past several decades, have been dominated by Western scholars, particularly from the United States. For years, the conventional scholarly and practical wisdom has been that concepts and precepts of communication and management are universal and hence can be applied across countries or cultures. This paradigm starting from Fayol (1937), Koontz and O'Donnell (1955), and Mintzberg (1973), to name a few scholars of organizational management, still persists (Carroll and Grillen, 1987; Osigweh, 1983). In the field of communication, culture has often been ignored, especially by those whose interests have been flexibility, direction, and speed of information flow (Berlo, 1960; Schramm, 1955; Shannon and Weaver, 1949). The Shannon-Weaver model for instance does not represent the meaning, purpose, or intention of the participants. Korzybski (1958) in describing the communication process in his semantic reaction model provided a non-Aristotelian conceptualization of communication that countered Shannon and Weaver. Still, Korzybski essentially overlooks the importance of cultural orientation in the communication process. Likewise, Berlo (1960), who garnered widespread appeal for the simplicity and clarity of his modification of the Shannon-Weaver model to include channels of communication, nonetheless fails to address the meaning and intention of the participants. As a result, Berlo only cursorily touches on factors that have relevance for the cross-cultural dimension in the communication process.

Nevertheless, the awareness or perception that the universalist view is parochial or nonfunctional in a global setting appears to be gaining ground. Scholars and practitioners are increasingly becoming sensitized to the fact that cultural factors heavily influence management practices (Adler, 1983; Child, 1981; Hofstede, 1980; Laurent, 1983; Maruyama, 1984; Triandis, 1982–83). Similar awakening has occurred in the field of business communication as well (Haworth and Savage, 1989; Kilpatrick, 1984).

Literature review

Despite the increasing interest in the subject noted above, until recently a relative paucity of work has existed on intercultural business communication. This should not, however, seem surprising considering that general communication as a discipline has only recently gained recognition in business studies. Even in the area of international business studies, research of intercultural business communication as a field in its own right has been notably absent. Thus, in such major reviews of the state of the field in international business research as Dymza (1984) and Hawkins (1984), business communication received no mention at all. Moreover, in the survey conducted by the editors of the *Journal of International Business Studies* identifying the top 20 articles in the field of international business (Ricks, 1985), only one (Hall, 1960) directly deals with business communication.

International *business* communication is a nascent field. For example, with the exception of Hildebrandt's collection of essays (1981) and Victor's *International Business Communication* (in press), almost no scholarly books or textbooks have appeared expressly on *business* communication. Instead, most of the important work on cross-cultural communication research, at least somewhat relevant to business, surfaces in a wide range of other disciplines ranging from comparative management, organizational behavior, and psychology to anthropology and foreign language studies. We have, therefore, selectively cited articles relevant to business from these disciplines to help lay a foundation devoted specifically to cross-cultural *business* communication.

For example, most of the work on intercultural communication which has had some business focus has occurred in the last three decades following the pioneering work of the anthropologist Edward Hall (1959). Hall has written on how the various cultures of the world affect people's behaviors and nonverbal communication. In addition to Hall's later work (1966, 1976, 1983), others have examined the field. Inkeles and Smith (1974) discussed the effects of 'modernity' in six nations. Bass, Burger, Doktor and Barrett (1979) examined the effects of different cultural values and social norms in twelve nations on managerial behavior (including communication practices). Jaggi (1979) and Kaker (1971) studied values such as need and authority as they operate in Indian organizations. Graham (1984) explored the differing stances of international business negotiators. Finally, Andre Laurent (1983, 1986), the French management researcher, studied management conception and cultural loyalties within the multinational corporation. All of these authors generally investigated the effects of cultural variables on people's values and behaviors in business and organizational contexts. Most recently, Limaye (1989) proposed that the two factors leading to success in cross-cultural business negotiations included both cognitive and affective aspects (knowledge and sensitivity) of an international executive's overseas preparation.

Empirical work in the intercultural arena is time-consuming, expensive, and requires coordination of many scholars across national boundaries. Initial efforts of the early eighties include the work of Bhagat and McQuaid

(1982), Child (1981), Hofstede (1980), and Ronen and Shenkar (1985). In recent years, the pace has picked up (Beck and Moore, 1985; Laurent, 1983, 1986; Triandis, 1988). Tayeb (1988) has emphasized the role of culture in shaping behavior of employees in organizations and, implicitly, its effect on human communication in business firms. Casimir (1985) and Fisher (1988) emphasize differing schemata, cognitive maps, or mindsets. Adler and Graham (1989) have alluded to interpersonal orientation indexes developed by earlier psychologists as predictors of success for international negotiators. Additionally, Albert (1983) and her colleagues have developed Intercultural Sensitizers (ICSs) and tested them with diverse groups.

Limitations of the existing work

Most work in this field suffers from five shortcomings:

1 Anecdotal treatment dominates the field (Chesanow, 1985; Harris and Moran, 1987; Kennedy, 1985; Snowden, 1986; Punnett, 1989). Anecdotal work on intercultural business communication, while useful for illustrating key concepts and contributing to the stock of information available, needs to be supplemented by rigorous empirical research.
2 However, much existing research lacks this rich conceptual basis (Borisoff and Victor, 1989; Condon and Yousef, 1985; Copeland and Griggs, 1985; Ricks, 1983; Valentine, 1988). Conceptual frameworks or strong theoretical underpinnings are a necessary characteristic of seminal and significant research of the kind mentioned at the beginning of this review (Shannon and Weaver, 1949; Korzybski, 1958; Berlo, 1960). Such work provides the heuristic and new paradigms that encourage further research in a field. But current work on cross-cultural business communication has paid little attention either (a) to adapt these seminal works on general communication to the needs of intercultural business or (b) to create new models more relevant to cross-cultural business exchanges.
3 Some limited empirical research on comparative or intercultural business communication has been conducted but usually on broader issues than business communication alone (Bass, Burger, Doktor and Barrett, 1979; Haneda and Shima, 1983; Hofstede, 1980; Kelley and Worthley, 1981; Laurent, 1983; Sathe, 1985; Torbjorn, 1985). Considerably more empirical work exists on cross-cultural business communication between two cultures only (e.g. Eiler and Victor, 1988; Halpern, 1983; Varner, 1988; Victor, 1987; Victor and Danak 1990, Zong and Hildebrandt, 1983), but such studies are too culture-specific and also treat only narrow slices of those cultures. As a result, it is debatable whether their findings can apply *across* cultures.

E. C. Stewart (1985) has studied the decision-making styles prevalent in business across several cultures and listed the technical style (common in the U.S.), the logical style (employed in Western Europe), the bureaucratic style (in which a committee is responsible for decisions), and the social collective style (prevalent in Japan). Likewise, R. H. Kilpatrick's (1984) survey of business communication, though limited to the more mundane aspects of business writing, represents an effort toward greater multinational empirical research. Even so, the corpus or sample of illustrations for both Stewart and Kilpatrick is broadly from the cultures of the industrialized nations of the world.

4 Another persistent weakness of the research on international management and, by extension, cross-cultural business communication lies in some scholars' assumption of comparability where none may exist. Similarly, these researchers assume that theories and models developed in one social system may be applicable or operative in another. Some non-Western scholars trained in Western universities and Western methods of social research have arguably been influenced in many cases by Western modes of thinking (Hamnett and Porter, 1983). In other words, the research of such Asian or African scholars has been tainted or contaminated to the extent that their theories are not native or indigenous to the soil. This flaw has been drawn attention to in some recent work (Adler, 1983; Adler and Graham, 1989; Hofstede, 1980; Osigweh, 1988).

5 The prevailing linear paradigm for communication models in Europe and North America is also limiting (Berlo, 1960; Shannon and Weaver, 1949). The complexity and sophistication of recent models have admittedly enhanced the older communication models, but even these ignore the uniqueness of cross-cultural communication. Bowman and Targowski (1987), for example, suggest a need for more elements than the traditional processive paradigm allows. In a later article (Targowski and Bowman, 1988) they actually develop a layer-based pragmatic communication process model covering more variables affecting the communication path than any earlier model. Nevertheless, they only indirectly address the role of cultural factors among their layer-based variables.

In a similar vein, Haworth and Savage (1989) developed a channel-ratio model specifically for intercultural communication. However, their accommodation of intercultural elements remains very limited as it is a one-variable-oriented model which is essentially a reduced reconfiguration of the Shannon-Weaver model. While their channel-ratio model is praiseworthy in focus and useful for analyzing one variable, it is inadequately comprehensive. Haworth and Savage, in short, fail to account fully for the multiple communication variables in the intercultural communication environment.

We therefore hypothesize:

Hypothesis 1: Traditional Western linear and process models of communication do not represent the complexity of cross-cultural communication.

Relevant issues and research gaps in intercultural communication

Cognitive frames

Triandis and Albert (1987) maintain that 'the basic ideas concerning cognitive frames are the same regardless of setting' (p. 265). Cognitive frames may, however, differ from culture to culture. Fisher (1988) emphasises the possibility of differing mindsets. Cognition as a human faculty is probably shared by all people across cultures, but cognitive schema and frames cannot be assumed to be identical in all cultures. The dominant values of a society, its ideologies, and its ways of looking at the world around it affect the nature, scope, and definitions of rationality and of the inquiry by researchers in that society (Kumar, 1976, p. 9). What is rational and logical thus apparently differs among cultures and countries because world views or perceptions differ radically among people around the globe. Harris and Moran (1987) cite such diversity as leading to cultural synergy. W. E. Deming's success in Japan in melding U.S. and traditional Japanese concepts supports this belief in cultural synergy. Such thinking is still relatively new: Few executives can think of the advantages that can accrue to an organization because of the cultural diversity of its employees (Adler, 1991).

Barnlund (1975, 1989) and Kumon (1984) expound upon the differences between the cognitive processing of information by Japanese and Westerners. Similarly, Adler, Doktor and Redding (1989, p. 42) emphasise the differences between Japanese and Western modes of reasoning. Teruyuki Kume's survey (1985) of North American and Japanese managerial attitudes toward decision-making lent empirical support to this contrast. Kume found Japanese business communication style to be indirect and agreement-centered with an 'intuitive' (p. 235) decision criterion. This style was diametrically opposite the North American communication style which Kume's data revealed to be direct and confrontation-centered with a 'rational' (p. 235) decision criterion. Kume, in short, showed North American business communication style to derive from a cultural emphasis on practical empiricism while Japanese business communication is shaped by the need to maintain group harmony. It can hence be hypothesized that:

Hypothesis 2: Businesspersons' perceptions of issues related to negotiations or communication events are influenced by their cognitive frames or unique world views.

Subjective and objective culture

The division between subjective culture (referring to values, behavioral norms, attitudes, and religion) and objective culture (referring to infrastructure, technology, and other 'material' objects) is important for understanding a group of people because that group's objective and subjective cultures put it apart from other identifiable groups. Communication differential across cultures can, for instance, be partly accounted for by a society's view of nature and technology. It influences people's roles, actions and stances toward one another in complex ways.

Communication scholars note frequently that technology (one aspect of objective culture) influences communication processes – who communicates with whom, how many times and into what medium within and among organizations (Borisoff and Victor, 1989; Calder, 1969; Drucker, 1970; Douglas, 1986; Ellul, 1964; Gregory-Smith, 1979; Huber and Daft, 1987; Illich, 1977; Rybczynski, 1983; Schiller, 1976). Some have also noted that advanced industrial nations heavily use electronically mediated communication technology and emphasize written communication over oral or face-to-face communication. They cite the United States, Canada and Germany as examples of this trend. But Japan, which has access to the latest communication technologies, relies more on face-to-face or oral communication than the written mode. We think that the determining factor is not the degree of industrialization, but whether the country falls into low-context or high context cultures as Edward Hall defines the categories (Hall, 1959). In high context cultures like that of Japan, a larger portion of the message is left unspecified and accessed through the context, nonverbal cues, and between-the-lines interpretation of what is actually said or written. In contrast, in the US, which is labeled as a low-context culture, messages are expected to be explicit and specific. More is spelled out than left for the receiver to deduce from the context. Hence we propose that:

Hypothesis 3: Relative emphasis either on written or oral communication is a function of whether the country has a high- or low-context culture.

We also propose, as a corollary, that:

Hypothesis 4: Business organizations in high-context cultures do not emphasize rules and regulations to the extent that business organizations in low-context cultures do.

Linear and circular (monochronic and polychronic) concepts of time

Varying attitudes to time in different cultures have been treated in past literature, particularly the linear or monochronic temporal conception dominant in the United States, Canada, and Northern Europe versus the more polychronic temporal orientation dominant in most of Latin America, Southern Europe, and most part of Asia and Africa (Doob, 1971; Fraser, 1987; Hall, 1959, 1983; Kluckhohn and Stodbeck, 1961; McClelland, 1961). The monochronic or linear temporal orientation of much of Northern Europe and English-speaking North America and its effects on communication are therefore fairly well known. For example, people in the monochronic cultures tend to follow the direct plan approach in good news or neutral business letters. In other words, members of these cultures come to the point very quickly with little introductory phrasing. Similarly, members of these monochronic cultures tend to value quick responses in discussions with little introductory phrasing or politenesses. More pointedly, monochronic cultures usually fragment tasks into predetermined units of time – scheduling – that limit the length and depth of business communication. All of these examples indicate a linear time perception.

By contrast, time is not linear in most other cultures. These polychronic cultures more frequently view time as flexible. Conversations and written communication can be more indirect or circular. Thus, a business talk can acceptably – indeed, in many cases must – go off on tangents to the main subject to place all information in its proper context. Polychronic cultures, therefore, are likely to view the direct plan approach of linear time conception as rude or so lacking in adequate development as to seem unclear.

As an extended example of differing attitudes toward time, Indian polychronic or circular perception of time can be contrasted with the linear orientation. The US linear perception regards time as a scarce resource. Once gone time can never be retrieved. The all-familiar concept of 'time is money' implies that a person's current activities take on prime importance, for the profitability of the future is dependent upon how effectively the present is used. In the same vein, future time is budgeted and its efficient use measured against the goals established in the present (Limaye and Hightower, 1982/83).

In contrast, the circular perception of time prevalent in India and many polychronic business cultures regards time as a renewable resource. Consequently, time is not considered subject to waste. This perception views time as repeating itself: Time has neither a beginning nor an end. Besides being a common religious concept in Hinduism and Buddhism, many agricultural societies shared this perception as well. Consistent with this view, value systems and priorities develop which are not governed by the mere passage of time (Meade and Singh, 1970; Limaye and Hightower, 1982/83). The polychronic perception of time allows Indian businesspersons to be unhurried during negotiations. In a dyadic communication situation, the other partly with the monochronic mindset, on the other hand, feels the pressure of deadlines. Hence our hypothesis:

Hypothesis 5: Differing time perceptions in various cultures may cause failures in business negotiations between participants who do not share identical attitudes to time.

Convergence versus divergence

A debate has been going on between universalists and relativists: Universalists maintain that organizations across the globe are converging to a point of homogeneity as far as macro issues are concerned (Child, 1981; Negandhi, 1985). Technological similarities, homogenization of consumer tastes, and interdependence of nations are causing organizational management to be more similar to one another than ever before. Advocates of this global view argue that contingencies of technologies, market conditions, and organizational structures have a greater impact on management styles and processes than cultural variations: 'Gone are accustomed differences in national or regional preference' (Levitt, 1983, p. 92). On the other hand, relativists like Hofstede (1980), Laurent (1983) and Heller and Wilpert (1979) maintain that organization management has been culture specific and continues to be so. The similarities are to be found chiefly in modern technologies of manufacturing processes and communication, while human resources management is widely divergent across culture clusters, formulated on the basis of work-related employee values and attitudes (Ronen and Shenkar, 1985). For instance, Adler *et al.* quote Fugisawa as saying that 'Japanese and American management is 95 percent the same, and differs in all important respects' (Adler, Doktor and Redding, 1989, p. 27). We therefore propose:

Hypothesis 6: Though technologies in business organizations are converging across cultures, meanings conveyed through them (that is, human communication styles) are not.

Even Child (1981) found important differences in behavior among workers coming from varying cultural backgrounds, and Laurent (1983) substantiated this finding in his investigation across countries. He found that attitudes and behaviors differed among multi-cultural employees in far-flung subsidiaries of the same multinational corporation. Hence we hypothesize (as a replication of Laurent's study):

Hypothesis 7: Culture is a more significant factor in influencing work-related values and communication behaviors than factors such as profession, and role (power position) within the organization.

Non-Western communication and management models

Some scholars of organizational behaviour and international business negotiations (Becker, 1971; Fisher, 1988; Kapoor, 1975) have expressed doubts about the validity of linear models (which have been a badge of the European and North American cognitive frame) when applied to management and communication in non-Western cultures. Becker's 'mosaic' model and Kapoor's 'context' model may foreshadow a trend which will persistently question the adequacy of current Western designs of communication.

The communication model that comes closest to extending beyond the limitations of the linear paradigm inherent in most Western communication theories is the Becker (1971) mosaic model. Becker described communication as a three-dimensional cube comprised of information bits randomly brought together as in a Rubik's cube. For Becker, communication is nonlinear, dependent instead on the relationship of information to other bits of information, cultural factors among them. In other words, the Becker mosaic model describes in three-dimensional terms the meaning of the message in relation to other marginally pertinent information. This represents a major break from the linear process model's emphasis on the sender and receiver relationship. The Becker mosaic model, however, leaves all communication as random; the mosaic is never complete. The tiles of the mosaic – Becker's information bits – are constantly added and taken away. This, in effect, ignores process altogether, leaving little room to predict those patterns of relationships created by the mosaic bits. Still, while Becker's mosaic model may be too random to be readily useful, it represents a major breakthrough for future scholars as they attempt to create a model for cross-cultural communication less limiting than the prevailing Western linear paradigm.

Ashok Kapoor's circular model for the context of negotiation (1975) provides another nonlinear approach to international communication. For Kapoor, international negotiation can be seen as the center of several concentric rings, much like the pebble dropped in a pond producing ripples of increasing size. Each ring represents a negotiation context that the international negotiator must incorporate into a communication strategy before progressing inward to the next ring. The outer ring involves individual perspective; the next ring involves environmental factors (economic, political, cultural and social); the next ring encompasses the 'four C's' (criteria, compromise, conflicting interests, common interests); and the internal ring refers to the situation itself.

Finally, Fisher (1988) adopts a nonlinear approach to general communication (with its major focus on international political negotiations) based to some extent on the fields of operations research and information systems. For Fisher, each culture programs its members to behave, think and communicate in a particular fashion. He calls these human programs mindsets. While Fisher does not thoroughly develop this concept into a specific model of communication, the move toward a systems approach (of which the traditional linear process approach is only a part) is useful as a basis for theorists wishing to devise nonlinear or extralinear models of business communication, models broad enough to encompass the elements of Fisher's mindsets, that is, the complexities of culturally-based behavioral differences affecting communication.

Baker, Fisher, and Kapoor have taken the first tentative steps toward formulating some prerequisites for generating a universal model, we think that culture-specific communication models might be the way to go initially. A comparison of culture-specific models may lead to culture-cluster models based on the similarities among specific models or approaches. These may in turn lead to more successful attempts toward a universal approach to mapping human communication which could satisfy the theoretical as well as practical criteria of an efficient model. Plurality of approaches may thus prove to be some feasible beginnings.

Different mindsets or cognitive maps of, say, the Orientals have also been noted by Adler and Graham (1989) and Osigweh (1989). The questions of the 1990s in this context may very well be these: How do we best go beyond linear models of communication? What paradigm(s) will adequately map the different world(s) of intercultural business communication? What models, nonlinearly conceived, will more accurately delineate the non-Western reality of the cultures of many Asian, Middle Eastern, and some Latin American countries and the organizational communication practices in those countries?

As mentioned above, in a solely U.S. context, the growing ethnic and cultural diversity of the U.S. work force will induce awareness of the differing work goals, attitudes and communication patterns of an increasingly diverse workforce. The numerical dominance in the United States work place of the white male – particularly of Anglo-Saxon or Northern European background – which has given the U.S. world of work a certain cultural homogeneity (a John Wayne type of masculine, individualistic, aggressive stamp) may gradually diminish (Graham and Herzberger, 1983; Johnston, 1987). The recent success of Japan, Korea and Singapore (among other rapidly industrializing countries) in world trade has forced upon the U.S. consciousness Oriental patterns of communication behaviour in business organizations. This awareness may encourage research in non-Western models of cognition, management behaviours, and communication processes.

Need for investigating additional cultural dimensions

Hofstede (1980), investigating the work-related values and attitudes of the employees in several subsidiaries of a large corporation, derived through factor analysis four dimensions of culture that he deemed as salient: Masculinity–Femininity, Individualism–Collectivism, Power Distance, and Uncertainty Avoidance. On the masculinity pole of the masculinity–femininity continuum are values such as productivity, competition, monetary gains and bigness, while on the femininity pole one finds values like quality of life, societal welfare, and cooperation. Individualism is associated with personal time, freedom on the job, challenge, and individual responsibility. Collectivism goes with supportive work environment, goal direction, and group responsibility. High power distance refers to top-down decision making, loyalty to the boss, and rigid hierarchical structure; low power distance translates into egalitarian work environment, flexible hierarchies, and participative management. High uncertainty avoidance leads to explicit (written) rules and regulations, a great need for long-range planning, and reliance on information systems. Low uncertainty avoidance, on the other hand, means very few formalized rules, low need for MIS, and less preoccupation with long-term planning.

These four dimensions are undoubtedly an important contribution to the study of cross-cultural organizational behavior and work-related values. Hofstede study also has had a great deal of impact on several subsequent scholars who have used his framework of the above four dimensions of culture as bases for their research. We however think that survey items different from those Hofstede generated might have yielded a different set of responses. A factor analysis of those responses might have revealed some other salient dimensions of culture that also affect employee values, behaviors, and communication flows in business organizations. Another major validation attempt is thus called for. Hence, we propose:

Hypothesis 8: More and different dimensions of culture are discoverable through administration of different sets of questionnaire items than Hofstede's.

It is well known that investigator's cultural bias can contaminate a survey design, but bias can be substantially reduced or controlled considerably and offset by multiple perspectives and more research into non-Western sources of values and work-related behaviors. Such research can unearth important Eastern values such as attachment to family, power of seniority, personal loyalty, respect for guests (a 'guest' defined in a broad sense to include the other business party), sense of duty, yearning and motivation for education, and a strain of altruism. Some of these can hardly be subsumed under Hofstede's four dimensions.

Beyond knowledge and sensitivity

Alder (1991) suggests that to minimize misinterpretation one should avoid 'premature closure' by emphasizing 'description rather than interpretation or evaluation ... Effective cross-cultural communication presupposes the interplay of alternative realities; it rejects the actual or potential domination of one reality over another' (p. 88). Similarly, mere knowledge or cognitive understanding of the history, economic conditions, and business practices of societies other them one's own may not ensure effectiveness in communication or success for international business managers. At the least, knowledge must be supplemented by sensitivity, by nonevaluative awareness and appreciation of diversity. One, however, needs to go beyond tolerance or acceptance of non-Western modes of thinking, values, and communication practices (either exhibited by business negotiators or by research scholars) because acceptance may not be enough (Limaye, 1989). It still may remain essentially a Western paradigm with Western standards, just a little more sensitized. Hence, our next hypothesis is as follows:

Hypothesis 9: New and more encompassing paradigms of cross-cultural business communication and management will entail re-examination and redefinitions of what constitutes communication effectiveness.

It may thus mean a redefinition of the current European and North American criteria of enterprise effectiveness and communication competence. This caution makes sense since 'organizations establish their criteria for effectiveness based on the dominant values operating in the culture' (Sekaran and Snodgrass, 1989). This may be one more argument for designing multiple approaches or models of communication based on individual cultures. Once effectiveness and success are redefined to cover non-Western cultural norms, the organizing structures and systems accomplish organizational effectiveness will also have to be modified to make them congruent with organizational effectiveness based on non-Western values. In other words, different means or processes (integrating systems) will have to be devised and put in place to attain newly defined enterprise effectiveness. Cameron, Kim and Freeman (1989) have reported that Brazilian universities have been managed effectively in their own context, though important concepts of North American management have been disregarded in the Brazilian case. Hence we propose:

Hypothesis 10: Organizational effectiveness must be defined and measured in culture-specific contexts and that identical standards of excellence cannot be applied across the board.

It is in this sense we believe that future paradigms for intercultural business communication must go beyond the principally Western linear models.

Conclusion

In this paper, we have extensively reviewed the scholarship in the field of cross-cultural business communication and pointed out the gaps in the research. We have also outlined a few significant directions which the scholarship in this field should take. New paradigms and redefinitions of some concepts to include non-Western world views and effectiveness criteria, we think, would greatly strengthen the catholicity and diversity of approaches in this field.

References

Adler, N. (1991). *International dimensions of organizational behavior* (2nd ed.). Boston: PWS-Kent.

Adler, N. J. (1983). Cross-cultural management research: The ostrich and the trend. *Academy of Management Review, 8,* 226–232.

Adler, N. J., Doktor, R and Redding, S. G. (1989). From the Atlantic to the Pacific century. In C. A. B. Osigweh (Ed.), *Organizational science abroad: Constraints and perspectives* (pp. 27–54). New York: Plenum Press.

Adler, N. J. and Graham, J. L. (1989). Cross-cultural interaction: The international comparison fallacy? *Journal of International Business Studies,* 515–537.

Albert, R. (1983). The intercultural sensitizer or culture assimilator: A cognitive approach. In D. Landis and R. Brislin (Eds.), *Handbook of intercultural training,* Vol. 2 (pp. 196–217), New York: Pergamon Press.

Almaney, A. J. and Alwan, A. J. (1982). *Communicating with the Arabs: A handbook for the business executive.* Prospect Heights, Illinois: Waveland Press.

Axtell, R. E. (1989). *The do's and taboo's of international trade: A small business primer.* New York: John Wiley & Sons.

Barnlund, D. C. (1989, March-April). Public and private self in communicating with Japan. *Business Horizons,* pp. 32–40.

Barnlund, D. C. (1975). *Public and private self in Japan and the United States: Communicative styles of two cultures.* Tokyo: Simul Press.

Bass, B. M., Burger, P. C., Doktor, R. and Barrett, G. V. (1979). *Assessment of managers: An international comparison.* New York: Free Press.

Beck, B. E. F. and Moore, L. F. (1985). Linking the host culture to organizational variables. In P. J. Frost et al. (Eds.), *Organizational culture* (pp. 335–354). Beverly Hills, CA: Sage.

Becker, S. (1971). Rhetorical studies for the contemporary world. In L. Bitzer and E. Black (Eds.), *The prospects of rhetoric.* Englewood Cliffs, N. J.: Prentice Hall.

Berlo, D. K. (1960). *The process of communication.* New York: Holt, Rinehart & Winston.

Bhagat, S. R. & McQuaid, S. J. (1982). Role of subjective culture in organisations: A review and directions for future research. *Journal of Applied Psychology*, 67, 653–685.

Bond, M. H., Leung, K. and Wan, K. C. (1982). How does cultural collectivism operate? The impact of task and maintenance contributions on renewal distributions, *Journal of Cross-cultural Psychology*, 13[2], 186–200.

Borisoff, D. and Victor, D. A. (1989). Cross-cultural awareness in conflict management. In *Conflict management: A communication skills approach*. Englewood Cliffs, N. J: Prentice-Hall, 120–164.

Bowman, J. P. and Targowski, A. S. (1987). Modeling the communication process: The map is not the territory. *The Journal of Business Communication*, 24(4), 21–34.

Calder, N. (1969). *Technopolis: Social control of the uses of science*. New York: Clarion/Simon & Schuster.

Cameron, K. S., Kim, M. U. and Freeman, Sarah J. (1989). Contradictions between Brazilian and U.S. organizations: Implications for organizational theory. In C.A.B. Osigweh (Ed.), *Organizational Science Abroad* (pp. 203–228). New YorK: Plenum Press.

Carroll, R. (1988). *Cultural misunderstandings: The French-American experience*. (Trans. C. Volk). Chicago: University of Chicago Press.

Carroll, S. J. and Grillen, D. J. (1987). Are the chemical management functions useful in describing managerial work? *Academy of Management Review*, 12, 38–51.

Casimir, F. L. (1985). Stereotypes and schemata. In W. B. Gudykunst, L. P. Stewart, S. Ting-Toomey (Eds.) *Communications, culture, and organizational processes* (pp. 48–47). Beverly Hills: Sage.

Chesanow, N. (1985). *The world-class executive*. New York: Rawson Associates.

Child, J. (1981). Culture, contingency and capitalism in the cross-national study of organizations. In L. L. Cummings and B. M. Staw (Eds.), *Research in organizational behavior*, Vol. 3 (pp. 303–356). Greenwich, CT: JAI Press.

Condon, J. C. (1985). *Good neighbors: Communicating with the Mexicans*. Yarmouth, Maine: Intercultural Press.

Condon, J. C. (1984). *With respect to the Japanese: A guide for Americans*. Yarmouth, Maine: Intercultural Press.

Condon, J. C. and Yousef, F. (1985). *An introduction to intercultural communication*. New York: Macmillan.

Copeland, L. and Griggs, L. (1985). *Going international: How to make friends and deal effectively in the global marketplace*. New York: Random House.

DeMente, B. (1989). *Chinese etiquette and ethics in business*. Lincolnwood, Illinois: NTC Business Books.

DeMente, B. (1988) *Korean etiquette & ethics in business*. Lincolnwood, Illinois: NTC Business Books.

DeMente, B. (1981). *The Japanese way of doing business: The psychology of management in Japan*. Englewood Cliffs, New Jersey: Prentice-Hall.

Direction of Trade Statistics Yearbook (1990). International Monetary Fund (IMF), Washington, D.C.

Doob, L. W. (1971). *Patterning of time*. New Haven: Yale University Press.

Douglas, M. (*1986*). *How institutions think*. Syracuse, New York: Syracuse University Press.

Drucker, P. F. (1970). *Technology, management and society*. New York: Harper.

Dymsza, W. A. (1984, Spring/Summer). Future international business research and multidisciplinary studies. *Journal of International Business Studies*, pp. 9–13.

Eiler, M. A. and Victor, D. (1988). Genre and function in the Italian and U.S. business letter. *Proceedings of the Sixth Annual Conference on Languages and Communication for World Business and the Professions*. Ann Arbor.

234   *Cross-cultural Management*

Ellul, J. (1964). *The technological society*. New York: Vintage.
Fayol, H. (1937). The administrative theory of state. (Sarah Greer, translator). In L. Gullick and L. Urwick (Eds.), *Papers on the science of administration*. New York Institute of Public Administration, Columbia University.
Fieg, J. P. (1980). *Thais and North Americans*. Yarmouth, Maine: Intercultural Press.
Fisher, G. (1988). *Mindsets: The role of culture and perception in international relations*. Yarmouth, Maine: Intercultural Press.
Fraser, J. T. (1987). *Time: The familiar stranger*. Amherst: The University of Massachusetts Press.
Graham, J. L. and Herzberger, R. A. (1983, July-August). Negotiators abroad – don't shoot from the hip. *Harvard Business Review*, pp. 160–168.
Graham, J. L. (1985). The influence of culture on the process of business negotiations: An exploratory study. *Journal of International Business Studies*, 81–96.
Gregory-Smith, D. (1979). Science and technology in East Asia. *Philosophy East and West*. 29, 221–236.
Hall, E. (1959). *The silent language*. Garden City, NY: Doubleday.
Hall, E. T. (1976). *Beyond culture*. New York: Anchor Press.
Hall, E. T. (1983). *The dance of life: The other dimension of time*. Garden City, New York: Anchor Press/Doubleday.
Hall, E. T. (1966). *The hidden dimension*. New York: Doubleday.
Hall, E. T. and Hall, M. R. (1987). *Hidden differences: Doing business with the Japanese*. Garden City, New York: Anchor Press/Doubleday.
Halpern, J. W. (1983). Business communication in China: A second perspective. *The Journal of Business Communication*, 20, 43–55.
Hamnett, M. P. and Porter, D. J. (1983). Problems and prospects in Western approaches to cross-national social science research. In D. Landis and R. W. Brislin (Eds.), *Handbook of intercultural training*. Vol. 1 (pp. 61–81). New York: Pergamon Press.
Haneda, S. and Shima, H. (1983). Japanese communication behavior as reflected in letter writing. *The Journal of Business Communication*. 20, 19–32.
Harris, P. and Moran, R. (1987). *Managing cultural differences* (2nd ed.). Houston, TX: Gulf Publishing.
Harrison, P. A. (1983). *Behaving Brazilian: A comparison of Brazilian and North American social behavior*. Cambridge, Massachusetts: Newbury House.
Hawkins, R. G. (1984, Winter). International business in academia: The state of the field. *Journal of International Business Studies*, 13–18.
Haworth, D. A. and Savage, G. T. (1989). A channel-ratio model of intercultural communication. *The Journal of Business Communication*, 26, 231–254.
Heller, R. A. and Wilpert, B. (1979). Managerial decision making: An international comparison. In G. W. England, A. R. Negandhi and B. Wilpert (Eds.), *Functioning organizations in cross-cultural perspective*. Kent, OH: Kent State University Press.
Hildebrandt, H. (Ed.) (1981). *International business communication: Theory, practice, teaching throughout the world*. Ann Arbor, MI: University of Michigan School of Business, Division of Research in collaboration with the Association of Business Communication.
Hofstede, G. (1980). *Culture's consequences: International differences in work-related values*. Beverly Hills, CA: Sage.
Huber, G. P. and Daft, R. L. (1987). The information environments of organizations. In F. M. Jablin, L. L. Putnam, K. H. Roberts and L. W. Porter (Eds.), *Handbook of organizational communication* (pp. 130–164). Newbury Park, CA: Sage.
Illich, I. (1977), *Toward a history of needs*. New York: Pantheon.

Inkeles, A. and Smith, D. (1974). *Becoming modern:Individual change in six developing countries.* Cambridge, MA: Harvard University Press.

Jaggi, B. (1979). Need importance of Indian managers. *Management International Review, 19*(1), 107–113.

Johnston, W. B. (1987). *Workforce 2000: Work and workers for the 21st century.* Indianapolis, IN: The Hudson Institute.

Kakar, S. (1971). Authority patterns and subordinate behavior in Indian organizations. *Administrative Science Quarterly, 16*, 298–308.

Kapoor, Ashok (1975). *Planning for international business negotiation.* Cambridge, Mass: Ballinger Publishing Company.

Kelley, L. and Worthley, R. (1981). The role of culture in comparative management: A cross-cultural perspective. *Academy of Management Journal, 24*, 164–173.

Kennedy, G. (1985). *Doing business abroad.* New York: Simon and Schuster.

Kilpatrick, R. (1984). International business communication practices. *The Journal of Business Communication, 21*(4), 33–43.

Kluckhohn, F. and Strodtbeck, F. (1961). *Variations in value orientation.* New York: Harper & Row.

Knapp, M. L. (1978). *Nonverbal communication in human interaction.* New York: Holt, Rinehart & Winston.

Koontz, H. and O'Donnell, C. (1955). *Principles of management.* New York: McGraw-Hill.

Korzybski, A. (1958). *Science and sanity: An introduction to non-Aristotelian systems and general semantics.* (4th ed.) Lakeville, Conn: The International Non-Aristotelian Library Publishing Company.

Kras, E. S. (1988). *Management in two cultures: Bridging the gap between U.S. and Mexican managers.* Yarmouth, Maine: Intercultural Press.

Kroeber, A. L. and Kluckhohn, C. (1952). *Culture: A critical review of concepts and definitions.* Cambridge, MA: Harvard University Press.

Kumar, K. (1976, June). Some reflections on transitional social science transactions. Paper presented at the *Mediating Person Workshops*, Honolulu, Hawaii. Quoted in Hamnett, M. P. and Porter, D. J. (1983). Problems and prospects in Western approaches to cross-national social science research. In D. Landis and R. W. Brislin (Eds.), *Handbook of intercultural training.* Vol. 1 (pp. 61–81). New York: Pergamon Press.

Kume, T. (1985). Managerial attitudes toward decision-making: North America and Japan. In W. B. Gudykunst, L. P. Stewart, S. Ting-Toomey (Eds.), *Communication, culture, and organizational processes* (pp. 231–251). Beverly Hills: Sage.

Kumon, S. (1984). Some principles governing the thought and behavior of Japanese contextuals. *Journal of Japanese Studies, 8*, 5–28.

Laurent, A. (1986). The cross-cultural puzzle of international human resources management. *Human Resources Management, 25*(1), 91–102.

Laurent, A. (1983). The cultural diversity of Western conceptions of management. *International studies of management and organization, 13*(1–2), 75–96.

Leppert, P. (1989). *Doing business with the Koreans: A handbook for executives.* Chula Vista, Calif: Patton Pacific Press.

Leppert, P. (1990). *Doing business in Singapore: A handbook for executives.* Chula Vista, Calif: Patton Pacific Press.

Levitt, T. (1983). The globalization of markets. *Harvard Business Review, 83*(3), 92–102.

Limaye, M. (1989). International negotiations: Watch those nuances. *Working Paper Series, 89*(6), College of Business Administration, Colorado State University.

Limaye, M. and Hightower, R. (1982/83). Intercultural Communication: Cultural

Values and Business Environment. University of Texas-Austin, Dept. of General Business Working Paper 82/83–3–7, College of Business, 1–28.

Maisonrouge, J. (1983). The education of a modern international manager. *Journal of International Business Studies*. *14*(1), 141–146.

March, R. M. (1988). *The Japanese negotiator: Subtley and strategy beyond Western logic.* Tokyo: Kodansha International.

Maruyama, M. (1984). Alternative concepts of management: Insights from Asia and Africa. *Asia Pacific Journal of Management*, *1*(2), 100–111.

McCaffrey, J. A. and Hafner, C. R. (1985, October). When two cultures collide: Doing business overseas. *Training and Development Journal*, pp. 26–31.

McClelland, D. (1961). *The achieving society*. New York: Irvington.

Meade, R. D. and Singh, L. (1970). Motivation and progress effects on psychological time in sub-cultures in India. *Journal of Social Psychology*. *80*, 3–10.

Mintzberg, H. (1973). *The nature of managerial work.* Englewood Cliffs, NJ: Prentice-Hall.

Negandhi, A. R. (1985). Management in the Third World. In P. Joynt and M. Warner, (Eds.), *Managing in different cultures* (pp. 69–97). Oslo, Norway: Universitetsforlaget.

Nydell, M. (1987). *Understanding Arabs: A guide for Westerners.* Yarmouth, Maine: Intercultural Press.

Osigweh, Yg., C. A. B. (1989). *Organizational science abroad: Constraints and perspectives.* New York: Plenum Press.

Osigweh, C. A. B. (1983). *Improving problem-solving participation: The case of local transnational voluntary organizations.* Lanham, MD.: Univ. Press of America.

Ricks, D. A. (1983). *Big business blunders.* Homewood, IL: Dow-Jones/Irwin.

Ricks, D. A. (1985, Spring/Summer). International business research: Past, present, and future. *Journal of International Business Studies*, 1–4.

Roberts, K. H. and Boyacigiller, N. A. (1984). Cross-national organizational research: The grasp of the blind men. *Research in Organizational Behavior*, 6, 423–475.

Ronen, S., and Shenkar, O. (1985). Clustering countries on attitudinal dimensions: A review and synthesis. *Academy of Management Review*, *10*, 435–54.

Rybczynski, W. (1983). *Taming the tiger: The struggle to control technology.* New York: Viking/Penguin.

Sanders, P. (1988) Global managers for global corporations. *Journal of Management Development*, *7*(1), 33–44.

Sathe, V. (1985). *Culture and related corporate realities.* Homewood, Illinois: Richard D. Irwin.

Schiller, H. I. (1976). *Communication and cultural domination.* White Plains, New York: M. E. Sharpe.

Sekaran, U. and Snodgrass, C. R. (1989). Organizational effectiveness and its attainment: A cultural perspective. In C. A. B. Osigweh (Ed.), *Organizational Science Abroad* (pp. 269–292). New York: Plenum Press.

Sekaran, U. (1983). Methodological and theoretical issues and advancements in cross-cultural research. *Journal of International Business Studies*, 61–73.

Seligman, S. D. (1989). *Dealing with the Chinese: A practical guide to business etiquette in the People's Republic today.* New York: Warner Books.

Shannon, C. and Weaver, W. (1949). *The mathematical theory of communication.* Urbana, IL: University of Illinois Press.

Snowden, S. (1986). *The global edge: How your company can win in the global marketplace.* New York: Simon and Schuster.

Statistical abstracts of the United States. (1990). National Data Book, U.S. Department of Commerce, Bureau of the Census, 110th edition.

Stewart, E. C. (1985). Cited in Triandis, H. C. and Albert, R. D. (1987). Cross-cultural perspectives. In F. M. Jablin, L. L. Putnam, K. K. Roberts and L. W. Porter (Eds.), *Handbook of organizational communication* (pp. 264–295). Newbury Park, CA: Sage.

Targowski, A. and Bowman, J. (1988). The layer-based, pragmatic model of the communication process. *The Journal of Business Communication, 25*(1), 5–24.

Tayeb, M. H. (1988). *Organizations and national culture: A comparative analysis.* London: Sage.

Ting-Toomey, S. (1985). Toward a theory of conflict and culture. In W. B. Gudykunst, L. P. Stewart and S. Ting-Toomey (Eds.), *Communication, culture, and organizational processes* (pp. 71–86). Beverly Hills, CA: Sage.

Torbjorn, I. (1985). The structure of managerial roles in cross-cultural settings. *International Journal of Management and Organization 15*(1), 52–74.

Triandis, H. C. (1988). Cross-cultural contributions to theory in social psychology. In M. H. Bond, *The cross-cultural challenge to social psychology.* Newbury Park, CA: Sage.

Triandis, H. C. (1982–83). Dimensions of cultural variations as parameters of organizational theories. *International Studies of Management and Organization, 12*(4), 139–169.

Triandis, H. C. and Albert, R. D. (1987). Cross-cultural perspectives. In F. M. Jablin, L. L. Putnam, K. H. Roberts and L. W. Porter (Eds.), *Handbook of organizational communication* (pp. 264–295). Newbury Park, CA: Sage.

Valentine, C. F. (1988). *The Arthur Young international business guide.* New York: John Wiley & Sons.

Varner, I. I. (1988). A comparison of American and French business communication. *The Journal of Business Communication, 25*(4), 55–65.

Victor, D. A. (1987). Franco-American business communication practices: A survey. *World Communication, 16*(2), 157–175.

Victor, D. A. (in press). *International business communication.* New York: Harper Collins Press.

Victor, D. A. and Danak, J. (1990). Genre and function in the U.S. and Indian English-language business letter: A survey. Paper presented at the Conference on Language and Communication for World Business and the Professions. Ypsilanti, Michigan.

Wik, P. (1984). *How to do business with the People's Republic of China.* Reston, Virginia: Reston Publishing Company.

Zong, B. and Hilderbrandt, H. W. (1983). Business communication in the People's Republic of China. *The Journal of Business Communication, 20*, 25–33.

Reproduced from Limaye, M. R. and Victor, D. A. (1991). Cross-cultural business communication research: state of the art and hypotheses for the 1990s. *Journal of Business Communication,* **28** (3), 277–99, by permission of *Journal of Business Communication.*

6.2 A channel-ratio model of intercultural communication: the trains won't sell, fix them please

Dwight A. Haworth and Grant T. Savage

General models of communication do not focus on problems arising from intercultural interactions, nor do these models address some practical needs of business persons. The purpose of this paper is to present a channel-ratio model to address those problems and needs. The channel-ratio model divides each communication channel into an explicit and implicit component. The ratio of explicit to implicit information in the channel is culturally and contextually determined, and intercultural communication problems may be analyzed in terms of mismatches between the channel ratios of the participants. Because the model is intended for business people who do not have a strong background in communication theory, the model incorporates explicit cues to problem areas in intercultural communication and has been kept as simple as possible for ease of retention.

This presentation first discusses the problems of communication models and then examines the needs of business communicators. Next, the assumptions of the channel-ratio model, its elements, and its dynamic operation are described. Examples of the model's application to verbal and non-verbal communication are given; the cited examples are from related literature, from the authors' intercultural experiences, and from focus groups that used the model to analyze their own intercultural communication experiences. Finally, the research and training potentials of the model are discussed.

Problems of communication models

The best known communication model is the Shannon–Weaver model (1949) in which the sender encodes and transmits a message and the receiver receives and decodes the message. Timm (1986) points out four major fallacies of this model: (1) it tends to focus primarily on the message preparation skills of the sender, (2) it ignores the inferences that the receiver may draw, (3) it implies that the receiver may not communicate when in fact communication occurs concurrently, and (4) it ignores the continuous bi-directional nature of oral communication. Further, the Shannon–Weaver model has no provision for nonverbal content which may make up a large part of an intercultural exchange (Asante, 1980). Such a model is difficult to apply because it omits many aspects of communication.

Bowman and Targowski (1987) delve beneath this criticism of the Shannon–Weaver model by noting the model's philosophical roots in Hart-ley's (1949) objectivist view of the communication process as the transmission of information. By focusing on the reception of intact signals, the Shannon–Weaver model equates communication with syntax. If the receiver can replicate the same signals in the same order as they were transmitted, communication occurs. However, as Bowman and Targowski note, this definition of communication ignores both semantic (the 'subjective' meanings the signals evoke) and pragmatic (the 'action' such subjective meanings entail) levels of analysis.

Campbell and Level (1985) propose a detailed model which allows for the influence of the sender's and receiver's value systems, incorporating both a syntactic and semantic level of analysis. Their model contains fifteen signifi-cant boxes, five noise boxes, and a web of connections. The model provides for most of the known or hypothesized influences on interpersonal communi-cations; however, the model has too many components to be easily retained by the person who is being trained to practice intercultural communications. Furthermore, although their model allows for the influence of the receiver's value system, the effects of the sender's value system or cultural biases on the process of message selection are not explicit.

Targowski and Bowman (1988) put forth a layer-based model that is slightly less complex. Their model parallels in many respects the Open Systems Interconnection reference model for computer data communication established by the International Standards Organization (Stallings, 1985). The Targowski and Bowman model has ten layers that address separately various communication factors. Like the boxes of the Campbell and Level model, the layers interact, but the nature of the interaction is not described. Further, these ten layers exceed the seven-plus-or-minus two rule for human cognitive activity and may create retention problems for the student or practitioner.

Berlo (1960) presents a model of communication which allows for multiple channels of communication, the influences of the sender's and receiver's phenomenal field (expressed as communication skills, attitudes, knowledge, social system, and culture), and the message. This model does not address specifically the implicit and explicit message(s) which may be sent, nor does it address the number of the explicit messages which may be apprehended or the amount of inference which the receiver may draw. However, Berlo's model does provide a framework which suggests that communication may occur in several channels simultaneously and that several channels may be used to transmit one message, elements which would be useful in a training model.

Many of the models reported in academic writing assume a scholarly sophistication, including a knowledge of related disciplines (Smith, 1962). Business people often lack the breadth of study needed to relate reductive or ambiguous models to the situation at hand. In some situations, the user may not have time to sort through the knowledge of various disciplines and relate this knowledge to a model which does not explicitly allow for such relationships. A practitioner's model then should show relationships that might only be implied in a scholar's model.

Needs of business people

Business people need a model that is complex enough to accommodate business situations and provide insights to problems. The model must contain enough elements that users easily can relate their personal experiences and training to the model. In the cross-cultural context, the model must allow for cultural and personal differences in communication behavior and give cues to help the user. Depending on the sophistication of the user, a model may suggest potential problem areas or it may suggest specific behavior which may be effective. While simplicity is desirable for ease-of-retention, a more complex model which can be related meaningfully to experience probably will be retained better and used more than a simpler, less meaningful model.

Asante and Vora (1980) criticize the intercultural communication emphasis on how U.S. citizens adjust to other cultures and argue for a more general approach that will be useful to all, regardless of native culture. In order to simplify consideration of cultural influences, we propose a model that is, in a sense, orthogonal to noncultural models. Components of this model subsume elements of other models in order to focus on cultural influences. Such influences we believe contribute to the misinterpretation which Bowman and Targowski (1987) acknowledge is possible.

Assumptions of the model

Seven well accepted and previously articulated assumptions about human communication are incorporated in the channel-ratio model. Communication is (1) a process involving (2) both purposive and expressive messages (3) composed of multi-unit and (4) multi-level signals that (5) depend upon the context for their meanings (Knapp, 1984). Moreover, (6) communication involves explicit and implicit meanings which are apprehended directly and indirectly inferred, respectively (Habermas, 1984). Hence, (7) communication competence is dependent upon the expressive and interpretive abilities of both interactants (Spitzberg and Cupach, 1984).

As a process, communication has no determinate beginning or end; rather, it is an ongoing exchange of messages between two or more people. People exchange both intended (purposive) and unintended (expressive) messages. Misunderstanding may occur, as MacKay (1972) has noted in his discussion of goal vs. nongoal directed signals, if expressive messages are interpreted as purposive messages and vice versa. Moreover, the possibilities for this misunderstanding may be heightened – or lessened – because messages are composed of multiunit signals.

Face-to-face communication involves verbal, paraverbal, kinesic, proxemic, olfactory, and other signals apprehended by the five senses. These multi-unit signals, simultaneously exhibited, provide a configuration which typically contains both expressive and purposive messages. (Because multiple signal configurations may occur either *within* or/and *across* channels, the term multi-unit signals is more precise than multichannel signals.) If multi-unit signals are congruent, the messages are more likely to be interpreted as intended. However, if these signals are incongruent, one or another of the conflicting messages are typically discounted (Watzlawick, Bevin and Jackson 1967.) This process of misinterpretation can be further exacerbated – or resolved – by the multilevel nature of communicative signals.

At least two levels of communication – the semantic and the pragmatic – are of significance in all relevant communication. In other words, every interaction involves not only signals directed toward the *semantics* of a shared concern or topic but also signals that comment about the communication itself (Ruesch and Bateson, 1951). These meta-communicative signals may be verbal but are often nonverbal, and they provide a framework (Goffman, 1974) for understanding the purpose of the interaction, for proceeding with the interaction, and for interpreting potentially confusing multi-unit signals. As such, meta-communication centers upon the *pragmatics* of the relationship between communicators. For example, such obtrusive signals as those involving turn-taking during a conversation can indicate whether a recommendation is well received (nodding 'yes' and gesturing 'go on'), ignored (interrupting and talking over), or disapproved (a frown and silence).

Of course the specific meanings of utterances – as intended or apprehended – often depend on the context. The context provides both speakers and listeners a more-or-less shared background which can alter the literal meaning of any utterance as well as lend significance to the unspoken. Here, we can distinguish at least two ways in which the context affects the meaning of messages (Knapp, 1984). One notion of context ties it closely to the ongoing interaction of the speaker and listener. Because the present conversation is incrementally built upon the exchange of messages, each new message is framed by that exchange and affects the interpretive framework for future messages. For example, a business person's utterance, 'Let's play ball,' has only a literal, generic meaning unless its conversational context of petty grievances about working together on a project with a colleague are considered. Another notion of context brings into play the background and orientation of the two people in the conversation. This broader sense of context as an overlapping phenomenal field is what permits the speaker to assume that saying 'Let's play ball' will convey a spirit of cooperativeness based on a shared background of schoolyard play and associated expressions.

Reliance on the context for determining the meaning of expressions and actions occurs in all conversations. However, the ratio of explicit messages vs. implied messages may vary from situation to situation and from culture to culture. The conversational context provides each communicator with a reference point for assessing the extent that implied messages are being inferred as expected. On one hand, to the extent that conversational responses indicate uptake of implied messages, the communicators can 'take-for-granted' some degree of overlap in their phenomenal fields of experience. On the other hand, if implied messages are not being responded to appropriately, both communicators must use more explicit messages to establish a shared ground of understanding.

Because many times implied or inferred messages are meta-communicative in nature, misinterpretation or ignorance of these messages can quickly sour the relationship between the conversational partners. Hence, the burden of rectifying misunderstood or discounted meanings falls on both communicators. Competence within a conversation is jointly achieved.

Elements of the model

Following the lead of Berlo's adaptation of the Shannon-Weaver model, our proposed model incorporates a sender and receiver (Smith, 1962). When applied to a communication event, the model includes Berlo's five channels – sight, sound (oral–aural), touch, taste, and smell – in two directions to accommodate the concurrent, two-way nature of interpersonal communication (Berlo, 1960; Smith, 1962). However, when used to analyze specific aspects of a communication, the model can show activity in a single one-way channel.

Communication Channel

The model shows a channel between sender and receiver which is one of five which may be active in any communication session. This channel may carry messages in several modes. For example, the oral–aural channel may carry,

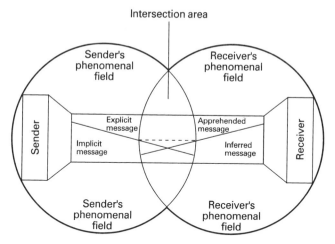

Figure 1   *Channel-ratio model of intercultural communication*

in addition to words, varying degrees of loudness, pauses, intonations, and inflections, all of which will add meaning to the denotations and connotations of the words. The content of the channel is the focus of the model.

The model shows the sender's coded message, or part of a message, in a channel. The message in the channel contains an explicit component and an implicit component which is shown by the division of the channel. The explicit contains both purposive and expressive behavior, the implicit component is made up of behavior which is absent but which conveys meaning within the conversational and cultural context. On the receiver's side, the channel is divided to show part of the total channel message is inferred and part is a portion of the explicit message apprehended by the receiver. As used in this context, 'apprehended' means the message is received, interpreted, and assimilated by the receiver. When a message is apprehended in this sense, it influences the receiver's behavior.

Phenomenal field

The phenomenal field is the ongoing combination of conscious and unconscious influences on the individual's communication behavior. The phenomenal field includes elements from Berlo's model: personal attitude, knowledge, and culture. The term 'knowledge' in this model includes the body of facts, skills, and experiences the individual has acquired, including knowledge of the other party which Hall (1976) emphasizes as being critically important. The phenomenal field is influenced by the individual's culturally conditioned perception of 'the subject or activity, the situation, and one's status in the social system' (Hall, 1976, p. 87). For this model, the influence of the cultural component of phenomenal field is a major factor. As discussed previously the phenomenal field provides the 'broader context' for implying and inferring meanings.

The first and most obvious influence of culture is on the sender's choice of symbols. Although the Berlo model has been critized for emphasizing the role of the sender-encoder, the sender-encoder is a key for understanding semantics in intercultural communications. The selection of the correct codes is paramount if explicit messages are to be interpreted as intended. The U.S. sojourner in Korea who beckons to a store clerk with the typical U.S. come-hither gesture may never be served because that particular gesture is used in Korea to call a dog. When the sender chooses to encode the message in native symbology, additional consideration must be given to choose symbols likely to be understood by the receiver. On the receiver-decoder side, similar care is necessary; although the code may be familiar, meaning should be ascribed only tentatively and verified through subsequent interaction.

Intersection area

The model shows an overlap in the phenomenal fields of the sender and receiver. This overlap area is intended to show the amount of knowledge common to both sender and receiver. Such common knowledge includes sets of symbols and meanings appropriate to the subject of the communication, specific knowledge about the topic, general background knowledge, cultural similarities, cultural awareness, information from previous interaction with the other party, and situational and environmental information. The overlap or intersection area is dynamic in any communication episode. As the topic of the conversation shifts, as the communicators develop an understanding of each other, and as the situation and environment change, the overlap area may increase or decrease. The dynamic intersection area gives the model its usefulness.

Dynamics of the model

The division of the channel is not constant. As an example, consider again the model shown in Figure 1, typical of the oral–aural channel. The division begins nearest the sender, with the channel divided so that the amount of *explicit* information is small relative to *implicit* information – a low E/I ratio. Moving away from the sender, the division is sloped so that the amount of explicit information increases and the amount of implicit information decreases. At the point when the channel crosses the boundary of the sender's phenomenal field circle, the E/I ratio reaches a maximum. A similar division occurs in the receiver's channel except the division is between apprehended explicit information and inferred information which will be called the A/I ratio. (The term E/I will be used to refer to this division in general and when referring to the sender; the term A/I will be used only to refer to the division of the receiver's channel.) Through the varying division of the channel, the model achieves its ability to accommodate dynamic interaction.

Communication episode

Within a communication episode, the point where the sender's channel enters the intersection area determines the E/I ratio on which the sender is attempting to communicate. Likewise, the point where the receiver's channel emerges from the intersection area determines the A/I ratio on which the receiver is trying to operate. Because of the way the oral–aural channel is divided, a sender and receiver with a large intersection area are able to engage in low E/I oral–aural communication. With a very small intersection area, the sender and receiver must resort to a high E/I ratio.

When a communication episode is initiated, typically there is a relatively small intersection area. In the model, the boundary of the intersection area is far from the participants, and the channel division indicates a high proportion of explicit information is required. As the episode continues, the communicators typically build mutual understanding, and the intersection area grows. This increasing overlap causes the boundary of the intersection area to move closer to both sender and receiver. This action results in the channel's crossing the boundary at a place where less explicit information is required, the messages have a lower E/I ratio, and the reception is at a lower A/I ratio.

Should the subject matter change, the communicators may find the intersection area suddenly smaller and higher E/I communication required. Failure to follow shifts of this nature leads to miscommunication. It is easy to visualize the sender who has failed to recognize a decrease in intersection area suddenly being the recipient of a relatively large number of explicit messages in the visual channel (also consistent with the high E/I requirement) for more information, a wrinkled brow, more attentive posture, an upward open palm, or other culturally appropriate signals for more explicit information. Of course, the sender must be sensitive to these messages, interpret them appropriately, and adjust the E/I ratio in the oral channel.

Cultural influences

The interpreted size of the intersection area is a critical element in any communication episode. It is subject to continuous change and may be misinterpreted by either party. An example of such an error would be a sender who believes the intersection area is large attempting to communicate at a lower E/I ratio than the receiver is expecting. Such errors aggravate the problems rising from culturally based differences in the channel ratios of the sender and receiver.

The magnitude of E/I ratio changes depends on the culturally determined division of the sender's and receiver's channels. Some cultures use subtle implication and inference – based on a shared context of experience and interaction – to exchange messages. These high context (HC) cultures, as Hall (1976) has termed them, can be contrasted to low context (LC) cultures which rely more on explicit and less on implicit messages to communicate. The division for a participant from an HC culture, may appear like a step function. According to Hall, in a familiar situation, someone from an HC culture (low E/I ratio) relies more on the context (lower E/I ratio) to convey meaning than someone from a LC culture. However, in an unfamiliar topic area, the person from an HC culture requires more explicit information and may rely less on the context (higher E/I ratio) than someone from a low context culture.

Among people from a low context culture, Hall (1976) suggests a relatively constant ratio is at work. In a familiar area, the person from an LC culture will operate at and require a higher E/I ratio than someone from an HC culture; however, in an unfamiliar area, the LC person will require and operate at a lower E/I ratio than someone from a high context culture.

Verbal examples

Table 1 presents an example of a high intersection exchange between a husband and wife as reported by Garfinkel (Ellis and Beattie, 1986, pp. 161–163). In this case, the sender and receiver are from the same culture and have the same division of the channel. Because of the large amount of common information and common experience, the intersection area is extensive. As a result, the sender relies on a large amount of implied information (a low E/I ratio), and the receiver infers a relatively large amount of information (a low A/I ratio). As indicated by the dashed line in Figure 2, only a small proportion of explicit information is expressed in the channel; the remainder of the channel carries implicit information. A successful

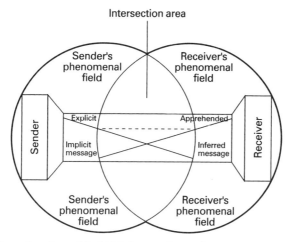

Figure 2   *Channel-ratio model of high intersection exchange*

dialogue occurs because the receiver's A/I ratio matches the sender's E/I ratio.

E/I-greater-than-A/I mismatches

In intercultural communication, even exchanges between communicators with relatively large intersection areas may go awry if one communicator uses greater explicitness than the other communicator requires. An English student who participated in an intercultural focus group, reported an example of over-explicitness in her interactions with a U.S. lab partner.[1] '[M]y chemistry lab partner, she . . . [would] tell me exactly step by step to do things. I'm on the same level she is, and I felt that she thought I was an idiot and didn't know what the difference between a test tube and a thermometer was.' Figure 3 shows a U.S. sender and an English receiver with the appropriate channel divisions. Because of channel-ratio differences between the U.S. native and the English person, the sender operated at a high E/I ratio and the receiver operated at a lower A/I ratio, resulting in the mismatch shown in Figure 3 and dissatisfaction for the receiver.

The following is an example of the type of intercultural communication problem explained by the model where even larger E/I and A/I ratio differences occurred. A Korean manufacturer contracted to produce H-O scale model trains for a United States distributor. After receiving the first shipment of model trains, the distributor sent the manufacturer a long, detailed list of discrepancies that had been found in the shipment. The discrepancies included both manufacturing flaws (welding faults, machine

Table 1   Example of high intersection exchange

What was said	*What was understood*
Husband: Dana succeeded in putting a penny in a parking meter today without being picked up.	This afternoon as I was bringing Dana, our four-year-old son, home from the nursery school, he succeeded in reaching high enough to put a penny in a parking meter when we parked in a meter zone, whereas before he had always had to be picked up to reach that high.
Wife: Did you take him to the record store?	Since he put a penny in a meter that means that you stopped while he was with you. I know that you stopped at the record store either on the way to get him or on the way back. Was it on the way back, so that he was with you or did you stop there on the way to get him and somewhere else on the way back?
Husband: No, to the shoe repair shop.	No, I stopped at the record store on the way to get him and stopped at the shoe repair shop on the way home when he was with me.
Wife: What for?	I know of one reason why you might have stopped at the shoe repair shop. Why did you in fact?
Husband: I got some new shoe laces for my shoes.	As you will remember, I broke a shoe lace on one of my brown oxfords the other day so I stopped to get some new laces.
Wife: Your loafers need new heels badly.	Something else you could have gotten that I was thinking of. You could have taken in your black loafers which need heels badly. You'd better get them taken care of pretty soon.

From H. Garfinkel (1967). *Studies in ethno-methodology*. New Jersey: Prentice-Hall, p. 34.

marks, etc.) and modelling errors (incorrect routing of pipes, wrong shape of cowcatcher, misplaced valves, etc.) The Korean manufacturer, using a culturally-based low A/I ratio, inferred more than was intended by the U.S. distributor; specifically, the manufacturer assumed that this communication was an attempt to justify a reduction in price. As a result, the manufacturer spent his effort on cutting the price and did nothing to correct the errors. Not long thereafter, the U.S. distributor cancelled the order, returned the shipment, and withdrew the letter of credit that had been established.

Shortly after this incident, the manufacturer invited a U.S. serviceman who was a model railroad enthusiast to visit his plant. This serviceman was able to explain that the type of model being produced would be sold to

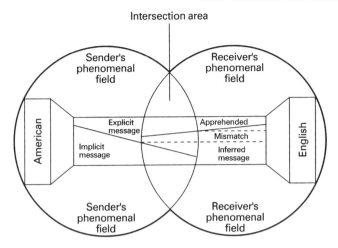

Figure 3   *U.S.A.–United Kingdom exchange described using the channel-ratio model*

serious enthusiasts who would not accept the kinds of flaws described no matter how much the price was cut. For the remainder of his tour of duty in Korea, the serviceman spent two weekends each month doing quality control checks on the models being produced and advising on the marketability of new products in the design and prototype stage.

E/I-Less-Than-A/I Mismatches

Another intercultural focus group provided an example of the problem that arises when the context changes. In this case the sender was an Israeli immigrant and the receiver was a native U.S. citizen. The U.S. native worked for the Israeli who owned two stores. Initially the U.S. native worked under the Israeli's supervision, and they developed a low E/I mode of communication. When the U.S. native was made manager of the second store, miscommunication developed over the amount of latitude the U.S. native had in discounting merchandise. Sales were lost because the U.S. native did not cut prices enough, and the Israeli owner blamed him for not cutting prices more, implying that the U.S. native should have inferred more from his position. The context had changed and the intersection area became much smaller, but the Israeli owner tried to continue to operate at the low E/I ratio. The U.S. citizen, faced with the new context, wanted more explicit information.

   Hall (1976) describes a similar low intersection exchange between a U.S. soldier and a Japanese houseboy who shines the soldier's brown shoes with black polish. The houseboy has little experience with shoes and how they

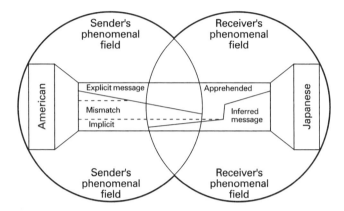

Figure 4   *U.S.A.–Japan exchange described using the channel-ratio model*

should be shined, having shined only black shoes; as a result, the intersection area is small as shown in Figure 4. Assuming that brown shoes will be shined with brown shoe polish, the U.S. sender attempts to operate at his normal E/I ratio, relatively lower than the Japanese receiver's A/I ratio, with the resulting mismatch shown in figure 4. Adequate communication occurs only when the sender increases the E/I ratio to match the A/I of the receiver by including the proper color of shoe polish.

These examples suggest that the result of a mismatch between the sender's E/I ratio and the receiver's A/I ratio will be unsatisfactory communication. The mismatch may occur in two ways, E/I-greater-than A/I or E/I-less-than-A/I. Hall (1976) discusses the result of excessive explicit information (E/I greater than A/I) and calls it 'low contexting someone.' The receiver may infer that he or she is being talked down to and may evaluate the relationship unfavorably. The English student and her U.S. lab partner are an example of this result. The U.S. soldier and the Japanese houseboy are an example of the opposite case, an E/I-less-than-A/I mismatch. In both cases, when the sender's E/I ratio does not match the receiver's A/I ratio, some adjustment must be made for satisfactory communication to occur.

Nonverbal examples

Only since 1945 has nonverbal communication become a significant field of scientific study. Both Wolfgang (1984) and Knapp (1978) acknowledge that much investigation remains to be done in regard to multi-cultural (and consequently intercultural) nonverbal behavior. They state that while there appears to be intercultural consistency of meaning in some facial expressions, the meanings of body positions and body motions seem to be culture specific. Intercultural nonverbal communication seems to be in the 'dictionary development' stage. We are aware of some of the meanings associated with specific behaviors of some cultures, but we do not have the equivalent of a U.S. 'Other Culture' dictionary for nonverbal behavior.

Through the E/I ratio, the model provides a means for assessing the relative importance of each channel in the transmission of a message. Knapp addresses the division of the message between channels when he states 'nonverbal behavior can repeat, contradict, substitute for, complement, accent, or regulate verbal behavior' (1978, p. 21). Further, he recognizes that meaningful nonverbal behavior occurs at both the intentional and the unconscious level. Both the intentional (purposive) and unconscious (expressive) are incorporated within the proposed model as explicit information; as before, implicit information is derived from the context.

However, different cultures focus for information upon different aspects of behavior which occur within the *same* context. For example, Kendon (1984, p. 88) reports that various studies of Italian and British subjects have shown that the Italian subjects were better able to identify and remember verbal descriptions of objects if those descriptions were accompanied by gestures. Gesturing, however, provided little information value to the British subjects. These studies show that explicit signals may have little meaning if the phenomenal field of the receiver is not attuned to those signals. In other words, even though the sender's nonverbal message may be explicit, the receiver must be aware of the code in order to apprehend it.

Like the verbal channel, the touch channel has a characteristic division (CD). Knapp (1978) indicates that some of the following factors influence the amount and kind of contact which is acceptable: social status, purpose of communication, role of sender and receiver, and gender of sender and receiver. These factors are the same as those which condition the content of the verbal channel.

Knapp (1978) cites Barnlund's study of U.S. and Japanese subjects which showed that the U.S. subjects engaged in almost twice the amount of touching as the Japanese. Figure 5 shows the touch channel in an exchange between a U.S. man and a Japanese man. Note that the division is sloped opposite the oral–aural channel; the explicit content increases as the participants become more familiar with each other.

This example demonstrates the use of the model to anticipate problems. Because the American sender is always inclined to a higher E/I ratio than the Japanese receiver's A/I ratio, with the attendant mismatch shown in Figure 5, the American business person may be cautioned against touching when dealing with Japanese businessmen.

The data for constructing a CD for the nonverbal channels is not available, except for occasional examples such as the previous illustration of touching. Knapp summarizes, ('We don't know much about the specifics of cultural

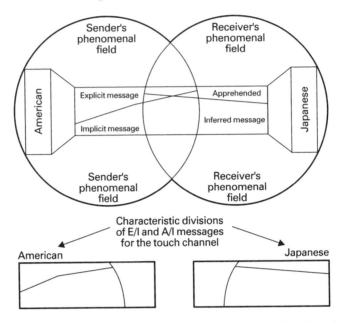

Figure 5   U.S.A.–*Japan touch channel described using the channel-ratio model*

differences in touching. We do know that there seem to be enormous differences ... (1978, p. 258).[2] A third focus group discussed such an example. The receiver is a male Chinese student who is tutoring U.S. students. The sender is a female U.S. student who has just earned a good grade on an examination after receiving tutoring from the Chinese student. She expressed her happiness with an embrace, as well as with words, to the consternation of the tutor. In this case, given the context, the Chinese CD of the touch channel was clearly at a much lower E/I ratio than the U.S. CD.

In his discussion of kinesics, Knapp (1978) cautions that his example is specific to white, upper-middle-class, adults in the U.S. His chapter on proxemics cites some cross-cultural experimental work, but the cited work gives mostly general results that allow only the grossest inferences about the CD of the visual channel. The treatment of the visual channel itself may be best addressed in terms of components which Knapp lists: environment, proxemics, appearance, kinesics, facial expression, and eye contact. Methods have been developed to analyze many of these components; in many cases all that is needed is the application of resources.

Discussion and implications

Although the channel-ratio model focuses on the E/I ratio and the intersection area, intercultural communicators must always look at the choice of symbols first. If the sender chooses language, gestures, or other behavior that may be misinterpreted by the receiver, then effective communication cannot be assumed, no matter what E/I ratios are operative. The existence of a common set of symbols is a requirement for an intersection area to exist; if no intersection area exists, there can be no communication.

Suggestions for intercultural business communication training

The channel-ratio model emphasizes cultural and contextual determinants of communicative behavior. By providing a framework in which cultural differences are compared and contrasted, business people are sensitized to culture and context. In so doing, the model may help offset the tendency to underestimate the influence of context and culture that is noted by Ehrenhaus (1983). The potential uses of the model in training follow from the cultural and contextual emphasis of the model. If trainees are being trained to operate in a foreign culture, the model may be used to prepare them for the different E/I ratio of the other culture. If the training is general, the model may be used as in this article, with a variety of examples to make the student aware of the ways intercultural communication may go awry.

Following Hall's lead, the model assumes that each culture has a characteristic division (CD) of the channel. When training business people to function in a specific foreign culture, trainees should be given a description of the characteristic division of their native culture and the CD of the target culture. By comparing the two CDs, trainees may be made aware of potential problem areas. In some cases, awareness of the other party's normal E/I ratio may be sufficient to avoid problems as would have been the case had the English student known that her U.S. classmate was not talking down to her but was merely trying to be helpful. In other cases, knowledge that specific information will not be made explicit by a participant from a low E/I culture may suggest that additional information be gathered before the conversation. The goal is not to alter the native E/I of trainees, but to make them aware of differences and to give them suggestions for coping with the differences. In addition, by being aware of the differences in the CDs of the parties in a conversation, trainees may recognize and correct problems as they emerge.

Specifically, trainees should be made aware of the ways to request background information which are acceptable within the host culture. Such instruction might include techniques for turn-taking in conversations, forms of address, and idioms for asking for clarification and explanation. Also, trainees should be exposed to videotapes or live interactions with natives from the host culture so that they may become attuned to the nonverbal signals natives use to manage conversations. For example, they should then be able to recognize nonverbal signals from others which indicate their messages are either too explicit or too implicit. Such training will enable business people to become better able to understand and manage the conversational context within a host culture.

In more general cross-cultural training, the model gives trainees a sensitivity to the taken-for-granted context underlying other cultures' interpersonal communication. Small, culturally heterogeneous groups have been found to be effective at developing examples of miscommunication explained by the model. (This technique was used by the authors to develop some of the examples for this manuscript.) Groups with greater cultural diversity tend to produce clearer, more interesting examples of how the general context may influence miscommunication. Moreover, by being aware of the kinds of problems the model identifies, trainees are able to identify the nature of the E/I mismatch without reference to specific CDs.

However, the trainee should be made aware of the variation possible in the CD of a culture. Within any culture, E/I norms may vary depending on such matters as the situation; the status, gender, and roles of the sender and receiver; and the subject of the communication. Among individuals in a culture, variances in the E/I ratios for similar situations occur because of personality or training. For example, some U.S. instructors acquire an habitually high E/I mode of oral–aural communication because they use it so much when teaching.

The model has additional pedagogical value in that it gives business people a relatively simple structure upon which to organize information. In doing so, the model may serve to pull together topics which appeared unrelated when first presented. Further, the model may indicate the general nature of information the business person does not have. The model is, therefore, a tool which may be used for independent study and observation.

Suggestions for intercultural business communication research

The channel-ratio model also satisfies in part a need enunciated by Gudykunst (1983, p. 15) when he called for theories in intercultural communication to provide 'conceptual fameworks that will give direction to the diverse research efforts taking place within it.' The model provides a structure on which to organize known information, and as a result, gaps in our knowledge are highlighted. By emphasizing the need to consider all five of the senses when communicating, this model highlights how the combination of messages must be considered by business people in order to understand the context of the conversation as well as the cultural context. Future research should focus holistically on inter-cultural communication, using among other frameworks, that offered by this model. For example, while this manuscript was being prepared, the lack of comparative information about nonverbal communication became clear as the model was extended to those areas.

The model itself poses several questions. Given a high E/I sender and a low A/I receiver, to what degree does the mismatch disrupt communication and in which channel, if any, does the receiver signal dissatisfaction? Is the channel used for the dissatisfaction signal dependent on the culture? Is the dissatisfaction signal itself dependent on culture? Which cultures are similar in these respects? These same questions are appropriate for the reverse situation, a low E/I sender and a high A/I receiver. Other questions follow logically. Within a culture, is the dissatisfaction signal and its channel dependent on context? What are the interaction effects between culture and context relative to a particular type of communication mismatch?

Given that communication is a two-way process, in which channels are feedback, agreement, disagreement, and support transmitted? What is the appropriate E/I ratio for feedback? To what degree do these two, feedback channel and feedback E/I ratio, vary with culture and context?

To apply the model in more than a general, qualitative sense, specific research to develop the characteristic division for each channel is required. Such research will depend on several antecedents. Before the CD may be developed, observations of communication behavior over a range of situations must be made in each culture. A starting point for data collection may be found in the soap operas and other dramatic programs broadcast on national television by various cultures across the world. Most, if not all, of these programs depict business people in various situations – including business lunches, business meetings, routine business and office interactions, and entertaining business partners. Even though these TV programs may distort and over-emphasize certain cultural norms (and de-emphasize others), they provide a rich source of information on many aspects of characteristic channel divisions within specific cultures. However, before observations such as these can be made, researchers should develop a set of standardized attributes to define and allow precise recording of the situations and behaviors of interest.

Pedagogically, the model should be evaluated in a variety of settings. In addition to the suggested training, the model may be useful in language training to guide students in making their communication more like that of native speakers. Conceivably, there are three distinctly different pedagogical applications for the model: in foreign language training, in culturally specific (nonlanguage) training, and in general intercultural communication training.

In conjunction with evaluating the model in each of these settings, a set of standardized tests could be developed to measure trainee learning and a follow-up evaluation questionnaire developed to be administered after the trainee enters the intercultural communication arena. Naturally, training materials relevant to the model should also be developed. All of these materials are necessary for conducting a two-treatment experiment to evaluate the effectiveness of the model.

Summary

The proposed model provides a structure to organize information about intercultural communication. The structure, which incorporates seven recognized assumptions about human communication, is based on the ratio between explicit information and implicit information in each of the five sensory channels. Culturally determined norms provide the basis for the ratio, and the communication context determines the appropriate value of the ratio at any moment during the communication episode. The culturally determined basis for the ratio is called the characteristic divisions for the channel. To the extent that the characteristic divisions of the sender's and receiver's channels are accurately known, possible intercultural communication problems may be identified.

The usefulness of the model in specific cross-cultural combinations may be limited because data about explicit and implicit channel content may not exist for one or more channels in one or both cultures. In such cases, the model serves to identify gaps in our knowledge which should be filled. Examples of such gaps and the questions which follow from them are discussed.

The model is intended to assist trainers and business people in organizing and relating information about specific cultures. Because it is intended that the model provide relevant insights to business people operating in the intercultural arena, the model has been crafted for ease of learning and retention. The application of the model to culture-specific training is discussed. Examples of communication problems and their analysis, drawn from training sessions, are used to demonstrate the application of the model to general intercultural communication training.

The potential for the model to improve the practice of intercultural communication and to foster needed research in intercultural communication is advocated. It is hoped that application of this model may not only help Koreans to sell toy trains, but also help U.S. business people to buy them.

Endnotes

1 The examples used here, and as indicated in other parts of this manuscript, are based on transcripts of six intercultural focus groups. The authors conducted these focus groups as part of a four-hour training workshop in May, 1988, for international management students from Africa, Asia, Europe, North America, and South America. Most of the participants were graduate students with significant business experience in their native countries, although some of the participants were undergraduates from the U.S. Each focus group included five to six participants, with representatives from three to four different countries. First, the six groups were briefed on the elements and dynamics of the model for approximately 20 minutes. Second, each group met for about 45 minutes to discuss and analyze – using the channel-ratio model – incidents of cross-cultural miscommunication that the members had experienced. Third, representatives from each focus group presented a 5- to 10-minute synopsis of the incidents discussed and analyzed by their respective focus groups. During these presentations, participants freely commented and inquired about the incidents and their analyses.
2 Although Knapp's remarks certainly are dated, they remain accurate. Computer searches of the psychological, sociological, and linguistic data bases revealed that little substantial work has been conducted since the mid-1970s in the intercultural study of touch. Moreover, those studies that have been conducted shed little light on adult cross-cultural communication. Almost all of the recent cross-cultural studies of touch have examined infant–mother interactions.

References

Asante, M. K. (1980). Intercultural communication: An inquiry into research directions. In *Communication yearbook 4*. New Brunswick, NJ: Transaction Books, pp. 401–410.

Asante, M. K. and Vora, E. (1983). Toward multiple philosophical approaches. In *Intercultural communication theory*. Beverly Hills: Sage Publications, pp. 293–298.

Berlo, D. K. (1960). *The process of communication*. New York: Holt, Rinehart and Winston.

Bowman, J. P. and Targowski, A. S. (1987). Modeling the communication process: The map is not the territory. *The Journal of Business Communication, 24*(4), 21–34.

Campbell, D. P. and Level, D. (1985). A black box model of communications. *The Journal of Business Communication, 22*(3), 37–47.

Ehrenhaus, P. (1983). Culture and the attribution process. In *Intercultural communication theory* (pp. 259–270). Beverly Hills: Sage publications.

Ellis, A. and Beattie, G. (1986). *The psychology of language and communication*. New York: The Guilford Press.

Goffman, E. (1974). *Frame analysis*. New York: Harper & Row.

Gudykunst, W. B. (1983). Theorizing in intercultural communication. In *Intercultural communication theory* (pp. 13–20). Beverly Hills: Sage Publications.

Habermas, J. (1984). Intermediate reflections: Social action, purpositive activity, and communication. In *The theory of communicative action: Reason and the rationalization of society*. T. McCarthy, Trans. Boston: Beacon Press.

Hall, E. T. (1976). *Beyond culture*. New York: Anchor Press.

258 *Cross-cultural Management*

Hartley, R. V. L. (1949). Transmission of information. *Bell System Technical Journal*, *28*, 535.

Kendon, A. (1984). Did gesture have the happiness to escape the curse at the confusion of Babel? In A. Wolfgang (Ed.), *Nonverbal behavior: Perspectives, applications, intercultural insights*. Lewiston, NY: C. J. Hogrefe, Inc.

Knapp, M. L. (1984). The study of nonverbal behavior *vis-à-vis* human communications theory. In A. Wolfgang (Ed.), *Nonverbal behavior: Perspectives, applications, intercultural insights*. Lewiston, NY: C. J. Hogrefe, Inc.

Knapp, M. L. (1978) *Nonverbal communication in human interaction*. New York: Holt, Rinehart, and Winston.

MacKay, D. M. (1972) Formal analysis of communicative processes. In R. A. Hinde (Ed.), *Non-verbal communication*. New York: Cambridge University Press.

Ruesch, J. and Bateson, G. (1951). *Communication: The social matrix of society*. New York: W. W. Norton.

Shannon, C. and Weaver, W. (1949). *The mathematical theory of communication*. Urbana, IL: University of Illinois Press.

Smith, R. L. (1962). General models of communication – Special Report No. 5. *Summer Conference of the National Society for the Study of Communication*.

Spitzberg, B. H. and Cupach, W. R. (1984). *Interpersonal communication competence*. Beverly Hills: Sage Publications.

Stallings, W. (1985). *Data and computer communications*. New York: Macmillan Publishing Company.

Targowski, A. S. and Bowman, J. P. (1988). The layer-based, pragmatic model of the communication process. *The Journal of Business Communication*, *25*(1), 5–24.

Timm, P. R. (1986). *Managerial communication*. Englewood Cliffs, NJ: Prentice-Hall.

Watzlawick, P., Beavin, J. D. and Jackson, D. D. (1967). *Pragmatics of human communication: A study of interactional patterns, pathologies, and paradoxes*. New York: W. W. Norton and Company.

Wolfgang, A. (1984). State of the art of nonverbal behavior in intercultural counselling. In A. Wolfgang (Ed.), *Nonverbal behavior: Perspectives, applications, intercultural insights*, Lewiston, NY: C. J. Hogrefe, Inc.

Reproduced from Haworth, D. A. and Savage, G. T. (1989). A channel-ratio model of intercultural communication: the trains won't sell, fix them please. *Journal of Business Communication*, **26** (3), 231–54, by permission of *Journal of Business Communication*.

7 International negotiation

7.1 Understanding the domain of cross-national buyer–seller interactions

Sudhir H. Kale and John W. Barnes

Conducting business across international boundaries requires interaction with people and their organizations nurtured in different cultural environments. Jain (1989) observes that more than any other function of a business, marketing is perhaps the most susceptible to cultural error. Consequently, it is in the area of international marketing that most of the 'international business blunders' occur (Colvin, Heeler and Thorpe 1980; Ricks 1983; Sheth 1983).

Scholars in marketing have been acutely aware that cultural differences across societies have to be taken into account when making marketing mix decisions (Clark 1990; Graham 1988; Jain 1989; Kreutzer 1988; Martenson 1987). Surprisingly, however, there is little in the literature that addresses the impact of culture on cross-national personal selling interactions, except for a very few notable exceptions (cf. Graham 1983, 1985; Graham et al. 1988; McGee and Spiro 1991; and for an excellent review see Cavusgil and Nevin 1981). With the increasing globalization of business for most industries, cross-cultural negotiations and interactions have become a 'fact of life' for many companies. With the push toward increasing economic co-operation, especially among Western European economies, the importance of understanding the cultural domain of personal selling becomes even more vital (cf. *Wall Street Journal*, 1989). The ever increasing opportunities to market products and services globally cannot be optimally capitalized upon unless the cultural domain of the buyer–seller dyad is better understood. The stage is set for researchers and practitioners to move beyond anecdotes, simplistic associations, and fragmented studies toward a better conceptual grasp of the various factors unique to cross-national personal selling.

The aim of this article is to provide a conceptual framework within which cross-national personal selling interactions can be studied, evaluated, and integrated. We propose that cross-national interactions are largely influenced by three distinct, yet highly inter-related constructs: national character, organizational culture, and individual personality. We further contend that research using each of these constructs has thus far been thwarted by the lack of a commonly acceptable and measurable typology for each construct. An understanding of the domain of each of these constructs for each actor in the dyad may be enhanced by the use of a parsimonious but quantifiable typology. Such a typology should facilitate better descriptive and normative theories of cross-national personal selling.

This paper has three broad objectives: (1) to explain the impact of national character, organizational culture and individual personality on dyadic sales encounters; (2) to suggest an appropriate typology with which to evaluate, analyze, and measure each of these constructs; and (3) to offer suggestions on how this three-construct conceptual framework can help practitioners to better comprehend cross-national sales negotiations.

A comprehensive conceptualization of the buyer–seller interaction process in an international context serves several functions. First, it encourages more systematic research that takes into account many interdependent phenomena relevant to understanding the buyer–seller interaction process. Second, it points out new areas of research that invariably originate from a comprehensive perspective. Finally, it can set an agenda of priority issues in this important area.

Conceptual framework

The foreign sales force of a multinational company could include three types of personnel: (1) the ex-patriate salesperson working in a foreign country; (2) the foreign salesperson working at home for a subsidiary of a foreign company; and (3) the 'cosmopolitan' salesperson – an expatriate who works in many foreign countries (Cateora 1990). The level of psychological overlap in communication between the buyer and the seller will vary across these three situations. Further, the impact of various factors constituting national character, organizational culture, and actor personality on the sales interaction will also vary. None of the earlier articles addressing cross-national personal selling issues have clarified in which of the three situations their findings or conceptual import applies. The framework developed for this article is equally applicable to all three situations. The level of abstraction of the proposed framework is such that it can be used for comparative studies, cross-national studies, and even domestic studies. The underlying constructs of this framework have been depicted in Figure 1.

A personal selling transaction can be visualized along two components: content and style (Sheth 1983; Steinberg and Miller 1975). Content refers to the substantive aspects of the interaction for which the buyer and seller come together. Sheth (1976, 1983) explains that the content of a personal selling interaction involves suggesting, offering, or negotiating a set of

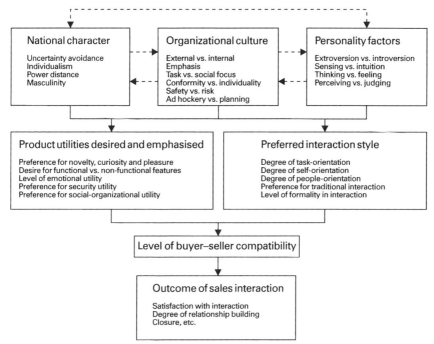

Figure 1 *Cultural and personality dimensions affecting cross-national buyer–seller interactions*

product-specific utilities and their expectations. Style, on the other hand, refers to the rituals, format, mannerisms, and ground-rules that the buyer and the seller follow in their encounter. A satisfactory interaction between the buyer and the seller (e.g. positive negotiation outcome, satisfaction with the negotiation process, etc.) will be contingent upon buyer–seller compatibility with respect to *both* the content and style of communication (cf. Spiro and Weitz 1990; Weitz 1981; Williams and Spiro 1985).

Although the dimensions of content and style offer a convenient approach to visualize an international sales transaction, past research has not clearly delineated their components (Sheth 1983; Weitz 1981). A broad review of literature in marketing, sociology, and psychology suggests that both the content and style of a dyadic interaction are shaped by (1) national character, (2) organizational culture, and (3) individual personality of actors. Further refinement in theory construction and successful practical application necessitates appropriate operational frameworks for assessing each of these constructs, and for appreciating their likely inter-relationships. A workable typology of these constructs is needed so that each construct may be succinctly defined, accurately measured, and meaningfully related with other constructs. Drawing on the literature in sociology, organizational behavior, and psychology, we suggest an appropriate framework within which each of the three constructs can be investigated.

National character

Culture has a profound impact on the way consumers perceive and behave (Clark 1990; Hall 1976, 1983). The level of aggregation of this construct, however, has always been somewhat problematic. In the realm of international marketing, culture has been typically visualized at the national level (Douglas and Dubois 1977; Graham 1985; Hoover, Green and Saegert 1978). Even here, operationalization has been difficult because of a wide divergence of definitions, each reflecting different paradigms from varying disciplines (e.g. psychology, sociology, anthropology, etc.). The key problem in any discussion of national cultures involves the confusion between etic and emic measures. Etic instruments are culture-free and can be employed in several countries or cultures (Elder 1976). Emic instruments, on the other hand, are designed to study a phenomenon within only a single country or culture (Berry 1969). Since etic instruments are often very difficult to develop, most past research has relied on emic measures, thus making cross-cultural comparisons all the more elusive.

In this regard, the construct of 'national character' seems most promising (Clark 1990). This construct incorporates both economic and cultural aspects; as such, it is ideally suited to studying marketing exchanges. As Duesenberry (1949) observed over four decades ago, all of the activities in which people engage are culturally determined, and nearly all purchases and economic exchanges are undertaken either to provide physical comfort or to implement the activities that make up the life of a culture.

Hofstede (1980) defines national character as the 'collective mental programming' of people in an environment. As such, it is not a characteristic of individuals, but of a large number of persons conditioned by similar background, education, and life experiences. In a similar vein, Clark (1990, p. 66) offers the following working definition, 'National character describes the pattern of enduring personality characteristics found among the populations of nations.' Researchers have identified several dimensions of national character (Eysenck and Eysenck 1969; Hall 1959; Hofstede 1980; Inkeles and Levinson 1969; Kluckhohn and Stodtbeck 1961). Of these, Hofstede's four-dimensional framework appears to be most comprehensive. These dimensions are uncertainty avoidance, individualism, power distance, and masculinity. The four dimensions show meaningful relationships with important demographic, geographic, economic, and political national indicators (Triandis 1982).

Uncertainty avoidance (UAI) assesses the way in which societies react to the uncertainties and ambiguities inherent in daily living. At one extreme, weak UAI societies socialize members to accept and handle uncertainty without much discomfort. People in these societies tend to accept each day as it comes, take risks rather easily, and show a relatively greater tolerance for opinions and behaviors different from their own. The other extreme – strong UAI societies – feel threatened by ambiguity and uncertainty. Consequently, such societies emphasize the strong need to control environment, events, and situations. Based on Hofstede's research, Belgium, Japan, and France display strong uncertainty avoidance. Denmark, Sweden, and Hong Kong could be characterized as weak UAI societies; the United States is somewhat in the middle.

The dimension of individualism (IDV) describes the relationship between an individual and his or her fellow individuals, the collectivity which prevails in society. One extreme contains societies with very loose ties between individuals. Such societies allow a large degree of freedom, and everybody is expected to take care of themselves and their nuclear family. The other extreme expects people to watch after the interests of their in-group and to hold only those opinions and beliefs sanctioned by the group. These collective societies show tight integration. The United States, Great Britain, and the Netherlands display strong individualism, while countries such as Ecuador, Pakistan, and Taiwan gravitate toward the other extreme.

Power distance (PDI) involves a society's solution to inequality. People possess unequal physical and intellectual capabilities, which some societies allow to grow into inequalities in power and wealth. Some other societies, those characterized by a small power distance, de-emphasize such inequalities and strive toward maintaining a relative equity in the distribution of power, status, and wealth. The Philippines, India, and France all display relatively large power distance. Austria, Israel, and Denmark depict relatively small PDI, while the United States lies in the mid-range of the PDI continuum.

Masculinity (MAS) pertains to the extent to which societies hold values traditionally regarded as predominantly masculine or feminine. Examples of 'masculine' values include assertiveness, respect for the super-achiever, and the acquisition of money and material possessions. 'Feminine' values include nurturing, concern for the environment, and championing the underdog. Japan, Austria, and Italy are examples of typically masculine societies, while Norway, Sweden, the Netherlands, and Denmark show strong feminine characteristics.

Each of these dimensions can be quantified and measured, allowing researchers a quantitative assessment of the degree to which two or more societies differ in their character. In this regard, Hofstede's framework and its etic dimensions are indeed preferable to some of the earlier systems of cultural classification (cf. Hall 1959, 1983; Inkeles and Levinson 1969; Parsons and Shils 1951).

Organizational culture

Organizational culture encompasses the pattern of shared values and beliefs which enables people within the organization to understand its functioning, and furnishes them with behavioral norms (Deshpande and Parasuraman 1986; Deshpande and Webster 1989; Sathe 1984; Wilkins 1983). The values inculcated by an organization along with the behaviors it prescribes should have a discernible impact on a salesperson's (or buyer's) content and style of interaction (Apasu, Jchikawa and Graham 1987; Deshpande and Webster 1989; Weitz, Sujan and Sujan 1986). Deshpande and Webster (1989) assert that the marketing concept in itself is a manifestation of a firm's organizational culture (also see Norburn *et al*. 1990).

While extremely crucial in its import, the construct of organizational culture has been quite difficult to operationalize. Multiple definitions have caused the concept to remain fuzzy and elusive. Furthermore, except for the last five years, empirical work in this area has been conspicuously lacking (cf. Hofstede *et al*. 1990). A notable attempt to identify and operationalize the dimensions of organizational culture from a broad-based perspective was undertaken by Reynolds (1986).

Based on the premise that reliable procedures for the measurement of organizational culture are sorely needed, Reynolds (1986) identified fourteen aspects of organizational culture based on earlier works by Ansoff (1979), Deal and Kennedy (1982), Harrison (1978), Hofstede (1980), and Peters and Waterman (1982). From a marketing perspective, five aspects seem to be vital, particularly in understanding dyadic interactions: (1) External versus Internal Emphasis; (2) Task versus Social Focus; (3) Conformity versus Individuality; (4) Safety versus Risk; and (5) Ad Hockery versus Planning. These five aspects of organizational culture are logically and empirically independent.

An organization with an external emphasis underscores the task of satisfying customers, clients, or whatever. The other end of this dimension places a relatively greater accent on internal organizational activities and a producer orientation. The outward orientation resulting from an external emphasis will make firms more market-driven as opposed to product-driven.

The dimension of task versus social focus contrasts the relative priorities of an organization between organizational work versus concern for the personal and social needs of its members. In recognition of the fact that an organization is a complex social system, firms with a social focus consciously try to accommodate the social needs of their members in terms of status, esteem, and a sense of belonging. Firms with a purely task-driven focus will strive toward almost robotic efficiency in the attainment of their financial and growth objectives.

The dimension of conformity versus individuality assesses an organization's degree of tolerance of distinctiveness and idiosyncrasy among its members. One extreme encourages homogeneity in work habits, dress, and even personal life while the other tolerates considerable within-group variation. Thus, firms emphasizing conformity portray a homogeneous organizational image, and strive toward the perpetuation of that stereotype. Firms which encourage individuality display an appreciation of diversity among their members, allowing greater latitude in member lifestyles and behaviors.

An organization's response to risk is an important dimension of organizational culture, particularly in a fluid and rapidly changing business environment. One extreme depicts the tendency to be cautious and conservative in adopting new methods and practices while the other is a predisposition to change when confronted with new challenges and opportunities. Firms motivated by safety will typically be slow in decisionmaking, particularly when it comes to decisions involving the global marketplace. In pursuit of safety, they will be prone to curtail the level of autonomy of their members. Firms thriving on risk will typically want to be pioneers, be it in product development or in entering new markets. They will also allow their executives a fair degree of autonomy, and a chance to learn through experimentation.

Ad hockery versus planning captures inter-organizational variations in the tendency to anticipate and plan for change. Some organizations create ad hoc responses to all changes, while others may opt for elaborate plans that anticipate most future scenarios. Planning-oriented firms will be typically drawn to elaborate forecasting, mathematical modelling, and economic analysis. Firms practicing ad hockery will rely less on forecasts and numbers, and more on intuition.

Reynolds (1986) uses a reliable and field-tested questionnaire to capture each of the five dimensions of organizational culture discussed above. With minor modifications, this questionnaire should prove effective in measuring organizational culture in marketing-related studies.

Personality factors

Dyadic communication takes place between individuals. Conditioned by the broader social environment at various levels (such as the family, school, and organization), people nevertheless exert their personality traits or individual preferences. The concept of personality has been called one of the 'great' topics of behavioral sciences (Wilkie 1986). Drawing on commonality among hundreds of different definitions, personality can best be defined as an individual's consistency in behaviors and reactions to events. The focus of this research lies in classifying individuals into 'types' of people. Kassarjian and Sheffet (1981) counted over 200 articles on personality in the marketing literature. Most of these focus almost exclusively on consumer behavior and employ popular tests such as the Edwards Personal Preference Schedule (EPPS), Horney's CAD Scale, the Minnesota Multiphasic Personality Inventory (MMPI), etc. In general, there has been a lukewarm response to the use of personality tests in consumer behavior studies. This is probably due to the inability of personality tests to consistently predict brand and product preferences. Wilkie (1986) concludes that although personality does not dominate all other factors that bear on consumer behavior, it does exert an influence. Given the face-to-face nature of most buyer–seller encounters, we believe that personality tests will have a greater applicability in understanding such interactions than they do in predicting brand preferences.

Most research on personality variables in personal selling looks at the relationship between salesperson personality and job performance (cf. Aaker and Bagozzi 1979; Bagozzi 1978; Churchill, Ford and Walker 1979; Teas, Wacker and Hughes 1979, and for a review of earlier work relating salesperson personality to on-the-job performance, see Weitz 1979. Buyer–seller similarity along dimensions involving personality and demographics has also been a topic of considerable interest to researchers in marketing (cf. Busch and Wilson 1976; Churchill, Collins and Strang 1975; Evans 1963. The findings thus far have been inconclusive, and more effort is needed toward a better understanding of the impact of buyer–seller similarity on the outcome of a sales transaction.

Research in social psychology suggests that personality dimensions significantly affect the effectiveness and outcome of dyadic communication (Padgett and Wolosin 1980; Runkel 1956). Individual personality exerts a significant influence on both the content and the style of dyadic interactions (Kroeger and Thuesen 1988). The proposed method of operationalizing actors' personalities within a dyad, and one that has not yet been operationalized in marketing studies, is the Myers–Briggs Type Indicator (MBTI). This approach is gaining considerable attention in the psychological, educational, and organizational disciplines (cf. Buchanan and Taylor 1986; Carlyn 1977; Giovanni, Berens and Cooper 1986; Keirsey and Bates 1978, Myers and Myers 1980; Moore 1987.

Based on Carl Jung's pioneering work on psychological types, the MBTI describes valuable differences in the ways people see the world, make decisions, choose careers, and communicate with one another. It identifies sixteen different patterns of preferences and action which are based on four dimensions: extroversion versus introversion (E or I), sensing versus intuition (S or N), thinking versus feeling (T or F), and perceiving versus judging (P or J). Figure 2 is a brief description of the sixteen personality types identified by MBTI.

Extroverts typically are oriented to the outer world of people and things; introverts gravitate toward their inner world of ideas and feelings. Thus,

		Sensing types (S)		Intuitive types (N)	
		Thinking (T)	Feeling (F)	Feeling (F)	Thinking (T)
Introverted types (I)		ISTJ Hard working, focused on facts, details, and results. Like structure, order, and privacy in work setting. Like tangible products and concrete accomplishments.	ISFJ Quiet, friendly, responsible and conscientious. Prefer organizations offering security and work-settings that are clearly structured with practical service-oriented outcomes.	INFJ Prefer quiet and organized work setting that allows time and space for reflection. Succeed by perseverance. Respected for their firm principles.	INTJ Decisive and intellectual, focused on designing future strategies and visions. Skeptical, critical, independent, determined and often stubborn.
		ISTP Prefer project-oriented work-settings. Active independent problem-solvers, unconstrained by rules. Usually interested in impersonal principles, the how and why of things.	ISFP Sensitive, modest, kind, and loyal. Shun disagreements. Often relaxed about getting things done. Place a high value on aesthetic needs.	INFP Care about learning, ideas, language, and independent projects. Hate competition and bureaucracy. Tend to undertake too much, then somehow get it done.	INTP Independent thinkers focused on solving complex problems. Quiet, reserved and impersonal. Little liking for parties or small talk.
Extroverted types (E)		ESTP Lively results-oriented people who use first-hand experience to solve problems. Enjoy technical problems for which they can use their powers of observation.	ESFP Lively, action-oriented, and harmonious. Like sports and making things. Find remembering facts easier than mastering theories.	ENFP Imaginative people focused on human possibilities. Crave novelty, variety, challenge and freedom from tight supervision. Idea-oriented and creative.	ENTP Enjoy working in environments that favor change, are flexible, reward risk, and focus on competency. Resourceful in solving challenging problems but may neglect routine assignments.
		ESTJ Task-oriented, structured, organized and hard-working. Prefer stability, predictability and efficiency. Not interested in subjects they see no use for.	ESFJ Warm-hearted talkative, popular, conscientious, born cooperators. Tend to operate on actual facts and realities like things to be organized.	ENFJ Sociable, popular, sensitive to praise and criticism. Like people-oriented, supportive, and organized work environment. Enjoy leading and facilitating teams.	ENTJ Results-oriented, tough-minded and independent. Demand efficiency from both the systems and people with whom they work. Often fiercely competitive.

Key: I = Introversion, E = Extroversion, S = Sensing, N = Intuition, T = Thinking, F = Feeling, J = Judgment, P = Perception
Source: Myers and Myers (1980) and Hirsh and Kummerow (1989)

Figure 2 *Thumbnail sketch of sixteen personality profiles*

while terms like sociability, interaction, and external focus would categorize an extrovert's life, apt descriptors for the lifestyle of an introvert's would be territoriality, concentration, and internal focus.

A sensing person shows a marked preference for facts whereas the intuitive person finds appeal in the metaphor and enjoys vivid imagery. Sensing types sniff out detail while intuitive people prefer to focus on the big picture. Words like sensible, down-to-earth, and practical would fit the sensing types. Intuitive types could be best described by words like imaginative, innovative, and ingenious.

The thinking–feeling dimension encompasses the basis for people's decision-making in life. While thinkers want to decide things logically and objectively, feelers base their decisions on more subjective grounds. Words like objective, principle, and analysis typify the decisionmaking of thinkers, while the feeler's decisionmaking could be characterized as subjective, value-based, and sympathetic.

The perceiving types tend to be flexible in life, always seeking more information. Persons who seek closure over open options are the judging types. Js prefer life to be settled, decided, and fixed; Ps opt for life to be in the pending, data gathering, and flexible mode. Judgers display a preference for organizing and controlling events of the outside world, whereas perceivers are primarily interested in observing and understanding such events.

Over two decades in wide use, the MBTI has been used to assess people's preferences in a variety of situations. In 1986 alone, over 1.5 million people took the test, 40% of them in the corporate world (Moore 1987). Companies such as Apple, AT&T, Citicorp, and 3M routinely use MBTI in their management development programs. Extremely simple in its administration, this test has nevertheless demonstrated convincing construct validity in relation to similar constructs on other scales such as the AVL, EPPS, PRI, and the Rokeach Dogmatism Scale. A review of the literature in social sciences suggests that in 1984, references to the MBTI occurred in at least twenty-three business journals, thirty education journals, twenty-four medical journals, thirty-seven psychology journals, eight science journals, three religious journals, and fourteen other specific professional journals (Willis 1987). These numerous studies have led scholars in psychometrics to conclude that, 'The MBTI is a good instrument based on its substantive theoretical and empirical bases' (Willis 1987, p. 334).

We therefore advocate the use of the Myers–Briggs typology in effectively discerning a person's preferences with regard to both the content and the style in a personal selling situation.

Interrelationships between constructs

As suggested in Figure 1, the constructs of national character, organizational culture, and individual personality collectively determine the preferred mode of content and style for each actor in the sales dyad. Furthermore, the manifested impact of any one construct will be tempered or amplified by the other two constructs. For example, an actor nurtured in a national character of high individualism may suppress his or her individualistic tendencies when functioning in a corporate environment characterized by strong conformity. Similarly, a perceiving type's behavior may be tempered by a planning-oriented organizational culture. Which behavioral characteristics are ultimately manifested in an interaction will ultimately depend upon the strength of national character, the robustness of corporate acculturation, and the strength of preferences along the four dimensions of personality.

In the organizational context, some self-selection in matching personality types to organizational cultures is evident (Deal and Kennedy 1982). Perceivers tend to gravitate to a company characterized by ad hockery and risks, whereas the sensing types tend to thrive in an organizational culture that emphasizes planning and safety. Extroverts will feel more comfortable in an organization with an external emphasis, whereas feelers will tend to choose organizations with a social focus (Hirsh and Kummerow 1989).

There will be a strong relationship between national character and individual personalities as well. A nation's character is, after all, shaped by the preferences and predispositions of its habitants. Clark (1990) visualizes national character as the pattern of enduring personality characteristics of a country's population. Thus, a society characterized by strong uncertainty avoidance would have relatively more judging types in its population than it would perceivers. One could also speculate that masculine cultures will have more thinkers than feelers in their populations. We will now take a closer look at how the three constructs in our framework affect the content and style in dyadic interactions.

Effect on sales interactions

Recall that the content of a sales interaction involves suggesting, offering, and negotiating a set of product-specific utilities and their expectations. *Functional Utility* is concerned with a product's performance, i.e. the value of a product as is solely determined by the functions it is designed to perform. *Social-Organizational Utility* (or disutility) results from the identification of a product with a selective set of demographic, socioeconomic, or organizational types, producing social imagery. *Emotional Utility* arises out of a product being associated with emotions and feelings such as respect, love, anger, and fear. *Epistemic Utility* has its roots in people's desire for novelty, curiosity, and the exploration of new product offerings. *Security Utility* deals with reduction of perceived risk associated with the purchase and consumption of products (cf. Sheth 1976).

A product typically contains a vector of each of these utilities, and consumers will strive to enhance the total perceived utility in their purchases. The relative importance that buyers and sellers place on the various utilities will be impacted by the three constructs suggested in Figure 1.

Communication style in the salesperson–customer dyad has received some attention in marketing literature (cf. Sheth 1976, 1983; Williams and Spiro 1985). Style refers to the rituals, ground-rules, mannerisms, and format followed in communication. *Self-Oriented Style* depicts the communication of one who is more concerned about his or her own needs than those of others, more interested in extrinsic as opposed to intrinsic rewards, and relatively open about airing his or her own status or esteem. *Task-Oriented Style* refers to a preference for accomplishing the transaction at hand with a minimum expenditure of time, money, and effort. *Interaction-Oriented Style* has been characterized by a preference for establishing a personal rapport with the dyadic partner, sharing things with others, and fostering the security of belonging. *Tradition-Oriented Style* implies a preference for following the rituals in a transaction that have been set by others and followed over the course of generations. National character, organizational culture, and personality of the participants in the dyad will have a significant impact on interaction style.

National character

The dimensions of uncertainty avoidance, individualism, power distance, and masculinity broadly shape the aspects of content and style for each actor in the sales dyad. A buyer conditioned (or programmed) in a national character of strong uncertainty avoidance should typically prefer uncertainty-reducing attributes in a product offering. Facets such as established brand name, superior warranty, and money-back guarantee should be very important in the choice processes of strong UAI societies. Thus, security utility will be valued more in strong UAI cultures than in weak UAI cultures. Similarly, 'environment-friendly' products such as biodegradable bags should find greater appeal in the relatively feminine Scandinavian countries than they would in masculine countries such as Venezuela and Italy.

Countries displaying high individualism (such as the United States) place a significantly greater emphasis on seeking variety and pleasure as compared to the relatively collectivist societies (such as Yugoslavia and Ecuador). Thus, product attributes designed to offer the epistemic utility will be more valued by American consumers than they would by consumers in Ecuador. Similarly, large power distance societies such as Venezuela and Mexico would emphasize the 'status' value of a particular product, rather than its functional utility, to a greater extent than would small power distance cultures such as Denmark and Austria.

The four dimensions of national character should also shape the preferred style of communication. Hofstede (1980) observes that cultures displaying strong uncertainty avoidance also experience greater stress and anxiety when compared to weak UAI societies. Anxiety is often manifested into the level of aggressiveness displayed in social interactions. Thus, people nurtured in weak UAI cultures should evince greater receptivity to a soft-sell approach and non-aggressive sales techniques. Strong uncertainty avoidance societies, on the other hand, would show relatively greater preference and tolerance for the hard-sell approaches. Collective societies aim at the welfare of everyone; individualistic societies focus on the relative maximization of self-interest. Graham *et al.* (1988) have investigated the use of the problem-solving approach (PSA) in sales negotiations. At one end of the PSA continuum are negotiation behaviors best characterized as cooperative, integrative, and interaction-oriented. At the other end of the scale are negotiation behaviors described as competitive and individualistic. The use of PSA should be more pronounced in low-IDV (or collective) societies than in high-IDV (or individualistic) cultures.

Power distance will also impact style by way of the role of each negotiator in a sales transaction. Schmidt (1979) and Graham (1988) have observed that in a large PDI society such as Japan, the seller has been considered 'little more than a beggar.' Thus, in terms of style, sellers will have to be respectful and subservient to their buyers in large-PDI societies. Another manifestation of power distance is the willingness to trust other people. Large PDI societies typically view others as a threat and, as a result, show less inclination to trust others. Conversely, people in small power distance societies feel less threatened by others and tend to trust them more. Accordingly, people in large power distance societies (e.g. the Arab countries) will discuss business only after developing trust in the salesperson. Thus, the no-nonsense task-oriented style of interaction may work well in the predominantly small PDI countries of Western Europe but would backfire in the Middle East. One could also surmise that cultures depicting strong uncertainty avoidance will show resistance to change, and may thus prefer the tradition-oriented style of interaction.

Organizational culture
Lebas and Weigenstein (1986) contend that 'culture control' is increasingly used to replace rules-based control in an attempt to enhance productivity within organizations. Organizational culture of the buyer and the seller firms should have a distinct impact on the content and style of sales interactions. An organization emphasizing an external orientation places singular emphasis on satisfying clients and customers. As opposed to a firm with internal emphasis, representatives of companies with external emphasis will use the problem solving approach, i.e. the interaction-oriented style, to a greater degree. The external emphasis also manifests itself in a relatively greater willingness on the part of the seller to modify the product offering in order to maximize a buyer's utility and convenience.

A task focus will drive a firm's employees toward the task-oriented style of interaction. A salesperson (buyer) reared in such an environment will strive to conclude the sales transaction with utmost efficiency. The emphasis will be toward concluding the interaction with a minimum expenditure of time, money, and effort. A culture emphasizing the social focus will show a relatively greater inclination for social chit-chat, building personal rapport, and for facilitating the socialization needs of each actor in the course of the sales transaction. The social and emotional utilities inherent in certain products will be valued higher by firms with a social focus as opposed to those with a task focus.

Representatives bred in a culture of conformity should elicit a preference for standardized sales presentations or 'canned approaches'. Company policies and procedures will determine the scope of the concessions offered, terms of contract, and even the rituals of the transaction. Companies practicing relatively high individuality will allow their representatives a high level of autonomy in behavior and decisionmaking during the sales negotiation process.

The dimension of safety versus risk will determine the relative importance of attributes such as the reputation of the selling firm, the creditworthiness of the buyer, the acceptable level of return privileges, and the desire for personal rapport between the buyer and the seller. A safety-conscious response to risk-taking may result in an emphasis on written contracts as opposed to oral agreements. Conversely, representatives of firms with greater risk tolerance will be more inclined to encouraging new suppliers, trying out new and innovative products, and accepting a certain level of ambiguity in sales contracts.

Finally, the content and style displayed in a sales transaction will also be impacted by the dimension of ad hockery versus planning. The planning culture will emphasize the need for non-ambiguous communication in conveying product benefits, warranty features, and contingency clauses. Representatives of firms with a preference for ad hockery will tend to negotiate in a manner that encourages flexibility in the role stipulation, delivery, and other aspects of sales negotiation. The interaction style of such representatives will be somewhat informal, and less task-driven when compared to the style of representatives from firms inculcating a planning orientation.

Personality

Weitz (1978, 1981) has emphasized the need for a contingency approach to sales transactions. Typically, a salesperson interacts with buyers spanning a whole spectrum of personalities. A salesperson's understanding of the buyer's personality should facilitate a selling approach that has a greater likelihood of success.

Extroverts like to socialize and engage in social chit-chat. Their orientation is toward the outer world of people and things. Introverts, on the other hand, are drawn more to their own inner world of ideas. It therefore follows that social-organizational utility (or disutility) would be more important to extroverts than it would be to introverts. Conversely, introverts are likely to value functional utility, i.e. the functional performance of a product, to a greater degree than would extroverts.

Extroverts will prefer the interaction-oriented style of communication. They will elicit preference for establishing a personal bond with their dyadic counterpart. Introverts, on the other hand, will probably prefer the task-orientation in sales interactions.

Sensing types will show a preference for quantifiable product performance data. They will be impressed by a factual presentation, full of charts, graphs, and statistics. Intuitive types, on the other hand, are more likely to be impressed by the use of metaphor and analogy. Given their fascination for non-routine objects and experiences, intuitives will probably value epistemic utility more than would the sensing types.

Thinkers will be swayed by a presentation strongly grounded in reasoning and logic. Feelers will be more comfortable with the use of emotional appeals such as the use of love, loyalty, fear, and responsibility. Emotional utility (or disutility), resulting from a product being associated with feelings such as anger, respect, love, and fear, will appeal more to feelers than to thinkers.

Judgers will be eager to close a sale, and thus conclude the transaction at the earliest opportunity. Perceivers, on the other hand, will display significant indecisiveness even in small purchases. Judgers will prefer irrevocable contracts, while perceivers will want to maximize flexibility. Judging types insist on being right and, as a result, may promote disagreements in a sales encounter. The perceiving types are more likely to be conversationalists and the discussion may go on and on, without any inclination for closure. Given their desire for organization and control, judgers will tend to dominate the sales interaction. Perceivers will tend to digress more, introducing into the conversation topics which may have little bearing on the transaction. Security utility inherent in a product will be valued more by judgers than by perceivers.

Measurement

The constructs of national character, organizational culture, and individual personality have all been operationalized using the typology suggested in this paper. However, this operationalization has appeared in non-marketing-related studies. Illustrations of how individual items may be constructed to measure underlying dimensions of national character, organizational culture, and individual personality have been listed in the Appendix.

Discussion

Managerial implications

Discussing buyer–seller interactions for the three-construct perspective discussed herein allows for visualizing of an array of scenarios ranging from 'most chance of success' to 'least chance of success'. This is illustrated in Figure 3.

The first level depicts a perfect match between the buyer and the seller along the three central constructs; the buyer and seller are congruent in their milieu of national character, organizational culture, and individual personality. Within this scenario, a harmonious transaction with the highest chance

Alternative matching scenarios		
National character	Organizational culture	Personality factors

MOST SUCCESSFUL

	National character	Organizational culture	Personality factors
1.	S*	S	S
2.	S S D	S D S	D* S S
3.	D D	S D	D S
4.	D	D	D

LEAST SUCCESSFUL

*S = Same between buyer and seller
*D = Different between buyer and seller

Figure 3   *Assessment of buyer–seller similarity*

of closure and greatest satisfaction with the interaction can be predicted. The content and style of the seller's communication mesh perfectly those of the buyer. Conversely, the most challenging scenario and the one with the least chance of success is denoted by a complete lack of congruence between the buyer and seller in the areas of national character, organizational culture, and individual personality. Should the seller fail to recognize this incongruence and act accordingly (cf. Spiro and Weitz 1990; Weitz 1978), a total mismatch in communication will occur, resulting in a virtual collapse of the transaction.

It is also necessary to stress that the relative importance of the dimensions of each of the constructs will, to some degree, be situationally determined. For example, cross-cultural buyer-seller differences on the dimension of power distance may be potentially crippling in one situation (e.g. a U.S. vendor selling a fairly generic product to a powerful Japanese buyer; Graham 1988), while in other cases they may not (e.g. if the seller of the same product is from a large PDI society such as Panama, and the buyer is from the U.S., a somewhat small PDI culture). Or, a lack of congruence in individual personalities will not dramatically affect the successful close if the seller is operating in an industry that could be considered a sellers' market (cf. Frazier and Kale 1989; 1986).

Situational factors aside, the importance of the three constructs discussed in this article has powerful managerial implications in at least three areas: (1) choosing national markets for doing business; (2) fine-tuning a firm's organizational culture; and (3) recruiting and training salespeople for overseas business. This conceptual framework also leads to the development of a 'selling sequence' to maximize the success rate of cross-national face-to-face selling transactions.

Choosing national markets
National character can be used as an important entry criterion along with such traditional criteria as population, per capita income or GNP, the existence of infrastructure, etc., with which to evaluate the attractiveness of various national markets (cf. Root 1987). Economics and infrastructure alone do not adequately predict a firm's chances of success in a foreign market. For instance, Canada and the United Arab Emirates (UAE) have somewhat similar per capita GNP figures. From a standpoint of similarity in national characters alone, one could postulate that a firm from the United States will find it easier to deal with buyers from Canada than it would with buyers from UAE.

Using the four dimensions of national character, major national markets of the world can be segmented into relatively homogeneous clusters. A company choosing national markets with a national character similar to its own (i.e. belonging to the same cluster) will have to undertake relatively little learning and acculturation to successfully sell its products within these markets. Conversely, if markets with radically dissimilar national characters are chosen, considerable investment in acculturation, recruitment, and training of personnel will be needed to successfully sell a company's products within these markets. Thus, if a firm has to choose between two markets with comparable levels of market potential, economic well-being, competition, and infrastructure facilities, it should first choose to enter that market where the 'cultural distance' is smaller (Johanson and Vahlne 1977).

Fine-tuning organizational culture
If a firm is operating in a group of culturally homogeneous countries that have a national character different from its own (such as a British trading company in Africa), it can fine-tune its organizational culture to better reflect the national character of its markets. While it may be difficult to change the underlying values comprising the organizational culture of the firm, adaptation in its marketing and management practices is indeed feasible (Hofstede *et al.* 1990). This will enhance the skills of the firm's boundary personnel in dealing with buyers who share a different national character.

Thus, differences in national character alone need not be a deterrent. The multinational firm can shape its organizational culture in a manner that would soften the adverse impact of such differences. Hindustan Lever Limited, a subsidiary of the Dutch conglomerate Unilever, has inculcated an organizational culture in its Indian subsidiary that takes into account the relatively low level of individualism, and the relatively large power distance within India. Similarly, Coca-Cola in Japan has adopted the collective orientation of Japanese society. Coke's sales are higher in Japan than in the United States, and senior executives indicate that at least part of this success is due to cultural adaptation on the part of Coca-Cola (Wilson 1980). Thus, if a particular national market is important enough to a multinational company, it should design the organizational culture within that subsidiary in a manner that considers the national character of that market. Conversely, some companies may try to export their own national character to their overseas subsidiaries. Japanese auto makers, for instance, have been some-what successful in incorporating elements of the Japanese national character into the organizational culture of their subsidiaries in America. However, in terms of the marketing to end-consumers, these companies still adapt their practices to the cultural psyche of an American.

Recruitment and training of salespeople
Many high-tech firms rely on cosmopolitan salespeople – expatriates who sell to customers in a number of different national markets. The products sold usually have a high unit price (e.g. aircraft and computer systems) and the salesperson's ability to develop successful relationships with the buyer becomes a critical determinant of success (cf. Dwyer, Schurr and Oh 1987). Also, the role of personal selling is greatest when an exporting firm sells directly to the end-user or to governmental agencies. Under these situations, the selling firms must rely heavily on person-to-person communication and oral presentations. Here, the empathy shown by the salesperson in the willingness to adapt his or her behavior to the psychological mind-set of the buyer assumes critical importance (Spiro and Weitz 1990).

A cosmopolitan salesperson needs to possess a 'flexible personality' (Simurda 1988). Though Weitz (1979) has questioned the utility of personal-ity trait measures for predicting sales performance, we are advocating the specific trait of flexibility, which is conceptually different from earlier trait measures. Spiro and Weitz (1990) have considered flexibility an important trait in the execution of adaptive selling. The concept of flexibility is similar to the construct of 'interpersonal orientation' discussed by Rubin and Brown (1975). People with low interpersonal orientation tend to behave consistently across intra- and cross-cultural situations. Conversely, people with high interpersonal orientation are sensitive to the interpersonal aspects of their relationships with others.

Noer [1975] suggests that the key attributes desired in salespeople involved in cross-cultural selling situations include openness and sensitivity to others, cultural sensitivity and awareness, ability to relate across cultures, awareness of one's own culturally derived values and a certain degree of resiliency to bounce back after setbacks. The Myers–Briggs Type Indicator suggests that perceivers are more likely to possess the attributes of flexibility, high interper-sonal orientation, and cultural sensitivity than are judgers. In their characteri-zation of judgers and perceivers, Keirsey and Bates (1978) describe the judgers as 'fixed' and the perceivers as 'flexible'. Furthermore, judgers like to plan their selling strategy a priori, whereas perceivers tend to follow an 'adapt as you go' approach. Finally, while the judger hungers for controlling the sales transaction, a perceiver will try hard to observe, understand, and adapt. Thus, perceivers are better equipped in dealing with self-monitoring, i.e. in the degree to which they alter their self-presentation in response to situational cues, than judgers (Snyder 1979). This adaptability gives perceivers an innate advantage in handling the various contingencies involved in cross-national selling (cf. Weitz 1981).

A prospective cosmopolitan salesperson should also possess extensive international knowledge or demonstrate the willingness to gain it (Simurda 1988). The more a person is aware of the enormous differences in morals, customs, beliefs, and lifestyles of various peoples around the globe, the less ethnocentric that person is likely to be. Such a person will typically demonstrate the willingness to modify his or her behaviors to suit the unique cultural and personality context of each selling task. Thus, the requisite flexibility and international awareness of a recruit could be used as critical criteria for selecting cosmopolitan salespeople. The task now is to train the salesperson for international selling.

Empirical evidence suggests that negotiators tend to change their usual behavior in cross-cultural negotiations (Adler and Graham 1989). With appropriate training in assessing the buyer's 'psychological field', the adaptive selling practices followed by a salesperson should become more effective (Merrill and Reid 1981). In international sales, knowing the customer means more than comprehending the customer's product needs; it includes knowing the customer's culture as well. At broad levels, this culture is shaped by national character and organizational culture. At the level of preferred ways of acting, an understanding of the customer's personality becomes important. We therefore suggest that international salespeople be given a thorough grounding in the constructs of national character, organizational culture, and individual personality.

Hofstede's dimensions of culture are intuitively appealing for practitioners. In management development programs conducted by the senior author, most managers reported that these dimensions broadened their understanding of the various cultures constituting the global environment. Many were able to relate their experiences with peoples of different nationalities to differences in their national character on the four dimensions.

The dimensions of organizational culture enhance a salesperson's understanding of the corporate values of his or her own organization, and those of the buyer. Organizational culture conveys a sense of identity to its members, and understanding a buyer's culture should smooth all phases of the sales presentation. We suggest that salespeople be trained in adapting their practices when dealing with a customer from a drastically different organizational culture.

Finally, the Myers–Briggs typology teaches a salesperson to appreciate other types, and to develop the requisite sensitivity in dealing with other types. With some proficiency in the characteristics of the sixteen different types, and with workshops designed to sharpen 'type watching skills' of participants, salespeople become quite adept at assessing a buyer's personality with a minimum exposure time.

These three constructs become convenient vantage points with which to understand the psychological mind-set of the buyer. The same constructs also provide a basis of self-assessment for the seller. Having developed a buyer's profile along national character, organizational culture, and individual personality dimensions, the salespeople can compare this profile with their own, and thus be able to determine areas where adaptation is needed. This leads to a sequential approach to cross-national selling.

The selling sequence Figure 4 is a flowchart that cosmopolitan salespeople could utilize in cross-national selling transactions. Salespeople trained in the three-construct framework suggested in this paper can follow this flow-chart in adopting a strategy for face-to-face interactions with buyers. Such an exercise should enhance their success rate in personal selling transactions.

A well-trained salesperson becomes aware of his or her own conditioning and personality. This awareness has been depicted in Figure 4 as 'self-appraisal'. The aim of self-appraisal is to develop a frame of reference whereby one's own communication preferences regarding content and style could be understood. Self-appraisal thus results in 'cultural self-awareness' (Root 1987). Dimensions discussed in this paper under personality, organizational culture, and national character become convenient headings under which to generate cultural and psychological self-awareness.

Impression formation involves understanding the buyer's position on the three constructs. Typically, national character and organizational culture can be assessed even before the seller meets with the buyer. Hofstede (1983) provides scores and ranks for fifty countries on the basis of their positions on the four dimensions of national character. The organizational culture of most large- and medium-sized companies can be gleaned from their press releases, annual reports, and from popular literature (cf. Deal and Kenndy 1982). For example, the annual report of American Express (1982) reads, 'Consumers of all ages are expecting much more from financial services . . . and it is our obligation to meet their needs.' This is an indicator of the external emphasis of the company. Similarly, the task-focus of Digital Equipment Corporation can be surmised from the company's 1990 annual report, 'Our worldwide operations have become more efficient. Six years ago, we had 32,000 manufacturing employees; today, with more than double the revenues, we have 29,300.' A salesperson trained in type-watching can assess a buyer's personality with a fair degree of accuracy in a relatively short period of interaction. An accurate impression of the buyer's psychologi-

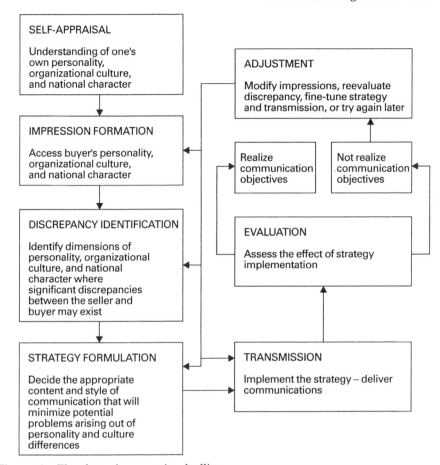

Figure 4 *Flowchart of cross-national selling*

cal mind-set can lay the foundation for relationship-building, which is so critical to face-to-face interactions.

The seller then needs to go through the mental exercise of 'discrepancy identification'. This involves comparing the buyer's estimated position on the various dimensions of the three constructs with one's own. This alerts the seller to potential problem areas in communication arising out of differences in personality and cultural conditioning. Strategy formulation involves a selection of means and methods designed to minimize the impact of problem areas identified in the earlier step. For instance, if the buyer is a feeler, and the seller is a thinker, the seller needs to modify his or her persuasion style. In this instance, the seller's preferred persuasion style is logical and impersonal, and this style may not gel well with the buyer. The appropriate style would be to appeal to the buyer's feelings and emotions, pointing out the people-benefits behind the seller's offering. Similar adjustments can be made on other dimensions as well. For instance, if the buyer happens to be from a country displaying strong uncertainty avoidance, or subscribes to an organizational culture displaying a strong inclination for safety, then the security utility in the product offering needs to be emphasized. What seems crucial for the seller is taking a quick perspective, and adapting the content and style of the sales presentation accordingly (Spiro and Weitz 1990).

Transmission involves implementation of the communication/persuasion strategy (cf. Weitz 1978). During the course of transmission, the seller should be sensitive to the verbal and non-verbal feedback received from the buyer. If the seller has correctly identified the buyer's mind-set as assessed by the three constructs, the persuasion strategy should be on target, and the feedback received from the buyer will be encouraging.

Assessing the effect of the communication strategy constitutes the 'evaluation' phase (cf. Weitz 1978). Continued interest in the presentation, readiness to close the sale, or seeking more information toward closure would all indicate that the seller's communication has been effective. If these and other communication objectives are realized, then the encounter has been successful. If not, the seller goes through the 'adjustment' process where buyer impressions, discrepancies, and strategy are re-evaluated, and the transmission modified. At the evaluation and adjustment phases, the seller always has the choice of cutting short the encounter and trying again at a future point in time. Regardless of the outcome, every encounter adds to the seller's repertoire of experiences, skills, strategies, and alternative transmission approaches.

Research implications

The basic premise of this article is that harmony along the constructs of national character, organizational culture, and individual personality will improve buyer–seller communication, thereby resulting in a positive sales outcome. Evans (1963) sought to validate the similarity hypothesis using demographic characteristics. While empirical research on the relationship between dyadic similarity and the likelihood of a sale has thus far yielded mixed results (cf. Busch and Wilson 1976; Churchill, Collins and Strang 1975; Woodside and Davenport 1974), several studies in the field of social psychology have demonstrated that social and psychological similarities in a dyad do improve communication (cf. Padgett and Wolosin 1980: Triandis 1960; Runkel 1956). However, the impact of improved communication arising out of salesperson–customer similarity on a positive sales outcome has yet to be conclusively established. Future research in cross-cultural sales interactions needs to validate the relationship between similarity and a positive sales outcome. The dimensions of each construct suggested in this article should be quite useful in assessing salesperson–customer similarity.

None of the three constructs proposed in this article, as operationalized herein, has received empirical treatment in the marketing discipline. It is therefore vital that the constructs be empirically tested in order to assess their relevance in explaining cross-cultural interactions. This is no easy task, as data collection in the international context is fraught with logistic and methodological problems (cf. Douglas and Craig 1983). However, the potential benefits resulting from an empirical assessment of these constructs far outweigh their costs.

Any discussion of national character has to grapple with the critical question of which cultural classification system to operationalize. We have suggested using the Hofstede (1980) framework because of its empirical base and its proven reliability characteristics. Some scholars have questioned the construct validity of this framework (cf. Triandis 1982). One of the reviewers, in commenting on the earlier draft of this article, observed:

> As well as Hofstede's scheme is grounded in previous theory, Hall's ideas reflect a deeper appreciation for culture as a construct . . . while I don't fault Hofstede for his approach, Hall's immersion in cultural anthropology may have yielded a more useful scheme.

A key area of research, therefore, is to assess the adequacy of Hofstede's dimensions of national character and to test his framework in relation to other competing typologies of cultural classification. Although marketing scholars like Redding (1987) and Riddle (1986) have praised the four-dimensional framework for its simplicity and quantifiability, cross-cultural researchers like Triandis (1982) have raised the possibility that the four dimensions may explain only a fraction of all the dimensions required to adequately explain cross-cultural differences. Also, Hofstede's (1980) questionnaire revolved almost entirely around work-related values. Questions spanning other contexts of peoples' lives were not included. If a questionnaire with a broader domain were designed, a few more underlying dimensions of culture might emerge. The task for researchers in marketing and international business is to use Hofstede's framework as a starting point with which to design a questionnaire with a wider context. Once the stability and adequacy of these dimensions are ascertained, this framework can be used in a variety of international business issues such as market segmentation, product planning, international promotion, and comparative studies on management and organizational behavior.

In a similar vein, the five dimensions of organizational culture we propose also need to be empirically investigated and compared to other frameworks depicting organizational culture. The marketing literature to date has evidenced no real attempt to operationalize the construct of organizational culture (except in a study by Apasu, Ichikawa and Graham 1987 which utilized the Rokeach framework). The few such attempts in the management and organizational behavioral literatures (cf. Hofstede *et al*. 1990; Posner, Kouzes and Schmidt 1985; Reynierse and Harker 1986; Reynolds 1986) have yet to influence organizational culture measurement in marketing. In setting the agenda for organizational culture and marketing, Mahajan, Varadarajan and Kerin (1987) have suggested that the next phase of development of the field of strategic market planning must involve a formal integration of organizational culture issues.

The degree of impact of organizational culture on buyer–seller interaction in particular is a topic worthy of attention, but has thus far been ignored in the marketing literature. In this regard, we feel that attempts by Weitz, Sujan and Sujan (1986) to include organizational culture concepts in their model of selling effectiveness are indeed noteworthy. We hope that this article will accelerate efforts to study organizational culture and its impact on buyer–seller interactions across both domestic and international contexts.

In the area of personality, we feel that researchers should not give up on personality-related studies to solve marketing problems. We agree with Wilkie's (1986) assessment that, when carefully executed, personality studies enhance our understanding of marketing issues (also see Spiro and Weitz 1990).

We are particularly excited about the application of MBTI in marketing. Extensively used and widely researched, this test is understandable, nonthreatening, and easy to administer. It has already been used in diverse contexts such as the work environment (Williams, Armstrong and Malcolm 1985), higher education (Provost and Anchors 1987), group behavior (Schemel and Borbely 1982), and counseling (Provost 1984). Across each of these contexts, MBTI has exhibited tremendous diagnostic and predictive abilities. A mere understanding of this typology should enhance the salesperson's tolerance and appreciation of different types, and thus lead to the development of empathy so crucial to successful face-to-face selling.

We have postulated a strong interactive relationship between national character, organizational culture, and individual personality. Further research is needed to assess the relative importance of these three constructs in terms of their impact on the outcome of a selling interaction. Differences in relative importance of the three constructs would necessitate a situational or contingency framework in that personality factors may exert a greater influence in some encounters, while organizational culture may emerge as being the most dominant in others. For instance, do personality factors tend to dominate the dynamics of a sales interaction in products and services involving a high degree of personal salience for the buyer (e.g. cosmetics)? Does the outcome of sales interactions involving customized industrial products tend to be dominated by compatibility in organizational cultures (e.g. computer software systems)? In most cases, it is likely that the national character roots may be so deeply embedded that they overshadow the influence of both the organizational culture and the personality of the actors in the dyad (cf. Laurent 1986).

Another question worthy of attention is the degree to which foreign country bias affects dyadic interactions (cf. McGee and Spiro 1991). While this article has focused on buyer–seller interactions, it raises some interesting questions for managing cross-national relationships in distribution channels as well. Here, it may be possible to inculcate in the relationship a synergistic culture, which may transcend the cultural milieu of the two entities in the dyad (Adler 1986). A comparative study of distribution channel relationships within two or more countries could also be facilitated by using this framework. This will enable researchers to identify which aspects of content and style are driven by national character and which are artifacts of personality, organizational culture or other environmental variables not covered under the framework presented in this article (cf. Frazier, Gill and Kale 1989; Kale 1986).

Conclusion

The problem of communicating with people in diverse cultures is one of the great creative challenges in international marketing (Ricks 1988). This is because cultural factors typically operate below the level of conscious awareness, they operate on an individual at several levels, and are therefore difficult to comprehend. Scholars and practitioners alike have come to the realization that it is culture that largely determines the way in which various phenomena are perceived, what one talks about, how one approaches others, and myriad other bits and pieces of behavior. This had led scholars in cross-cultural communication to believe that 'culture is communication' (Barnlund 1989; Hall 1959; Kale 1991).

We have proposed a general framework within which to investigate cross-national personal selling transactions at three levels. Drawing from evidence in several disciplines, we suggest that the degree of compatibility between the two actors in a sales dyad with regard to their national character, organizational culture, and individual personality will largely determine the overall compatibility in their communication. This compatibility, in turn, will determine the degree of success achieved by the seller.

For each of these constructs, there exist field-tested measurement instruments. While our thoughtful search has led us to recommend the Hofstede framework for national character, the Reynolds typology for organizational culture, and the MBTI for personality, we do not rule out the efficacy of other competing frameworks for measuring the three constructs. Scholars in marketing and international business are urged to utilize, validate, and refine the various instruments in their studies of cross-national negotiation and other issues. An interdisciplinary approach to cross-national selling such as the one suggested in this article further reinforces Dunning's plea for a greater integration of international business knowledge across various specialized areas (Dunning 1989). From a managerial standpoint, the practical applications and intuitive appeal of the proposed three-construct framework are indeed exciting. This framework should assist practitioners in the areas of selecting national markets, shaping an appropriate organizational culture, and the recruitment and training of cosmopolitan salespeople.

Above all, we believe that scholars in marketing should focus greater attention to studying cross-national marketing issues. In the early stages of such research, there will always be some false starts, a weak integration across various research programs, and instances of inadequate attention to some basic methodological issues (Deshpande and Webster 1989). Also, in the foreseeable future, there will continue to be the ongoing debate concerning which typology to use, and which borrowed concept to apply. As Frijda and Jahoda (1974) perspicaciously observe, 'Cross-cultural research is like virtue – everybody is in favor of it, but there are widely differing views of what it is and ought to be.' In this regard, we hope the framework we propose will yield a number of thought-provoking ideas and a healthy debate on the relative merits of the typologies suggested. We believe that despite the obvious constraints involving cross-national and cross-cultural research, sustained efforts by way of further conceptualization and empirical assessment will advance theory development in this important area.

Appendix: Illustrative measures of national character, organizational culture, and personality dimensions

		Strongly agree	*Agree*	*Undecided*	*Disagree*	*Strongly disagree*
National character						
Uncertainty avoidance						
1	Rather than elaborate planning for life, I prefer to take each day as it comes.*	1	2	3	4	5
2	Written rules and regulations tend to interfere with my productivity at work.*	1	2	3	4	5
Individualism						
1	Decisions made by individuals are usually of higher quality than decisions made by groups.	1	2	3	4	5
2	Having considerable freedom to adopt my own approach to the job is important to me.	1	2	3	4	5
Power distance						
1	Lower level employees are often afraid to express disagreement with their superiors.	1	2	3	4	5
2	Those in power should try to appear as powerful as possible.	1	2	3	4	5
Masculinity						
1	A corporation should do as much as it can to solve society's problems.*	1	2	3	4	5
2	Earnings and recognition at work are relatively more important than friendly atmosphere and co-workers' cooperation.	1	2	3	4	5
Organizational culture						
External vs. internal emphasis						
1	At work, the major emphasis of my company is on meeting outside demands of customers, clients, or whoever.	1	2	3	4	5
2	My company encourages me to try to get customers or clients to discuss their needs with me.	1	2	3	4	5

APPENDIX   (continued)

	Strongly agree	Agree	Undecided	Disagree	Strongly disagree
Task vs. social focus					
1 At my company, organizational work is always more important than concern for the personal and social needs of workers.	1	2	3	4	5
2 My company encourages fostering a real sense of belonging among all employees.★	1	2	3	4	5
Conformity vs. individuality					
1 My company is flexible enough for each individual to exercise his/her creativity.★	1	2	3	4	5
2 Depicting a homogeneous corporate image among its executives is important to my company.	1	2	3	4	5
Safety vs. risk					
1 My company could be characterized as risk-averse.	1	2	3	4	5
2 When it comes to adopting new methods or practices, my company takes a very cautious approach.	1	2	3	4	5
Ad hockery vs. planning					
1 Rather than making elaborate plans for the future, my company follows an 'adapt-as-you-go-approach'.	1	2	3	4	5
2 My company believes that the only way to deal with environmental changes is to anticipate them and to plan for them.★	1	2	3	4	5
Individual personality					
Extroversion vs. introversion					
1 Rather than initiate conversation when among a group of people, I wait to be approached.★	1	2	3	4	5
2 I find that I can speak easily and at length with strangers.	1	2	3	4	5
Sensing vs. intuition					
1 I tend to trust my experience more than my hunches.	1	2	3	4	5

APPENDIX   (continued)

	Strongly agree	Agree	Undecided	Disagree	Strongly disagree
2 I believe a strong sense of reality is a greater virtue than a vivid imagination.	1	2	3	4	5
Thinking vs. feeling					
1 Consistency of thought is more appealing to me than harmonious human relationships.	1	2	3	4	5
2 In dealing with others, being fair-minded is more important than being sympathetic.	1	2	3	4	5
Judging vs. perceiving					
1 The ability to organize and be methodical is more admirable than the ability to adapt and make do.	1	2	3	4	5
2 Rather than setting deadlines for myself, I prefer to work just whenever.*	1	2	3	4	5

* The scores for these items are reversed.
Source: Adapted from Hofstede (1980); Harrison (1979); Reynolds (1986), and Keirsey and Bates (1978).

References

Aaker, David A. and Richard P. Bagozzi. 1979. Unobservable variables in structural models with an application in industrial selling. *Journal of Marketing Research*, 16 (May): 147–58.

Adler, Nancy J. 1986. *International dimensions of organizational behavior*. Belmont, CA PWS Kent.

Adler, Nancy J. and John L. Graham, 1989. Cross-cultural interaction: The international comparison fallacy? *Journal of International Business Studies*, 20(3): 515–37.

American Express, 1982. *1982 annual report*. New York: American Express Company.

Ansoff, H. Igor. 1979. *Strategic management*, New York: John Wiley & Sons.

Apasu, Yao, Shigeru Ichikawa and John L. Graham, 1987. Corporate culture and sales force management in Japan and America. *Journal of Personal Selling & Sales Management*, 7(3): 51–62.

Bagozzi, Richard P. 1978. Sales performance and satisfaction as a function of individual difference, interpersonal, and situational factors. *Journal of Marketing Research*, 15 (November): 517–31.

Barnlund, Dean C. 1989. *Communication styles of Japanese and Americans: Images and realities*. Belmont, CA: Wadsworth.

Berry, John W. 1969. On cross-cultural comparability. *International Journal of Psychology*, 4(2): 119–28.

Buchanan, Dale R. and Jane A. Taylor, 1986. Jungian typology of professional psychodramatists: Myers–Briggs Type Indicator. *Psychological Reports*, 58(2): 391–400.

Busch, Paul and David T. Wilson 1976. An experimental analysis of a salesman's expert and referent bases of social power in the buyer-seller dyad. *Journal of Marketing Research*, 13 (February): 3–11.

Carlyn, Marcia, 1977. An assessment of Myers–Briggs Type Indicator. *Journal of Personality Assessment*, 41(5): 461–73.

Cateora, Philip R. 1990. *International marketing* (seventh edition). Homewood, IL: Richard D. Irwin.

Cavusgil, S. Tamer and John R. Nevin, 1981. The state of the art in international marketing: An assessment. In Ben Enis and Kenneth Roering, editors, *Review of marketing*, Chicago, IL. American Marketing Association.

Churchill, Gilbert A., Robert H. Collins and William A. Strang 1975. Should retail salespersons be similar to their customers? *Journal of Retailing*, 51(3): 29–42.

Churchill, Gilbert A., Neil M. Ford and Orville C. Walker, 1979. Personal characteristics of salespeople and the attractiveness of alternative rewards. *Journal of Business Research*, 7(1): 25–50.

Clark, Terry, 1990. International marketing and national character: A review and proposal for an integrative theory *Journal of Marketing*, 54(4): 66–79.

Colvin, Michael, Roger Heeler and Jim Thorpe, 1980. Developing international advertising strategy. *Journal of Marketing*, 44(4): 73–9.

Deal, Terrence and Alan A. Kennedy, 1982. *Corporate culture*. Reading, MA: Addison-Wesley.

Deshpande, Rohit and A. Parasuraman, 1986. Linking corporate culture to strategic planning. *Business Horizons*, 29(3): 28–37.

Deshpande, Rohit and Frederick E. Webster, Jr. 1989. Organizational culture and marketing. Defining the research agenda. *Journal of Marketing*, 53(1): 3–15.

Digital Equipment Corporation. *1990 annual report*. Maynard, MA: Digital Equipment Corporation, Inc.

Douglas, Susan P. and C. Samuel Craig. 1983. *International marketing research*. Englewood Cliffs, NJ: Prentice-Hall.

Douglas, Susan P. and Bernard Dubois, 1977. Looking at the cultural environment for international marketing opportunities. *Columbia Journal of World Business*, 12(4): 102–9.

Duesenberry, James S. 1949. *Income, saving, and the theory of consumer behavior*. Cambridge, MA: Harvard University Press.

Dunning, John H. 1989. The study of international business: A plea for a more interdisciplinary approach. *Journal of International Business Studies*, 20(3): 411–36.

Dwyer, F. Robert, Paul H. Schurr and Sejo Oh. 1987. Developing buyer–seller relationships. *Journal of Marketing*, 51(2): 11–27.

Elder, Joseph W. 1976, Comparative cross-national methodology. In Alex Inkeles, editor. *Annual review of sociology*, Palo Alto, CA: Annual Reviews. Inc.

Evans, Franklin B. 1963. Selling as a dyadic relationship – A new approach. *American Behavioral Scientist*, 6(6): 76–9.

Eysenck, Hans J. and Sybil B. G. Eysenck. 1969. *Personality structure and measurement*. London, U.K. Routledge and Keagan Paul.

Frazier, Gary L. and Sudhir H. Kale. 1989. Manufacturer–distributor relationships: A sellers' versus buyers' market perspective, *International Marketing Review*, 6(6): 7–26.

Frazier, Gary L., James D. Gill and Sudhir H. Kale. 1989. Dealer dependence levels and reciprocal actions in a channel of distribution in a developing country, *Journal of Marketing*, 53(1): 50–69.

Frijda, Nico and Gustav Jahoda. 1974. Quoted in Michael Cole and Sylvia Scribner, editors, *Culture and thought: A psychological introduction*. New York: John Wiley & Sons.

Giovanni, Louise, Linda Berens and Sue Cooper. 1986. *Introduction to temperament* (second edition). Del Mar, CA: Prometheus Nemesis.

Graham, John L. 1983. Brazilian. Japanese and American business negotiations. *Journal of International Business Studies*, 14(1): 47–61.

Graham, John L. 1985. Cross-cultural marketing negotiations. A laboratory experiment. *Marketing Science*, 4(2): 130–46.

Graham, John L. 1988. Deference given the buyer. In Farok J. Contractor and Peter Lorange, editors, *Comparative strategies in international business*. Lexington, MA: Lexington Books.

Graham, John L. Dong Ki Kim. Chi-Yuan Lin and Michael Robinson. 1988. Buyer–seller negotiations around the Pacific Rim. *Journal of Consumer Research*, 15(1): 48–54.

Hall, Edward T. 1959. *The silent language*. Garden City, NY: Doubleday & Company, Inc.

Hall, Edward T. 1976. *Beyond culture*. New York, NY: Anchor Press.

Hall, Edward T. 1983. *The dance of life*. New York, NY: Anchor Press.

Harrison, Roger. 1978. Questionnaire on the cultures of organizations. In Charles Handy, editor. *The gods of management*. London, U.K.: Souvenir.

Hirsh, Sandra and Jean Kummerow. 1989. *Life types*. New York: Warner Books.

Hofstede, Geert. 1980. *Culture's consequences: International differences in work-related values*. Beverly Hills, CA Sage Publications.

Hofstede, Geert 1983 Dimensions of national cultures in fifty countries and three regions. In Jan B. Deregowski, S. Dziurawrec and R. C. Annis, editors, *Expiscations in cross-cultural psychology*, Lisse, Austria: Swets and Zettlinger: B. V.

Hofstede, Geert, Bram Neuijen, Denise D. Ohayv and Geert Sanders 1990. Measuring organizational cultures: A qualitative and quantitative study across twenty cases. *Administrative Science Quarterly*, 3 (June): 286–316.

Hoover, Robert J., Robert T. Green and Joel Saegert, 1978. A cross-national study of perceived risk *Journal of Marketing*, 42(3): 102–8.

Inkeles, Alex and Daniel J. Levinson, 1969. National character: The study of modal personality and sociocultural systems. In Gardner Lindzey and Elliot Arenson, editors. *The handbook of social psychology*. Vol 4. Reading, MA. Addison-Wesley.

Jain, Subhash C. 1989. Standardization of international marketing strategy: Some research hypotheses. *Journal of Marketing*, 53(1): 70–9.

Johanson, Jan and Jan-Erik Vahlne. 1977. The internationalization process of the firm: A model of knowledge development and increasing foreign market commitments *Journal of International Business Studies*, 8(1): 23–32.

Kale, Sudhir H. 1986. Dealer perceptions of manufacturer power and influence strategies in a developing country. *Journal of Marketing Research*, 23 (November): 387–93.

Kale, Sudhir H. 1991. Culture-specific marketing communications: An analytical approach. *International Marketing Review*, 8(2): 18–30.

Kassarjian, Harold H. and Mary J. Sheffet. 1981. Personality and consumer behavior: An update. In Harold H. Kassarjian & Thomas S. Robertson, editors, *Perspectives in consumer behavior*. Glenview, IL: Scott Foresman.

Keirsey, David and Marilyn Bates, 1978. *Please understand me: Character and temperament types*. Del Mar, CA: Prometheus Nemesis.

Kluckhohn, Florence R and Fred L. Stodtbeck, 1961. *Variations in value orientations.* Westport, CT: Greenwood Press.

Kreutzer, Rolf T. 1988. Marketing-mix standardisation. An integral approach in global marketing. *European Journal of Marketing*, 22(10): 19–30.

Kroeger, Otto and Janet M. Theusen, 1988. *Type talk.* New York: Delacorte Press.

Laurent, Andre, 1986. The cross-cultural puzzle of international human resource management. *Human Resource Management.* 25(1): 91–102.

Lebas, Michael and Jane Weigenstein. 1986. Management control: The role of rules, markets, and culture. *Journal of Management Studies.* 23(3): 259–72.

Mahajan, Vijay, P. Rajan Varadarajan and Roger A. Kerin. 1987. Metamorphosis in strategic market planning. In G. L. Frazier and J. N. Sheth, editors, *Contemporary views on marketing practice.* Lexington, MA. Lexington Books.

Martenson, Rita, 1987. Is standardisation of marketing feasible in culture-bound industries? A European case study, *International Marketing Review*, 4(3): 7–17.

McGee, Lynn W. and Rosann L, Spiro. 1991. Salesperson and product country-of-origin effects on attitudes and intentions to purchase. *Journal of Business Research*, 22(1): 21–32.

Merrill, David W. and Roger H. Reid. 1981. *Personal styles and effective performance.* Radner, PA: Chilton.

Moore, Thomas 1987. Personality tests are back. *Fortune*, March 30: 74–81.

Myers, Isabel B and Peter B. Myers 1980. *Gifts differing*, Palc Alto. CA: Consulting Psychologists Press.

Noer, David M. 1975. *Multinational people management*, Washington, DC: Bureau of National Affairs.

Norburn, David, Sue Birley, Mark Dunn and Adrian Payne. 1990. A four nation study of the relationship between marketing effectiveness, corporate culture, and market orientation. *Journal of International Business Studies.* 21(3): 451–68.

Padgett, Valette R and Robert J Welosin, 1980. Cognitive similarity in dyadic communication. *Journal of Personality and Social Psychology*, 39(4): 654–9.

Parsons, Talcott and Edward A Shils, editors. 1951. *Toward a general theory of action.* Cambridge, MA: Harvard University Press.

Peters, Thomas and Robert Waterman, 1982. *In search of excellence*, New York: Harper & Row.

Posner, Barry Z., James Kouzes and Warren H. Schmidt, 1985. Shared values make a difference: An empirical test of corporate culture. *Human Resource Management*, 24(2): 249–309.

Provost, Judith A. 1984. *A casebook: Applications of the Myers–Briggs Type Indicator in counseling.* Gainesville. FL: Center for Applications of Psychological Types.

Provost, Judith A. and Scott Anchors. 1987. *Applications of the Myers–Briggs Type Indicator, in higher education.* Gainesville, FL: Center for Applications of Psychological Types.

Redding, Gordon S. 1987. Research on Asian cultures and management: Epistemological issues. *Asia Pacific Journal of Management*, 5(1): 89–96.

Reynierse, James H. and John B Harker, 1986. Measuring and managing organizational culture. *Human Resource Planning*, 9(1): 1–8.

Reynolds, Paul D. 1986. Organizational culture as related to industry, position, and performance: A preliminary report. *Journal of Management Studies*, 23(3): 333–45.

Ricks, David A. 1983. *Big business blunders: Mistakes in multinational marketing.* Homewood. IL: Dow Jones-Irwin.

Ricks, David A. 1988. International business blunders: An update. *Business and Economic Review*, 34(2): 11–4.

Riddle, Dorothy I. 1986. *Service-led growth: The role of the service sector in world development.* New York: Praeger Publishers.

Root, Franklin D. 1987. *Entry strategies for international markets*. Lexington, MA: Lexington Books.

Rubin, Jeffrey Z. and Bert R. Brown, 1975. *The social psychology of bargaining and negotiation*. New York: Academic Press.

Runkel, Philip J. 1956. Cognitive similarity in facilitating communication. *Sociometry*, 19(3): 178–87.

Sathe, Vijay, 1984. Implications of corporate culture. A manager's guide to action. *Organizational Dynamics*, 12(2): 4–23.

Schemel, George J. and George Borbely. 1982. *Facing your type*. Gainesville. FL: Center for Applications of Psychological Types.

Schmidt, Klaus D. 1979. *Doing business in Taiwan and doing business in Japan*. Menlo Park CA: Business Intelligence Program. SRI International.

Sheth, Jagdish N. 1976. Buyer–seller interaction. A conceptual framework. In Beverlee B. Anderson, editor, *Advances in consumer research*. Cincinnati, OH Association for Consumer Research.

Sheth, Jagdish N. 1983. Cross-cultural influences on the buyer–seller interaction/negotiation process. *Asia Pacific Journal of Management*, 1(1): 46–55.

Simurda, Stephen J. 1988. Finding an international sales manager. *Northeast International Business*, 1 (September): 15–6.

Snyder, Mark. 1979. Self-monitoring processes. In Leonard Berkowitz, editor, *Advances in experimental psychology*, Vol 12. New York: Academic Press.

Spiro, Rosann L. and Barton A. Weitz. 1990. Adaptive selling. Conceptualization, measurement, and nomological validity. *Journal of Marketing Research*, 16 (August): 355–69.

Steinberg, Mark and Gerald R. Miller. 1975. Interpersonal communication: A sharing process. In G. H. Hanneman and W. J. McEwen, editors, *Communication and behavior*. Reading, MA: Addison Wesley.

Teas, R. Kenneth, John G. Wacker and R. Eugene Hughes. 1979. A path analysis of causes and consequences of salespeople's perceptions of role clarity. *Journal of Marketing Research*, 16, August: 355–69.

Triandis, Harry C. 1960. Cognitive similarity and communication in a dyad. *Human Relations*, 13(2): 175–83.

Triandis, Harry C. 1982. Review of culture's consequences: International differences in work-related values, *Human Organization*, 44(1): 86–90.

Wall Street Journal. 1989. Euro-man: As 1992 approaches, the old world takes on a new look. Special supplement, September 22.

Weitz, Barton. 1978. Relationships between salesperson performance and understanding of customer decision making. *Journal of Marketing Research*, 15(4): 501–16.

Weitz, Barton. 1979. A critical review of personal selling research. The need for a contingency approach. In Gerald Albaum and Gilbert Churchill, editors, *Critical issues in sales management: State-of-the-art and future research needs*. Eugene, OR: University of Oregon.

Weitz, Barton. 1981. Effectiveness in sales interactions: A contingency framework, *Journal of Marketing*, 45(1): 85–103.

Weitz, Barton, Harish Sujan and Mita Sujan. 1986. Knowledge, motivation, and adaptive behavior: A framework for improving selling effectiveness. *Journal of Marketing*, 50(4): 174–91.

Wilkie, William L. 1986. *Consumer behavior*. New York: John Wiley & Sons.

Wilkins, Alan L. 1983. The culture audit. A tool for understanding organizations. *Organizational Dynamics*. 12(2): 24–38.

Williams, Cecil D., David Armstrong and Clare Malcolm. 1985. *The negotiable environment*. Del Mar. Ca.: Prometheus Nemesis.

Williams, Kaylene C. and Rosann L. Spiro. 1985. Communication style in the salesperson–customer dyad. *Journal of Marketing Research*, 22 (November): 434–42.

Willis, Carl G. 1987. Myers–Briggs Type Indicator. In Daniel G. Keyser and Richard C. Sweetland, editors, *Test critiques compendium*. Kansas City, MO: Test Corporation of America.

Wilson, Ian R. 1980. An American success story – Coca-Cola in Japan. In Mark B. Winchester, editor, *The international essays for business decision makers*, Vol 8. Dallas, TX: The Center for Business.

Woodside, Arch G. and William J. Davenport. 1974. The effect of salesmen similarity and expertise on consumer purchasing behavior. *Journal of Marketing Research*, 11 (May): 198–202.

Reproduced from Kale, S. H. and Barnes, J. W. (1992). Understanding the domain of cross-national buyer–seller interactions. *Journal of International Business Studies*, First quarter, 101–132, by permission of *Journal of International Business Studies*.

7.2 Negotiation: lessons from behind the Bamboo Curtain

Paul S. Kirkbride and Sara F. Y. Tang

The People's Republic of China (PRC) was, under Mao Tse-tung, a relatively closed society from 1949 until 1976. The death of Mao and the overthrow of the 'Gang of Four' led to a more open leadership under Hua Guo-feng, and later Deng Xia-ping. China increasingly opened its doors to tourists, foreign businessmen and joint-venture partners. One of the results of the 'Four modernisations' (of industry, service and technology, agriculture and national defence), as articulated in the 1978 'Ten-Year Economic Plan' and the 'Ten Principles' of Premier Zhao Ziyang in 1981, was an increase in business, finance and trade links with the rest of the world. An example of these increasing links is provided by the expansion of joint ventures. As Li Kui-wai [1] has noted, the PRC 'undertook 169 projects in 1981 in co-operation with foreign companies, absorbing a total of US 1,435 million dollars in foreign investment'. Similarly Pye has noted that 'in the first nine months of 1985, US companies formed more than 800 joint ventures with state enterprises in the People's Republic of China' [2]. This trend was temporarily halted by the events in China (including the Tiananmen Square incident) during the summer of 1989 which resulted in the exodus of foreign businessmen and investors. However it appears that most are returning or have returned and the current Chinese leadership under Li Peng are still stressing the importance of their business links with the Western world.

In view of these trends and such figures it is not surprising to find that the last few years have seen a sudden upsurge in interest in China by Westerners. In particular, there has been an extensive interest in the processes of negotiation with the Chinese. Some of the literature deals with the general aspects of trading and business practices in such a different culture [3], while some deals more specifically with cross-cultural aspects of negotiation and the Chinese negotiating style [4]. There seems to be a consensus in the literature that, despite their isolation for many years and their lack of business experience, the Chinese in the PRC are very good negotiators. For example, Pye [5] argues that 'the Chinese may be less developed in technology and industrial organisation than we are, but for centuries they have known few peers in the subtle art of negotiating. When measured against the effort and skill the Chinese bring to the bargaining table, American executives fall short'. Similarly, Warrington and McCall [6] take the view,' ... endorsed by those who have had dealings with China – that the Chinese are tough, shrewd, tenacious negotiators'.

We would not necessarily support the assertion of negotiation superiority but we would suggest that certain aspects of Chinese negotiation style are very different to Western approaches. This creates problems for the cross-cultural negotiator. As Pye [7] has concluded, 'unquestionably the largest and possibly the most intractable category of problems in Sino-American business negotiations can be traced to the cultural differences between the two countries'. We would, however, take a more optimistic view and instead seek to focus on positive aspects in terms of what Western negotiators can learn from the different styles of their Chinese counterparts. What behaviours contribute to the success of Chinese negotiators and what lessons can Western negotiators learn from them?

Characteristics of successful negotiators and Chinese styles

There is, of course, a massive literature in the West dealing with negotiation. It ranges from the popular bookstall level [8] through the managerial [9] to the academic. Here one finds a host of different approaches from political science [10], social psychology [11], organisations [12], industrial relations [13], and management theory [14]. In addition, one can refer to the specially designed training packages in audio visual or video formats [15].

It is not possible to review this literature here but we can extract from it a set of common 'key injunctions' or rules for successful negotiation. These are:

- Always set explicit limits or ranges for the negotiation process.
- Always seek to establish general 'principles' early in the negotiation.
- Always focus on potential areas of agreement and seek to expand them.
- Avoid taking the negotiation issues in sequence.
- Avoid excessive hostility, confrontation and emotion.
- Always give the other party something to 'take home'.
- Always prepare to negotiate as a team.

One of the most fascinating things for us about such a list of bargaining rules is how closely they parallel natural Chinese negotiation styles which are themselves influenced by wider Chinese values. In simple terms, one of the advantages possessed by Chinese negotiators is that they do these things fairly naturally.

Bargaining ranges

The negotiation literature is replete with advice on the need to set bargaining ranges. For example, Lewicki and Litterer [16] suggest that, 'negotiation is the process of establishing an agreement somewhere between two resistance points within a positive settlement range' and, therefore, a key part of the planning process is to be able to 'specifically define an objective (target point) and a "bottom line" (resistance point)'. A common failing of Western negotiators is setting the resistance point (or fall back position) too close to the target point and thus retaining very little room for the necessary process of movement during the negotiation process.

This is a fault less common among Chinese negotiators and is a result of their general preference for compromising as a method of conflict resolution [17]. It may be suggested that parties who expect to reach compromise solutions in the bargaining process will correspondingly give themselves greater room for manoeuvre and movement by setting higher and more extreme initial demands and offers. This would contrast with those (such as Westerners) who might prefer confrontational styles and retain greater expectations of resolving the conflict on or near their own terms. In such situations the negotiator might have an initial demand or offer which is nearer to the potential compromise [18].

Principles

One well known industrial relations negotiation training package [19] lays great stress on the need to establish central principles early in the negotiations. These are labelled 'key commitments' and defined as 'the fundamental element which underpins each crucial settlement point. In other words it is the principle or point of argument which, if accepted, means that the settlement point will almost certainly be yours'. They are seen as useful in determining your strategy, concentrating discussion on your own side of the negotiation, and extending the potential area of agreement or 'common ground' between the parties. Thus they are things which need to be achieved in the early stages of the negotiation process. These commitments have to be achieved by processes of persuasion and argument. They are, therefore, represented in the negotiation process by the use of 'legitimising principles' [20] which are articulated on the level of rhetoric [21]. Thus effort needs to be directed at getting as much agreement as possible on these 'commitments' or 'principles' before launching into your detailed proposals, as general agreement by the other side at this stage can serve to bind them at a later one. As the training package [22] puts it, 'as you achieve your commitments and deny him his, the basis of the final settlement moves in your favour'.

Many observers of negotiations in the PRC [23] have noted that Chinese negotiators, at the early stages of the negotiation, often 'seek agreement on generalities, dwelling on overall considerations, and avoiding specific details as much as possible, leaving, as they like to say,' concrete arrangements 'to later negotiations'. To some extent this form of behaviour may be culturally influenced in that it avoids or postpones direct conflict and confrontation over specific and substantive items [24]. However, as Frankenstein [25] points out, often 'much of what transpires at this stage is mistakenly regarded by the non-Chinese side as mere rhetoric' and unimportant. But for the Chinese side, these declarations are an important step; they establish a framework for the negotiations and provide ammunition should the foreign negotiators go beyond the boundaries. In fact, this general tactic of focusing on general principles has several advantages. These include the fact that the very wording of such principles can often make it possible to extract movement from the other party later. Also, as Pye [26] has noted, 'a second advantage for the Chinese is that they can, at times, quickly turn an agreement on principles into an agreement on goals and then insist that all discussion on concrete arrangements must foster those agreed-upon-goals'.

Common ground

Many negotiation handbooks stress the need to focus more on what unites the parties than on what divides them. For example, Hawver [27] advises negotiators to 'take pains to build firmly on the foundation of common ground before moving on to confront differences between the parties'. From the results of their study of 'skilled' and average negotiators, Rackham and Carlisle [28] report that 'the skilled negotiators gave over three times as much attention to common ground areas as did average negotiators'. Thus the skilled process of negotiation can be seen as the progressive expansion of common ground until agreement is reached. As another training package [29] notes, 'it is useful in negotiation to think of common ground in terms of position and in terms of people'. Negotiators should return to common ground if negotiations appear to be stalled or in order to launch any new proposal.

A study of Chinese negotiating behaviour reveals several ways in which this particular injunction is followed. Firstly, we have already referred to the Chinese habit of seeking agreement on general principles early in the negotiation which can be seen as an attempt to establish a form of 'macro-level' common ground. Secondly, the natural Chinese preference for compromise as a conflict resolution mechanism [30] points to a greater willingness to focus on areas of potential agreement.

However, we need to be aware of the precise meaning of compromise in relation to Chinese negotiation. In the West compromise is generally seen as a process of horse-trading, trade-offs, give and take, and mutual concessions. It represents therefore, not a win-win solution (as provided by collaboration) but a half win-half win situation. However, the Chinese, as Pye [31] notes, 'apparently see less inherent merit than Americans do in the concept of compromise . . . Instead, the Chinese prefer to hold up for praise ideals of mutual interests, of joint endeavours, and of commonality of purpose'. The effect is that the Chinese will set high opening positions and be willing to move to a compromise position (as with all negotiators) but 'when they reach the point of settlement they prefer to play down the fact of retreat by both sides and play up the idea that all along both sides have mutual interests that have finally been recognized'. Thus for Westerners, compromise is acknowledged as a necessary but sub-optimal solution where concessions are articulated and justified by identifiable concessions from the other side. For Chinese compromise is acknowledged as the reconciliation of mutual interests through a commonality of purpose and thus an optimal solution.

Sequential versus holistic bargaining

Rackham and Carlisle [32] discuss the difference between what they term 'Sequence Planning' and 'Issue Planning'. Sequence planning refers to the process where the negotiator plans and attempts to discuss and negotiate a series of linked issues in a pre-determined logical sequence. Issue planning instead refers to the alternative process of dealing with issues independently and not in any pre-determined sequence. From their detailed research, they found that 'skilled negotiators tended to plan around each individual issue in a way which was independent of any sequence. They would consider issue C, for example, as if issues A, B and D didn't exist. Compared with the average negotiators they were careful not to draw sequence links between a series of issues'. However, not all Westerner negotiators are as skilled as the better ones in this study. Indeed the general tendency is to prefer sequential negotiation and the fragmentation of issues. As Graham and Herberger [33] have observed, 'Americans usually attack a complex negotiation task sequentially – that is, they separate the issues and settle them one at a time. . . . Thus, in an American negotiation, the final agreement is a sum of the several concessions made on individual issues, and progress can easily be measured. . . . In other countries, particularly Far Eastern cultures, however, concessions may come only at the end of a negotiation. All issues are discussed with a holistic approach – settling nothing until the end'.

We can trace this difference to two aspects of Chinese psychology which come together to provide a distinct natural advantage. Firstly, it has been noted that Chinese people tend to have a holistic proclivity [34]. As Yang [35] has argued, 'Chinese people, especially adults, tend to display a cognitive style of seeing things or phenomena in wholes rather than in parts while Westerners tend to do the reverse. This proclivity may, in turn, be related back to traditional Chinese values and thus 'regarded as an application of the Chinese spirit or principle of harmony in the realm of the intellect. In this spirit, the Chinese will try to synthesize the constituent parts into a whole so that all parts blend into a harmonious relationship at this higher level of perceptual organisation' [36]. Secondly, there is the relatively high tolerance for uncertainty in Asian countries noted by Hofstede [37]. Together these tendencies lead to a holistic approach to negotiation and bargaining.

Confrontation

A corollary of our earlier injunction about common ground is that the negotiator should not seek to unnecessarily and excessively confront the other side to the detriment of achieving the goals of the negotiation process. Rackham and Carlisle [38] found from detailed research that their skillful negotiators generally avoided the use of both 'irritators' and 'defend/attack' spirals. Irritators are statements or words which upset or irritate the other side and thus serve to further divide the parties rather than unite them in agreement. This would include, for example, the gratuitous use of the term 'reasonable' to refer to one's own position and 'irrational' to refer to the other party. Defending/attacking behaviours refer to the use of emotional language to attack the other party or defend one's own position. This usually results in reciprocation and escalation which only serves to make future agreement more difficult. Our own research [39] would suggest that Western negotiators tend to adopt more aggressive, competitive and confrontational styles than their Chinese counterparts.

This can be partly explained by the differences in cultural traditions and heritage. There are a number of 'key' cultural values in Chinese society which reinforce a less confrontational approach to conflict resolution. The Confucian notions of 'Li' and 'Jen' together lead to conformity being a central value in Chinese society [40]. This conformity, together with its associated collectivist orientation [41] leads individuals to consider the relationship between themselves and the other party as one of the crucial factors in any conflict or negotiation situation. Thus there is a tendency for the Chinese to avoid confrontation for fear of disturbing these relationships and their mutual dependence. Similarly, the Confucianist concept of 'Chung Yung' from the Doctrine of the Mean asks individuals to adapt themselves to their collectivity; to control their emotions; and to avoid conflict and competition. In such a culture the disturbance of these inter-personal relationships gives rise to powerful feelings of 'shame' [42]. As a result of these cultural values the Chinese generally exhibit levels of assertiveness and confrontation. They thus tend to engage in less extreme verbal posturing, less emotive language, and in generally lower levels of verbal interaction. In terms of negotiation this is represented by less open argumentation and debate. This phenomenon has been traced back by Becker [43] who suggests that the Chinese avoidance of open argumentation and debate is a function of geo-demographic factors, socio-linguistic roots and philosophical traditions.

Face

It is generally recognised in most negotiating manuals that in many situations the parties may negotiate together in the future. For this reason alone there is a need to ensure that the other negotiator is able to gain something from the negotiation in order to maintain 'face'. Thus a training package on negotiation [44] lists as a convention of bargaining that 'a means of saving face should be preserved in defeat'. Or, as Vic Feather (ex-General Secretary of the TUC) used to say rather more vividly, 'always leave the other fellow with the bus fare home!'

Goffman [45] defined face in his classic article as 'the positive social value a person effectively claims for himself by the line others assume he has taken during a particular contact. Face is an image of self delineation in terms of approved social attitudes'. The face mechanism operates to influence a person to behave in a certain way that reinforces his social position as well as others. The influence of face in social interactions is universal but is particularly important to the Chinese [46]. Hu [47] subdivided face into two dimensions – 'Lien' and 'Mien-tzu'. The former one is normally ascribed while the latter is more achieved than ascribed. A person is socially condemned if he has no 'Lien' and is seen to be unsuccessful and low in status if he has no 'Mien-tzu'. They are externally mediated and people interact with a purpose to add, give, take, compete, exchange or borrow 'face'. In negotiating situations, aggressive behaviour from either party can easily injure the 'face' of the other party. As not giving face to a person is perceived as denying the person's pride and dignity, Chinese will hesitate to engage in such aggressive actions under normal circumstances. In addition, the adoption of face-giving or face-saving behaviour in conflict situations is valued as a means of maintaining group harmony.

Teamwork

Many negotiations are conducted by teams rather than individuals. In such situations there is the potential for chaos and conflict resulting from different approaches being pursued by the different individuals. It is not surprising therefore, that many negotiation manuals stress the importance of good team organisation. They usually stress the need for the team members to play different roles (such as Negotiator, Recorder and Analyst) and to provide empathetic support for each other. They also stress the need for team discipline. For example, 'members of the team should discipline themselves so that the team is united and purposeful' [48]. The fact that such advice is necessary perhaps signals that such behaviour is unusual. We would argue that it is unusual because it runs counter to the core Western value of 'individualism'. Hofstede [49] has argued that the presence of this value results in a preference for individual decisions and desires for independent and autonomous expression.

   In contrast Chinese societies are characterised by collectivism, and thus co-operation and collaboration in teams is a more natural form of behaviour. For example, Hofstede has noted that collectivism appears to be related positively to a preference for group decisions and negatively to the use of individual initiative [50]. In respect of negotiation in the PRC, Pye [51] has noted that 'at the substantive sessions the Chinese negotiating teams are almost always larger than American or even Japanese teams'. However, size is not the only difference. Pye has also noted that there is a paradoxical contrast in the character of typical Chinese and American negotiating teams. In the preliminary stages, it is the Chinese who stress personal interaction and friendship; when serious negotiating begins the Chinese side usually becomes highly bureaucratized, requiring co-ordination with layers of hierarchical committees and senior officials. Americans at the early stages may use elaborate teams in making technical presentations, but when serious negotiating begins the American instinct is to move toward a one-to-one relationship [52].

Conclusion

We have tried to suggest in this paper that Chinese negotiators, because of their cultural background, generally adopt and practice some of the desired negotiating behaviours derived from our negotiation injunctions. Thus we would suggest that there is much that Western negotiators could usefully learn from their Chinese counterparts. This is not to say, of course, that all Chinese are 'good' negotiators. We are not asserting that *all* Chinese negotiators behave in these culturally influenced ways, as culture is only one mediating variable on negotiation style. Differences between cultures are differences of degree and one can always find exceptions to the general rule. The events in the summer of 1989 in China can be taken to illustrate both the cultural underpinnings of the some of the key negotiation injunctions that we have identified and the fact that some (less experienced) Chinese negotiators do transgress these injunctions.

On 18 May 1989, as Gorbachev was leaving Shanghai for Moscow at the end of his historic but disrupted state visit, Li Peng, the Chinese Prime Minister, finally, and at his own instigation, agreed to meet representatives of the students camped in Tianenmen Square in an attempt to end the demonstration. The student leaders agreed and came to press their demands for apologies for a People's Daily editorial, recognition of their independent student 'union', and dialogue with the authorities. The 'negotiation', broadcast by state television, was unsuccessful and, two days later, martial law in Beijing was announced.

The chances of these negotiations being successful were, of course, slim in any event. But the behaviour of the student representatives soon ensured that a breakdown would occur. They failed to focus on common ground, appeared to adopt an 'all-or-nothing' approach, and were extremely confrontational. In a Chinese sense they failed to give 'face' to the other side. Even their style of dress appeared designed to irritate. Wu'er Kaixi arrived in a pair of striped pajamas while Wang Dan appeared in a leather jacket and a red headband scrawled with slogans. Li Peng began with a conciliatory tone apologising for the lateness of the meeting, but was soon interrupted by Wu'er Kaixi. 'This meeting is not only a little late but it is too late. . . . The topic of discussion should be decided by us' [53].

He went on to directly challenge deep seated cultural values. '. . . to solve the present problem, the government should forget 'face' and associatiated matters . . . should admit its own mistakes . . . we have some opinions about Li Peng, not a personal criticism . . . we have some opinions about you because you are the government leader' [54]. The conflict swiftly escalated and Li Peng began to reply in a similar manner. 'There is complete chaos in Beijing. Moreover, the turmoil has spread throughout the country . . . I can state that during the past few days, Beijing has been in a state of anarchy. I don't want to blame Wu'er Kaixi and Wang Dan but . . .' [55]. What is interesting in this example is the way in which counter-cultural behaviours serve to surface the deep cultural roots of 'normal' Chinese negotiating behaviour.

We are also not seeking to assert that the Chinese are 'super' negotiators, because there are, in fact, aspects of 'good' negotiating practice which run counter to Chinese culture. For example, the findings of Rackham and Carlisle [56] which suggest that 'skilled' negotiators use extensive behaviour 'labelling' and display of feelings, runs counter to Chinese culture which favours lower levels of verbal interaction, less direct signalling of intentions, and less sharing of feelings or information [57]. As Pye notes, historically, 'Chinese diplomats have preferred to play their cards very close to their chests and suggest inflexibility until the moment of accommodation' [58].

As a final point, it is interesting to note that much negotiation training in the West is really concerned with modifying certain culturally influenced behaviours. Similarly the implication is that similar training in Chinese societies would involve seeking to change certain Chinese culturally determined behaviours. We have certainly found from our joint experience in running negotiation training seminars for large organisations in Hong Kong, that one has to stress rather different skills and phases of the negotiation process in the Chinese case than one would in the West. In short there is no one culture which provides the ideal 'recipe' for negotiation. All cultures have certain strengths but have much to learn from others.

References

1 Li, K. W., *Financing economic development in China, 1978–1984.* Discussion Paper No 41, Department of Economics, University of Hong Kong, pp. 28, 1984.
2 Pye, L. W., The China trade: Making the deal. *Harvard Business Review.* July/August, p. 74, 1986.
3 Such as: Frankenstein, J., Trends in Chinese business practice: Changes in the Beijing wind. *California Management Review*, 29, 1, pp. 148–160, 1986; Hendry, S. R., The China trade: making the deal work. *Harvard Business Review*, July/August, 75/81–84, 1986; Lockett, M., China's special economic zones: The cultural and managerial challenges. *Journal of General Management* 12, 3, pp. 21–31, 1987; Pye, L., *op. cit.*, 1986; Reeder, J. A., When West meats East: Cultural aspects of doing business in Asia. *Business Horizons*, Jan/February, pp. 69–74, 1987; Saunders, J. and Choi, T. H., Trade with China and Japan. *Management Decision* 24, 3 pp. 7–12, 1986; Warrington, M. B., Doing business in China: Britons may have the advantage. *Management Decision*, 21, 6, pp. 25–30, 1983.
4 For example, Pye, L. *Chinese commercial negotiating style.* New York: Oelgeschlager, Gunn and Hain, 1982; Shenkar, O. and Ronen, S., The cultural context of negotiations: the implications of Chinese interpersonal norms. *Journal of Applied Behavioural Science*, 23, 2, pp. 263–75, 1987; Warrington, M. B. and McCall, J. B. Negotiating a foot into the Chinese door. *Management Decision*, 21, 2, pp. 3–13, 1983.
5 Pye, L., *op. cit.* p. 74, 1986.
6 *op. cit.* p. 11.
7 Pye, L., *op. cit.* p. 20, 1982.
8 For example, Cohen, H., *You can negotiate anything*, New Jersey: Lyle Stuart,

1980; Nierenberg, G. I., *The art of negotiating*. New York: Pocket Books, 1981; Schatzki, M., *Negotiation: The art of getting what you want*. New York: Signet, 1981.

9 Atkinson, G. G. M., *The effective negotiator*. London: Quest, 1975.

10 Fisher, R. and Ury, W., *Getting to yes: Negotiating agreements without giving in*. Boston: Houghton-Mifflin, 1981.

11 Morley, I. and Stephenson, G., *The social psychology of bargaining*. London: Allen and Unwin, 1977; Rubin, J. Z. and Brown, B. R., *The social psychology of bargaining and negotiation*. New York: Academic Press, 1975.

12 Bazerman, M. H. and Lewicki, R. J., *Negotiating in organizations*. Beverly Hills: Sage, 1983.

13 Stevens, C. M., *Strategy and collective bargaining negotiations*. New York: McGraw-Hill, 1963.

14 Lewicki, R. J. and Litterer, J. A., *Negotiation*. Homewood, Illinois: Irwin, 1985.

15 Employment Relations, *An introduction to negotiation*. Cambridge, U.K.: Employment Relations Limited, 1980; Employment Relations, *Collective bargaining*. Cambridge, U.K.: Employment Relations Limited, 1981.

16 Lewicki and Litterer, *op. cit*. p. 58, 1985.

17 See for example, Kirkbride, P. S., Tang S. F. Y. and Westwood, R. I., *Chinese bargaining and negotiating behaviour: The cultural effects*. Working Paper No 23, City Polytechnic of Hong Kong, 1988. Tang S. F. Y. and Kirkbride, P. S. Developing conflict management skills in Hong Kong: An analysis of some cross-cultural implications, *Management Education and Development*, 17, 3, pp. 287–301, 1986.

18 Graham, J. L. and Herberger, R. A., Negotiators abroad – Don't shoot from the hip, *Harvard Business Review*, July/August, pp. 160–68, 1983.

19 Employment Relations, *op. cit*. p. 36, 1980.

20 Armstrong, P. J., Goodman, J. F. B. and Hyman, J. D., *Ideology and shop-floor industrial relations*, London, Croom Helm, 1981.

21 Kirkbride, P. S. and Durcan, J. W., Bargaining power and industrial relations, *Personnel Review*, 16, 2, pp. 3–11, 1987.

22 Employment Relations, *op. cit*. p. 36, 1980.

23 Pye, L., *op. cit*. p. 40, 1982.

24 Kirkbride, Tang, and Westwood, *op. cit*, 1988.

25 Frankenstein, *op. cit*. p. 149, 1986.

26 Pye, L., *op. cit*. p. 42, 1982.

27 Hawver, D. A., *How to improve your negotiating skills*. New York: Alexander Hamilton Institute, Inc., 1982.

28 Rackham, N. and Carlisle, J., The effective negotiator – Part 2. *Journal of European Industrial Training*, 2, 7, p. 3, 1987b.

29 Employment Relations, *op. cit*. p. 38, 1980.

30 Kirkbride, Tang, and Westwood, *op. cit*, 1988.

31 Pye, L., *op. cit*. p. 77, 1982.

32 Rackham and Carlisle, *op. cit*. p. 4, 1978b.

33 Graham and Herberger, *op. cit*. p. 164, 1983.

34 Hwang, C. H., Studies in Chinese personality: A critical review. *Bulletin of Educational Psychology*, 15, pp. 227–40, 1982.

35 Yang, K. S., Chinese personality and its change. In M. H. Bond, (Ed.), *The psychology of the Chinese people*, Hong Kong, Oxford University Press, p. 147, 1986.

36 Yang, *op. cit*. p. 148, 1986.

37 Hofstede, G., *Culture's consequences: International differences in work related values*. London: Sage, 1984.

38 Rackham, N. and Carlisle, J., The effective negotiator – Part 1. *Journal of European Industrial Training*, 2, 6, pp. 6–11, 1978a and Rackham, N. and Carlisle, J., The effective negotiator – Part 2. *Journal of European Industrial Training*, 2, 7, pp. 2–6, 1978b.

39 Tang and Kirkbride, *op. cit*, 1986.

40 Redding, S. G., Cognition as an aspect of culture and its relation to management processes: An exploratory view of the Chinese case. *Journal of Management Studies*, 17, pp. 127–48, 1980.

41 Hofstede, *op. cit*, 1984.

42 Benedict, R., *The chrysanthemum and the sword.*, London: Secker and Warburg, 1947.

43 Becker, C. B., Reasons for the lack of argumentation and debate in the Far East. *International Journal of Inter-Cultural Relations*, 10, pp. 75–92, 1986.

44 Employment Relations, *op. cit.* p. 34, 1980.

45 Goffman, E., On face-work: An analysis of ritual elements in social interaction, *Psychiatry*, 18, 3, pp. 213–31, 1955.

46 Lin, Y. T., *My country and my people.* Hong Kong: Heineman, 1977.

47 Hu, H. C., The Chinese concepts of face, *American Anthropologist*, 46, pp. 45–64, 1944.

48 Employment Relations, *op. cit.* Note 5, 1981.

49 Hofstede, *op. cit*, 1984.

50 *op. cit.* p. 166.

51 Pye, L., *op. cit.* p. 53, 1982.

52 *op. cit.* p. 55.

53 Fathers, M. and Higgins, A. *Tiananmen: The rape of Peking*. London: Independent/Doubleday, p. 72, 1989.

54 Fong, L. T. (Ed)., *Democracy movement.* Hong Kong: Ming Pao Publishing (In Chinese), p. 73, 1989.

55 *op. cit.* p. 73.

56 Rackham and Carlisle, *op. cit*, 1978.

57 Becker, *op. cit*, 1986.

58 Pye, L., *op. cit.* p. 69, 1982.

Reproduced from Kirkbride, P. S. and Tang, S. F. Y. (1990). Negotiation: lessons from behind the bamboo curtain. *Journal of General Management*, **16** (1), 1–13, by permission of *Journal of General Management*.

Part Four

Acculturation: adapting to other cultures

Acculturation

One definition of acculturation is that of Berry (1980, p. 215): 'changes induced in (two cultural) systems as a result of the diffusion of cultural elements in both directions'. In other words, whenever individuals from two cultures come together, for example by working together or through living in a different country, a change takes place whereby individuals adapt or react to the other culture. Such cultural exchanges take place in international mergers and acquisitions.

Mergers and acquisitions

The first reading in Chapter Eight (Olie, 1990) points to some of the issues and problems involved, by reference to the merger or acquisition relationship of the organizations concerned. This contrasts two dimensions: cooperation–dominance, and low–high integration needs. Not all acquisitions, for example, require a high integration of cultures, the acquired company being kept at arm's length. However, when there is a need for a high level of integration then an acquired company may have to accept the dominant culture of its acquirer, or in the case of a merger, may have to develop a 'third' culture, drawing on the synergies of the two partners.

This first reading therefore sets the scene. The second reading provides a more detailed analysis of the acculturation process within mergers and acquisitions (Nahavandi and Malekzadeh, 1988). This analysis is based on a model which looks for congruence between the acquired firm's and acquirer's modes of acculturation. This, in turn, is based on four modes of integration: adaption (but not losing cultural identity), assimilation (adopting the culture of the other), separation (remaining independent and retaining own culture) and deculturation (losing cultural and psychological contact, usually leading to the disintegration of the company as a cultural entity). The degree of congruence, as a result of the level of compatibility between the two cultures, defines the extent of acculturation stress. This is a factor in the successful implementation of a merger or acquisition.

The problems of expatriate acculturation

The problems of expatriate assignment failures are well documented by the two readings in Chapter Nine (Mendenhall and Oddou, 1985; Hiltrop and Janssens, 1990), both indicating contributing factors and offering possible solutions in selection and training.

For Mendenhall and Oddou (1985) an analysis of expatriate acculturation involves the consideration of four dimensions: self-orientation, others-orientation, perceptual dimension and cultural-toughness. The first dimension involves factors which strengthen self confidence. They discuss 'reinforcement substitution', which involves the ability to replace familiar activities with those drawn from the host culture, stress reduction activities, and technical competences as part of the self-oriented dimension. The others-oriented dimension involves the ability to develop relations, and willingness to use language to communicate to develop relationships rather than simply for job-related utility. The perceptual dimension involves the management of causal attribution and cognitive evaluation in interpreting host nationals' behaviour. The contextual factors are summed up in the cultural-toughness dimension. Simply stated, some national cultures are more difficult to penetrate than others, for guest nationals from countries whose culture appears to be widely different.

Hiltrop and Janssens (1990) delineate three broad factors associated with expatriate performance: personal characteristics, characteristics of the expatriate's family and factors related to the subsidiary–parent company relations. Specifically, personal attributes are technical ability, stress tolerance, flexibility, communication skills and cultural empathy. Adaptability of spouse and children is a major factor in expatriate failure and needs to be addressed at the selection stage. Subsidiary–parent relations may cause conflicts of interest for the expatriate where the objectives of the parent do not coincide with the needs and expectations of the subsidiary.

The implications of these factors are discussed in each of the readings, and recommendations made for selection and training.

References

Berry, J. W. (1980) 'Social and cultural change', in H. C. Triandis and R. W. Brislin (eds), *Handbook of Cross-cultural Psychology*, Vol 5, 211–79. Boston: Allyn and Bacon.

Hiltrop, J. M. and Janssens, M. (1990) 'Expatriation: challenges and recommendations', *European Management Journal*, Vol 8, No 1, March, 19–26.

Mendenhall, M. and Oddou, G. (1985) 'The dimensions of expatriate acculturation: a review', *Academy of Management Review*, Vol 10, No 1, 39–47.

Nahavandi, A. and Malekzadeh, A. R. (1988) 'Acculturation in mergers and acquisitions', *Academy of Management Review*, Vol 13, No 1, 79–90.

Olie, R. (1990), 'Culture and integration problems in international mergers and acquisition', *European Management Journal*, Vol 8, No 2, 206–15.

8 Cultural exchange in mergers and acquisitions

8.1 Culture and integration problems in international mergers and acquisitions

René Olie

Introduction

Mergers and acquisitions continue to be important vehicles for organizational growth. A merger wave is sweeping through Europe. In most countries, the number of domestic mergers and acquisitions increased drastically in the past few years. In addition, many companies started teaming up in cross-border alliances such as joint ventures, cooperative agreements and mergers and acquisitions to achieve Europe-wide market shares, economies of scale or the critical mass to allow high R&D expenditures. Cross-border acquisitions of British firms increased by almost 80% between 1986 and 1988. The increase for French firms was even more overwhelming: an increase from 20 to 195 in just one year. An important reason behind the increased merger activity is '1992'. For many firms the disappearance of barriers in Europe creates new opportunities and challenges, but also means threats from non-familiar competitors.

Mergers and acquisitions are a significant strategic alternative to internal growth of firms, because they enable firms fast penetration of new and foreign markets, obtain economies of scale more quickly and or acquire necessary know-how and skilled personnel. Yet, the success of an acquisition strategy is not guaranteed. On the contrary, many financial studies regarding domestic mergers show that on average the profitability gains from mergers and acquisitions are limited or nonexistent. Some mergers may be profitable, but others never reach their financial goals. Estimates of success rates vary between 40 and 60%, while failure rates are estimated between 20 and 50%, often implying divestures. In addition, in between success and failure is a category of approximately 20% of ventures that can be qualified as 'uninteresting'. Some reports on the effectiveness of mergers are even more pessimistic, stating that one half to two thirds of all mergers and acquisitions simply do not work. Despite these somewhat alarming figures, we must compare these results with alternative strategies such as greenfield investments and the starting up of new activities in internal growth.

Similar figures are found for international mergers. For example, Kitching [1] found that of 407 European acquisitions by US firms in the period between 1965 and 1970 only fifty per cent could be termed as successful. Well-known are examples of international cooperation and cross-border mergers that proved to be unsuccessful in the seventies, such as Dunlop-Pirelli, Hoogovens-Hoesch, the non-merging of Citroën-Fiat, or state-controlled ventures such as the Franco-British Concorde project ('At no time was it ever a marriage').

In spite of the incidence of this type of external growth, the evidence on the reasons of the success or failure of mergers and acquisitions is not abundant. Most research focuses on the strategic fit, i.e. the degree of relatedness between the two firms. The more related firms usually perform better than the unrelated ones. In addition, failures are often ascribed to a poor choice of merger partners due to inappropriate pre-merger analysis or to faulty motives. These studies suggest that more planning is needed and a better assessment of the potential partner will lead to more positive outcomes. The outcome of the merger nevertheless is not only dependent upon these 'static' parameters. Environmental conditions change and can have a profound effect upon the stability of the merger in question. Changing market conditions, technological developments and government policy have at least an equal impact upon the outcome of the combine. Indeed these factors may even be more important in the case of international mergers.

Another explanation for the lack of success of mergers and acquisitions points to the problems in the integration phase. It has been estimated that one third of all merger failures are caused by faulty integration [2]. Most mergers suffer in the beginning from what is termed as the post-merger syndrome.

Culture-related problems are often part of this integration process. In an assessment of Dutch mergers and acquisitions it appeared that financial issues may dominate the pre-merger phase, but personnel and culture problems are the prominent problems during the implementation. Of the 73 mergers investigated in the period between 1986 and 1988, 50% reported problems in relation with personnel and cultural issues [3]. Many mergers suffer to some extent from a set of symptoms in the integration period of what is called the postmerger syndrome [4]. On an individual level managers and employees show simultaneous fight–flight responses, a resistance to change, resentment of the acquired company's managers and a focus on personal security rather than organizational goals. Furthermore, people go through a culture shock, and cultural differences are often cited as a source of hostility. At the organizational level, the syndrome is visible through a tendency to not pass information or problems up or down, a tendency among top management on both sides to not communicate with their respective organization, and conflicts between the acquired organization often quite intense. Furthermore, there is a tendency towards a decrease in earnings and productivity, but also a tendency towards high rates of turnover. The syndrome is, among others, affected by the amount of change that is required of the organization.

Culture-related phenomena in relation with different types of mergers and acquisitions

Cultural differences often seem to lie at the root of merger failures. They are often part of the problems that give problems in the integration of the merger. Organizational cultures tend to follow lines of the industry and the country. The organizational culture of a bank will be very comparable to another bank in the same country, but very different to an organization in the seashore industry. Likewise, these differences occur also according to country culture. Illustrative is the overall long-term orientation of Japanese organizations in comparison with American firms in the same industry. Sony's former president Akio Morita, for example, once said that American firms have a planning horizon of just ten minutes. Thus, some organizations are more difficult to combine than others, some combinations of firms will be more synergistic than others. The effect of these differences, however, will be moderated by several factors related to the degree of change and the extent in which this change is regarded favourably. Three factors seem to be important:

(a) The degree of integration between the two organizations. Integration between the two participating firms can range from weak to strong. Postcombination integration efforts tend to be minimal, for example, in the case of financial integration in which only financial systems and reporting relations may be modified. The other extreme is operational integration which involves significant changes for the target firm or partner firm. It may be obvious that in the latter type the significance of culture and cultural differences will be increased in the integration period. In general, resistance to cultural change is related to the degree of change involved; the more radical the change, the greater the likely resistance. Especially when the desired changes involve many shared assumptions, more central assumptions and a movement toward a more alien, sometimes less intrinsically appealing culture [5].

(b) The kind of cultural exchange [6]. In most mergers and acquisitions a unilateral adoption of culture, practices and identity from the acquiring firms by the acquired firm takes place. Organizations become fully integrated in the operations of the parent firm. Often they lose their separate corporate identity. This unilateral exchange of cultural elements is called assimilation. The other extreme of acculturation is integration, which in this respect means a mutual exchange of cultural elements.

In some cases, the exchange of cultural elements is neither between these two opposites, as in the example of financial integration or in the case of financial take-overs. In cases in which a stronger integration between the participating organizations is required, but unilateral flow of organizational culture is not possible, such as in a merger or joint venture, are more based upon cooperation, than domination. Cooperation characterizes also the prevailing dynamism in some acquisitions more than domination.

The positioning on this dimension is strongly determined by the power differential between the firms which is defined by their initial negotiating power based on assets, resources and access to alternative strategies. Furthermore, the motives and needs of the acquiring party or merging parties are important in deciding which acculturation mode will be followed.

Combining the integration mode and the acculturation/cooperation–domination mode, four main types of mergers and acquisitions can be distinguished. These are depicted in Figure 1. The positioning of organizational combinations on these two dimensions will vary according to the motives and expectations, as well as the bargaining power of the two firms. For example, the greater the firms resources, the better the bargaining position. In reverse, the greater the need of a partner ('white Knight rescue') the more disadvantageous for its bargaining position. The greater the power differential, the greater the possibility for a firm to unilaterally impose its structure and culture on the other firm. A small firm can still strike a balance to a certain extent with a larger firm because of its special assets. In addition to these motives, expectations and bargaining power, external conditions like industry structure and competitive behaviour can have an effect upon the configuration.

Acquisitions which are characterized by a slight power differential or whose dominant mode is cooperation, and simultaneously show a low extent of integration with the acquiring firm, are mostly found in unrelated/conglomerate mergers. In this the acquiring firm leaves the acquired firm alone, changing little or none of its management or operations. This happens in so-called financial takeovers or in acquisitions that are the result of a diversification strategy in order to spread risk. The acquisition of the Dutch firm Hendricks, a firm specializing in biotechnology by British Petroleum, is the result of a strategy to secure its position in future markets. Because of the lack of know-how in the field and the reputation of the acquired firm, the latter is mostly left to its own. The acquired firm maintains its corporate identity, personnel changes are minimal and, as said before, limited control is exerted by the acquiring firm. Culture related conflicts therefore tend to be minimal.

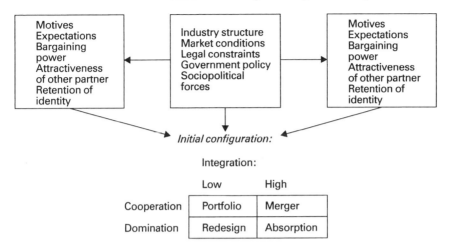

Figure 1 *Different forms of mergers and acquisitions*

The second type is the merger, often described as a marriage. These marriages, however, are very difficult to realize since they involve two partners of more or less equal strength which have decided to blend their operational and managerial functions. This implies that both firms are confronted with a change of corporate identity and organizational culture. Neither of the two companies have the power to unilaterally impose its own structure and culture on the other company. Since both companies are equal, they have to develop a 'third culture'. Not many international examples of this kind exist. Royal Dutch/Shell and Unilever (both Dutch-English) are successful examples. Other examples are SAS (Scandinavian countries), Agfa-Gevaert (German-Belgian) and Hoogovens-Hoesch (Dutch-German). Recent examples are Amro Bank-Generale Bank (Dutch-Belgian), which already exploded in its premerger period, Asea-Brown Boveri (Swedish-Swiss) and Leyland Daf Trucks (English-Dutch).

The third combination is the absorptive acquisition. As in the merger type the goal is to create synergy, therefore integration needs are strong. Only in this case a clear power difference exists between the two organizations. This type is most frequent among horizontal acquisitions.

The fourth type is also characterized by a clear power differential. Although synergy is not the objective in this type of combination, the acquiring party may still exert its influence and force its management methods upon the target firm. This may happen in cases in which the acquiring management believes it can transfer its management know-how and techniques to other (related) industries. Often management of the acquired firm is replaced.

We must realize that this is a rather crude classification; not all mergers and acquisitions can be fitted into these four types. For example, vertical acquisitions will be somewhere halfway on the integration dimensions. However, the four types give an indication of the extent and type of postmerger integration difficulties in general, and of culture-related problems in particular. The role of culture-related problems will be minor in unrelated mergers or acquisitions in comparison, while significant in cases in which no unilateral flow of cultural elements can take place, though integration needs are strong. Changes in both organizations take place and a third culture needs to be developed to overcome disparities. In contrast, in acquisitions that are characterized here as redesign and absorption mergers, only one company is undergoing changes. Due to the power differential, there is one dominant culture that has to be accepted. The impact of cultural processes in these types can vary according to a third set of factors:

(c) The extent to which the own cultural identity of the firm is valued and the other firm's culture is regarded as attractive [7]. In general, problems in the integration period will be minor when wishes and needs from both the acquiring and acquired party coincide.

Problems will arise when the retention of the own cultural identity does not go along with an assimilation tendency from the side of the acquiring firm. Similarly, problems are bound to occur when the partner's culture is not valued as an attractive option, which may happen in hostile takeovers. Organizations may give up their identity freely when an organization has not been very successful and members perceive that their strategies, goals and values, derived from their culture, are hindering the organization's performance.

When forced to give up their identity, organization members resist openly or show resignation, but at a deeper level continue to resist. The result is a split culture: an organization with different subcultures. An excellent illustration is provided by Linda Smircich's study [8] about an insurance company which was part of a much larger organization serving agriculture. At a certain moment new professionals were brought in after the demotion of its president. This led to the development of two distinct subcultures: the first was represented by the original staff, of the 'inside group'; the second consisted of the newly recruited professionals, the 'outside group'. These professionals had strong ideas about what was needed in the new organization. 'This is how we did it at . . .' was a common phrase. Due to such differences, genuine concerns were not given the attention they deserved. The parent group eventually decided to reabsorb the insurance company into the main company. The example also shows that acquisitions which may start as portfolio or redesign acquisitions may finally end up as absorption acquisitions.

The positive attitude towards the acquisition or merger and the other partner is found to have a profound influence and is an important predictor of the merger's success. Although mergers are based more on cooperation than acquisitions, this does not automatically imply a positive attitude towards the other partner. There are several reasons why a merger is not adopted wholeheartedly by one of the partners. This may be the case when the merger is more a result of a defensive strategy in which no other alternative options are available. In addition, there may exist differing ideas about retention of old identities within the same firm. Middle management may not be as convinced of the merger as top management is. The attitude of middle management in this is relatively important because it is they who usually have to bring about the merger. A third reason for a less positive attitude is when the merger is advocated by outside parties. This may be the case in state-controlled enterprises or firms which rely heavily on government orders.

In sum, the extent of integration and the acculturation mode were identified as major determinants of which specific set of culture-related problems in the post-combination period can be expected. These in turn are defined by firm-specific variables such as motives, including strategies, needs and bargaining power. Variables, specific of the external environment, such as firm structure, further set the constraints for the chosen configuration. In addition, the need to retain one's own culture and the attractiveness of the other party determine the intensity of these problems.

The role of culture in international mergers and acquisitions

So far nothing has been said specifically about the international aspects of mergers and acquisitions. It may be clear that the suggested classification of combinations is relevant for both domestic and international mergers and acquisitions, except that in the latter some external conditions will come to play a bigger part. National culture is not seen here as an environmental condition (which may be partly correct too), but as incorporated in the firm's needs and motives. The influence on the chosen configuration can be quite strong. For example, Kogut and Singh [9] found in their study, in which they analyzed the different entry modes of foreign firms in the United States, that the choice for acquisition was negatively related to the cultural distance of its home country and the cultural characteristic of risk avoidance. Thus, Japanese firms strongly opted for joint venture agreements instead of acquisitions of wholly owned firms in the United States.

Integration in international mergers and acquisitions will probably be more troublesome, especially for absorption and redesign acquisitions when pressures for assimilation increase. This is because a culture is central to a group's identity and view of reality; as a result it is not given up lightly. This may apply to an organization within the same country and will even be more valid when organizations from different countries are involved.

So far, we have used the term culture both for organizational and national levels alternately, yet its implication is somewhat different. Both uses of the term culture refer to a *social* process of understanding and interpreting the world surrounding us. Culture is often compared to a lens through which we perceive the world. When we depict culture as an onion, the outer layers are the organizational culture. The organizational culture is embodied in symbols, rituals and heroes [10]. Symbols are words, gestures and objects. Corporate identity programmes are, for example, part of this symbolic level of culture. The symbolic level further includes manners of speaking and dress habits. Rituals refer to social rules and norms which need to be followed in a certain environment, while heroes are persons that are used as role models. They possess characteristics that are highly valued in an organization. National culture, in contrast, relates to the more central layers. Values represent this side of the spectrum: they are feelings of right and wrong, good and evil, beautiful and ugly, rational and irrational. It is believed that these values are already acquired in early childhood and are resistant to change in later years. National cultural values are more part of ourselves than we usually realize. As with an iceberg, most of it remains under the surface; organizational cultures refer more to the elements that can be seen instead. A society's values are formed in its history and they tend to be transferred from generation to generation, reinforced by social institutions. In a similar way, organizational cultures are also formed in early history; the founders often play an important role in its creation [11].

Research indicates that the dominant values in a national culture have a profound effect upon organizations and organizational behaviour. For example, French and Italian firms tend to have strong centralized hierarchical structures in which patriarchal influence of the patronage is strongly felt. In contrast, Northern European firms, such as Dutch and German firms, are more decentralized. National cultures may further influence the formalization of an organization, its decision-making style and its strategy, as we have seen in the example above. The national culture also has a profound effect upon the organizational culture of its national organizations. This effect is achieved through the values of the organizational leaders and members that are brought into the organization. Organizations can, however, possess distinct cultures in terms of symbols, rituals and heroes within the same country. IBM has a very distinct corporate identity from that of Ford or Du Pont, yet all three are US companies.

In the case of a foreign acquisition, both the companies' organizational culture, which is characteristic of the firms' identity, and elements of the host national culture are brought in. As we have seen earlier, cultural clashes will tend to be minimal when coordination is of a financial nature, but will increase when closer integration is imperative.

The international merger is a special case. In foreign takeovers, potential cultural conflicts will be solved through the bargaining power of the dominant partner. Such is impossible in a merger in which both partners are roughly of equal size or importance. There are two cultures or value patterns which are more or less compatible with each other. No dominant 'home culture' is available which can provide a frame of reference. This case is similar in many respects to joint ventures where the management is shared between the two partners. In this case a third culture has to be developed by the two partners. On the basis of research on national cultures we may, for example, argue that some cultures can be more easily combined than others [12]. Because of weak success of German–Dutch mergers in comparison with some British–Dutch ventures, it is, for example, argued that the latter combination creates a cultural synergy, while the former creates an anergy. A few examples of cultural differences in international ventures:

The American managers of a U.S. subsidiary of a Japanese bank showed great difficulties with the absence of clearly stated, measurable performance targets on the part of their Japanese superiors. The philosophy of the Japanese bankers was markedly different to that of their own. As one of the Japanese bankers stated: 'If only I could get these Americans to understand our philosophy of banking. To understand what the business means to us, how we feel we should deal with our customers and our employees. What our relationship should be to the local communities we serve. How we should deal with our competitors, and what our role should be in the world at large. If they could get that under their skin, then they could figure out for themselves what an appropriate objective would be for any situation . . . and I would never have to tell them, never have to give them a target' [13].

A similar experience comes from a British–American joint venture. The board of directors of this company consisting of American and British managers, continually disagreed vehemently about the amount of data required before a decision could be made. The British could not understand why the Americans wanted all those numbers. The Americans, on the other hand, believed the British were totally flying blind [14].

A final example of different working methods comes from a German–Dutch merger. Discussions in board meetings showed a lack of synergy. A favourite expression was that the Dutch liked basic discussions, while Germans favoured basic decisions instead.

Culture is not to be viewed only as a simple variable that societies or organizations possess. It must simultaneously be understood as an active, living phenomenon through which people create and recreate the worlds in which they live. Culture is a lens through which we perceive the world surrounding us; it is a sensemaking process, a frame of reference that guides our actions and thoughts. In acquisitions such as absorption and redesign acquisitions this frame of reference is supplied by the parent organization. In mergers it has to be recreated.

Additional specific obstacles in the integration of international mergers and acquisitions

Cultural differences are not the only problems in the integration of international organizations, and especially in mergers, that hinder an effective integration. Due to their different environment, legal conditions, tax problems and the role of governments may be important obstacles to achieve a merger. Once they are resolved, they may continue to play a role in the integration and process of the merger. Those national governments which are at first lenient towards an international merger, may start to reconsider their stance when confronted with worsening industry conditions. Or it may actually hinder effective integration to favour one of the partners with subsidies, financial help unilaterally, or to change the legal conditions in general. In a way these specific obstacles are related to an inadequate European integration so far. Many of these obstacles played a role in European cross-border mergers in the seventies, such as Hoogovens-Hoesch in the steel industry, Fokker-VFW in the aircraft industry. Just recently, a planned merger between the Amro Bank, a Dutch bank, and the Generale Bank in Belgium was cancelled partly for reasons of a lack of legal harmonization in Europe. However, these are probably not the main reasons why international mergers are so difficult to accomplish.

Previously, we discussed the existence of a merger syndrome in domestic mergers and acquisitions. Such a syndrome can also be identified at the international level. Apart from cultural difference as a source of problems, resistance to change, the perceived threat of concentration and nationalism are identified as problems. Not surprisingly, these problems tend to have a nationalistic bias. For one of the characteristics of culture is that it creates a form of ethnocentrism: we tend to regard activities that do not conform to our established views of doing business as abnormal and deviant.

In an investigation among 150 top managers of international firms [15], human factors were found to be of prime importance. The first was management's reluctance to implement changes per se. This resistance showed itself in two ways. The first was a resistance to change in working methods. Management will be reluctant to modify its own policies and procedures, because one is convinced that one's own way is the best since it has been effective in the past. Each partner will insist on his way of doing business. A second manifestation of resistance is the opposition against any alienation of the national character of the environment. A second issue was the perceived threat to one's personal position after the concentration. The typical concern of top management is to retain its freedom and to remain 'one's own boss'. A further concern is often the fear that a deteriorating national economic situation will put them at a competitive disadvantage in relation to their foreign partners. In contrast, the fear of middle management is that of rationalizations and losing career opportunities. This fear in international link-up is exacerbated by unfamiliarity of middle managers with their foreign counterparts. Interviewees in Mazzolini's research reported inferiority complexes with regard to foreign managers. These were mostly reported with reference to German managers, which was generated by the postwar economic success of Germany. In case of rationalizations, the company would get rid of them and retain the more capable, hard-working German managers instead. More than superior managerial skill, the Germans were viewed as having remarkable working potential, having the ability to discipline themselves and to produce an outstanding collective effort. As lay-offs are mostly avoided in international link-ups because of the sensitivity of the issue, the fear of losing career opportunities may well be the most serious problem here.

A third human issue in international acquisitions and mergers is nationalism. All kinds of animosities and prejudices between countries in Europe exist which have an historical basis. Strongest animosities were reported in Mazzolini's investigation in relation with Germany, due to the Second World War. A second source of nationalism is a nationalism for its own sake, i.e. a bias in favour of maintaining the national identity of organization on the grounds of managerial and economic chauvinism.

The foregoing makes clear that the integration of a merger or takeover in the international field is full of problems and that these ventures are not very stable in their first few years. Its stability may not only be endangered by internal struggles, but also by external forces, such as changing economic conditions, legal regulations which forces to adopt a new configuration. In the next section, the integration process is discussed in relation with international mergers. In Figure 2, which is an extension of the model presented in Figure 1, this process is visualized.

A dynamic model of merger stability

In a merger two formerly independent organizations unite into a single organization with a common and co-equal identity, hierarchy, system and power. Although the firms A and B may bring in distinct motives, expectations, and resources, there may be small power of resource differentials, which rules out possibilities for a clear acquisition of one by the other. In the case of international ventures the choice for the merger mode may be partly motivated by external conditions. For example, the industry structure, such as the lack of potential acquisitions candidates, or because national governments refuse to let a strategic industry be taken over. For example, during the 1960s and 70s the role of multinational corporations was heavily criticized because of their part in taking decisions outside a country which could

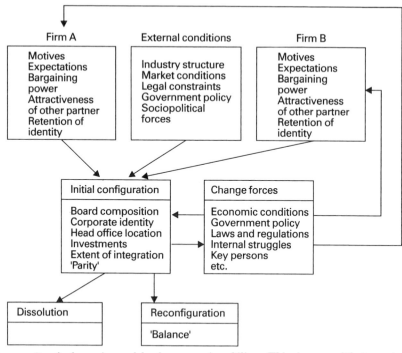

Figure 2 *A dynamic model of merger instability. This is a modified version of Harrigain's model of joint venture stability*

significantly affect their well-being, the removal from the local money market of high-potential stock, the threat to labour of moving operations from one country to another, the limitations of career opportunities, and the blocking of national research efforts. The creation of cross-border mergers instead of a foreign acquisition helped to circumvent many of these problems for firms who wanted to expand internationally.

The additional set of factors in relation with international business ventures, such as differing labour conditions, including workers participation, the attitude of political parties and the differing laws and regulations may further have an effect upon the actual form of the configuration.

The objective in a merger is to achieve a synthesis of the management systems and identities of the two organizations. Roughly there are two extremes in this: on the one extreme, a loosely coupled structure, in which the participating companies coexist under an umbrella organization, leaving most of the original organizations intact. This solution is possible when the two partner firms have few overlapping activities, or are able to agree upon a division of tasks and responsibilities. This was the case with AGFA-Gevaert. The division of market between the two companies was fairly clear cut; Agfa had always had a good name in the amateur market, and Gevaert on the industrial side – in fact, it was this complementary interest which encouraged them to discuss merger in the first place. In the other extreme, the two organizations are closely interwoven; they are combined in a new structure. Enka, a German – Dutch merger (previously named Enka-Glanzstoff) chose to integrate its activities as much as possible. Especially, departments such as purchasing, sales and distribution were integrated. Consequently, such an operation also involved the relocation of departments and the transfer of managers across the national border.

Because the organizational parties regard themselves as co-equals, the initial configuration of international mergers is often characterized by parity. Every indication that one of the parties is dominating the venture is avoided. This parity is applied to management positions, the composition of the management board, the issue of presidency, new investments and the location of the head office. To ensure a balance of control, agreements usually specify that managerial key positions will be staffed on a 50–50 basis. In addition, the two parties will demand that an equal share of new investments will be channelled into their home countries. An important issue is also the location of a head office or the place for coordinating teams to meet. In case a single head office is chosen, it is usually located somewhere in the middle. The coordinating teams in the Agfa-Gevaert merger started to meet at a hotel equidistant from both main plants. The head office of Fokker and VFW was located in Düsseldorf, a place which is somewhere between the main plants in Amsterdam and Bremen. The appointment of a single president who acts as an ultimate authority is often regarded as an infringement of the balance of power. In most cases two presidents are appointed who alternately preside meetings in the respective home countries.

In addition, a new name is chosen for the merged firms, e.g. Estel for the steel merger Hoogovens – Hoesch. More often the new name is a combination of the old corporate identities. Here difficulties often start with the problem which name is to precede. Both partners are attached to their own, and equally valid arguments can be produced to support either partner's case. In the case of Agfa–Gevaert a fixed order of names was chosen. The joint name was to appear on all advertising and packing, but the trade mark used was to depend on which product was being promoted; Agfa for consumer goods, Gevaert for technical and industrial products. In other cases this issue is solved through a flexible order of the names. Thus it became Enka–Glanzstoff BV for the Dutch part of the organization and Glanzstoff–Enka AG for the German part when these two firms merged in 1969. A similar compromise was found in the aircraft merger Fokker–VFW (or VFW–Fokker). Very often, the corporate identity of the new firm proves to be a very emotional issue. A illustrative example is the name of the Franco-British aircraft joint venture which was Concorde for the French and Concord for the British. Memoranda were circulated saying that the 'official

British spelling was Concord and that deviations in the form of an additional "e" were not permitted' [16].

Paradoxically, in contrast with the goal behind every merger of creating a new common identity which will be profitable to both, both parties tend to think in terms of separate entities with diverging interests and – sometimes – opposing goals rather than in terms of cooperation in order to achieve this higher goal.

Managers and employees have to relinquish their old identities and shed their loyalties to the new firm. There is, however, a tendency to stick to the old corporate identities. As we have seen, this may be because of emotional reasons because the firm provides an identity on which one is proud or for nationalistic reasons why people would attach to a certain identity. Attachment to the old structures is further explained by political and strategic reasons. There are usually powerful groups of people in any organization whose particular interest is to maintain the status quo. The chief executive of an apparently independent organization seems to have more status than the manager of a division. Reorganizations probably imply the loss of status, and in some cases involve even the loss of one's job. As a result, resistance to change may be quite strong. As a manager of an international merger noted: 'Tacit political factions developed to sabotage the consolidation: managers avoided any collaboration and pointed to the administrative frictions to demonstrate the inadvisability of the collaboration'[17].

The shifting of loyalties may be one of the most difficult aspects to achieve in a merger. For example, in the proposed bank merger between Amro bank and Generale, this argument was named as the most important reason eventually to refrain from the merger.

Thus there exists a strong tendency to favour solutions that satisfy partial interests instead of the interest of the whole group. Conflict may arise when parties bargain over decisions which may decrease one party's power and control while increasing the other's parity in the initial configuration is often a necessity to minimize these conflicts. These win–lose battles may turn into lose–lose battles when self-serving actions are undertaken. Once started, self-serving actions lead to a vicious circle of mutual distrust that is most difficult to break. These conflicts are exacerbated by cultural differences which provide ethnocentric lenses and which often result in the attribution of negative meanings to the behaviours in the other organization. The famous dictum: 'when people perceive situations as real, they are real in their consequences', is then often appropriate. If unchecked, the mutual distrust usually increases in intensity until the venture is irretrievably poisoned.

In conclusion, it may be clear that the first stage in a merger is full of potential conflicts and that the initial configuration is very unstable because of intrinsic factors: not only because of win–lose battles over integration efforts, but also because of the organizational lay-out in which numerical parity proves to be ineffective. As it seldom happens that both companies are in the possession of equal resources of management talent, the international merger may suffer from a top management which is not staffed with the most competent persons. For this reasons some transnational corporations such as Shell and Unilever have gradually abandoned the concept of absolute numerical parity after several years. A related problem concerns the number of members in the top management of the new organization. In general, top managers will not agree to a deterioration of their pre-merger status. Consequently, often both managing committees are simply put together. In their effort to find enough legitimate tasks for the extended top management, the partners may tend to split tasks that logically belong together. The resulting overcompartmentalization can severely impede the management coordination and communication. Similarly, as long as a sense of unity is not achieved, people start to think in terms of competition, rather than in terms of cooperation.

The goal of a merger, however, is to overcome these separate identities and loyalties and disparate goals through the establishment of a common identity. In cultural terms this means to create a shared sense of reality. The function of a group ultimately hinges upon the ability to create such a shared sense of reality. Top management plays a crucial role in this process. It needs a very determined and strong-minded management to make the dramatic changes sometimes required and to bridge the conflicting interests of the two groups. The loss of these key-persons that have promoted the merger often has a disastrous effect upon the outcome of the merger.

Central in a cross-border merger is its concept of binationality. The exact parity in the new firm not only satisfies power needs, but also conveys symbolically the message that both partners are equal. However, parity is not a permanent solution because it creates efficiency problems. We can see that the initial configuration in which strict parity dominates, is gradually abandoned. Parity is then replaced by the concept of balance. As stated by a German top manager of a Dutch–German merger: 'We do not necessarily need exact parity on our Board of Management. But what we need is an organization and a top management that assures participation of both nationalities in the major decision making processes of the group in a manner that is convincing inside and outside the company'. In this merger the original German and Dutch organizations became more integrated through one chairman, one board instead of two with alternating chairmen and, in addition, one single name. These in turn, not only added to the economic and administrative efficiency, they also helped to further increase a sense of common identity. A similar effect has the use of a common management development programme. In order to emphasize binationality, however, often not all operations are integrated. As Shell and Unilever, this company retained both head offices. Since the location of a head office is easily associated with decision power, the presence of two head offices has a symbolic value stressing the binationality of the firm.

In sum, it is argued that due to differing loyalties and identities, as well as different motives, needs, expectancies, bargaining power and values that the two firms will bring into the combine, conflicting interests continue to exist over a long time. The integration of an international merger is a process of many years rather than months. Despite its seemingly economic ineffectiveness, the emphasis on parity promotes the sense of cooperation. Separately identifiable interests will gradually decrease and the initial configuration undergoes changes and becomes more resistant to internal frictions. However, this process may also be interrupted prematurely when extrinsic factors in the starting period gain a decisive influence. Important conditions may be: the loss of key persons or worsening economic conditions.

Existing separate loyalties can be more rapidly overcome by introducing common management programs, integration of tasks and responsibilities for managers or by creating common quantifiable goals and projects.

References

1 Kitching, J., Winning and losing with European acquisitions, *Harvard Business Review*, March–April. 1974, p. 124–136.
2 Kitching, J., Acquisition in Europe: causes of corporate success and failure. *Business International*, 1973, p. 20–35.
3 *Kenmerken van Overnames tussen Nederlandse ondernemingen*, Reitsma & Wertheim, 1988.
4 Bastine, D. T., Ven, van de A. H., Managerial and organizational dynamics of mergers and acquisitions, unpublished paper, University of Minnesota, 1986.
5 Buono, A. F. and Bowditch, J. L., *The human side of mergers and acquisitions*, Jossey-Bass, London, 1989.
6 Bastien, D. T. and Ven, van de A. H., *op. cit.*
7 Nahavandi, A., Malekzadeh, A. R., Acculturation in mergers and acquisitions, *Academy of Management Review*, 1, 1988, p. 79–90.
8 Smircich, L., Concepts of culture and organizational analysis, *Administrative Science Quarterly*, 28, 1983, p. 339–358.
9 Kogut, B., Singh, H., *Entering the United States by acquisition or joint venture, country patterns and cultural characteristics*, Reginald H. Jones Working Paper, Wharton School, 1986.
10 Hofstede, G., Organising for cultural diversity, *European Management Journal*, December 1989.
11 Schein, E., *Organizational culture and leadership*, Jossey-Bass, San Francisco, 1985.
12 Hofstede, G., *Culture's consequences*, Sage, San Francisco, 1980.
13 Ouchi, W., *Theory Z*, Addison-Wesley, Reading, Massachusetts, 1981, p. 34.
14 Killing, J., *Strategies for joint venture success*, Praeger, New York, 1983.
15 Mazzolini, R., *European Transnational concentrations*, McGraw-Hill, London, 1974.

16 Hochmuth, M. S., *Organizing the transnational*, Sijthoff, Leiden, 1974.
17 Mazzolini, R., *op. cit.*
18 Olins, W., *The corporate personality*, Design council, London, 1978.

Reproduced from Olie, R. (1990). Culture and integration problems in international mergers and acquisitions. *European Management Journal*, **8** (2), 206–15, by permission of *European Management Journal*.

8.2 Acculturation in mergers and acquisitions

Afsaneh Nahavandi and Ali R. Malekzadeh

Mergers have proven to be a significant and increasingly popular means for achieving corporate diversity and growth. The effectiveness of this strategy depends upon extensive planning and careful implementation (Blake and Mouton, 1984; Jemison and Sitkin, 1986; Salter and Weinhold, 1979). Most of the research on mergers has focused on strategic and financial fit between the acquirer and the acquired firms, though some research has dealt with the integration of various organizational systems, such as technology and management control systems (e.g. see Shrivastava, 1986).

These lines of research, although essential to an understanding of mergers, leave other important aspects relatively unexplored. With a few exceptions (e.g. Sales and Mirvis, 1984; Shrivastava, 1986), the role of sociocultural factors and the processes involved in merging two organizations as cultural entities have not been studied thoroughly (Jemison and Sitkin, 1986; Schein, 1985). Issues related to organizational fit and the management of human resources have received some attention (e.g. Barrett, 1973; Hayes, 1979; Sutton, 1983); however, much of the research has been prescriptive and relatively atheoretical, and few models that are applicable across different organizations have been proposed.

The role of acculturation in mergers is addressed in this paper and an interdisciplinary acculturative model of the planning and implementation of mergers as a strategic alternative is proposed. It is proposed that the degree of congruence between the preferred modes of acculturation for the acquirer and the acquired company will affect the success of the implementation of the merger. Other organizational systems such as structure, technology, and control systems are not specifically addressed. This model deals with diversification through acquisitions rather than diversification through internal means (i.e research and development). Theories from cross-cultural psychology are adapted to explain the processes of cultural adaptation and acculturation in mergers.

Review of existing research

Organizational culture

Culture is defined in many different ways (for a review see Jelinek, Smircich and Hirsch, 1983). Each of the various definitions emphasizes a particular focus and level of analysis (for some examples see Deal and Kennedy, 1982; Pettigrew, 1979; Smircich, 1983; Tagiuri and Litwin, 1968; Van Maanen, 1979). With a few exceptions (e.g. Schein, 1984, 1985), the definitions of culture, however, fail to recognize it as a multidimensional, multilevel concept.

Most of the definitions of culture focus on the beliefs that members of an organization share. Although the term often is used as if organizations have a monolithic culture, most firms have more than one set of beliefs influencing the behavior of employees (Sathe, 1985). These various subcultures within one organization may be divided along occupational, functional, product or geographical lines; such subcultures may be enhancing, orthogonal, or counter to one another (Sathe, 1985).

In this paper culture is defined as the beliefs and assumptions shared by members of an organization. It is assumed that although a firm may have a dominant culture, many subcultures may coexist and interact. Researchers and practitioners focus on different subcultures depending on their interests. However, understanding the culture of any company involves identifying and deciphering the various subcultures and gaining insight into how they interplay to influence organizational behavior and decision making.

Organizational culture has been used as an independent variable to explain differences in managerial styles and organizational practices (e.g. Roberts, 1970; Bhagat and McQuaid, 1982). It also has been used as an internal variable focusing on the cultural elements within organizations (e.g. Deal and Kennedy, 1982; Tichy, 1982). Culture also has been used to explain the success of some organizations (e.g. Peters and Waterman, 1982). In fact, some researchers suggest that fit between culture and strategy is an essential element in organizational effectiveness (Ackerman, 1984; Schwartz and Davis, 1981). Of particular interest in the study of mergers has been the use of culture as a variable assumed to influence the implementation of strategic decisions (Davis, 1984; Schwartz and Davis, 1981; Shrivastava, 1986) or as a determinant of strategy (Ackerman, 1984; Shrivastava, 1985). Most of the studies attempting to identify the factors that affect the success of mergers as a strategic alternative mention the importance of more subtle issues (e.g. Jemison and Sitkin 1986; Lubatkin, 1983, 1987; Marks, 1982). However, there appears to be a gap between the research about the various classifications of mergers and the research about the role culture plays in the overall implementation of mergers.

Mergers in strategic management research

In strategic management, mergers are most commonly classified on the degree of relatedness of two firms. Although this approach was developed for studying overall corporate diversification strategies, without distinguishing between internal and external means of diversification (Rumelt, 1974, 1982; Wrigley, 1970), it, along with Ansoff's corporate growth model (1965), is used in the study of strictly external diversifications (mergers) as well (i.e. Chatterjee, 1986; Lubatkin, 1987; Montgomery and Wilson, 1986). The research on relatedness has shown that although unrelated acquisitions can be successful (Montgomery and Wilson, 1986), firms that diversify into related businesses through internal or external means, on the average, outperform those that diversify into unrelated ones (Hawks, 1984; Kusewitt, 1985; Rumelt, 1974).

The choice of the degree of relatedness between the two firms in mergers depends upon the motives behind the merger. These motives can include achieving operating synergies in production, in marketing, in scheduling, in managerial experience, or in compensation systems (Chatterjee, 1986; Lubatkin, 1983). Also, many companies merge in order to achieve financial synergies such as risk reduction through diversification (Steiner, 1975) and access to more favorable financial terms (Lubatkin, 1983, 1987).

To obtain these synergies, a firm must select a merger target that is in varying degrees related to its business. Depending on the type of merger and the motive, the acquiring company must decide on an implementation strategy. That strategy determines the extent to which the various systems of the two firms will be combined and the degree to which the employees of the companies will interface.

For example, in unrelated mergers, the goal is to achieve financial synergy, thereby requiring little if any integration of the operations of the two companies (Shrivastava, 1986) and minimal contact between their employees. As the degree of relatedness decreases (e.g. in vertical or unrelated mergers), managers may be less willing to intervene in the business of the acquired unit (Walter, 1985). Therefore, the acquirer may impose changes only in the acquired unit's financial systems (Shrivastava, 1986). On the other hand, in related mergers, the acquirer is more likely to impose its own culture and practices on the acquired company (Walter, 1985), thereby initiating extensive interaction among the employees of the two firms. In these instances, the acquirer considers itself knowledgeable about an industry or the product, and it perceives a need to reduce duplication and to achieve economies of scale (Shrivastava, 1986).

Overall, achieving operating synergies has been less than successful (Galbraith and Stiles, 1984; Kitching, 1967). Problems such as differences in managerial styles or compensation systems (Lubatkin, 1983; Scherer, 1980), resistance by the members of both firms to changes in the structure (Pitts, 1976), and the differences in the firms' personnel characteristics and employees' willingness to adapt to the culture and practices of the other company (Jemison and Sitkin, 1986; Lubatkin, 1983) have been suggested as possible obstacles for achieving the desired synergies. Jemison (1986) indicated that research about the implementation of mergers is fragmented and he suggested that a process-oriented, long-term view is necessary. Shrivastava (1986) focused particularly on the importance of postmerger integration of the two companies in determining the success of the merger. He identified three different levels of integration: (a) procedural, (b) physical, and (c) managerial and sociocultural. Whereas the first two types of integration have been discussed in the literature, because of the complexity of the variables involved, sociocultural and managerial integration has not been examined thoroughly (Shrivastava, 1986).

Integration at the managerial and sociocultural level requires contact between the employees of the two companies. Where change occurs, it may affect the members of the acquired firm most strongly because they often are expected to adapt to the practices of the acquirer (Jemison and Sitkin, 1986; Sales and Mirvis, 1984). Processes that involve mutual influence of two autonomous systems and firsthand contact between members of two groups have received considerable attention in anthropology and cross-cultural psychology under the topic of acculturation (e.g. Berry, 1980; Chance, 1965; Redfield, Linton and Herkowitz, 1936; Social Science Research Council, 1954).

Acculturation in anthropology and cross-cultural psychology

The study of acculturation in anthropology and cross-cultural psychology dates to the 1880s. Acculturation is generally defined as 'changes induced in (two cultural) systems as a result of the diffusion of cultural elements in both directions' (Berry, 1980, p. 215). The process occurs at the group and individual levels in the three stages of contact, conflict, and adaptation (Berry, 1983). Although acculturation is considered to be a balanced two-way flow, members of the one culture often attempt to dominate members of the other (Berry, 1980; Keesing, 1953).

Though the concept of acculturation was developed to explain events involving societal groups, it can be applied to industrial or social organizations as well, because the two share many defining characteristics. Both industrial and social organizations exist and adapt within a specified environment and have well-defined boundaries that encompass a number of individuals who interact and are interdependent to varying degrees (Sales and Mirvis, 1984). They have a functional and adaptive quality and provide their members with a system of shared symbols and cognitions to deal with each other and with the outside world.

However, in organizations, the various systems such as structure and technology affect the organization and its members more directly. Furthermore, when a societal group is forced to interact with another, the members do not have the option of not acculturating and refusing contact as readily as organization members do. In organizations, members can choose not to accept the culture of the other organization by simply leaving the organization, or the acculturation process can be bypassed if most members of the acquired company are fired. More importantly, the concept of acculturation as it is used in cross-cultural research focuses on the desires of the members of the culture that is being invaded; it also focuses on the way in which these members adapt to the intruder. However, in mergers, the motive for the merger and the type of merger, both factors associated with the acquirer, cannot be overlooked.

Modes of acculturation

Berry (1983, 1984) identified four modes through which acculturation takes place. These modes define ways in which two groups adapt to each other and resolve emergent conflict. In the case of mergers, the characteristics of the acquired and the acquiring companies determine which mode of acculturation will be triggered.

Integration

Integration is triggered when members of the acquired firm want to preserve their own culture and identity and want to remain autonomous and independent. Berry (1983) suggested that integration as a mode of acculturation leads to structural assimilation of two cultures, but little cultural and behavioral assimilation. London (1967) argued that although integration involves interaction and adaptation between two cultures and requires mutual contributions by both groups, it does not involve loss of cultural identity by either. As a result, the acquired company's employees try to maintain many of the basic assumptions, beliefs, cultural elements, and organizational practices and systems that make them unique. At the same time, they are willing to be integrated into the acquirer's structure. However, integration can take place only if the acquirer is willing to allow such independence. Overall, integration leads to some degree of change in both groups' cultures and practices; the flow of cultural elements is balanced because neither group tries to dominate the other.

Assimilation

In contrast to integration, assimilation is always a unilateral process in which one group willingly adopts the identity and culture of the other (Berry, 1983, 1984). Therefore, the members of the acquired firm willingly relinquish their culture as well as most of their organizational practices and systems (Sales and Mirvis, 1984), and they adopt the culture and systems of the acquirer. This may occur in an acquired firm that has been unsuccessful, one in which employees and managers perceive that their culture and practices are dysfunctional and hindering organizational performance. Therefore, following the merger, structural as well as cultural and behavioral assimilation will occur. Overall, the acquired firm will be absorbed into the acquirer, and it will cease to exist as a cultural entity.

Separation

Separation as a mode of acculturation involves attempting to preserve one's culture and practices by remaining separate and independent from the dominant group (Berry, 1983). Separation is likely to take place when members of the acquired organization want to preserve their culture and organizational systems and they refuse to become assimilated with the acquirer in any way or at any level. These members resist any attempt at adaptation and conciliation, and they try to remain totally separate from the acquirer. If allowed to do so, they will function as a separate unit under the financial umbrella of the parent company. Overall, separation means that there will be minimal cultural exchange between the two groups, and each will function independently.

Deculturation

The fourth mode of acculturation is 'deculturation' or 'marginality'. Deculturation involves losing cultural and psychological contact with both one's group and the other group, and it involves remaining an outcast to both (Sales and Mirvis, 1984). Deculturation occurs when members of the acquired company do not value their own culture and organizational practices and systems, and they do not want to be assimilated into the acquiring company. As a result, the acquired company is likely to disintegrate as a cultural entity. Berry (1983) suggested that '. . . it is accompanied by a great deal of collective and individual confusion . . . and by feelings of alienation, loss of identity, and what has been termed acculturative stress' (p. 69).

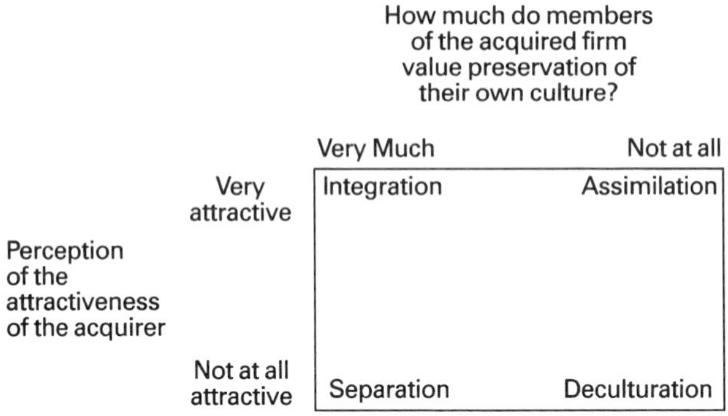

How much do members
of the acquired firm
value preservation of
their own culture?

	Very Much	Not at all
Very attractive	Integration	Assimilation
Not at all attractive	Separation	Deculturation

Perception
of the
attractiveness
of the acquirer

Figure 1   *Acquired firm's modes of acculturation. (Note: This model is a modified version of one developed by Berry, 1983)*

Factors that determine the course of acculturation

The concept of acculturation presented above addresses the different ways through which the culture, organizational practices, and systems of two companies can be combined. It is suggested that when two groups come in contact, total absorption of one into the other is by no means the only mode of adaptation. The course of acculturation depends on the way in which the acquirer and the acquired companies approach the implementation of the merger. From the acquired company's point of view, the degree to which members want to preserve their own culture and organizational practices and the degree to which they are willing to adopt the acquirer's culture and practices will determine their preferred mode of acculturation (see Figure 1).

The variables in Figure 1 can be measured by asking members of the acquired organization the extent to which they seek positive relations with the acquirer and the extent to which they perceive their own culture to be valuable and worth retaining (for an anthropological example see Berry, Wintrob, Sindell and Mawhinney, 1982). Furthermore, cross-cultural psychologists (e.g. Sommerlad and Berry, 1970) have used scales increasing identification with one or the other culture as measures of attitudes toward acculturation. In addition to questions related to attitudes toward one's own and the acquirer's culture, observation of organizational events and critical incidents can be used to estimate attitudes toward one's culture and toward the acquirer's culture (e.g. Sales and Mirvis, 1984). These methods provide information about how members of the acquired company would like to acculturate to the acquirer.

In the case of the acquirer, the culture, particularly the degree to which the firm is multicultural and the diversification strategy regarding the type of merger (i.e. degree of relatedness), will determine the preferred mode of

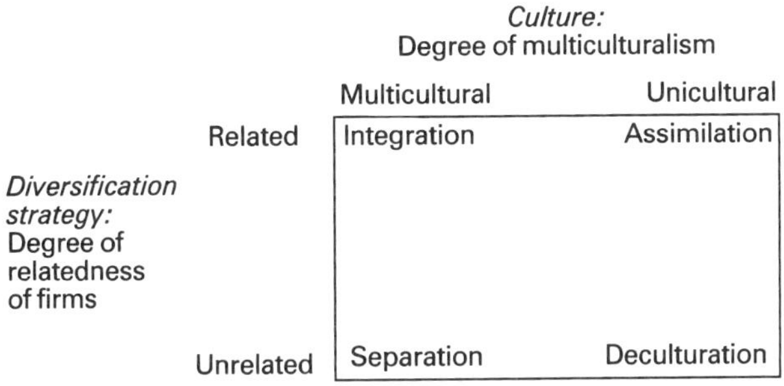

Culture:
Degree of multiculturalism

		Multicultural	Unicultural
	Related	Integration	Assimilation
Diversification strategy: Degree of relatedness of firms			
	Unrelated	Separation	Deculturation

Figure 2   *Acquirer's modes of acculturation*

acculturation (see Figure 2). The term multiculturalism refers to the degree to which an organization values cultural diversity and is willing to tolerate and encourage it. If an organization simply contains many different cultural groups, it is considered to be a plural organization; if in addition, the organization values this diversity, it is considered to be multicultural (Sales and Mirvis, 1984). If an acquirer is unicultural and, therefore, emphasizes conformity and rewards adherence to unique goals, strategies, and organizational practices, it is more likely to impose its own culture and management systems on a new acquisition. If the acquirer is multicultural, it is likely to consider diversity an asset and therefore will allow the acquired firm to retain its own culture and practices.

The second variable that determines the course of acculturation for the acquirer is the diversification strategy regarding the type of merger – the degree of relatedness between the acquirer and the acquired firms. If the merger is with a firm in a related business, the acquirer is more likely to impose some of its culture and practices in an attempt to achieve operating synergies. On the other hand, an acquirer is less likely to interfere with the culture or practices of an unrelated acquisition (Walter, 1985).

The degree of multiculturalism of an organization can be measured by observing organizational events and examining oral and written records of ways in which groups with different cultures have been managed. For example, the way in which a previous acquisition was handled can indicate the culture of an acquirer. If the members of the acquired organization were forced to change many of their practices and everyday behaviors, the acquirer is likely to be unicultural. Overall, the extent of change imposed on individuals or groups who are different from what an organization considers as acceptable provides an index of the degrees of multiculturalism.

Measures of relatedness have been developed and used extensively in strategic management research (for a review see Venkatraman and Grant, 1986; for some examples see Christensen and Montgomery, 1981; Hawks, 1984; Rumelt, 1974, 1982). These measures can be used to assess the degree of relatedness of the two businesses and to provide information regarding

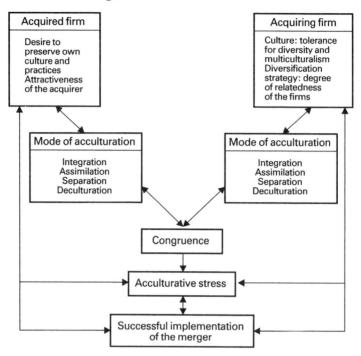

Figure 3   *Acculturative model for the implementation of mergers*

the second determinant of acculturation from the point of view of the acquirer.

Acculturative model for the implementation of mergers

The concepts presented in this paper provide a new approach for increasing our understanding of some of the underlying elements that affect the implementation of mergers. A general model is introduced in Figure 3. The basic contention of the model is that given that the members of the two organizations may not have the same preferences regarding a mode of acculturation, the degree of agreement (congruence) regarding each one's preference for a mode of acculturation will be a central factor in the successful implementation of the merger.

It is proposed that when two organizations agree on the preferred mode of acculturation for the implementation of the merger, less acculturative stress and organizational resistance will result, making acculturation a smoother process. Acculturative stress is defined as '. . . individual states and behaviors that are mildly pathological and disruptive . . .' (Berry, 1980, p. 261). Such stress and disruption is the result of contact with another group (Berry, 1983; Berry and Annis, 1974). Congruence can take place even if the cultures and practices of the two organizations are considerably different.

Incongruence which occurs when the two organizations do not agree on the mode of acculturation is likely to lead to high amounts of acculturative stress and disruption for both individual and group functioning. A high degree of acculturative stress would indicate a poor resolution of the conflict that is triggered when the two firms come in contact. Measures of acculturative stress developed for use in cross-cultural studies (e.g. Cawte, Bianchi and Kiloh, 1968; Mann, 1958) can be adapted for use in organizational research. As a result of incongruence, key managers and other valued employees may leave, active resistance to adopting any of the acquirer's systems may occur, and overall, the conflict will not be resolved in a way that would be beneficial to either of the organizations involved. On the other hand, congruence will result in minimal acculturative stress, and it will help to facilitate the implementation of the merger.

The last feature of the model presented in Figure 3 is its dynamic nature. The model suggests that the mode of acculturation that occurs, the process of implementation, and the outcome of the merger will, in turn, affect the cultures and practices of the two organizations. For example, an acquired firm's members' desire to preserve their culture and practices may change as a result of contact with a very successful and attractive acquirer. On the other hand, the degree of multiculturalism of an an acquiring firm may change as a result of the outcome of various mergers. The dynamic nature of the model suggests that over time two merger partners may each move from one mode of acculturation to other modes and, therefore, the degree of congruence between each one's preferences may change.

Propositions concerning the role of acculturation in the implementation of mergers are presented in Table 1.

Discussion and implications

The existing failure rate of mergers suggests that neither academicians nor practitioners have a thorough understanding of the variables involved in planning and implementing a successful merger. Aside from the financial and operational considerations, the model presented draws attention to the concept of cultural adaptation both during and after a merger. It is suggested that a successful merger involves not only thorough financial and strategic analysis and planning, but also planning regarding congruence between the

Table 1   Propositions concerning the role of acculturation in mergers

---

Preferred mode of acculturation for the acquired company:

1 When members of an acquired organization value their culture and organizational practices and want to preserve them, and they perceive an acquirer as attractive, integration will be their preferred mode of acculturation.

2 When members of an acquired organization do not value their culture and practices and do not want to preserve them, and they perceive an acquirer as attractive, assimilation will be their preferred mode of acculturation.

3 When members of an acquired organization value their culture and practices and want to preserve them, and they do not perceive an acquirer as attractive, separation will be their preferred mode of acculturation.

4 When members of the acquired organization do not value their culture and practices and do not want to preserve them, and they do not perceive an acquirer as attractive, deculturation will be their preferred mode of acculturation.

Preferred mode of acculturation for the acquirer:

1 When an acquirer is multicultural and the merger is with a related company, integration will be most likely mode of acculturation.

2 When an acquirer is unicultural and the merger is with a related company, assimilation will be the most likely mode of acculturation.

3 When an acquirer is multicultural and the merger is with an unrelated company, separation will be the most likely mode of acculturation.

4 When an acquirer is unicultural and the merger is with an unrelated company, deculturation will be the most likely mode of acculturation.

Congruence and successful implementation:

1 If there is congruence between the two companies regarding the preferred mode of acculturation, minimal acculturative stress will result and the mode of acculturation triggered by the contact between the two companies will facilitate the implementation of the merger.

2 If there is incongruence between the two companies regarding the preferred mode of acculturation, a high degree of acculturative stress will result and the mode of acculturation triggered by the contact between the two companies will hinder the implementation of the merger.

---

two companies' preferences about the implementation strategy for the merger.

Role of the acquired company

One of the shortcomings of much of the previous research about merger effectiveness has been to focus on the acquirer and its objectives and strategies at the expense of the role of the acquired company. The typical approach to merger implementation has been to expect the acquired firm either to adjust or to adapt to the acquirer. However, the active resistance that often accompanies mergers is evidence that the desires and preferences of the members of the acquired firm cannot be ignored (Walter, 1985). The concepts of acculturation and congruence suggest that many of the problems associated with postmerger integration of two firms can be avoided or managed if they agree on the mode of acculturation.

Furthermore, given that organizations typically encompass several different subcultures, one or more of the modes of acculturation may be triggered simultaneously. As a result, acculturation may take different courses for various subgroups within the acquired organization, and different degrees of congruence are likely to result for each subculture. This possibility suggests that the various subcultures must be understood by the acquirer, and that each may need to be managed differently.

Fit between strategy and culture

The model presented in this paper also questions one frequent recommendation related to strategic management. As mentioned earlier, much of the research about the concept of relatedness has found that related companies tend to outperform unrelated ones. Such results have given way to broad strategic recommendations for companies to diversify into related businesses so that they can take advantage of operating synergies. However, the success of some unrelated acquisitions (Montgomery and Wilson, 1986) shows that stringently adhering to this recommendation may deprive companies of opportunities. Missing from the research is precise information regarding the reasons why related or unrelated acquisitions succeed. No empirical data are available regarding the way in which successful and unsuccessful acquisitions have been managed. Focus has been on the link between diversification strategy (e.g. relatedness) and outcome (e.g. financial performance); the process has been ignored.

The acculturative model of merger implementation provides hypotheses regarding how mergers with firms with varying degrees of relatedness can be successful. For example, an unrelated acquisition can be managed successfully if the acquired business is left separate (separation mode) according to its employees' desires. This mode corresponds to the original goal of an unrelated merger, which is to achieve financial rather than operating or managerial synergy. The concept of congruence and the issue of fit between strategy and culture for the acquirer can explain some of the performance differences in related and unrelated mergers.

Focus on process

Many researchers agree that the main objective of any merger is to improve the performance of the combined companies (Lubatkin, 1983). Often, the measures that are used to evaluate merger performance rely on financial data and focus on the profitability of the organizations (Kusewitt, 1985; Chatterjee, 1986). This financial approach to effectiveness takes a general, one-shot, outcome-oriented view of mergers. In light of criticisms of such a view (e.g. Jemison, 1986; Jemison and Sitkin, 1986; Montgomery and Wilson, 1986), the need to develop process-oriented models of postmerger integration is evident (Shrivastava, 1986). The model presented here encourages focusing on the dynamic processes by which the acquired and the acquiring firms resolve the conflict that arises as a result of their contact. It draws attention to the meshing of people, cultures, and organizational practices as a determinant of a successful merger.

Future research

Research concerning this model should take two approaches. First, the propositions should be tested; this also would involve further development and adaptation of existing measures. Second, because the model identifies only three major variables more theoretical exploration is required. Other organizational elements and systems, such as structure, leadership, managerial style, and control systems may have an impact on the choice of the preferred acculturation mode and the course of acculturation.

Aside from methodological and theoretical developments, the concepts of acculturation and congruence suggest interesting research and practical issues. For instance, given that incongruence between the preferred modes of acculturation for the acquired and the acquiring companies is likely to take place, are some mismatches of modes easier to manage than others? Would incongruence be more manageable if the acquirer prefers integration and if the acquired wants to be assimilated, rather than the former preferring assimilation and the latter integration? Furthermore, some mismatches of the preferred modes may be so incongruent that the movement toward congruence may be painstakingly slow, or impossible. Clarifying the above issues and their determinant factors may help to plan and manage the acculturation process in mergers.

References

Ackerman, L. D. (1984) The psychology of corporation: How identity influences business. *Journal of Business Strategy*, 5(1), 56–65.

Ansoff, H. L. (1965) *Corporate strategy*. New York: McGraw-Hill.

Barrett, P. F. (1973) *The human implications of mergers and take-overs*. London: Institute of Personnel Management.

Bhagat, R. S. and McQuaid, S. J. (1982) Role of subjective culture in organizations: A review and directions for future research. *Journal of Applied Psychology Monograph*, 67, 653–685.

Berry, J. W. (1980) Social and cultural change. In H. C. Triandis and R. W. Brislin (Eds.), *Handbook of cross-cultural psychology* (Vol. 5, pp. 211–279). Boston: Allyn & Bacon.

Berry, J. W. (1983) Acculturation: A comparative analysis of alternative forms. In R. J. Samuda and S. L. Woods (Eds.), *Perspectives in immigrant and minority education* (pp. 66–77). Lanham, MD: University Press of America.

Berry, J. W. (1984) Cultural relations in plural societies: Alternatives to segregation and their sociopsychological implications. In N. Miller and M. B. Brewer (Eds.), *Groups in contact* (pp. 11–27). Orlando, FL: Academic Press.

Berry, J. W. and Annis, R. C. (1974) Acculturative stress: The role of ecology, culture and differentiation. *Journal of Cross-Cultural Psychology*, 5, 382–406.

Berry, J. W., Wintrob, R. M., Sindell, P. S. and Mawhinney, T. A. (1982) Psychological adaptation to culture change among the James Bay Cree. *Le Naturaliste Canadien*, 109, 965–975.

Blake, R. R. and Mouton, T. S. (1984) *Solving costly organizational conflicts: Achieving intergroup trust, cooperation and teamwork*. San Francisco: Jossey-Bass.

Cawte, J., Bianchi. G. N. and Kiloh, L. G. (1968) Personal discomfort in Australian aborigines. *Australian New Zealand Journal of Psychiatry*, 2, 69–79.

Chance, N. A. (1965) Acculturation, self-identification, and personality adjustment. *American Anthropologist*, 67, 372–393.

Chatterjee, S. (1986) Types of synergy and economic value. The impact of acquisitions on merging and rival firms. *Strategic Management Journal*, 7, 119–140.

Christensen, H. and Montgomery, C. A. (1981) Corporate economic performance: Diversification strategy versus market structure. *Strategic Management Journal*, 2, 327–343.

Davis, S. M. (1984) *Managing corporate culture*. Cambridge MA: Ballinger.

Deal, T. E. and Kennedy, A. A. (1982) *Corporate culture* Reading, MA: Addison-Wesley.

Galbraith, C. S. and Stiles, C. H. (1984) Merger strategies as response to bilateral market power. *Academy of Management Journal*, 27, 511–524.

Hawks, E. T. (1984, October) *Strategic diversification and economic performance: An empirical examination of security-market determined measures of performance*. Paper presented at the meeting of the Strategic Management Society, Philadelphia.

Hayes, R. H. (1979) The human side of acquisitions. *Management Review*, 68(11), 41–46.

Jelinek, M., Smircich, L. and Hirsch, P. (1983) Introduction: A code of many colors. *Administrative Science Quarterly*, 28, 331–338.

Jemison, D. B. (1986) *Strategic capability transfer in acquisition integration*. (Working Paper No. 913). Stanford University, Graduate School of Business.

Jemison, D. B. and Sitkin, K. (1986) Corporate acquisitions: A process perspective. *Academy of Management Review*, 11, 145–163.

Keesing, F. (1953) *Cultural change: An analysis and bibliography of anthropological sources to 1952.* Stanford, CA: Stanford University Press.

Kitching, J. (1967) Why do mergers miscarry? *Harvard Business Review*, 45(6), 84–101.

Kusewitt, J. B., Jr. (1985) An exploratory study of strategic acquisition factors relating to performance. *Strategic Management Journal*, 6, 151–170.

London, H. (1967) Liberalising the white Australia policy: Integration, assimilation or cultural pluralism? *Australian Outlook*, 21, 38–346.

Lubatkin, M. (1983) Merger and the performance of the acquiring firm. *Academy of Management Review*, 8, 218–225.

Lubatkin, M. (1987) Merger strategies and stockholder value. *Strategic Management Journal*, 8, 39–53.

Mann, J. W. (1958) Group relations and the marginal man. *Human Relations*, 11, 77–92.

Marks, M. L. (1982) Merging human resources: A review of current research. *Mergers and Acquisitions*, 17(2), 38–44.

Montgomery, C. A., and Wilson, V. A. (1986) Mergers that last: A predictable pattern? *Strategic Management Journal*, 7, 91–96.

Peters, T. J. and Waterman, R. H., Jr. (1982) *In search of excellence: Lessons from America's best-run companies.* New York: Harper & Row.

Pettigrew, A. M. (1979) On studying organizational cultures. *Administrative Science Quarterly*, 24, 570–581.

Pitts, R. A. (1976) Diversification strategies and organizational policies of large diversified firms. *Journal of Economics and Business*, 28, 181–188.

Redfield, R., Linton, R. and Herkowitz, M. J. (1936) Memorandum on the study of acculturation. *American Anthropologist*, 38, 149–152.

Roberts, K. H. (1970) On looking at an elephant: An evaluation of cross-cultural research related to organizations. *Psychological Bulletin*, 74, 327–350.

Rumelt, R. (1974) *Strategy, structure, and economic performance.* Cambridge, MA; Harvard University Press.

Rumelt, R. (1982) Diversification strategy and profitability. *Strategic Management Journal*, 3, 359–369.

Sales, A. L. and Mirvis, P. H. (1984) When cultures collide: Issues of acquisition. In J. R. Kimberly and R. E. Quinn (Eds.), *Managing organizational transition* (pp. 107–133). Homewood, IL: Irwin.

Salter, M. S. and Weinhold, W. A. (1979) *Diversification through acquisition*, New York: Free Press.

Sathe, V. (1985) *Culture and related corporate realities.* Homewood, IL: Irwin.

Schein, E. H. (1984) Coming to a new awareness of organizational culture. *Sloan Management Review*, 25(2), 3–16.

Schein, E. H. (1985) *Organizational culture and leadership.* San Francisco: Jossey-Bass.

Scherer, F. M. (1980) *Industrial market structure and economic performance.* Chicago: Rand McNally.

Schwartz, H. and Davis, S. M. (1981) Matching corporate culture and business strategy. *Organizational Dynamics*, 10(1), 30–48.

Shrivastava, P. (1985) Integrating strategy formulation with organizational culture. *Journal of Business Strategy*, 5(3), 103–111.

Shrivastava, P. (1986) Postmerger integration. *Journal of Business Strategy*, 7(1), 65–76.

Smircich, L. (1983) Concepts of culture and organizational analysis. *Administrative Science Quarterly*, 28, 339–358.

Social Science Research Council (U.S.) (1954) Acculturation: An exploratory formulation. *American Anthropologist*, 56, 973–1002.

Sommerlad, E. and Berry, J. W. (1970) The role of ethnic identification in distinguishing between attitudes towards assimilation and integration of a minority racial group. *Human Relations*, 23, 23–29.

Steiner, P. O. (1975) *Mergers: Motives, effects, policies.* Ann Arbor, MI: University of Michigan Press.

Sutton, R. I. (1983) Managing organizational death. *Human Resource Management*, 22, 391–412.

Tagiuri, R. and Litwin, G. H. (1968) *Organizational climate: Exploration of a concept.* Boston: Harvard University, Graduate School of Business.

Tichy, N. M. (1982) Managing change strategically: The technical, political, and cultural keys. *Organizational Dynamics*, 11(2), 59–80.

Van Maanen, J. (1979) The self, the situation, and the rules of interpersonal relations. In W. Bennis (Ed.), *Essays in interpersonal dynamics* (pp. 41–101). Homewood, IL: Dorsey Press.

Venkatraman, N. and Grant, J. H. (1986) Construct measurement in organizational strategy research: A critique and proposal. *Academy of Management Review*, 11, 71–87.

Walter, G. M. (1985) Culture collision in mergers and acquisitions. In P. J. Frost, L. F. Moore, M. R. Louis, C. C. Lundberg and J. Martin (Eds.), *Organizational culture* (pp. 301–314). Beverly Hills, CA: Sage.

Wrigley, L. (1970) *Divisional autonomy and diversification.* Unpublished doctoral dissertation, Harvard University, Graduate School of Business.

Reproduced from Nahavandi, A. and Malekzadeh, A. R. (1988). Acculturation in mergers and acquisitions. *Academy of Management Review*, **13** (1), 79–90, by permission of *Academy of Management Review*.

9 Expatriation and cultural adaptation

9.1 The dimensions of expatriate acculturation: a review

Mark Mendenhall and Gary Oddou

During the past two decades personnel administrators in multinational corporations (MNCs) have been plagued by a persistent, recurring problem: significant rates of the premature return of expatriate managers (Baker and Ivancevich, 1971; Henry, 1965; Misa and Fabricatore, 1979; Tung, 1981, Zeira, 1975).

The inability of expatriate managers to adjust to the host culture's social and business environment is costly in terms of management performance, productivity in the overseas operation, client relations, and operations efficiency. It has been estimated that the expatriate failure rate from 1965 to the present has fluctuated between 25 percent and 40 percent (Henry, 1965; Misa and Fabricatore, 1979; Tung, 1981), with the average cost per failure to the parent company ranging between $55,000 and $85,000, depending on the international exchange rate and location of assignment (Misa and Fabricatore, 1979). Misa and Fabricatore note that

> The costs involved in expatriate assignments that don't work out can be staggering. Assuming a moderate early return rate of 25% and $55,000 per family, the expense amounts to more than a million dollars for 100 expatriate family units (1979, p. 42).

There are also 'invisible' costs due to a manager's failure overseas: the loss of self-esteem and self-confidence in the expatriate's managerial ability and the loss of prestige among one's peers.

Despite the clear need for effective selection and training policies and programs for expatriates, personnel directors have consistently employed rigid and simplistic methods in selecting and training expatriate managers (Baker and Ivancevich, 1971; Tung, 1981; Zeira, 1975).

Problems in expatriate selection and training

An ingrained practice of personnel directors when selecting potential expatriates is the use of the 'domestic equals overseas performance' equation. The assumption behind this formula is that: 'Managing [a] company is a scientific art. The executive accomplishing the task in New York can surely perform as adequately in Hong Kong' (Baker and Ivancevich, 1971, p. 40.). 'Technical expertise' or 'having a successful track record' is overwhelmingly the primary selection criterion of American MNCs (Baker and Ivancevich, 1971; Miller, 1972, 1973; Tung, 1981; Vassel, 1983).

As the result of such beliefs, most MNCs send the expatriate and his/her family abroad soon thereafter, without any acculturation training whatsoever (Baker and Ivancevich, 1971; Tung, 1981; Vassel, 1983; Zeira, 1975). When companies do administer acculturation training, it often is too general or is not followed up with an evaluation of its effectiveness (Tung, 1981; Zeira, 1975). A variety of reasons are given by personnel directors for not investing in predeparture training:

1 A feeling that such training programs are generally ineffective (Baker and Ivancevich, 1971; Schnapper, 1973; Tung, 1981; Zeira, 1975).
2 Past dissatisfaction with the training program on the part of expatriate trainees (Brislin, 1979; Schnapper, 1973; Zeira, 1975).
3 The time between selection and departure is short, and there is not enough time to expose the expatriate to in-depth acculturation training (Baker and Ivancevich, 1971; Tung, 1981).
4 The view that because the expatriate's assignment is temporary, it does not warrant training expenditures (Tung, 1981).

Also, many personnel administrators believe that the dimensions of acculturation are simply not known well enough to devise sound selection instruments and/or training programs (Baker and Ivancevich, 1971). To a large degree they are correct in holding this view. Management researchers have largely failed to study systematically the psychological, social, and behavioral concerns of managing overseas operations (Adler, 1983a, b; Tung, 1981).

A clearer understanding of the key factors that constitute the expatriate acculturation process would aid personnel directors in the design of (1) selection instruments that are predictive of expatriate acculturation and (2) acculturation training programs that would address the relevant factors of acculturation and train the expatriates in the necessary skills relevant to those factors. In addition to the business world, knowledge about – and effective training based on – the key factors of expatriate acculturation also would help the military, the Foreign Service, the Peace Corps, and a large number of religious organizations that rely on expatriates to manage their overseas operations.

The field of expatriate selection and training, then, currently suffers from two basic problems: (1) an inadequate understanding of the relevant variables of expatriate acculturation and, therefore, (2) the use of inappropriate selection and training methods.

The purpose of this paper is to: (1) review the extant literature on expatriate acculturation in order to pinpoint the key factors or dimensions involved in the cross-cultural adjustment process, and (2) discuss the implications of this study's findings for the selection and training of expatriates in MNCs. The review was not limited to the management and/or organizational behavior fields. Included in this review were studies from anthropology, social psychology, cross-cultural psychology, and sociology; however, only *empirical* studies that *directly* investigated the dependent variable of expatriate acculturation or effectiveness were reviewed.

From the review of the literature, four dimensions emerged as components of the expatriate adjustment process. These are: (1) the 'self-oriented' dimension; (2) the 'others-oriented' dimension; (3) the 'perceptual' dimension; and (4) the 'cultural-toughness' dimension.

The self-oriented dimension

This dimension includes activities and attributes that serve to strengthen the expatriate's self-esteem, self-confidence, and mental hygiene. This dimension is composed of three subfactors: (1) 'reinforcement substitution', (2) 'stress reduction', and (3) 'technical competence'.

Reinforcement substitution

Reinforcement substitution involves replacing activities that bring pleasure and happiness in the home culture with similar – yet different – activities that exist in the host culture (David, 1976). For example, virtually all cultures value the general categories of art, sports, cuisine, music, dance, architecture, history, the family, and so on. However, all cultures' manifestations of those activities are not the same – the American expatriate may value baseball, steak and potatoes, and jazz; the new culture he/she is assigned to may value soccer, traditional folk music, or raw fish.

The expatriate who is able to find parallel substitutes for his/her interests and activities in the new culture is more likely to be successful in adjusting to that new culture. Culinary adaptability, for example, was found by Mumford (1975) to be an important aspect of expatriate acculturation.

Brein and David noted that the most striking feature of their sample of well-adjusted expatriates was that:

> They succeed in expanding and enriching their repertoire of reinforcing activities, drawing freely from the Brazilian culture to substitute for these typically North American sources of personal gratification which are unavailable or inappropriate in Brazil (1973, p. 1–2).

Thus learning to enjoy, for example, soccer and rugby as a player or a spectator instead of baseball and football, or learning to value raw fish and yakisoba rather than hamburgers and french-fries, or appreciating traditional folk music rather than jazz or country and western music is important to the expatriate acculturation process.

Stress reduction

Cross-cultural theorists have long believed that the entrance into an unfamiliar culture produces stress within the expatriate (Byrnes, 1966; Oberg, 1960). Recent studies to indicate that the ability to deal with stress is important to expatriate adjustment (Abe and Wiseman, 1983; Bardo and Bardo, 1980; Graham, 1983; Hammer, Gudykunst, and Wiseman, 1978; Hautaluoma and Kaman, 1975; Hawes and Kealey, 1981; Ratiu, 1983).

Hautaluoma and Kaman (1975) reported that well-adjusted expatriates in Afghanistan were better able to cope with the stress of ambiguous interpersonal relations and were more impervious to depression and loneliness than were poorly adjusted expatriates. Japanese adapting to the U.S. culture were found to be more successful if they were effective in dealing with psychological stress (Abe and Wiseman, 1983). Also, Hawes and Kealey (1981) found that the ability to cope successfully with 'day-to-day life overseas' emerged as an impotant variable in the acculturation process. This 'coping' involved social adaptation to other expatriates and adapting to the new physical environment, including limitations in housing, services, entertainment, climate, or other conditions that might cause stress.

Ratiu (1983) reported that well-adjusted expatriates seem to have 'stability zones' to which they can retreat when conditions in the host culture become overly stressful to them. Examples of such 'stability zones' are meditation, writing in diaries, engaging in favorite pastimes, and religious worship. Such temporary withdrawals, Ratiu notes, 'produce a rhythm of engagement and withdrawal in the manager's involvement with unfamiliar environments' (1983, p. 144). Such withdrawals, then, allow the expatriate to acculturate gradually to the host culture by utilizing a familiar psychological support system to assuage the initial effect of culture shock.

Technical competence

All expatriates are assigned overseas to accomplish some kind of task – whether it be building a dam, running a business, converting others to one's religion, or teaching English. Confidence in one's ability to accomplish the purpose of the overseas assignment – and possessing the necessary technical expertise to do so – seems to be an important part of expatriate adjustment (Hays, 1971; Tung, 1981).

Hawes and Kealey (1981) surveyed 160 technical advisors and 90 spouses in 26 projects in 6 countries. A factor analysis performed on the resulting data revealed 'technical expertise' to be a significant dimension in acculturation. Hautaluoma and Kaman (1975) and Harris (1973) reported similar findings in Afghanistan and Tonga, respectively. Bardo and Bardo (1980) also found that well-adjusted expatriates consistently reported more feelings of expertise in their jobs than did poorly adjusted expatriates.

The others-oriented dimension

This dimension encompasses activities and attributes that enhance the expatriate's ability to interact effectively with host-nationals. It consists of two subfactors: (1) 'relationship development' and (2) 'willingness to communicate'.

Relationship development

The ability to develop long-lasting friendships with host-nationals emerged as an important factor in successful overseas adjustment (Abe and Wiseman, 1983; Brein and David, 1971; 1973; Hammer *et al.*, 1978; Harris, 1973; Hawes and Kealey, 1981; Ratiu, 1983), accounting for large portions of the variance in the factor analytic studies studying adjustment (Hammer *et al.*, 1978; Harris, 1973). Establishing close relationships with host-nationals has the same effect on the expatriate that a mentor has on a new employee; that is, the experienced person guides the neophyte through the intricacies and complexity of the new organization or culture, protecting him/her against faux pas and helping him/her enact appropriate behaviors. Brein and David noted that expatriates in Brazil with host-national mentors were able to overcome their 'problems by relying on their interpersonal relationships with Brazilian friends' (1973, p. 3).

A trusted mentor can provide helpful feedback that can aid immensely in understanding worker expectations and attitudes in the new culture. The mentor also can provide information and support that aids the expatriate in adjusting to the culture outside of the workplace as well. Hammer *et al.* reported:

> Sojourners who are able to establish meaningful relationships with people from the host culture are more likely, it would appear, to integrate themselves into the social fabric of the host culture and to more effectively satisfy their own basic needs and concerns of friendship, intimacy, and social interaction (1978 p. 388).

Willingness to communicate

Two recent factor analytic studies (Abe and Wiseman, 1983; Hammer *et al.*, 1978) found that the ability to communicate with host nationals is important to cross-cultural adjustment (for a review see Barrett and Bass, 1976). Major (1965) reported that the expatriate's confidence and willingness to use the host culture's language had a greater influence on successful adjustment than did actual level of fluency in the foreign language.

Brein and David (1973) found that well-adjusted Peace Corps volunteers in Brazil learned Portuguese in order to 'get to know' and become more familiar and intimate with their Brazilian hosts. These expatriates 'collected' what Brein and David term 'conversational currency' – anecdotes, jokes, poems, proverbs, movie and sports stars' histories and statistics, and so on. These 'conversational coins' were then used during conversation with host-nationals – they were injected into the conversation in order to promote camaraderie and to show their hosts that they were 'one-of-the-guys' even though they were Americans.

Abe and Wiseman (1983) found similar results with American and Japanese expatriates. In Ratiu's research well-adjusted expatriates reported a willingness to engage in 'considerable observation and listening, experimentation and risk-taking, and, above all, active involvement with others' (1983, p. 141).

If facility in a foreign language is viewed as a necessary tool to be used to get host-national subordinates to do what one wants them to do, then adjustment may be minimal; however, if language skills are viewed as a means to create and foster interpersonal relationships or as a means to understand the dynamics of a new culture, then language skill is a useful help toward expatriate adjustment. Communication skills, then, as they relate to adjustment, seem to be related to an expatriate's: (1) willingness to use the host-nationals' language; (2) confidence in interacting with people; (3) use of conversational currency; and (4) desire to understand and relate with host-nationals.

The perceptual dimension

The ability to understand why foreigners behave the way they do is important in adjusting to an unfamiliar cultural environment. The ability to make correct attributions about the reasons or causes of host-nationals' behavior allows the expatriate to predict how they will behave toward him/her in the future, thus reducing uncertainty in interpersonal and intercultural relations. However, research shows that people from different cultures often misinterpret each other's behavior because of learned cultural differences in their perceptions and evaluations of social behaviors (Everett and Stening, 1980; Triandis, Vassilou and Nassiakou, 1968). For reviews see Benson (1978); Brein and David (1971); Oddou and Mendenhall (1984); Triandis, Malpass and Davidson (1973); and Stening (1979).

Other researchers studying expatriate adjustment have found results in congruence with the above conclusions (Arensburg and Niehoff, 1971; Hammer *et al.*, 1978; Ratiu, 1983). Ruben and Kealey (1979) studied the relationship between interpersonal and social behaviors and patterns of success and failure in expatriate adjustment. Technical advisors and their spouses in Kenya were posttested a year after receiving training in interpersonal skills. Well-adjusted expatriates were nonjudgmental and nonevaluative when interpreting the behavior of host-nationals. This nonjudgmental approach in the cognitive evaluation of host-nationals led to clearer information transmission between the expatriates and host-nationals and in better interpersonal relationships with them as well.

Well-adjusted expatriates make 'looser' or less rigid evaluations about why others behave as they do (Detweiler, 1975), and they are more willing to update their perceptions and beliefs as new data arise. They also tend to seek out such informative data more than do maladjusted expatriates (Ratiu, 1983).

To date, little is known of the cognitive dynamics that lead to correct versus incorrect attributional or evaluative processing in cross-cultural settings (Oddou and Mendenhall, 1984). Some models have been proposed (Detweiler, 1978; Jones and McGillis, 1976; Kelley, 1973; Mendenhall and Oddou, 1984), but the extent to which they account for – and predict – attribution/evaluation processes in cross-cultural settings has yet to be empirically validated. However, the implications of the above research for expatriate adjustment are self-evident, and some training programs have included the evaluation of perceptions as an important component of their design (Brislin, 1979; Fiedler, Mitchell and Triandis, 1971; Mendenhall and Oddou, 1982).

The cultural-toughness dimension

The cultures of some countries seem to be more difficult to adapt to than do the cultures of other countries (Jones and Popper, 1972; Pinfield, 1973; Torbiorn, 1982; Tucker and Schiller, 1975). Torbiorn (1982) found that expatriates expressed high levels of dissatisfaction in their overseas assignment for India/Pakistan, Southeast Asia, the Middle-East, North Africa, East Africa, and Liberia in the areas of job satisfaction, levels of stress and pressure, health care, housing standards, entertainment, food, and skill of co-workers. Also, greater cultural barriers were reported for South-east Asia, Japan, Africa, and the Middle East than for other world regions.

Tucker and Schiller (1975) found similar results with U.S. Navy personnel. Instances of early return among Navy personnel assigned overseas were more frequent at some overseas bases than at others.

Graham (1983) reported that of the racial/cultural groups he studied (Japanese, Chinese, Maori, Samoan, Tongan, and Caucasian), the Samoans had a more difficult time in adjusting to the Hawaiian lifestyle than did the rest of his sample. He noted that the gap between Fa's Samoa (the Samoa Way) and the host culture was greater than the gaps between the home cultures of the rest of sample and the host culture. Thus, how well the expatriate adjusts to his/her overseas experience seems to be in part related to the country of assignment.

The above four dimensions of expatriate adjustment seem to hold generally for female as well as for male expatriates. Torbiorn (1982) reported that for the most part there were no differences across sexes in his study of Swedish expatriates; he did, however, find one difference in the area of 'perceived isolation'.

Perceived isolation refers to the emotional impact of having one's social needs go unsatisfied over an extended period. Torbiorn (1982) reported that 13 percent of female expatriates (wives of male expatriate managers) in his study indicated a marked sense of isolation, and a total of 50 percent expressed some degree of perceived isolation. His male respondents did not indicate significant levels of perceived isolation.

Torbiorn suggests that this discrepancy is not due to innate sex differences in the adjustment process but to 'the role and habits of life in the host country which apply particularly to women' (1982, p. 38). Useem's (1966) findings support Torbiorn's view. Useem found that the role expectations for males in the expatriates' home culture and those for males in the Indian culture were more congruent than were role expectations for females. It appears that some cultures may be extra 'culturally-tough' for women to adapt to because of an inherent 'male-dominated' value system within those cultures.

Discussion

Two major propositions can be derived from this study's findings; one regarding the future direction for expatriate selection and the other regarding future directions for expatriate acculturation training.

Proposition 1. Expatriate acculturation is a multidimensional process rather than a one-dimensional phenomenon; thus, *selection procedures of MNCs should be changed from their present one-dimensional focus on 'technical competence' as being the primary criterion toward a 'multidimensional make-up' and should focus on criteria relating to the self-oriented, others-oriented, perceptual, and cultural-toughness dimensions.*

Proposition 2. Proposition 2 is a natural outgrowth from Proposition 1. For comprehensive preparation of expatriates for living and working abroad, *acculturation training programs should orient expatriates in each of the four dimensions outlined in Proposition 1.*

In order to carry out the above propositions, the following action proposals should be considered by personnel directors.

Proposals for enhancing the expatriate selection process

The expatriate selection process should focus on the evaluation of the applicant's existing strengths and weaknesses in the dimensions of expatriate acculturation outlined above.

The Self-Oriented Dimension. It is likely that personnel administrators in MNCs already have effective means of evaluating the technical expertise of potential expatriates; historically, this has been their prime focus in the selection process. Another option for evaluating this dimension is the use of psychological tests and evaluation devices. Numerous instruments that are designed to measure stress levels in people are available to personnel staffs; indeed, many MNCs likely have in-house stress reduction programs already in place. These existing programs can be utilized for evaluating potential expatriates' ability to handle stress.

The Perceptual Dimension. A variety of psychological tests are available that measure the rigidity and flexibility of an individual's perceptual and evaluative tendencies (Howard, 1974). Among them are the cognitive rigidity test, the *F*-test, the Guilford–Zimmerman Temperament survey, and the Allport–Vernon Study of Values. Presently, few personnel administrators in MNCs make use of psychological instruments in their selection process (Baker and Ivancevich, 1971; Tung, 1981); however, the results of such tests, in conjunction with data from other sources, provide a more comprehensive view of each expatriate's potential for successful acculturation.

The Others-Oriented Dimension. In order to gauge potential expatriates' degree of others-orientation, in-depth evaluations from the applicant's superiors, subordinates, friends, and acquaintances can be collected and analyzed. In addition, it would be useful to utilize professional evaluations of an applicant's interpersonal skills from a psychiatrist and/or clinical/counseling psychologist. Professional evaluations have been used by the Peace Corps to aid in its selection process (Henry, 1965).

Another way to evaluate potential expatriates' self-oriented, others-oriented, and perceptual dimensions is to adapt existing selection technology to the overseas selection process. For example, assessment centers can be designed specifically to test participants' intercultural, perceptual, and interpersonal aptitude. Assessment centers have not, to this point, been widely used for expatriate selection; their use in this regard, however, seems to be potentially fruitful in terms of collecting behavioral data to coincide with that collected from psychological tests and evaluations from others.

The Cultural-Toughness Dimension. In concert with the above methods, the personnel staff should take into account the 'toughness' of the culture of the country to which the future expatriate will be assigned. Data gathered on the host country's political, legal, socioeconomic, business, and cultural systems should be compared to those systems as they exist currently in the United States. For an assignment in a country that is 'culturally tough' the personnel director should be satisfied that the applicant scored high enough on the battery of evaluation devices to handle the assignments. For assignments to cultures similar to those of the United States (e.g. United Kingdom, Australia, New Zealand) the personnel director may not feel the need to demand significantly higher scores from an applicant before recommending him/her for the job.

A training program that specifically deals with the subfactors of the dimensions of expatriate acculturation is crucial to the preparation of the expatriate. Very few of the training programs currently in use by personnel staffs of MNCs and by external consultants offer comprehensive coverage of all the dimensions and their subfactors (Brislin, 1979). These training programs, however, can be combined or 'integrated' with each other to provide the necessary coverage. Gudykunst, Hammer, and Wiseman (1977) combined six different training approaches and compared the subsequent acculturation levels of trainees who received the integrated training with those of trainees who received one-dimensional training. They found that the integrated training produced greater levels of expatriate acculturation than did the one-dimensional training. Thus, when designing expatriate acculturation training programs, the personnel staff of MNCs should create integrated training programs that cover all of the important dimensions of acculturation.

In order to implement these selection and training considerations, the personnel staffs of MNCs must be supported institutionally. MNCs would be well advised to support more effective selection and training in their overseas staffing by adopting the following organizational guidelines.

1 As in any major OD effort, it is vital that top management support both institutionally and politically an emphasis on rigor and depth in the selection and training of expatriates.
2 The length of time budgeted for the selection and training processes must

be increased. In order for this to happen, the personnel director must have accurate forecasts of human resource needs in foreign subsidiaries. Too often expatriates are selected hurriedly because of an unforseen staffing crisis in an overseas operation.

3 The selection and training process must include the spouse of the expatriate. The findings of this study showed that the dimensions of acculturation are the same for men and that women, in male-dominated foreign cultures and women may have more challenges to overcome than men. This state of affairs argues strongly for the inclusion of the spouse in the MNC's selection process. Comprehensive acculturation training should be required of all expatriates and their spouses. Any school-age children should be included in the predeparture training programs as well – their adjustment will be no less of a challenge than will that of their parents.

4 Finally, expatriate selection and preparation for overseas assignments should begin early in a manager's career. In order to provide for future overseas staffing needs, corporate recruiters should have a clear mandate from top management to hire 'internationally-oriented' MBA graduates. Once hired, the career paths of these individuals should be carefully planned to prepare them for future service abroad. As overseas staffing positions arise, then, there will be a larger pool of internationally oriented and interculturally prepared managers from which to select that is presently the case within MNCs.

References

Abe, H. and Wiseman, R. L. A cross-cultural confirmation of the dimensions of intercultural effectiveness. *International Journal of Intercultural Relations*, 1983, 7, 53–68.

Adler, N. J. Cross-cultural management research: The ostrich and the trend. *Academy of Management Review*, 1983a, 8, 226–232.

Adler, N. J. Cross-cultural management: Issues to be faced. *International Studies of Management and Organization*, 1983b, 13, 3–45.

Arensberg, C. M. and Niehoff, A. H. *Introducing social change; A manual for community development*, 2nd ed Chicago: Aldine-Atherton, 1971.

Baker, J. C. and Ivancevich, J. M. The assignment of American executives abroad; Systematic, haphazard, or chaotic? *California Management Review*, 1971, 13(3), 39–41.

Bardo, J. W. and Bardo, D. J. Dimensions of adjustment for American settlers in Melbourne, Australia. *Multivariate Experimental Clinical Research*, 1980, 5, 23–28.

Barrett, G. V. and Bass, B. M. Cross-cultural issues in industrial and organizational psychology. In M. D. Dunnette (Ed.), *Handbook of industrial and organizational psychology*. Chicago: Rand-McNally College Publishing, 1976, 1639–1686.

Benson, P. G. Measuring cross-cultural adjustment: The problem of criteria. *International Journal of Intercultural Relations*, 1978, 5, 21–37.

Brein, M. and David, K. H. Intercultural communication and the adjustment of the sojourner. *Psychological Bulletin*, 1971, 76, 215–230.

Brein, M. and David, K. H. *Improving cross-cultural training and measurement of cross-cultural learning [Vol. 1]*. Denver: Center for Research and Education, 1973.

Brislin, R. W. Orientation programs for cross-cultural preparation. In A. J. Marsella, G. Tharp and T. J. Ciborowski (Eds.), *Perspectives on cross-cultural psychology*. Orlando, FL: Academic Press, 1979, 287–304.

Byrnes, F. C. Role shock: An occupational hazard of American technical assistants abroad. *The Annals*, 1966, 368, 95–108.

David, K. H. The use of social learning theory in preventing intercultural adjustment problems. In P. Pedersen, W. J. Lonner and J. Draguns (Eds.), *Counseling across cultures*. Honolulu: University of Hawaii Press, 1976, 123–137.

Detweiler, R. On inferring the intentions of a person from another culture. *Journal of Personality*, 1975, 43, 591–611.

Detweiler, R. Culture, category width, and attributions: A model building approach to the reasons for cultural effects. *Journal of Cross-Cultural Psychology*, 1978, 9, 259–284.

Everett, J. E. and Stening, B. W. Intercultural interpersonal perceptions: A study of Japanese and Australian managers. *Japanese Psychological Research*, 1980, 22 42–47.

Fiedler, F., Mitchell, T. and Triandis, H. The culture assimilator: An approach to cross-cultural training. *Journal of Applied Psychology*, 1971, 55, 95–102.

Graham, M. A. Acculturative stress among Polynesian. Asian, and American students on the Brigham Young University – Hawaii campus. *International Journal of Intercultural Relations*, 1983, 7, 79–100.

Gudykunst, W. B., Hammer, M. R. and Wiseman, R. L. An analysis of an integrated approach to cross-cultural training. *International Journal of Intercultural Relations*. 1977, 1, 99–110.

Hammer, M. R., Gudykunst, W. B. and Wiseman, R. L. Dimensions of intercultural effectiveness: An exploratory study. *International Journal of Intercultural Relations*, 1978, 2, 382–393.

Harris, J. G., Jr. A science of the South Pacific: Analysis of the character structure of the Peace Corps volunteer. *American Psychologist*, 1973, 28, 232–247.

Hautaluoma, J. E., & Kaman, V. Description of Peace Corps volunteers' experience in Afghanistan. *Topics in Culture Learning*, 1975, 3, 79–96.

Hawes, F. and Kealey, D. J. An empirical study of Canadian technical assistance. *International Journal of Intercultural Relations*, 1981, 5, 239–258.

Hays, R. D. Ascribed behavioral determinants of success-failure among U.S. expatriate managers. *Journal of International Business Studies*, 1971, 2, 40–46.

Henry, E. R. What business can learn from Peace Corps selection and training. *Personnel*, 1965, 42(4), 17–25.

Howard, C. G. Model for the design of a selection program for multinational executives. *Public Personnel Management*, 1974, 3(2), 138–145.

Jones, E. E. and McGillis, D. Correspondent inference and the attribution cube: A comparative approach. In J. Harvey, W. Ickes and R. Kidd (Eds.), *New directions in attribution research [Vol. 1]*. Hillsdale, NJ: Erlbaum, 1976, 389–420.

Jones, R. R. and Popper, R. Characteristics of Peace Corps host countries and the behavior of volunteers. *Journal of Cross-Cultural Psychology*, 1972, 3, 233–245.

Kelley, H. H. The processes of causal attribution. *American Psychologist*, 1973, 28, 107–128.

Major, R. T., Jr. A review of research on international exchange. Unpublished manuscript. The Experiment on International Living, Putney, VT, 1965.

Mendenhall, M. and Oddou, G. The A-R-C approach to expatriate training. Workshop presented at the Rocky Mountain Psychological Association, Albuquerque, 1982.

Mendenhall, M. and Oddou, G. An information processing model of expatriate adjustment. Working Paper, No. 18, College of Business Administration Research Center, Loyola Marymount University, 1984.

Miller, E. L. The overseas assignment: How managers determine who is to be selected. *Michigan Business Review*, 1972, 24(3), 12–19.

Miller E. L. The international selection decision: A study of some dimensions of managerial behavior in the selection decision process. *Academy of Management Journal*, 1973, 16, 239–252.

Misa, K. F. and Fabricatore, J. M. Return on investment of overseas personnel. *Financial Executive*, 1979, 47(4), 42–46.

Mumford, S. J. Overseas adjustment as measured by a mixed standard scale. Paper presented at the meeting of the Western Psychological Association, Sacramento, 1975.

Oberg, K. Culture shock: Adjustment to new cultural environments. *Practical Anthropology*, 1960, 7, 177–182.

Oddou, G. and Mendenhall, M. Person perception in cross-cultural settings: A review of cross-cultural and related literature. *International Journal of Intercultural Relations,* 1984, 8, 77–96.

Pinfield, L. T. Sociocultural factors and inter-organizational relations. *Academy of Management Proceedings*, 33rd Annual Meeting, Boston, 1973.

Ratiu, I. Thinking internationally: A comparison of how international executives learn. *International Studies of Management and Organization*, 1983, 13, 139–150.

Ruben, B. D. and Kealey, D. J. Behavioral assessment of communication competency and the prediction of cross-cultural adaptation. *International Journal of Intercultural Relations*, 1979, 3, 15–47.

Schnapper, M. Resistances to intercultural training. Paper presented at the Thirteenth Annual Conference of the Society for International Development, San Jose, Costa Rica, 1973.

Stening, B. W. Problems in cross-cultural contact: A literature review. *International Journal of Intercultural Relations*, 1979, 3, 269–313.

Torbiorn, I. *Living abroad: Personal adjustment and personnel policy in the overseas setting*. New York: Wiley, 1982.

Triandis, H. C., Malpass, R. S. and Davidson, A. R. Psychology and culture. *Annual Review of Psychology*, 1973, 24, 355–378.

Triandis, H. C., Vassilou, V. and Nassiakou, M. Three cross-cultural studies of subjective culture. *Journal of Personality and Social Psychology*, 1968, 8, (4, Part 2).

Tucker, M. F. and Schiller, J. E. Final task report for an assessment of the screening problem for overseas assignment (Task Order 75/53/B). Denver: Center for Research and Education, 1975.

Tung, R. L. Selection and training of personnel for overseas assignments. *Columbia Journal of World Business*, 1981, 16(1), 68–78.

Useem, R. H. The American family in India. *The Annals*, 1966, 368, 132–145.

Vassel, B. Ten ways to improve performance in your overseas operation. Paper presented at the Annual OB Conference, Brigham Young University, 1983.

Zeira, Y. Overlooked personnel problems of multinational corporations. *Columbia Journal of World Business*, 1975, 10(2), 96–103.

Reproduced from Mendenhall, M. and Oddou, G. (1985). The dimensions of expatriate acculturation: a review. *Academy of Management Review*, **10**, 39–47, by permission of *Academy of Management Review*.

9.2 Expatriation: challenges and recommendations

Jean Marie Hiltrop and Maddy Janssens

Introduction

The past few years have witnessed a marked upsurge of interest in the topic of expatriation. Some suggest that this increase is the direct result of a rapid increase in both the number and size of multinational corporations (Ronen, 1986). Others argue that the increase stems primarily from organizations' heightened sensitivity to the financial and emotional costs association with expatriate failure (Zeira and Banai, 1985). Whatever the reason, the fact remains that the available research on expatriation has risen substantially in the last few years, as has awareness of the specific human resource management practices that may help multinational companies succeed in employing expatriates to manage their foreign operations.

This article gives an overview of current state of knowledge with respect to the topic of expatriation. This is done in an effort to identify: (1) the major difficulties that expatriate managers face in the international assignment, and (2) the specific human resource management practices that may be employed in order to help individual managers and their families deal effectively with the challenges of expatriation.

Known facts about expatriation

To begin with, let's examine those aspects of expatriation about which we feel fairly confident. Five such 'facts' can be identified in the literature.

1 We know that the demand for expatriates is increasing. As Zeira and Banai (1985) point out, the rapid growth of multinational companies and especially joint ventures in developing countries has produced a renewed demand for executives capable of serving outside their countries and willing to do so. The reasons for this renewed demand vary from company to company. For example, some organisations tend to staff key managerial positions in foreign subsidiaries with home-country nationals because they

believe, justifiably or not, that these managers possess qualities and characteristics which are not possessed by host-country nationals. These characteristics include familiarity with corporate objectives, loyalty to the company, and adherence to its style of management. Other firms apply this staffing policy only to most significant managerial positions or under certain circumstances; for instance, when the company is in the process of establishing new subsidiaries, or when there is a shortage of skilled professionals in the host country. Whether the need to use expatriate managers is justified or not, the fact remains that there is a significant increase in the number of managers working abroad, creating a rapid growth in the volume of expatriate employment.

2 We also know that expatriates are expensive to employ. Although a full explanation of the costs associated with expatriate employment is beyond the scope of this article, it is important to note some considerations. To begin with, expatriate managers typically earn substantial allowances in the form of premiums for relocation, cost-of-living differentials, travel expenses, childrens' education, and so forth. These allowances may increase base salaries by 25 to 100% (Franco, 1973). For example, one American investment bank, about 65 of whose executives are located in Britain, reckons that in the 1987 tax year this cost the company $2.5 million.

In addition, most multinational companies make up to their employees the amount of money they lose by paying higher taxes when working abroad. When these tax equalization costs are combined with relocation costs, the cost of travel between the subsidiary and the parent company, and the premiums paid for foreign assignments, it has been estimated that the average cost of employing executives abroad is roughly twice as high as he or she would cost in a comparable position at home (Schollhammer, 1969). Thus, the financial costs of employing home-country nationals abroad are significant.

3 We know that completing an international assignment presents expatriate managers and their families with a variety of difficulties and challenges. As Ronen (1986) points out, international assignees frequently operate in an environment that is culturally, politically, economically, and legally different from those experienced in their home country. It is not surprising then that studies of international staffing indicate that expatriates often develop symptoms of transfer anxiety, culture shock, social dislocation, adaptation problems, and feelings of abandonment (Brooke and Remmers, 1977; Zeira and Harari, 1977). Expatriates and their families also sometimes face a new world of social customs and are potentially at odds with their own value systems and living habits (Ronen, 1986). For example, a recent article in *The Economist* (1988) looked at Americans living in Britain and found that:

Day-to-day existence in Britain can take some getting used to; no all-night supermarkets, inefficient showers, lousy telephones and, some find, slapdash service where the general attitude is 'we can't do that'. One women was astonished to be told that it would take 12 months for her new sofa to be delivered. In the event it took eight months.

Apparently, attitudes to work also differ:

An American television executive working for a British company was jokingly advised to do her late-night work at home rather than in the office, as it might 'demoralise' her English colleagues (*The Economist*, 1988, p. 23).

Thus, when expatriates face host-country nationals and their different behavioural norms and expectations, tension may rise. Some expatriate managers may insist on using their own standards to judge others' behaviour. However, as time goes on, successful expatriates will presumably start to realize that the assumptions that guided behaviour at home are no longer applicable.

4 We know that the failure rate of expatriate managers is high. For example, a massive study of Swedish expatriates (covering 639 managers in 26 countries) showed that 25% returned home before the end of their assignment and that problems of cultural adaptation were the most common reason offered by managers for their early repatriation (Torbiorn, 1982). As one executive recalled: 'There's some kind of traumatic reaction to it. It evidenced itself in my insomnia. There was something there . . . waking up at 4 a.m. every morning.' (Adler, 1986, p. 195).

Studies of expatriation in the U.S. have reported even higher failure rates. For example, Desatnick and Bennet (1978) found that 50% of U.S. expatriates do not complete their assignments in developed countries; and the proportion rises to 70% in developing countries. This is consistent with the findings of Tung (1987) which showed lower failure rates among European and Japanese firms than in U.S. multinationals. Thus, while it is difficult to define failure precisely and the estimates should not be taken as hard data, it is clear that the assignment of managers abroad is a difficult process and one that generally cannot be deemed successful (Kobrin, 1988).

5 Finally, we know that premature repatriation is costly both to the company and to the manager who terminates a foreign assignment. As noted by Misa and Fabricatore (1979): 'The costs involved in expatriate assignments that don't work out can be staggering. Assuming a moderate return rate of 25% and $55,000 per family, the expense amounts to more than a million dollars for 100 expatriate family units' (p. 42). Similarly, the average cost of relocating an expatriate manager and his or her family has been found to range between $55,000 and $150,000, depending on the nature of the job, the person involved and the country of assignment

(Copeland and Griggs, 1985; Hill, 1977). Clearly, if the expatriate then returns early, most of that money has been wasted.

In addition to the financial losses from an aborted assignment, there are also psychological costs for the manager. As noted by Mendenhall and Oddou (1985), an expatriate who fails to complete his or her assignment abroad may suffer loss of self-esteem, a severe career setback, and the loss of prestige among peers. Thus, a great deal is at risk, and when the financial costs of expatriate failure are added to the psychological costs to managers and their families it is clear that preventing selection mistakes must be a priority for any company sending people on foreign assignments.

Factors associated with successful expatriation

Having established that the failure rate of expatriates is high, we might next logically consider how this failure rate, and the costs associated with premature repatriation, can be reduced. Yet it would be inappropriate to seek solutions without clearly identifying the major causes of expatriate failure. The next consideration should therefore be an overview of the factors that have been found to be associated with expatriate performance. These factors can be organised into three categories: (1) personal characteristics of the expatriate manager; (2) characteristics of the expatriate's family; and (3) factors related to the subsidiary–parent company relations.

Personal characteristics

A number of studies have considered the personal characteristics of successful expatriate managers (e.g. Miller, 1972; Kapoor and McKay, 1971). Most of these studies suggest that successful expatriates have superior intelligence, self-confidence and a strong drive for responsibility and task completion. In Phatak's (1974) terminology:

> Ideally, it seems, he (or she) should have the stamina of an Olympic swimmer, the mental agility of an Einstein, the conversational skill of a professor of languages, the detachment of a judge, the tact of a diplomat, and the perseverence of an Egyptian pyramid builder. And if he is going to measure up the demands of living and working in a foreign country he should also have a feeling for culture; his moral judgments should not be too rigid; he should be able to merge with the local environment with chameleon-like ease; and he should show no signs of prejudice.

Although many of these characteristics are considered essential by those responsible for expatriate recruitment and selection (Miller, 1972), researchers have criticized this list of necessary qualities for an international assignment because they fail to predict expatriate performance to a significant degree (Haemmerli, 1978). On the other hand, when considered together, the research to date does indicate that certain personal characteristics are potentially critical for managers' expatriate performance, and that a manager must possess a number of skills if he or she is to live and work successfully in a foreign environment. These characteristics and skills include:

1 *Technical ability* Obviously the expatriate must have the necessary technical knowledge and skills to do the job. Confidence in one's ability to accomplish the purpose of the overseas assignment seems to be an important part of expatriate adjustment (Hays, 1971; Tung, 1981).
2 *Stress tolerance* As noted earlier, expatriates and their families frequently operate in an environment that is personally highly stressful. To begin with, separation from friends, leaving one's home country, and drastic changes in one's culture environment generally create an experience of stress or emotional disturbance. As a result, many expatriates develop symptoms of transfer anxiety, culture shock, social dislocation, 'exile complex' (feeling abandoned by headquarters), frustration and disappointment (Brooke and Remmers, 1977; Zeira and Harrari, 1977).

   Recent studies (e.g. Torbiorn, 1982; Adler 1986) indicate that experienced expatriates have found many highly effective and creative mechanisms for coping with the stress of intercultural adaptation. For example, one expatriate family made a rule forbidding complaints during meals; they only allowed positive statements about the new physical environment, culture or other conditions that might cause stress and frustration.

   In addition, many of the most effective expatriates create 'stability zones' for coping with the problems of cultural adaptation (Ratiu, 1983). That is, when conditions in the host culture become overly stressful, they briefly retreat into an environment that closely recreates home. Examples of successful stability zones are playing a musical instrument, keeping a diary, watching video-movies in one's native language, or going to an international club and only talking with other compatriots. As Ratiu (1983) point out, such temporary withdrawals produce a rhythm of engagement and withdrawal in the manager's involvement with unfamiliar environment.
3 *Flexibility* There is evidence that expatriates who are able to find substitutes for their interests and activities at home, are more likely to be successful in adjusting to the new culture (Mendenhall and Oddou, 1985). Examples of replacing activities are learning to value raw fish and yakisoba rather than hamburgers and french-fries, discovering new hobbies such as

scuba diving in the Pacific and hill walking in the Himalayas, or appreciating indigenous music rather than rock-and-roll. They replace activities that bring pleasure in the home culture with similar – yet different – activities in order to help the expatriate enjoy more fully his or her experience in the host culture.

4 *Communication skills* Research (e.g. Abe and Wiseman, 1983; Hammer *et al.*, 1978, Harris, 1973) shows that it is important for expatriates to relate well with host nationals both in business and socially. This requires the ability to get along with people, the willingness to work with others, and most of all respect for the host national's religious and political beliefs.

   Successful expatriation also requires the willingness to learn and use the local language. For example, Brein and David (1971) found that expatriates who knew the local language collected 'conversational currency' – anecdotes, jokes, poems, proverbs, sports stars and so on. These conversational coins were then used during conversation with host nationals in order to show their hosts that they were 'one of the guys' even though they were members of a foreign country.

5 *Cultural empathy* Clearly, the ability to understand why foreigners behave the way they do is important in adjusting to a new cultural environment. All too often, adaptation problems arise because expatriates are unable to face a new world of cultural patterns that are potentially at odds with their own value systems and living habits (Furnham and Bochner, 1989). For example, expatriates sometimes fail to learn when 'yes' means 'yes', when it means 'maybe' and when it means 'no'; what to focus on and what to ignore. As a result, when they face host-country nationals and their different behavioural assumptions and expectations, tensions rise.

   Even performing the simplest of actions may produce unexpected and seemingly unintelligible responses from the new cultural environment (Ronen, 1986). For example, Triandis (1975) relates how an American visitor asked his Greek acquaintance what time they should come to his house for dinner. The Greek villager replied 'any time'. Now in American usage the expression 'any time' is a non-invitation that people give to appear polite but which they hope will not lead to anything. The Greek, however, actually meant that the Americans would be welcome any time, because in his culture putting limits on when a guest can come is deemed insulting.

   To deal with such problems, expatriates have to differentiate idiosyncratic behaviour from behaviour reflecting a cultural pattern (Adler, 1986). This requires learning what are the local habits, communicating with people about their everyday lives and values, and avoid making rigid evaluations about why others behave as they do. As Adler (1986) points out, the most successful expatriates constantly recognize that they may not fully understand the situation and that they must find ways to get reliable information and expertise. They 'know that they do not know'. They also recognize that they are in a difficult situation and that they will not act as effectively overseas as they did at home – especially in the initial stages.

Other expatriates and host nationals who have previously faced and dealt effectively with the same or similar problems can often best empathize with the newcomer's difficulties. This heightened individual awareness and enhanced knowledge of the local scene may give the expatriate the ability to understand local behaviour better and to be more objective in his views of local life.

Adaptability of the spouse

Although personal characteristics are important, a variety of studies suggest that the adaptability of a manager to be effective in a foreign subsidiary depends to a large extent upon how happy the manager's spouse and children are in the foreign environment (e.g. Gaylord, 1979; Howard, 1980; Tung, 1982). To be sure, many of the wives describe themselves as having hours and hours on their hands with nothing to do. They are bored and they don't have a meaningful role to fulfill.

In addition, the expatriate's spouse often becomes more immersed in the culture than the manager, and the challenges for successful adjustment are both different and greater. For example, she may have to find out all the essential elements of running a household, the arrangements for servants, the best places to go for groceries, to beat down the price or not, and even where to purchase products on the black market. She must deal with the foreign culture in the most immediate, every day basis (Harvey, 1985).

During the first months, the spouse may find that other people's behaviour doesn't make sense and, even more disconcerting, that her own behaviour doesn't produce the expected results. The constant frustration of not understanding and not being able to get simple things done, isn't easy to deal with.

It's the constant minor frustrations ... the phone never works, the electric power is variable, and, oh yes, filling the water bottles at 4 a.m., just to be sure that we'd have some water. (Adler, 1986, p. 229).

Experience indicates that most people get used to the irritations of a limited water supply, frequent electrical blackouts or other physical factors. However, loneliness and isolation are more difficult to cope with. Most expatriate wives leave their family and friends at home in order to follow their partner to the foreign country. This separation causes a spouse to want more time, attention and companionship from her husband. However, the expatriate often works long hours to deal with the unfamiliar working conditions of his new assignment. Hence, he cannot spend as much time as is necessary to reduce family anxiety and dissatisfaction (Adler, 1986).

Wives of 'fast-trackers' are also often reluctant to get involved in the new community because there is constant uncertainty as to whether they will be moved again and how long they will be in one place (Harvey, 1985).

In sum, the impact of the international transfer is more severe on the spouse than on the expatriate manager. While the expatriate manager retains his company and job structure, the spouses of expatriates frequently must give up their friends, job and career. For them, the hardest task of all is creating a meaningful life overseas. They have to answer to questions as: What do I really want to do? How can I continue doing the things that I find most important even while I am no longer living at home?

Subsidiary-parent company relations

In addition to these adaptation problems of the family, expatriates frequently must deal with problems stemming from the relationship between corporate headquarters and the foreign subsidiary. In multinational companies with ethnocentric organizational structures, the task of expatriate managers predominantly is to implement the objectives and policies that headquarters formulate (Perlmutter and Heenan, 1974). Unfortunately, those objectives and policies may conflict with the subsidiary's needs and expectations. For example, the subsidiary may want to reinvest most of the profits generated into its own operations. This goal, however, may be incompatible with the company's global strategy. For instance, the parent company may prefer to repatriate the profits and use the revenue to invest in another subsidiary or location. Clearly, such differences of opinion may create role conflict for expatriate managers (Rahim, 1983). As Ronen (1986) notes, the expatriate may end up caught in the middle. In addition, conflicts of interest between the subsidiary and the corporation may affect expatriate performance. After all, if the corporate headquarters impose constraints on the subsidiary's decision making processes, they also diminish the expatriate's ability to handle local problems.

Another factor influencing the effectiveness of expatriation involves the so-called 'information gap' between expatriates and their colleagues at home (Chorafas, 1967). Because corporate headquarters are outside the host country, head office managers often overlook the need to communicate with their colleagues abroad. As a result, expatriate managers frequently end up missing information concerning important activities at home. According to one study, more than two thirds of expatriates complain of suffering from this information gap phenomenon (Howard, 1974). These employees, in believing that their colleagues treat them as if they were 'out of sight, out of mind', often feel professionally unproductive and personally dissatisfied. They ultimately regard their foreign assignment as dysfunctional and too costly in personal and professional terms (Ronen, 1986).

Implications for human resource management

Based on the foregoing analysis of the factors associated with successful expatriation, the following implications can be drawn for the management of foreign assignments.

Selection

Companies should select effective, rather than marginal, employees for overseas assignments. A well thought-out selection system increases the likelihood of the best candidate for the job.

To be successful in selection, personnel officials should not just focus on the technical competence of the candidates; they should also assess personal characteristics such as adaptability, ability to communicate, emotional stability, relational skills etc. (Mendenhall, Dunbar and Oddou, 1987). Staffing overseas assignments calls for more comprehensive procedures where technical competence together with relational/cross-cultural/interpersonal skills must be considered.

Tung's (1988) research suggests that criteria for selecting international managerial candidates should vary according to the country of the foreign assignment and the managerial level of the job. When the differences between the two cultures are great and the job requires extensive interaction with members of the local community, attributes such as 'adaptability, flexibility in new environmental settings, maturity and emotional stability, and communication' become more critical and should become dominant factors in the selection decision. When the cultural differences are insignificant and the degree of interaction is low, selection should be based primarily on technical task variables.

Pucik and Katz (1986) suggest another contingency approach based on the type of information and control required by the job. According to these authors, technically competent expatriates are most effective when information is objective (understandable to persons with the appropriate professional training regardless of their national origin) and when control is bureaucratic. In contrast, expatriates who have internalized the corporate culture work best when information is social and control is normative.

Another surprisingly underutilized criterion for the selection of expatriates is the adaptability potential of the spouse and other family members. As noted earlier, the adaptability of the spouse is one of the most important reasons for expatriate failure. Yet, Tung (1988) found that only 40% of the companies included in her study, interviewed the spouse of the candidate.

In addition to assessing the adaptability of the spouse, the company should conduct a 'family screening process'. Important factors that need to be looked at in this process are: the level of marital stability, responsibilities for aged parents, the presence of learning disabilities in a child, behavioural problems in teenagers, and the strength of family's ties to the community, friends, other family members (Harvey, 1985; Mendenhall and Oddou, 1985).

Training

Once the screening process is completed, companies should offer formal training programmes to prepare expatriates and their families for their overseas assignments. Even the most careful selection does not eliminate the need for training.

A number of studies (White, 1971; Johnson and Carter, 1972; Samozar, Porter and Jain, 1981; Whetten and Cameron, 1984) indicate that the managerial skills needed to be effective in a domestic position are not sufficient to be successful in an international assignment. Apparently, human relations skills, understanding the host culture, and the ability to adapt are the most important skills needed by expatriates (Johnson and Carter, 1972).

Despite the clear need to minimize the expatriate manager's culture shock, few companies (Tung, 1988) offer formal training programmes to help managers deal with adaptation problems. Apparently, most companies that offer cross-cultural training use environmental briefing programmes. However, such programmes have proved inadequate in preparing trainees for assignments which require extensive contacts with members of the local community. To prepare expatriates better, companies should sponsor more comprehensive cross-cultural training programmes such as 'culture assimilator training, critical incidents, sensitivity training, field experiences, etc. (Brislin, 1979).

Support during the assignment

To minimize the risk of expatriate failure, companies should allow expatriates sufficient time to adapt to the foreign environment. The pressure to produce immediately in an overseas assignment compounds to the demands imposed on the expatriate and may negatively affect performance on the job. As Zeira and Harari (1977) recommend, expatriates should be exempted from active management duties in the first six months of arrival in a foreign country. Their performance should be assessed on the basis of long-term profitability, rather than on short-term results.

Furthermore, companies should establish and coordinate a support system that attend specifically to the needs and aspirations of expatriate employees (Tung, 1988). This 'social network' helps to reduce the 'out of sight, out of mind' dilemma by providing organizational information on the politics and day-to-day activities of the headquarters.

The support system should also monitor the training and development needs of expatriates. By providing continuous management training, companies ensure that expatriates improve their technical knowledge or capacity to manage others in cross-cultural work settings.

Repatriation

Expatriates who return to their home country after an extended period of time are faced with a number of problems. Brislin and Van Buren (1974) observed that returnees are frequently surprised and many are highly disappointed by what they experience at home. Although, they do not expect anything unfamiliar when returning, they often find that the country and the organization have changed considerably since taking up their foreign assignment. As a result, a number of expatriates and their families experience what Murray termed a 'cultural shock in reverse' (1973).

Adler (1986) notes that the professional re-entry can be especially difficult. Most managers expect the international assignment to help them in their career; yet, research (Hazzard, 1981) shows that fewer than half of the expatriates are promoted upon their return. Many expatriates find their overseas jobs more challenging: they miss the greater responsibility, the authority and the professional freedom in decision making.

There are a variety of ways in which companies can deal with re-entry problems. For example, companies can develop a succession plan that identifies subsequent job positions upon repatriation. Six months prior to the termination of the international assignment, an internal position search should be initiated (Mendenhall, Dunbar and Oddou, 1987). It is also important that an expatriate with extensive responsibility overseas is not given a temporary or less important assignment after re-entry.

Noer (1974) suggests a godfather approach to minimize re-entry problems. The task of the 'godfather' manager is to maintain an umbilical cord relationship to the expatriate during his assignment, to communicate with him, and to secure a position for him when he returns.

How companies are dealing with repatriation problems is perhaps not the most important question. The key issue is to involve the expatriate in determining what position will be most suited to his/her needs after the international assignment.

References

Abe, H. and Wiseman, R. L., A cross-cultural confirmation of the dimensions of intercultural effectiveness, *International Journal of Intercultural Relations*, 7, 1983, 53–68.

Adler, N. J., *International Dimensions of Organizational Behaviour*, Boston: Kent Publishing Company, 1986.

Brein, M. and David, K. H., International communication and the adjustment of the sojourner, *Psychological Bulletin*, 76, 1971, 215–230.

Brislin, R. W., Orientation programs for cross-cultural preparation. In A. J. Marsella, G. Tharp and T. J. Ciborowski (Eds.), *Perspectives on cross-cultural psychology*, Orlando, FL: Academic Press, 1979, 287–304.

Brislin, R. W. and Van Buren, H., Can they go home again? *International Educational and Cultural Exchange*, vol. 1, no. 4, 1974, 19–24.

Brooke, M. Z., and Remmers, H. L. (Eds.), *The International Firm*, London: Pitman, 1977.

Chorofas, D. N., *Developing the International Executive*, AMA Research Study No. 83, American Management Associations, 1967.

Copeland, L. and Griggs, L., *Going international*, New York: Random House, 1985.

Desatnick, R. L. and Bennet, M. L., *Human Resource Management in the Multinational Company*, New York: Nichols Publication Company, 1978.

Franco, L. G., Who manages multinational enterprises? *Columbia Journal of World Business*, 8, 1973, 33–37.

Furnham, A. and Bochner, S., Culture Shock: *Psychological reactions to unfamiliar environments*, London: Routledge, 1989.

Gaylord, M., Relocation and the corporate family, *Social Work*, May 1979, 186–191.

Haemmerli, A., *Women in International Business*, Paper presented at the Women in International Business Conference, New York, July 11, 1978.

Hammer, M. R., Gudykunst, W. B. and Wiseman, R. L., Dimensions of intercultural effectiveness: An exploratory study, *International Journal of Intercultural Relations*, 2, 1978, 382–393.

Harris, J. G., A science of the South Pacific: Analysis of the character structure of the Peace Corps volunteer, *American Psychologist*, 28, 1973, 232–247.

Harvey, M. G., The executive family: An overlooked variable in international assignments, *Columbia Journal of World Business*, Spring 1985, 84–93.

Hays, R. D., Ascribed behavioural determinants of success–failure among U.S. expatriate managers, *Journal of International Business Studies*, 2(1), 1971, 40–46.

Hazzard, M. S., *Study of the Repatriation of the American International Executive*, New York: Korn/Ferry International, 1981.

Hill, R., East is Still East, *International Management*, May 1977, 15–18.

Howard, C. G., How relocation abroad affects expatriates' family life, *Personnel Administrator*, November 1980, 71–78.

Howard, C. G., Model for the design of a selection program for multinational executives, *Public Personnel Management*, March–April, 1974, 138–145.

Johnson, M. B., and Carter, G. L., Training needs of Americans working abroad, *Social Change*, 1972.

Kapoor, A. and McKay, R. J., *Managing International Markets: A Survey of Training Practices and Emerging Trends*, Princeton: Darwin Press, 1971.

Kobrin, S. J., Expatriate reduction and strategic control in American Multinational Corporations, *Human Resource Management*, 27(1), 1988, 63–75.

Mendenhall, M., Dunbar, E. and Oddou, G., Expatriate selection, training and career-pathing: A review and critique, *Human Resource Management*, 26(3), 1987, 331–345.

Mendenhall, M. and Oddou, G., The dimensions of expatriate acculturation: A review, *Academy of Management Review*, **10**, 1985, 39–47.

Miller, E. L., The selection decision for an international assignment: A study of the decision-maker's behaviour, *Journal of International Business Studies*, 3(2), 1972, 49–65.

Misa, K. F. and Fabricatore, J. M., Return on investment of overseas personnel, *Financial Executive*, 47(4), 1979, 42–46.

Murray, J. A., International personnel repatriation: Cultural shock in reverse. *MSU Business Topics*, 2(3), 1973, 59–66.

Noer, D. M., Integrating foreign service employees to home organisations: The godfather approach, *Personnel Journal*, January 1974, 45–51.

Perlmutter, H. V. and Heenan, D. A., How multinational should your top managers be?, *Harvard Business Review*, 52, 1974, 121–132.

Phatak, A. V., *Managing Multinational Corporations*, New York: Praeger Publishers, 1974.

Pucik, V. and Katz, J. H., Information, control, and human resource management in multinational firms, *Human Resource Management*, 25, 1986, 121–132.

Rahim, A., A model for developing key expatriate executives, *Personnel Journal*, April 1983, 312–317.

Ratiu, I., Thinking Internationally: A Comparison of How International Executives Learn, *International Studies of Management and Organization*, 13, 1983, 139–150.

Ronen, S., *Comparative and Multinational Management*, New York: Wiley, 1986.

Samovar, L. A., Porter, R. E. and Jain, N. C., *Understanding Intercultural Communication*, Belmont, CA: Wadsworth, 1981.

Schollhammer, H., The compensation of international executives, *MSU Business Topics*, Winter 1969.

The Economist, *New New England: An Occasional Series on Foreigners in Britain Looks at Americans*, 1988, p. 27.

Torbiorn, I., *Living Abroad: Personal adjustment and personnel policy in the overseas setting*, New York: Wiley, 1982.

Triandis, H. C., Culture training, cognitive complexity and interpersonal attitudes, in Brislin, R. W., Bochner, S. and Lonner, W. J. (Eds.), *Cross-cultural Perspectives on Learning*. New York: Wiley, 1975.

Tung, R. L., *The new expatriates*, Cambridge, MA: Ballinger, 1988.

Tung, R. L., Selection and training procedures of U.S. European, and Japanese multinationals, *California Management Review*, 25, 1982, 57–71.

Whetten, D. A. and Cameron, K. S., *Developing Management Skills*, Glenview, IL: Scott Foresman, 1984.

White, A. F., *Preparation of managers for cross cultural assignments*, Unpublished master's thesis, Sloan School and Management, MIT, Cambridge, MA, 1971.

Zeira, Y. and Banai, M., Selection of expatriate managers in MNCs: The host environment point of view, *International Studies of Management and Organization*, 15(1), 1985, 33–51.

Zeira, Y. and Harari, E., Managing third country nationals in multinational corporations, *Business Horizons*, October, 1977, 83–88.

Reproduced from Hiltrop, J. M. and Janssens, M. (1990). Expatriation: challenges and recommendation. *European Management Journal*, **8** (1), 19–26, by permission of *European Management Journal*.

Part Five

International management learning

Cultural difference in management learning

The first stage in developing international managers requires an understanding of how managers from different cultural backgrounds learn. There has been considerable work undertaken in the United States (notably Kolb, 1976) and in the UK (notably Honey and Mumford, 1982) in identifying different learning styles of managers, but little study of differences across cultures (see Jackson, 1993, for a consideration of the issues involved). The first reading in Chapter Ten (Hayes and Allinson, 1988) provides an introduction to the study of differences in learning styles across cultures by looking at East African, Indian and United Kingdom managers. A consideration of such differences must be fed into the development process at the beginning, in order to determine the best strategies for learning for managers from different cultural backgrounds.

In the second reading of Chapter Ten Hughes-Weiner (1986) shows how the Kolb (see 1976) learning cycle may be used in cross-cultural learning programmes, using the cross-cultural context to qualify the four learning orientations described by Kolb, as follows:

- *Concrete experience* People from different cultural backgrounds will have different experiences, which could, for example influence their readiness for classroom learning.
- *Reflective observation* People from different cultural backgrounds may have different assumptions about what they observe and understand through experience, which has implications for the bodies of knowledge which learners start with.
- *Abstract conceptualization* People from different cultures may have different cognitive frameworks which may result in drawing inappropriate conclusions from what they see and experience outside their own cultures.
- *Active experimentation* People from different cultures may behave differently which may lead to misinterpretations of the meanings of behaviour outside their own cultures

From a consideration of how the Kolb learning cycle may be employed in international management learning they draw conclusions about how cross-cultural learning may be designed and managed, focusing on interpersonal relations, task accomplishment, personal goals, and learning how to learn.

European management learning

The final reading in this chapter sets the scene for management learning within the context of the challenges of European management. Tijmstra and Casler (1992) look at the imperative for developing a distinctly European approach to management, and then look at the implications of this for the competences required of such managers, and their development needs. They examine critically what is needed from the suppliers of management training: namely the business schools, particularly pan-European schools such as EAP and European networks of national business schools. They also look at what is required from the business organizations themselves, particularly in terms of support for the Europeanization and internationalization process which both organizations and managers should be going through.

This final reading, therefore, brings together many of the themes explored in this text, and particularly focuses on the need to develop a cross-cultural breed of European managers capable of working within the context of evolving transnational organizations, dealing with new concepts of strategic development and of new organization forms and mindsets. We could also add the ability to work with different management styles and patterns of motivation, the ability to deal with conflicting ethical and value considerations in transactions across cultures, the ability to negotiate effectively in an international situation with a thorough understanding of cross-cultural communication, and the ability to deal with the difficulties of the acculturation process in mergers and acquisitions or in expatriate assignments.

References

Hayes, J and Allinson, C. W. (1988) Cultural differences in the learning styles of managers', *Management International Review*, Vol 28, No 3, 75–80.

Honey, P. and Mumford A. (1982) *The Manual of Learning Styles*, Maidenhead: Peter Honey.

Hughes-Weiner, G. (1986) 'The "learn-how-to-learn" approach to cross-cultural orientation', *International Journal of Intercultural Relation*, Vol 10, 485–505.

Jackson, T. (1993) *Organizational Behaviour In International Management*, Oxford: Butterworth-Heinemann.

Kolb, D. A. (1976) *The Learning Styles Inventory*, Boston, MA: McBer and Co.

Tijmstra, S. and Casler, K. (1992) 'Management learning for Europe', *European Management Journal*, Vol 10, No 1, March, 30–8.

10 Management learning in an international context

10.1 Cultural differences in the learning styles of managers

John Hayes and Christopher W. Allinson

Building on the work of Dewey, Lewin and Piaget, Kolb [1, 2] developed a theory of experiential learning. A central theme of his theory is that the learning process is not the same for everybody. He suggests that as a result of genetic qualities and the demands of environmental circumstances most people develop learning styles which emphasize some learning abilities over others. This paper reports a study which focuses attention on the effect of one aspect of environmental circumstance, culture.

Kolb and Fry [3] argue that important agents of socialization such as family, school and work influence the development of learning style. At a more macro level there is reason to expect that economic factors, religion, settlement patterns, educational structures, forms of government and other social forces would produce environmental frameworks which could influence personal development. Consequently, nationality could be related to the development of learning style.

Early research evidence on the importance of national differences is offered by Haire *et al.* [4] and England [5]. Haire studied 3641 managers from 14 countries and found that about one third of the variability in managerial attitudes was due to individual differences whereas two thirds could be attributed to national differences. England, after examining the personal value systems of 1,000 managers in five countries found that only one third of the variation in value systems could be attributed to national differences. Nevertheless nationality still emerged as an important factor.

Knowledge about the way people from different countries go about learning and mastering the work tasks they are confronted with could be of considerable value to those responsible for designing, presenting and evaluating management development and training activities for an international clientele. Honey and Mumford [6] argue that the closer the match between an individual's preferred learning style and the learning activities to which he or she is exposed, the more likely the individual is to learn.

The study

This study tests the hypothesis that culture will account for differences in learning style by comparing the learning styles of mid-career managers from three different cultures. While Haire *et al.* and England found that nationality was an important factor accounting for differences in attitudes and values it was felt, when designing this study, that account should be taken of Bhagat and McQuaid's [7] argument that cross cultural differences offer a more fruitful basis for research than national differences, and Hofstede's [8] caution against treating names of countries as residues of undefined variance in the phenomena found. Two countries may be very similar in ecology and climate and, for example, through a common legacy of colonialism, have a similar language and legal, educational and governmental infrastructure but may be markedly different in terms of beliefs, attitudes and values. Even within one country there may be many different cultures. Gay and Abrahams [9] citing the work of Hanners [10], argue for example that Blacks in America exist in a cultural world which is sufficiently distinct in most realms of life to be more usefully regarded as a separate culture rather than a sub culture. The concept of subjective culture, advanced by Triandis *et al.* [11], which refers to a group's characteristic way of perceiving its social environment, is seen to provide the most useful way of defining and interpreting similarities and differences among people.

In this study national cultures are differentiated in terms of the four main dimensions identified by Hofstede [12]. He conducted an important cross-cultural study of work-related values which offers a framework for analysing similarities and differences in the subjective culture of two or more countries and a way of grouping together countries which have similar subjective cultures. He analysed data about the beliefs and values of over 60,000 people working for a single multinational company in 40 countries around the world and identified four main dimensions along which national cultures differ. These are Power Distance, (a dimension concerned with human inequality) Uncertainty Avoidance (concerned with the tolerance for uncertainty), Individualism–collectivism, (concerned with the relationship between the individual and the collectivity which prevails in a given society), and Masculinity–Femininity (concerned with the extent to which the dominant values in society are 'masculine', that is assertive, the acquisition of money and things, and *not* caring for others, the quality of life, or people).

Honey and Mumford's Learning Style Questionnaire [13] is used to assess learning style but, rather than reporting scores for the four learning styles normally measured by the LSQ, data, following Allinson and Hayes [14], is presented for two dimensions of learning style. The 'Analysis' dimension, with positive loadings on the LSQ's Theorist and Pragmatist scales, measures the extent to which the learner adopts a theory building and testing, as opposed to intuitive, approach. The 'Action' dimension, with a positive loading on the Activist LSQ scale and a negative loading on the Reflector LSQ scale, measures the extent to which the learner adopts a trial and error, as opposed to contemplative, approach. Test–retest reliability coefficients for these two sub-scales were significant at $P < 0.001$ over both a two week and six month interval.

Kolb's original Learning Style Inventory (Kolb [15]) was rejected as a measure of learning style in favour of the Honey and Mumford LSQ. It was felt that subjects from different cultures could have experienced difficulty discriminating between the meaning of some of the 36 words which have to be rank ordered in the Kolb inventory in terms of how they characterize learning style. The Honey and Mumford LSQ is based on more universally recognizable statements of managerial behaviour. Cognisance of a further criticism of Kolb's L.S.I., levelled by Freedman and Stumpf [16], also weighed the balance in favour of the LSQ. Ranking and scoring methods for the LSI result in the four dimensions being dependent on one another, thus high scores on one dimension necessitate lower scores on the others.

According to Allinson and Hayes [17] the LSQ may be preferable to the LSI as a measure of learning style for a number of reasons. First, it seems more capable of actually measuring something. Whereas the LSI apparently has no clear factor structure, the LSQ was able to distinguish similar cognitive dimensions in two independent samples, British and Indian. Second, the distribution of its scores is closer than that of the LSI to what might be expected theoretically. Third, it may be more reliable. Temporal stability coefficients for the LSQ appear to be superior to those reported for the LSI. Finally, it has better face validity. Whilst a number of the SLI items do not inspire confidence as indicators of learning style, the behavioural statements contained in the LSQ at least look as though they measure what they are supposed to be measuring.

The Myers–Briggs Type Indicator (Myers [18]) was also considered as a possible measure of learning style but was rejected for the reasons of length and complexity advanced by Sugarman [19]. She argues that in situations in which learning styles are of particular concern, the MBTI may be too sophisticated and may cause confusion, however, when used for other purposes the MBTI's learning style implications may warrant consideration.

The Honey and Mumford LSQ was administered to 95 mid-career managers from 19 countries who had participated in the project based M.B.A. programme offered by Leeds University. This sample contained two reasonably sized subsamples of managers, 40 from India and 28 from East Africa. Data for a similar group of 127 British middle managers was provided by Honey [20]. The value of Hofstede's four indices for these three cultures is presented in Table 1.

Inspection of Table 1 reveals that the three cultures differ least in terms of Uncertainty Avoidance. It is low in both the United Kingdom and India and

Table 1   Value of the four indices (with rank order, $n = 53$) for the three countries/ regions included in the study

Country	Power Distance		Uncertainty Avoidance		Individualism		Masculinity	
	Index	*Rank*	*Index*	*Rank*	*Index*	*Rank*	*Index*	*Rank*
East Africa	64	(31–32)	52	(17–18)	27	(18–19)	41	(14–15)
India	77	(42)	40	(9)	48	(30)	56	(30–31)
United Kingdom	35	(10–12)	35	(6–7)	89	(48)	66	(41–42)

only moderate in East Africa. The greatest difference appears to be related to Individualism. The United Kingdom is the most individualistic and East Africa the least, but all three cultures are clearly different from each other. A similar pattern of difference is also evident in terms of Masculinity. The United Kingdom is the most masculine culture and East Africa is the most feminine. India and East Africa are both much higher than the U.K. in terms of Power Distance. It would appear therefore that in a number of important respects managers from India, East Africa and the United Kingdom come from different cultural settings.

Results

Some descriptive statistics for each of the two dimensions of learning styles, Action and Analysis, are presented for East Africa, India and the United Kingdom in Table 2.

Inspection of Table 2 suggests that there are important differences in learning style between all three cultures. India appears to be much higher on Analysis than either East Africa or the United Kingdom and all three cultural groups present differences on the Action sub scale. Action scores are highest for British and lowest for East African managers.

Inequality of sample variances made it necessary to adopt nonparametric methods of analysis. The Kruskal–Wallis one-way analysis of variance presented in Table 3 confirms a difference in learning style between the three groups.

All possible comparisons were examined using the Mann–Whitney U-test and a more detailed picture of the differences is presented in Table 4.

The Z scores for Action show significant differences between East Africa and India, East Africa and the United Kingdom, and India and the United Kingdom. Z scores for Analysis show significant differences between India and East Africa, and India and the United Kingdom, but not between East Africa and the United Kingdom.

Table 2 Descriptive statistics for LSO subscales

Sample	n	Subscale	Mean	Mode	Median	SD	Range (0–40)
East Africa	28	Action	11.71	10	10.0	3.56	7–19
		Analysis	28.32	21	28.5	5.05	20–37
India	40	Action	13.95	11	13.5	4.76	3–25
		Analysis	31.03	34	31.5	3.85	18–37
United Kingdom	127	Action	16.60	13	16.0	5.53	5–32
		Analysis	28.05	29	29.0	4.36	9–38

Table 3 Group differences (Kruskal–Wallis one-way analysis of variance)

Samples	n	Action Mean Rank	Analysis Mean Rank
East Africa	28	57.25	91.45
India	40	85.22	130.56
United Kingdom	127	111.01	89.19
		$X^2 = 23.47*$	$X^2 = 16.89*$

$* \, p < 0.001.$

Table 4 Group differences in LSO scores (Mann–Whitney U-Test)

Samples	Action	Analysis
East Africa v India	$Z = -2.30*$	$Z = -2.48*$
East Africa v United Kingdom	$Z = -4.46***$	$Z = -0.07$
India v United Kingdom	$Z = -2.61**$	$Z = 4.15***$

$* \, p < 0.05; ** \, p < 0.01; *** \, p < 0.001.$

Discussion

In the post war years there has been an enormous increase in the demand for professional, administrative and managerial manpower in developing countries around the world. Independence led to a rapid indigenisation of the civil service in many countries and political and economic factors has speeded indigenisation in the private sector. The rapidity with which local human resources had to be developed made it attractive for both governments and multi nationals to import western human resource development practices which had been demonstrated to be effective in their country of origin.

The belief that the way people think and learn is the same, irrespective of culture, appears to be widely held. Greenfield [21. p. 225] expressed surprise that qualitative differences between western thinking and that of tranditional societies has rarely been explored when it is so clearly implicit in the work of anthropologists such as Boas, Durkheim, Mauss, Mead and Wharf. He illustrates the lack of concern for qualitative differences by pointing to Piaget's classic work on cognitive development which is based on experiments in which age alone is varied. Where Piaget's work has been extended to non-western societies the emphasis has been almost entirely quantitative and has been confined to timetable studies which have examined the 'lag' in the development of 'foreign' children in contracts to children in western society (see Flavell [22]).

In the area of management Hofstede [23] argues strongly for the non-universality of theory and practice. Thinking and theory are bounded by cultural conditioning. This has important implications for the design of organisations, for management practices and for the kinds of manager that management development programmes should be attempting to produce to work in different cultures.

The results of this study advance the argument a step further and raise questions about not only the aims and content of management development activities in different cultures but also about the nature of the learning process and the design of learning environments employed. Kolb and Fry [24] present evidence that people with different learning styles prefer different learning environments. They surveyed over 100 students who had completed an introductory experientially oriented course on human factors in management and found that students with different learning styles reacted very differently to such elements as structure, authority and opportunity for peer interaction. These findings are reflected in the work of Carter [25] who argues that a mismatch between preferred learning style and work environment will result in dissatisfaction and poor performance. More research is required into the relationship between learning styles, learning environments and learning outcomes. It may well be that the kind of learning environments and activities which promote effective learning in some cultures may not promote the same outcomes in other cultures where different learning styles predominate. This could have important implications for the design of learning environments, the composition of training groups and the location of training (in host country, regional centre or home country) undertaken by transnational organisations. In establishing that there are important cultural differences in the learning style of managers, this study lays the foundation for further, work in this area.

References

1 Kolb D. A. (1973): On management and the learning process. M. I. T. Sloan School Working Paper, No. 652–73.
2 Kolb D. A. (1984): *Experiential Learning*, New York, Prentice Hall.
3 Kolb D. A. and Fry R. (1975): Towards an applied theory of experiential learning. In C. Cooper (Ed.) *Theories of Group Processes*, New York, Wiley pp. 33–58.
4 Haire M., Ghiselli E. E., and Porter L. W. (1966): *Managerial thinking: An international study*, New York, Wiley.
5 England G. W. (1976): *The manager and his values: An international perspective.* Cambridge, Mass.: Ballinger.
6 Honey P. and Mumford A. (1983): *Using Your Learning Styles*, Maidenhead, Honey.
7 Bhagat R. S. and McQuaid S. (1982): Role of subjective culture in organizations: a review and directions for future research. *Journal of Applied Psychology*, Vol 67, pp. 653–685.
8 Hofstede G. (1984): *Culture's Consequences: international differences in work-related values* (abridged edition), London, Sage.
9 Gay G. and Abrahams R. D. (1973): Does the pot melt, boil or brew; Black children and white assessment procedures. *Journal of School Psychology*, 11, 4, pp. 330–340.
10 Hannerz U. (1969): *Soulside*, New York, Columbia University Press.
11 Triandis H. C., Vassiliou V., Vassiliou G., Tanaka Y. and Shanmugam A: (Eds.) (1972): *The analysis of subjective culture*, New York, Wiley.
12 Hofstede, G. (1984): *op. cit.*
13 Honey P. and Mumford A. (1982): *The Manual of Learning Styles*, Maidenhead, Honey.
14 Allinson C. and Hayes J. (1988): The learning style questionnaire: An alternative to Kolb's inventory? *Journal of Management Studies* 25, 6 (in press).
15 Kolb D. A. (1976): *Learning Style Inventory: Technical Manual*, Boston, McBer.
16 Freedman R. D. and Stumpf S. A. (1978): What can one learn from the Learning Style Inventory? *Academy of Management Journal* 21, pp. 275–282.
17 Allinson C. and Hayes J. (1988): *op. cit.*
18 Myers I. B. (1975): *Manual: The Myers–Briggs Type Indicator*. Palo Alto, CA: Consulting Psychologists Press.
19 Sugarman L. (1985): Kolb's model of experiential learning: touchstone for trainers, students, counsellors and clients. *Journal of Counselling and Development*, 64, pp. 262–268.
20 Honey P. (1986): private communication.
21 Greenfield P. M. (1966): On culture and conservation, Chapter 11 in J. S. Bruner *et al. Studies in Cognitive Growth*. London, Wiley.
22 Flavell J. H. (1963): *The developmental psychology of Jean Piaget*, Princeton: Van Nostrand.
23 Hofstede G. (1980): Motivation, Leadership and Organization: Do American Theories Apply Abroad? *Organizational Dynamics*. Summer, pp. 42–63.
24 Kolb D. A. and Fry R. (1975): *op. cit.*
25 Carter S. (1985): Is this the stuff that marketeers are made of? *European Journal of Marketing* Vol 9, No 6, pp. 53–64.

Reproduced from Hayes, J. and Allinson, C. W. (1988). Cultural differences in the learning styles of managers. *Management International Review*, **28** (3), by permission of *Management International Review*.

10.2 The 'learning how to learn' approach to cross-cultural orientation

Gail Hughes-Wiener

Introduction

No person can be completely prepared for interaction in another culture. Therefore, the best preparation a sojourner can have is to go beyond learning specific cultural information, to 'learn how to learn' about other cultures. Although such learning may best develop over years and ideally should be started in elementary or secondary school (Hughes, 1983), this approach is also appropriate for use in more intensive intercultural orientation programs (e.g. summer institutes, in-country programs), as well as college-level courses designed to prepare intercultural trainers and educators.

Every orientation program will have somewhat different needs, depending on its context and participants. However, this paper presents some general considerations in designing cross-cultural orientation programs incorporating a 'learning how to learn' approach. As a basis for this discussion, Kolb's 'Learning Cycle' (1976) will be adapted and expanded for use as an implied theory of learning and of learning how to learn.

Learning how to learn as an approach to program planning

Although there has been some attention given by intercultural trainers to the importance of learning-how-to-learn (Casse, 1980; Wight and Hammons, 1970; also see the intercultural orientation papers by Bennett, 1986; McCaffery, 1986; and Paige, 1986), it has been neither well-defined as an approach, nor used on a widespread basis for orientation programs.

The term 'learning how to learn' was perhaps first used in an article by Harlow (1949) which describes the formation of 'learning sets' in experiments with both monkeys and children. Over a series of individual but related problems, subjects developed the ability to transfer their learning from early problems to later ones. In this way they had apparently developed a strategy which enabled them to identify the procedures necessary for solving the type of problem involved, and had mastered the skills to implement the procedures successfully, i.e. they had learned how to learn.

Based on these assumptions, we define learning-how-to-learn (LHTL) as the acquisition of new strategies, skills and procedures to attain one's goals efficiently and effectively.[1] Programs which use a LHTL approach both directly teach and indirectly model the principles of effective learning. Here, the approach will be applied to program planning (orientation), and we first consider the learning processes from which it is derived.

Learning theory as a basis for the learning-how-to-learn approach

A major difficulty in developing this approach is the lack of sophisticated theoretical conceptualization and concomitant empirical evidence. Most research on learning has been restricted to the 'micro-level' – on physiological processes rather than learning procedures (see psychology texts such as Travers, 1977; Smith, Sarason and Sarason, 1982; and Coon, 1983). When considering the 'macro-level' processes of learning in designing orientation programs (i.e. determining goals, objectives, and topics; selecting and sequencing instructional materials and activities, identifying evaluation methods appropriate for the kinds of participants anticipated), trainers are limited, restricted primarily to testing information that is still primarily at the level of speculation.

David Kolb's 'Learning Cycle' (1976) hypothesizes a number of qualitatively different tasks which are performed in the process of learning. I have found it to be more comprehensive and easier to use than other theories and formats such as Bloom's taxonomy (Bloom *et al.*, 1956), which is presently more familiar to educators. Also, although a great deal of research will be required to validate something of the magnitude of the Learning Cycle, that which has been conducted so far has been supportive (Kolb, 1984). For these reasons, this paper will use Kolb's theory of learning as the basis for developing a learning-how-to-learn curriculum and instructional methodology for cross-cultural orientation programs.

---

[1] In his discussion of cognitive functions, Blumenthal (1977) describes the construct of a decision-making 'Executive' which plans, strategizes, monitors, and evaluates behavior. It's a sort of generic problem-solver. An alternative definition of learning how to learn might be the development of more efficient and effective. Executive abilities.

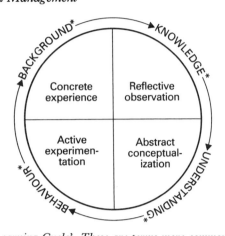

Figure 1   *Kolb's 'Learning Cycle'. These are terms more commonly used by educators, which I am using to describe Kolb's (1976) Learning Cycle quadrants*

An adaptation of Kolb's 'Learning Cycle' as a theory of learning

Kolb (1976) theorizes that when people learn something new, they go through a 'cycle' which involves four broad types of processes. These are the quadrants of his Learning Cycle: Concrete Experience, Reflective Observation, Abstract Conceptualization, and Active Experimentation, also referred to as Background, Knowledge, Understanding, and Behavior. These quadrants are shown in Figure 1, in circular rather than linear form to indicate that the learning process can start with any of the four processes.

Although Kolb presents the Cycle as a representation of universal learning processes, the steps should be applied differently in cross-cultural situations when different values and frames of reference are involved, if they are to be successful. A description of each quadrant as applied to intercultural learning is given below.

Concrete Experience ('Background') Concrete Experience refers to one's experiences in life, in the 'real world'. The competencies acquired through previous learning, in combination with their motivation and personal qualities (i.e. abilities, traits and attitudes), determine students' needs and their 'readiness' for further learning. People with different backgrounds, such as those from other cultures, are likely to have had quite different experiences, and are likely to vary in their 'readiness' for academic learning or for intercultural learning.

Reflective Observation ('Knowledge') Reflective Observation involves perceiving and responding to information. Since information is selected or filtered by perceptual frameworks, this quadrant is closely related to Abstract Conceptualization (see Albert, 1986). However, 'knowledge' relies on introspection and the sensory cognitions of perceiving, storing, and retrieving data, whereas 'understanding' often requires formal reasoning skills. Due to the variety of behavior patterns, artifacts, and institutions in different cultures, people from different societies are likely to acquire different bodies of knowledge and to make different assumptions about what is true.

Abstract Conceptualization ('Understanding') This quadrant refers to the development of concepts, generalizations, and theories by making inferences about the relationships among facts or data assumed to be facts. The construction of these explanatory models or conceptual frameworks enables learners to: (a) select the information collected in the Knowledge quadrant; (b) organize information most relevant to the frameworks, also in the Knowledge quadrant; and (c) interpret information to diagnose situations in the Behavior quadrant; as well as (d) achieve the psychological satisfaction of being able to make sense of the world around them. However, since people from different cultures have different cognitive frameworks, they may use inappropriate frameworks in cross-cultural situations, or may focus on irrelevant information, while ignoring important cues, resulting in incorrect interpretations.

Active Experimentation ('Behavior') In this quadrant, learning occurs through the manipulation of concrete objects and from interaction with people, with an emphasis on practical skills and overt behaviors. It involves diagnosing particular situations to select appropriate behavioral repertoires, and then performing the selected behaviors. Since cultures differ in behavioral patterns, cross-cultural situations may be mis-diagnosed, resulting in inappropriate responses. Alternatively, situations may seem unfamiliar and confusing, in which case sojourners may not know how to respond. Even when they know what to do, new behaviors may be difficult to perform smoothly.

Completing the Cycle Sojourners test the effectiveness of their behavior in achieving goals and incorporate their new knowledge, understandings, behaviors, and accompanying attitudes into situations arising in real life. Once the new learning is internalized, it becomes part of their 'readiness' for yet further learning. Having gone through the Cycle, the experience base (Quadrant 1) is now changed, and subsequent observations, conceptualizations, and behavioral experiments will be permanently altered. See the articles by Bennett (1986) and McCaffery (1986) for more information about the Cycle.

An extrapolation of Kolb's 'Learning Cycle' as an implied theory of learning how to learn

People do not have to be taught how to learn. Learning occurs quite naturally from earliest childhood by infants who have never heard of the Learning Cycle! However, people do not always learn as efficiently and as effectively as they could, and they sometimes 'learn' wrong things! Kolb theorized that understanding the quadrants of the Learning Cycle would help people to identify their strengths and weaknesses and enable them to become better learners.

Simply proceeding through the quadrants does not produce an effective learner. After all, it is of little use to gather biased information, to use monocultural cognitive frameworks in multicultural situations, or to act exactly as you would at home when you're in another country! Logical analysis suggests that successful use of the Learning Cycle entails acquiring not just any learnings – it entails acquiring appropriate, goal-related learnings.

Participants who have acquired appropriate learning in each quadrant will need to be able to draw on knowledge stored in memory and activate culture-relevant frameworks and behaviors that have become routinized. With the right strategy, the process of achieving a goal will be quite automatic. If, however, goal-related competencies have not been acquired, as is almost always the case in an unfamiliar environment, sojourners will need to learn them. To do this, they must: (1) know what they need to learn (i.e. they must have procedures for identifying goal-related knowledge, understandings and behaviors); (2) know how to learn it (i.e. they must have strategies for acquiring new intercultural competencies); and (3) be able to learn it (i.e. they must have the skills to implement the procedures and strategies).

Descriptions of these learning procedures, strategies, and skills are given below, followed by a discussion of their relevance to cross-cultural situations. The principles suggested have been conceptually derived from learning theory. They are related to cognitive psychology theory and research (see Miller, Galanter and Pribram, 1960, for a discussion of hierarchical mental plans which include strategies, procedures, skills and cognitions; Simon, 1967, for the philosophy of information processing theory; and Blumenthal, 1977, for a description of a cognitive 'Executive' which plans and monitors behavior). They are also related to social psychology research (see Shaw, 1981, regarding the importance of clear goals and 'goals paths').

Effective learning procedures

Learning procedures refer to the methods used to identify learning objectives – the selection of intercultural knowledge, understandings, and behaviors to be learned.

Concrete Experience [*'Background'*] Students learn more efficiently when they have clear goals (Simon, 1969; also Shaw, 1981). In a classroom situation the teacher is responsible for assessing needs and setting appropriate goals and objectives. However, outside the classroom context, learners identify their own objectives. Like a good teacher, they should identify their overriding purpose and (from research, theory, and experience) the factors necessary to achieve that purpose. Their goals should correspond to the factors, and objectives should relate to the knowledge, understandings, and skills they need to make progress towards achieving the goals, given their present circumstances. Students must possess a high level of self-awareness to do this effectively.

Reflective Observation (*'Knowledge'*) Due to the 'Knowledge Explosion', there is more information available about most topics than anyone can handle. Thus when students need to acquire information, they can do so most efficiently if they 'know what to look for' – i.e. if they know what kinds of information can help them achieve their goals and where they can find it (e.g. journals and major works in the field, 'native informants', institutions and agencies). Concepts, generalizations, and theories drawn from the 'Understanding' quadrant can provide appropriate 'cognitive maps' to help them identify important features of the environment (Tolman, 1948). To ensure that the information is accurate and balanced, students will need to recognize the biases of their sources, use sources representing different points of view, and challenge the truth of their own assumptions. These procedures will require some analytical skills as well as data-gathering skills related to library research, observations, listening, and communication skills. They also require an awareness of one's own assumptions and emotional reactions, an openness to new information, and the ability to cope with the stress of 'information overload'.

Abstract Conceptualization (*'Understanding'*) Students need to interpret their environment accurately if they are to know what to do to achieve their goals. To do this, they must have more than static cognitive maps which enable them to know what to look for. Rather, they must have dynamic conceptual models of reality (what Blumenthal, 1977, calls 'schemata') which can explain events and predict how various actions are likely to affect a given situation. People often make generalizations and form theories unconsciously, through inductively processing information in their environment. In different circumstances, however, existing models may not be appropriate. Thus, students must learn to identify and test their implicitly-held cognitive theories, and make modifications or even construct new ones when necessary. Such a 'cognitive shift' is very difficult for most people, as it challenges long-cherished beliefs and values, and it entails a period of uncomfortable disorientation and ambiguity, requiring self-awareness and intellectual openness in addition to highly-developed analytical skills.

Active Experimentation ('Behavior') Students must make a correct diagnosis of a particular situation if they are to make an appropriate response. Their diagnosis depends on having an accurate interpretation of the situation (from the 'Understanding' quadrant) and their response rests on the diagnosis and objectives. If students receive negative reactions to their behavior, they may have behaved inappropriately due to acting on false assumptions. Alternatively, if they are attempting new behaviors, they might not have performed them correctly. The development of new behaviors involves observing and modeling others, then experimenting with, refining, and practicing the behaviors. (See Hilgard and Bower's description of information processing theory and TOTE feedback units, 1975.) Students will need some courage and flexibility to attempt this process. A sense of humor can alleviate the frustrations and awkwardness which are likely to arise, and a realization that mistakes are a necessary part of learning can help them cope with feelings of ineptness.

Besides diagnostic skills, students will need the interpersonal, technical, and motor skills necessary to perform the relevant behaviors. They must also have the decision-making skills to make choices about how to respond when issues arise, such as when they are asked to act in ways that conflict with long-held beliefs and values.

Completing the Cycle Students will need to evaluate their progress toward attaining the goals they had set, as well as identify any unintended effects of their behavior. Doing this will require obtaining feedback through their own observations, the verbal and nonverbal responses of others, and if desired, through more formal methods such as interviews and the administration of surveys. Positive feedback will reinforce successful behaviors, and negative feedback will help students assess their learning needs for the next time they go through the Learning Cycle. However, negative feedback can be threatening to one's self-esteem, and defensiveness is a common reaction. Students will be more motivated to endure the discomfort if they can see that being honest with themselves will make it easier to build on their strengths and improve areas of weaknesses. (See Atkinson, 1972, and Hilgard and Bower, 1975, for the importance of feedback.)

Effective learning strategies

Effective strategies are plans which select the most appropriate methods to attain objectives in a given situation. Cross-cultural learning strategies enable sojourners to acquire the new intercultural knowledge, understandings, and behaviors identified by the procedures described in the previous section.

In terms of the development of general learning strategies, it should be noted that Quadrant III ('Understanding') is the pivotal quadrant for learning how to learn. Cognitive models are essential for gathering information efficiently, for without knowing what to look for, the student is like a newborn, bombarded with sensory data but unable to determine what they mean. On the other hand, the use of invalid models will result in inaccurate interpretations of events and ineffective behavior. Thus, after students identify their goals (Quadrant I), they should learn to recall, locate or construct appropriate frameworks for analyzing their environment. With an accurate understanding of the situation, it usually becomes relatively easy to acquire whatever new information and behaviors they need to achieve their goals. However, students must know where to obtain accurate feedback, emotional support, and assistance in developing new skills.

Learning strategies should be selected for their relevance to the learning situation. Situations in which the student's conceptual frameworks can not be taken for granted – (i.e., situations in which their cognitive frameworks need modification; situations in which core beliefs and values are challenged and new frameworks must be constructed; and 'unknown' situations) require strategies demanding a high degree of cultural awareness and tolerance for ambiguity. These strategies would test the validity of their existing frameworks through 'hypothesis refinement' methods (Seelye, 1974).

Learning Skills

Learning skills refer to the ability to perform the cognitive operations and physical behaviors identified by learning strategies and procedures. Effective learning demands assessment, planning, and evaluation skills to identify needed cross-cultural competencies, and diagnostic and decision-making skills to select appropriate strategies. Other cognitive, technical, interpersonal, and motor skills may be required, depending on the strategies and procedures used. In addition, a number of personal qualities with skill components (i.e. self-awareness, a tolerance for ambiguity, a multicultural perspective, etc.) are frequently desired. Skills likely to be associated with different specific procedures and strategies were identified in the sections above.

Effective learning in intercultural situations is more complex and stressful than learning in one's home culture. In addition to the unusually high degree of personal self-awareness required to learn effectively on one's own in any setting, sojourners will need a great deal of cultural self-awareness – an understanding of their own cultural patterns and preferences (see J. Bennett, 1986). Orientation programs which have a learning-how-to-learn approach will need to prepare their participants to use the most demanding of the procedures, skills and strategies discussed in relationship to Kolb's Learning Cycle. Suggestions as to how this might be done will be given in the program planning sections, which comprise the remainder of this paper.

Implications for cross-cultural orientation programs

The implications of the LHTL approach for cross-cultural orientation programs will be discussed by considering its application to each component of program planning – establishing the purpose and goals of the program, designing the curriculum, instructional planning, program management, and program and participant evaluation.

The purpose and goals of cross-cultural orientation programs

As may be inferred from Brislin and Pedersen (1976), the major purpose of cross-cultural orientation programs is to improve the performance and satisfaction of participants when they interact with another culture. While specific goals should be set according to the particular needs of participants, there are general goals that are included in most orientation programs and mentioned in the cross-cultural training literature as summarized by Dinges (1983) and Gudykunst and Hammer (1983). These three goal areas – interpersonal relations, task accomplishment, and personal goals – roughly correspond to the three dimensions identified by Hawes and Kealey (1979)[2] and by Kealey and Ruben (1983)[3] as the most important dimensions of intercultural effectiveness in overseas settings.

---

[2] Hawes and Kealey (1979) refer to these as 'professional effectiveness', 'intercultural interaction and training', and 'personal/family adjustment and satisfaction' (pp. 160–165). A key component of the 'personal satisfaction' dimension is 'engaging in enjoyable activities', which involves pursuing personal interests.

[3] Kealey and Ruben (1983) reviewed studies of Peace Corps Volunteers, overseas businessmen, technical assistance personnel, and military personnel, to identify the components of 'professional competence, intercultural interaction, and psychological adjustment' (pp. 155–164). They write that the main focus has been on adjustment.

Programs wishing to incorporate a LHTL approach should include a fourth goal – the goal of teaching participants how to continue learning after the program is over – so that they will be better equipped to accomplish their tasks, enhance their interpersonal relations, and realize their personal goals on their own in the new culture.

Curriculum design

In all but specialized programs, the four goals identified above can provide a broad framework for curriculum development. General objectives relating to the Background, Knowledge, Understanding, and Behavior quadrants of the Learning Cycle will be suggested for each goal. These will be derived from research results, intercultural theory, and the theory of learning how to learn. From these, specific objectives should be selected for individual programs which take into account participants' intercultural experiences, competencies, and personal qualities, as well as their interest in interacting with people from other cultures.

1 *Interpersonal Relations* According to a recent review of the literature (Dinges, 1983; also see Paige, 1986, for a short summary), cultural knowledge, cross-cultural understanding, and a number of intercultural behavioral skills and situational variables are important in fostering good intercultural relations. Some personal qualities, such as openness, flexibility, a sense of humor, and pluralistic values and attitudes are also helpful.

   Knowledge objectives should focus on helping participants to acquire realistic expectations of the target culture(s) (Kealey and Ruben, 1983). According to attribution theory, the expectations which are most important to intercultural relations are those which involve different interpretations of behavior (Triandis *et al.*, 1972). As argued by Hughes (1983), information about roles and role relationships should be more useful in preparing sojourners for what they're likely to encounter than information about the institutions of a society – their economic, political and educational systems, fine arts, etc. Participants may benefit from knowing what intercultural relations problems to expect (see Brislin's 18 themes, 1986), and the implications of situational variables (see Paige's summary, 1986). They should also be prepared for possible affective responses to cultural differences, such as anxiety and culture shock (Barna, 1983).

   According to Triandis (1975), a society's beliefs and values (i.e. its 'subjective culture') can serve as effective frameworks for learning to understand another culture. Brislin's intercultural themes (1986), Hughes' (1983) eclectic theory of intercultural relations, and Triandis' (1975) theory of isomorphic attribution are other frameworks which may be useful.

The major objective of the Behavior quadrant is to enable participants to interact with another culture by being able to act in accordance with its norms, or to create new 'third culture' patterns which incorporate elements of both host and home cultures. The issues involved in this choice, noted earlier, should be discussed. Roles and role relationships which participants are likely to experience – restaurant customer, guest, friend, etc. – may provide frameworks for diagnosing situations and experimenting with responses.

A number of diagnostic and interpersonal skills are integral to intercultural interaction.[4] Among these are communication and group process skills, hypothesis refinement, and coping with cultural differences. Each of these is in turn comprised of 'micro-skills'. For example, communication skills involve such things as listening, perception-checking, perspective-taking ('empathy'), and nonverbal communication (Wight and Hammons, 1970); conflict resolution includes the setting of superordinate goals, bargaining and negotiation (King, 1976).

2 *Task Accomplishment* Little research has been conducted on cross-cultural task effectiveness. To the extent that the processes of adjusting to a task culture is similar to those of adjusting to other aspects of a target culture, orientation participants should benefit from acquiring realistic expectations of: (a) the roles and role relationships of the task culture in which they will be working; (b) cross-cultural interpersonal problems which are likely to arise; and (c) situational variables which may affect their job performance or satisfaction. As with learning about the broader culture, it would be most efficient to concentrate on the differences which sojourners are likely to encounter between the home and host task cultures. Additional occupation-specific knowledge, understandings, behaviors and qualities may be required, depending on the nature of the tasks involved. Teachers will need somewhat different preparation than missionaries or businessmen, for example.

Relevant intercultural themes, intercultural relations theory, or other frameworks could be selected for helping students to understand their task culture. Additional frameworks will be needed for the occupations involved

---

[4] Although the skills and component micro-skills which are related to intercultural relations have not been well-established, the ones listed here have been frequently mentioned in the training materials of intercultural organizations (American Field Service Research Department, 1983; Canadian International Development Agency, 1979; Experiment in International Living – Batchelder and Warner, 1973; Experiment in International Living – Fantini, 1984; Peace Corps – McCaffery and Edwards, 1982; Peace Corps – Wight and Hammons, 1970; and Youth for Understanding, n.d.), in the writings of cross-cultural trainers (Casse, 1979; Hoopes and Ventura, 1979; Ruben and Kealey, 1979; and Weeks, Pedersen and Brislin, 1979), and in the writings of educators (Hoopes, 1980; King, 1976; Pasternak, 1979; Pusch, 1979; Seelye, 1974; and Smith and Otero, 1977).

– philosophies of learning for teachers, marketing principles for business-men, etc.

Sojourners should also learn the new or modified roles involved in performing their tasks successfully in another culture(s). The exact nature of the skills required depends on the task culture and on the work situation. Those new to an occupation will need to master all essential task-related skills, and should be referred to other sources of assistance if necessary. Those who have had comparable occupations at home could focus on developing skills to cope with the difficulties that are likely to arise due to cultural and situational differences. Decisions concerning whether to perform new behaviors with which one disagrees may be particularly knotty, as the issues are more difficult to avoid when they arise on the job. Participants should be helped to understand the perspectives of the host culture, but all points of view should be given serious consideration, and the students must feel free to make their own decisions.

3 *Personal Goals* Orientation participants are likely to be interested in different aspects of another culture. Some may want to learn traditional dancing; others may be interested in politics, in becoming fluent in the language, etc. At minimum, participants should think about their interests and what the other society has to offer to help them make the most of their experience. Success in achieving personal goals is important to sojourner satisfaction, and is probably important to their effectiveness in tasks and intercultural relations, as well (Hawes and Kealey, 1970; Kealey and Ruben, 1983).

4 *Learning How to Learn* Programs should teach participants how to use the conceptually-derived principles of effective learning discussed earlier in this paper. They should develop learning strategies, procedures, and skills which will enable them to reach their goals in cross-cultural situations. If possible, participants should learn to use strategies which enable them to test and modify their conceptual frameworks and create new ones if necessary. They should be able to use relevant criteria to identify effective procedures, and they should improve their learning skills to implement the procedures. Important learning skills include those relating to planning and evaluation, as well as the hypothesis refinement skills of information-gathering, reasoning, and situational and behavioral diagnosis. Learning on one's own also requires an unusually high degree of motivation and the personal qualities mentioned in relationship to the intercultural goals.

Participants may benefit from a basic understanding of Kolb's Learning Cycle and the theory of learning how to learn. They should be able to use the Learning Cycle as a mnemonic for remembering criteria and identifying their own strategies. It may also enhance participants' understanding of learning principles if they can see how they have been used to identify the program's intercultural goals and objectives. The program should also model the principles in its instructional methods and program management, to be considered in the next sections.

Instructional Planning

After the curriculum design – the broad outline of what should be taught – has been developed, attention should be given to instructional planning. As in curriculum design, the Learning Cycle can serve as a format for developing the instructional design. Some examples will be given of how the Learning Cycle might be used to improve the teaching of the program goals. Space demands that this discussion be very brief; but hopefully, it will provide a sufficient idea of the approach for you to be able to apply it to your own program in greater detail.

Using the Learning Cycle to Teach Intercultural Relations, Task Accomplishment, and Personal Goals An assessment of participants' 'readiness' – their existing knowledge, skills and attitudes – should be made upon entry into the program. Almost everybody has had some sort of intercultural experiences with people of another nation, ethnic group, religion, political party, or social class, or who differ in some major aspect of world view or lifestyle. Thus, most participants will be able to see the relevance of intercultural relations to their lives. A good way to begin a program would be to have them discuss their own cultural identities and intercultural experiences. They could then consider the importance these identities and experiences have had in their lives. This requires gathering factual information about specific cases and cultures which will help participants to identify essential features of a culture which are important for effective learning (Hilgard and Bower, 1975). Readings, case studies, 'critical incidents', and 'culture assimilators' can supplement students' own experiences. (See Brislin, 1986, and Albert, 1986, for information about culture assimilators.)

These culture specifics could form a basis for the development of concepts and generalizations which would have greater usefulness and applicability, such as the three goals and 18 intercultural themes mentioned in the curriculum section of this paper. This, then, would move students into the Understanding quadrant. If we would like participants to be able to use this understanding to improve their own relationships with others, we will need to move them even further, into the Behavior quadrant. Here, participants will need to diagnose situations in order to identify relevant intercultural principles. They will also need to practice using and refining their intercultural skills. Drills and 'experiential' methods such as simulations, role-plays, and skits should prove useful here. (See McCaffery, 1986, for a list of experiential activities.) Students will complete the cycle when they go beyond the protective instructional environment to test their newly-acquired skills and understandings in the 'real world'.

Participants' task skills should also be assessed early in the program. If they will be going to another culture as a student or as an employee, the desire to do a good job should be highly motivating. The program could help participants conduct a 'task analysis' to identify competencies they will need, and a 'systems analysis' to obtain information about cultural and institutional differences they'll be likely to encounter. They could learn from others who have completed similar experiences – returnees who've worked in the same organization, if possible. As with intercultural relations, skills practice and situational diagnosis should be included. If participants will need to acquire technical skills that the program can not provide and are hard to learn on one's own (e.g. language proficiency, computer literacy, teaching competencies), they should arrange to obtain them elsewhere.

Since for most programs, individual goals are likely to incorporate the greatest diversity of individual differences, it is a good area in which to have students practice their learning skills by asking them to devise a plan for pursuing their own interests. The plan should identify one of several personal goals, with learning objectives for Quadrants II, III, and IV of Kolb's Learning Cycle. It should also describe appropriate strategies and procedures for attaining their goals, including sources of information and assistance. Participants should also consider how to determine the extent to which the information they gather is complete and correct, and how to measure their progress in language, koto-playing or whatever – Quadrant I. (A journal, checklist, or graph may be appropriate here, or procedures to obtain feedback from others.) Some components of the plan should be ones they can complete during the course of training; others should be included that they will need to continue after the program is over.

Orientation leaders will need to find ways in which to combine these three 'content goals' into an integrated instructional design. In doing so, they should again consider the overriding purpose of the program and apply the principles of the Learning Cycle toward that end. Some ideas follow.

Using the Learning Cycle to Teach Participants How to Learn As with other information, knowledge of effective learning strategies must be applied if it is to be remembered. By applying the Learning Cycle to the three goals just discussed, instructors should simultaneously improve the teaching of these goals and provide a chance for students to experience the Learning Cycle in action. However, we want participants to do more than to understand learning strategies – we want them to be able to USE learning strategies. For the best results in learning how to learn, participants will need to practice implementing the strategies, skills and procedures.

Although academicians like to pursue things in a neat, rational order, usually starting with Background and ending with Behavior, the world is not always so orderly. A way to help participants to become more flexible learners would be to give them practice in using different strategies. Sometimes specific information could stimulate the formulation of generalizations, using inductive processes; other times, students could be asked to apply intercultural themes or principles to particular cases, using deduction. Sometimes students could be asked to participate in a role-play or simulation, after which their behavior is analyzed; other times, they could be given information which they are asked to apply to their performance in a role-play; etc.

Participants should practice simple strategies which use their existing cognitive frameworks before attempting the more difficult cognitive and paradigm shifts. A caveat: the direction from simple to complex should not be from meaningless parts to meaningful wholes, but from simplified wholes to complex wholes (Hilgard and Bower, 1975). Since cognitive and paradigm shifts involve looking at something in a different way and coming up with new explanations and solutions, participants should be rewarded for divergent thinking when attempting these strategies. Especially as those who take risks are likely to make a lot of mistakes, innovative participants will need to be praised for their creativity (Hilgard and Bower, 1975).

According to research, the amount of time spent on a task is positively associated with achievement related to that task (Smith, 1985). Thus, programs should spend the most time on the objectives which they consider most important. Since the purpose of most orientation programs is one which ultimately involves interpersonal interaction, this suggests that, although the full cycle of learning processes should be addressed, the most time and attention should be given to the intercultural and learning skills of the Behavior quadrant. Concomitant with this emphasis, more use should be made of instructional methods involving practice and experimentation, as well as direct and vicarious experiences (see McCaffery, 1986, for a description of skills training). People do not learn a skill simply by practicing it, however – they must receive feedback concerning their effectiveness and in complex skills, the learner must know the procedure or principle involved (Smith, 1985). Learning with understanding also is more permanent and more transferable than rote learning (Hilgard and Bower, 1975). For this reason, skills should not be practiced out of context, but should be taught in relationship to cognitive frameworks as when they are used to implement intercultural learning strategies.

Finally, more than needing to know HOW to learn, participants must WANT to learn. For this reason, the program must go beyond being relevant and well-organized. A well-conceived curriculum design must be brought to life by instructional activities which are interesting, which excite in participants a sense of adventure and a desire to keep learning.

Program management: designing the 'hidden curriculum'

Program management refers to the behavioral rules and patterns that are followed in the orientation program. It includes such things as the role of the instructor (authority? facilitator? diagnostician?), the instructor's relationship with students, and the norms which participants are expected to follow. In classroom settings, it could be referred to as the 'classroom culture'.

Program management is part of the organizational structure necessary to deliver instruction, but it is not usually considered to be part of instruction itself. However, social learning theory suggests, that management is a part of instruction whether we like it or not (Bandura, 1977). Social reinforcement and role modeling are shaped – usually subconsciously – by program management, and are among the most potent of teaching methods (see Boocock, 1972; also Banks, 1976; and Shipman, 1975, for discussions of the importance of social factors in education). In fact, many believe that 'the medium is the message', and that the messages communicated implicitly through program management have more impact than messages communicated explicitly through direct instruction – thus it's sometimes thought of as the 'hidden curriculum' (Overly, 1970).

For this reason, it is important that care be taken to model the behavior that orientation leaders are trying to teach. Instructors should be able to implement the principles of good cross-cultural communication and conflict resolution in their interactions with students, and should assist students in applying those principles to situations which may arise. This will help to convey the relevance of intercultural relations and will push students further along the Learning Cycle by demonstrating ways in which intercultural knowledge, understanding and skills can be applied to the 'real world' Instructors should also model the skills and attitudes important in learning how to learn. Rather than rigidly adhering to a set body of knowledge, they should be open to new ideas and raise questions about unanticipated events. They should address problems by demonstrating their ability to diagnose situations, formulate and test hypotheses, and evaluate their effectiveness. And perhaps most of all, they should express their curiosity and enthusiasm for other cultures and for intercultural interaction.

Program and participant evaluation

The 'learning-how-to-learn' (LHTL) approach to cross-cultural orientation described in this paper has been conceptually derived. Empirical data from program evaluation and research should be obtained to determine its validity.

Detailed overviews of designs and methods pertaining to program and participant evaluation can be obtained elsewhere. See Blake and Heslin (1983); Renwick (1979); and Triandis (1977) from the cross-cultural training literature. From education and psychology, such works as Mehrens and Lehmann (1984), Worthen and Sanders (1973), and The Joint Committee on Standards for Educational Evaluation (1981) may be helpful. Communication, accountability, utilization, and other special concerns of the new field of program evaluation are described in Anderson and Ball (1980). For those interested in affective outcomes, see *How to Measure Attitudes* by Henerson, Morris, and Fitz-Gibbon (1978). However, due to some highly technical components of testing and program evaluation, novices should not rely on these works alone, but should seek professional assistance.

Conclusion

In this paper, three major goals commonly held by sojourners – interpersonal relations, task accomplishment, and personal interests – were addressed, with attention given both to making progress towards these goals, and to a fourth goal of continuing intercultural learning after the program is over. Since this fourth goal – that of 'learning how to learn' – permeates the entire program, it may be termed as 'approach'. Through the 'learning how to learn approach', orientation participants will go beyond both the culture-specific and the culture-general information, to acquire the procedures, skills and strategies required to learn about culture and intercultural interaction.

Although 'learning how to learn' is compatible with existing cross-cultural and instructional theory and research, its effectiveness is yet to be determined. The author calls upon orientation leaders to adapt this approach for use in the programs they design, and to conduct formal, rigorous evaluations of these programs.

References

Albert, R. D., Conceptual Framework for Development and Evaluation of Cross-Cultural Training Programs, *International Journal of Intercultural Relations*, **10**, 2, 1986.

American Field Service Research Department (1983). *American field service orientation handbook* (Third ed.). New York: Intercultural Press.

Anderson, S. B. and Ball, S. (1980). *The profession and practice of program evaluation*, San Francisco, CA: Jossey-Bass Publishers.

Atkinson, R. C. (1972). Ingredients for a theory of instruction. *American Psychologist*, 27, 921–931.

Bandura, A. (1977). *Social learning theory*. Englewood Cliffs, NJ: Prentice-Hall.

Banks, O. (1976). *The sociology of education* (Rev. ed.). New York: Schocken Books.

Batchelder, D and Warner, E., Eds. (1973). *Beyond experience: The experiential approach to cross-cultural education*. Brattleboro, VT: The Experiment Press.

Bennett, J., Modes of Cross-Cultural Training: Conceptualizing Cross-Cultural

Training as Education, *International Journal of Intercultural Relations*, **10**, 2, 1986.

Boocock, S. S. (1972). *An introduction to the sociology of learning.* Boston, MA: Houghton Mifflin Company.

Blake, B. F. and Heslin, R. H. (1983). Evaluating cross-cultural training. In D. Landis and R. W. Brislin (Eds.), *Handbook of intercultural training* (Vol. 1). New York: Pergamon Press.

Bloom, B. S., ed., *et al.*, (1956). *Taxonomy of educational objectives: Handbook I, cognitive domain.* New York: David McKay Company.

Blumenthal, A. L. (1977). *The process of cognition.* Englewood Cliffs, NJ: Prentice-Hall.

Brislin, R. W., A Culture General Assimilator: Preparation for Various Types of Sojourns, *International Journal of Intercultural Relations*, **10**, 2, 1986.

Brislin, R. W. and Pedersen, P. (1976). *Cross-cultural orientation programs.* New York: Gardner Press.

Canadian International Development Agency (1979). *Adaptation Program*, Hull, Quebec: CIDA Briefing Centre.

Casse, P. (1980). *Training for the cross-cultural mind.* Washington, D.C.: SIETAR.

Coon, D. (1983). *Introduction to psychology: exploration and application* (3rd ed.). New York: West Publishing Company.

Dinges, N. (1983). Intercultural competence. In D. Landis and R. W. Brislin (Eds.), *Handbook of intercultural training* (Vol. 1). New York: Pergamon Press.

Fantini, A. E., Ed. (1984). *Getting the whole picture.* Brattleboro, VT: The Experiment in International Living.

Fedigan, L. (1979). School-based elements related to achievement: A review of the literature. (ERIC Document Reproduction Service No. ED1 181042, microfiche).

Gudykunst, W. B. and Hammer, M. R. (1983). Basic training design: approaches to intercultural training. In D. Landis and R. W. Brislin (Eds.), *Handbook of intercultural training* (Vol. 1). New York: Pergamon Press.

Harlow, H. F. (1949). The formation of learning sets. *Psychological Review*, **56**, 51–65.

Hawes, F. and Kealey, D. J. (1979). *Canadians in development: an empirical study of adaptation and effectiveness on overseas assignment.* (Technical Report). Ottawa: CIDA Communications Branch, Briefing Center.

Henerson, M. E., Morris, L. L. and Fitz-Gibbon, C. T. (1978). *How to measure attitudes.* Beverly Hills, CA: Sage Publications.

Hilgard, E. R. and Bower, G. H. (1975). *Theories of learning.* Englewood Cliffs, NJ: Prentice-Hall.

Hoopes, D. (1980). *Intercultural education.* (Phi Delta Kappa Fastback. 142). Bloomington, IN: Phi Delta Kappa Foundation.

Hoopes, D. and Ventura, P. Eds. (1979). *Intercultural Sourcebook: Cross-cultural training methodologies.* Pittsburgh, PA: Intercultural Network, Inc.

Hughes, G. F. (1983). Intercultural education in elementary and secondary schools. In D. Landis and R. W. Brislin (Eds.), *Handbook of intercultural training* (Vol 3). New York: Pergamon Press.

Joint Committee on Standards for Educational Evaluation (1981). *Standards for evaluations of educational programs, projects, and materials.* New York: McGraw-Hill Book Company.

Kealey, D. J. and Ruben, B. D. (1983). Cross-cultural personnel selection criteria, issues, and methods. In D. Landis and R. W. Brislin (Eds.), *Handbook of intercultural training* (Vol. 1). New York: Pergamon Press.

King, D. (1976). *Conflict, Part C. Global perspectives: A humanistic influence on the curriculum.* New York: Center for Global Perspectives.

Kolb, D. (1976). *Learning style inventory*. Boston: McBer & Co.

Kolb, D. (1984). *Experiential learning*. Englewood Cliffs, NJ: Prentice-Hall.

McCaffery, J., Independence Effectiveness: A Reconsideration of Cross-Cultural Orientation and Training, *International Journal of Intercultural Relations*, 10, 2, 1986.

McCaffery, J., and Edwards, D. (1982). *Cross-cultural training for peace corps volunteers*. (Information Collection & Exchange Manual TR-07). Washington, D.C.: Peace Corps.

Mehrens, W. A. and Lehmann, I. J. (1984). *Measurement and evaluation in education and psychology* (3rd ed.). New York: Holt, Rinehart and Winston.

Miller, G. A., Galanter, E. and Pribram, K. H. (1960). *Plans and the structure of behavior*. New York: Holt, Rinehart & Winston.

Overly, N., Ed. (1970). *The unstudied curriculum: Its impact on children*. Washington, D.C.: ASCD.

Paige, R. M., Trainer Competencies: The Missing Conceptual Link in Orientation, *International Journal of Intercultural Relations*, 10, 2, 1986.

Pasternak, M. C. (1979). *Helping kids learn multicultural concepts: A handbook of strategies*. Champaign, IL: Research Press Co.

Peterson, P. and Walberg, H. J., eds. (1979). *Research on teaching: Concepts, findings, and implications*. Berkeley, CA: McCutchan Press.

Pusch, M. D., ed. (1979). *Multicultural education: A cross-cultural training approach*. LaGrange Park, IL: Intercultural Network, Inc.

Renwick, G. (1979). *Evaluation handbook*. LaGrange, IL: Intercultural Network, Inc.

Ruben, B. and Kealey, D. (1979). Behavioral assessment of communication competency and the prediction of cross-cultural adaptation. *International Journal of Intercultural Relations*, 3, 15–47.

Seelye, H. N. (1974). *Teaching culture: Strategies for foreign language educators*. Skokie, IL: National Textbook Company.

Shaw, M. E. (1981). *Group dynamics: The psychology of small group behavior* (Third ed). New York: McGraw-Hill Book Company.

Shipman, M. D. (1975). *The sociology of the school* (2nd ed.). London, England; Longman.

Simon, H. (1969). *The sciences of the artificial*. Cambridge, MA: MIT Press.

Smith, B. O. (1985). Research bases for teacher education. *Phi Delta Kappan*, 66, 685–690.

Smith, G. R. and Otero, G. G. (1977). *Teaching about cultural awareness*. Denver, CO: Center for Teaching International Relations, University of Denver.

Smith, R. E., Sarason, I. G. and Sarason, B. R. (1982). *Psychology: The frontiers of behavior* (2nd ed.). New York: Harper & Row.

Tolman, E. C. (1948). Cognitive maps in rats and men. *Psychology Review*, 55, 189–208.

Travers, R. M. W. (1977). *Essentials of learning* (4th ed.). New York: MacMillan.

Triandis, H. (1975). Culture training, cognitive complexity and interpersonal attitudes. In R. W. Brislin, S. Bochner and J. W. Lonner (Eds.), *Cross-cultural perspectives on learning*. New York: Halsted Press Division. John Wiley & Sons.

Triandis, H. (1977). Theoretical framework for evaluation of cross-cultural training effectiveness. *International Journal of Intercultural Relations*, 1, 19–45.

Weeks, W., Pedersen, P. and Brislin, R. W., eds. (1977). *A manual of structured experiences for cross-cultural learning*. Washington, D.C.: SIETAR.

Wight, A. R. and Hammons, M. A. (1970). *Guidelines for peace corps cross-cultural training: Part II. Specific methods and teaching techniques*. Washington, D.C.: Office of Training Support, Peace Corps.

Worthen, B. R. and Sanders, J. R. (1973). *Educational evaluation: theory and practice.* Worthington, Ohio: Charles A. Jones Publishing Co.
Youth for Understanding (n.d.). Developing a dual perspective. New York: Unpublished training materials.

Reproduced from Hughes-Weiner, G. (1986). The 'learning how to learn' approach to cross-cultural orientation. *International Journal of Intercultural Relations*, **10**, 485–505, by permission of *International Journal of Intercultural Relations*.

10.3 Management learning for Europe

Sybren Tijmstra and Kenneth Casler

Today, business managers and their organisations around the world operate in a challenging, complex environment, one in which flexibility, adaptability and responsiveness are key factors of survival. As Europe changes economically, socially, and politically, as it grows more interdependent, a new business organisation is emerging, bringing with it a new management philosophy and business practices. 'European' management – as opposed to North American and Japanese management – is now becoming recognisable. Its innovative approaches to business strategy, organisational structure and operational issues arise from the specific nature of the European context.

European businesses are by no means out of the race for a world position, nor are they straggling far behind the frontrunners. The novelty is that they are attempting to run under a new banner – a European one – in order to unlock new potential and generate competitive advantage which should benefit European industry as a whole. This cannot happen in a state of national competition and economic fragmentation. Economic convergence is imposing new ways of thinking about products and services, innovative approaches to markets, changes in business organisation and operations: put simply, a European model of business and management.

The need for European managers

Like the USA and Japan, Europe wants to be seen as a supplier of high value added, high intellectual content products and services.[1] Such products require large capital investments and sophisticated know-how to develop and market. The expertise of well-educated professionals, with backgrounds in high technology and advanced science, is especially vital. Also, critical mass in terms of financial leverage, production volumes and market size are essential in sustaining viable positions both in the Home Market and in the World Market.

For Europe, this means that fragmented, national markets must be transcended to achieve the necessary critical mass. Accepting a process of transnationalisation in nearly every business function (from research and development, procurement and logistics to human resource management) is simply a necessity, at all levels of responsibility. Business managers and their organisations must develop the flexibility, adaptability and responsiveness to face and benefit from the transnational market conditions in Europe today.

European diversity, concentration and integration

Social and cultural diversity is, and will remain, a dominant feature of European society. In every respect, this diversity is a resource that we must learn to tap. In business, the variety of existing organisational forms and management styles, different entrepreneurial attitudes and human relations in the workplace[2] pose definite challenges but also offer many opportunities to learn and to create new wealth. This diversity will also stretch our imaginations. To quote one recent article: 'the creation of effective trans-European business organizations requires new managerial approaches and systems'.[3]

European integration is a key accelerator in this process of transnationalisation which affects all levels of management today. The political pressure from European institutions to reduce economic fragmentation is intense and is reflected in efforts to complete the Single Market and Monetary Union. Likewise Community programmes to establish a European Social Charter and Statutes for a European Company will change the way in which business operates. Gradually, these pressures to build a new socio-economic and political framework will transform the business environment and lead to fundamental changes in the management mentality in Europe.

Men and organisations need to internationalise profoundly

This transformation is a dynamic, open-ended process, affecting countries all across Europe, and not just the European Community. In this context managers need a greater international awareness and cross-cultural competence than before. International companies have always depended on a mobile corps of professionals and managers for their operations. A small team of expatriate managers have traditionally gained access to the top management and boardroom positions of such firms. Now the difference between international companies and European companies is that the latter need competent, international managers at all levels of the organisation. They must be armed with the skills and attitudes to operate in different cultural contexts, with people speaking different languages and holding different assumptions about life and work.

European managers can no longer work in geographical or functional isolation. They need to share their expertise throughout the organisation, frequently crossing national borders and language barriers. As more task forces and project groups include international team members, and as the transnational dimension of product development, production and marketing intensifies, internationalism – i.e. international awareness, sensitivity and competence – becomes the critical factor of success in the corporate culture in Europe. Management development for European and international responsibility becomes a particularly strategic issue.

European management and managers

The Europeanisation of organisations, management teams and management approaches is affecting the larger companies adopting pan-European business strategies, but also a growing number of small and medium-sized companies are concerned by M&A activity, strategic alliances, subcontracting arrangements and comakership relationships. Many of the critical issues which management will be grappling with in Europe in the 1990s have been discussed in recent publications. Among them are:[4]

- achieving improved productivity, product/service quality, and organisational flexibility
- introducing new/more science and technology into products and services
- managing integrated R&D, production and marketing through 'organic' work systems (task forces, project teams)
- stimulating and organising 'intrapreneurship' in international business networks
- developing and managing the firm's international human resources.

European companies will need to tackle these issues, paying special attention to the impact of the transnational/European dimension on business strategy, organisational structure, operating processes and procedures, and human resource and management development policies. As van Dijck[5] points out, these companies will need to

- focus more on international processes than structures
- facilitate international networking
- allow for 'subtle and informal mechanisms' of control and coordination to encourage cross-cultural collaboration

- build corporate identity and commitment across borders in order to achieve a common vision shared values and a coherent style within the organisation.

Companies, regardless of size, which take a strategic commitment to the European marketplace will need to bring their management approach in line with these new realities.

Different strategies lead to different management approaches

Since it can easily find itself in a variety of geographic and socio-political contexts, a European company's decision to serve specific markets has obvious implications for its business practices. A decision to position business operations for Europe, especially when this involves managing product development, manufacturing operations and customer relations in and across different countries, will have critical consequences for the company's organisational structure, operational processes, management approach and style, and human resource requirements.

European management is different from American and Japanese management

European management will differ considerably from both American and Japanese management. Thurley and Wirdenius (1989) argue that there are three reasons for this. Firstly, European management involves mediating, and capitalising on the diversity of European cultures. Through education and experience we inherit a cultural paradigm which embraces assumptions and convictions (values) about appropriate thought and action in management situations.

Secondly, the European Community is a novel political entity very unlike the United States of America or other existing federations. Since the precise framework and membership of the European polity cannot be stabilised in the face of political and economic transformations in central and eastern Europe today, the contours of the business environment in which companies operate may remain uncertain and in flux for years to come.

Finally, companies operating in Europe are facing serious competitive challenges resulting from political, social and economic developments in the European 'Community' and from economic globalisation trends which are shaking the foundations of industralised society world-wide. European companies will necessarily undergo a transformation in all areas to achieve competitiveness.

The emergence of a European management approach has obvious implications for the profile, education, development and management of Europe managers, It has been suggested[6] that the European manager will have five characteristics which derive from operating in a transnational context:

- An ability to comprehend the European business environment, and specifically its cultural, social, political and economic complexity.
- An ability to imagine, create and lead new forms of business (networks, task forces, coordinating units) which span borders and bridge cultures
- An ability to build commitment to a corporate identity and mission shared by all members of the organisation whatever their original cultural values
- An ability to win the support of 'national' stakeholders in the company's different countries of operation
- An ability to accept and pursue transnational mobility to achieve a European career path.

Underlying these characteristics are several important assumptions about the European manager. This person will probably:

- have a solid core of *technical and managerial competence* providing him/her with fundamental confidence in his/her ability to take up challenges. This expertise will reduce personal stress levels and also make him/her acceptable to colleagues.
- display a genuine *enthusiasm and empathy for different peoples and cultures* and a willingness to discover and accommodate divergent approaches to situations and problems. This means that he/she will have the language and cultural skills to overcome communications barriers and the personal skills to achieve goals and results in all European countries.
- be self-aware, conscious of *his/her own personal values and cultural orientation*. He/she will be mindful of the impact of his/her own bias on personal relations and performance in different cultural settings and will remain open to the values and preferences of these other cultures.
- be *willing and keen to accept changes* in the professional environment throughout his/her career. This flexibility and adaptability are hallmarks of a genuinely international personality.

National cultures and identities will remain a characteristic feature of European management throughout the 1990s and beyond. It is essential, therefore, that managers recognise and accommodate through their personal and professional thought and action the multiconformity – i.e. the many enlightening differences and complementarities – of Europe.

Management learning for Europe: the education and development of European managers

The current process of Europeanisation is creating individual and organisational learning opportunities that must be structured and supported in order for European management to emerge successfully. Pre-career education and post-experience development of European managers is an imperative and a challenge. The imperative is to transform national managers at senior and middle levels into European business leaders. The challenge is how.

The Europeanisation of managers includes four important aspects of learning: awareness, knowledge, skills, and attitudes (see Table 1). Knowledge of Europe and its social, political and economic environment is a 'hard' aspect, based on learnable facts. Short training courses can provide effective solutions to the need to form a European knowledge base. Attitude, in contrast, is a soft element, based on profound, unconscious, feelings (values), both personal and societal, shared by members of the same culture or cultural cluster. It takes a long time to instil attitudes and an equally long time to modify them. Development programmes and on-the-job experience are effective in attitude formation.

Awareness of Europe,[8] and sensitivity to its differences and similarities, is expanded through knowledge, exposure and experience. In this respect its formation results from both short- and long-term efforts to learn about Europe. Skills for European management (including leadership and cross-cultural communication and language skills) can be learned and developed intensively on the job. Thus, through education, experience and development it is possible to achieve the transformation of national managers into European managers.

There are three specific learning areas in which business leaders need to be developed for European management responsibilities. They are:

(1) The European business environment
(2) European management dynamic, and
(3) Europeanisation processes (cf. Figure 1).

Table 1

	Hard aspects	*Soft aspects*
Awareness	X	X
Knowledge	X	
Skills	X	X
Attitudes		X

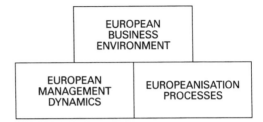

Figure 1

EUROPEAN BUSINESS ENVIRONMENT

SOCIO-POLITICAL DETERMINANTS	ECONOMIC DETERMINANTS
BUSINESS SECTOR DETERMINANTS	TECHNOLOGICAL DETERMINANTS

Figure 2

Each of these areas has several dimensions that the European manager needs to integrate and learn to be effective transnationally.

European business environment

Firstly, the European business environment is structured by a number of elements, which are knowledge-based (cf. Figure 2). An awareness and understanding of these determinants is *sine qua non* a necessity if the manager is to operate successfully across Europe.

Socio-political elements include the national heritage (history, culture, language) of each country of operation. They also include supra-national efforts made within the European Community to integrate member states (e.g. institutions, legislation, regulation). These factors are, in fact, both hard and soft and include legal obligations (e.g. employee involvement) as well as attitudes to work, leisure, and the environment in each country. All must be considered in business decisions. In comparison with Japanese and American management issues, it may be said that there is a specific 'learnable' European response to these issues.

Economic factors include national and Europe-wide industry dynamics as well as efforts to construct a single integrated economic community by 1993. Price controls, investment incentives, social charges etc. will differ from country to country until harmonisation is achieved. Europe is far more fragmented than either the United States or Japan in this respect; European managers will require a specific knowledge base on European economic issues and must be open to new developments and change. Europe's economic fragmentation is likely to persist beyond 1993 and the ultimate framework will concern far more than the 12 member states of the European Community.

In regard to technological development, current internationalisation trends are introducing greater harmonisation across industrialised societies and rapidly reducing the technological gap. Masaru Ibuka, co-founder of Sony, has claimed that the age of technological leadership for the competitive edge is over. On the contrary, the competitive edge now lies in the *marketing* of the technology. In Europe as a whole technological sophistication may vary from country-to-country and business sector-to-business sector, but there are strong and definite harmonisation trends. More important is the gradual convergence of life style in Europe and indeed around the globe which will have considerable impact on business sector and market dynamics throughout Europe, particularly in the area of marketing.

Although there still persist substantial differences between sectors in European countries, the effect of concentration trends and European integration will be to smooth out many of the local differences over the long run. In respect of technology and business sectors therefore, globalisation trends may be moving American, Japanese and European managers in fairly similar directions, particularly in terms of the complexity and diversity that they need to manage. However, Europeans are likely to gain a competitive advantage for world markets with their knowledge of and sensitivity to culturally diverse markets formed in the home market, where they learn to respond creatively, accurately and rapidly to customers in many countries.

European Management Dynamics

A second area of learning of crucial importance to national managers, is the dynamics of national approaches to management in European countries (cf. Figure 3). This covers the spectrum of soft management issues from business practices to leadership styles and personal values at work. There are two major determinants which illustrate the diversity of European management. They are:

• The diversity of business cultures in Europe, where culture is understood to consist of the traditions, practices and values of both individuals and organisations, and
• The spectrum of management values, by which is meant the patterns of

EUROPEAN MANAGEMENT DYNAMICS

BUSINESS CULTURES	MANAGEMENT VALUES

Figure 3

management behaviour which result from different educational systems, organisational models and business practices.

The tapestry of business cultures in Europe is rich. Managers who operate transnationally need to understand and work within a mosaic of values and practices.[9] They need to be creative, to recognise and adjust to diverse patterns of thought, judgement, perception and behaviour and to be able to work with many different people, members of different 'national' and organisational cultures.

An ability to read and understand cultural orientation across a broad spectrum of people and businesses in Europe is the hallmark of a European manager. It is best developed through exposure to different leadership styles, work styles, communication and collaboration styles. This ability forms not only part of the individual's managerial know-how but also part of the organisation's knowledge base. A transnational business needs to build a management team whose members are both culturally sensitive and sufficiently international in origin to ensure that the 'corporate culture' reflects the complex cultural environment in which it operates.

Management values are the sum of many factors: from individual preferences and attitudes about work and people at work, to specific organisational cultures and business practices they also include an individual's technical knowledge and skills. The European environment is rich in terms of its different conceptions of what a manager is and does. The diverse national systems of management education and training, the different personnel recruitment and career management practices, corporate organisation and management development policies all play a role in shaping the profile of the European manager. The European manager needs an understanding of this diversity in order to achieve both personal and professional goals. Organisations need a sophisticated knowledge of management recruitment, motivation and development practices around Europe in order to attract management potential and retain valuable members of its international management team, offering challenging, attractive careers.[10]

Europeanisation processes

There is a third area of learning about European management which concerns companies whose competitive advantage no longer lies exclusively at the national level but at the level where corporate vision and strategic decisions are European. Such transnational firms are developing innovative organisational structures, flexible management processes, effective cross-cultural communication systems and supra-national corporate identities to fulfill their missions (cf. Figure 4). They are able to synergise the contributions made by the different organisational units and people wherever they are located. To lead such an organisation the management team needs an awareness of European differences and similarities, on the one hand, and creative leadership and cross-border know-how, on the other. The ability and willingness to learn *all the time* is critical.

Firms across Europe will be experimenting with flatter organisational structures and decentralised units which enjoy autonomy and entrepreneurial responsibility in an integrated network. Increasingly such structures will rely on sophisticated but subtle planning and control coordination centres at the European level. It is of utmost importance in such organisational structures to achieve commitment to the corporate mission through shared values and a strong corporate identity. Competent, sensitive leadership is of the essence.

When the transnational dimension imprints the organisation, the complexity of its operations is magnified and effective communications become critical to operational success. The transnational organisation and the members of its management team will need cross-cultural communication skills to achieve its mission. These will necessarily include a knowledge of the languages and cultures in which the organisation operates, and an attitude of cooperation and learning to effectively bond the employees of the organisation wherever they work. People in different countries with differing personal and organisational values will have special need of bonding.

EUROPEANISATION PROCESS

TRANSNATIONAL STRUCTURES	TRANSNATIONAL PROCESSES
EUROPEAN IDENTITY	CROSS-CULTURAL COMMUNICATION

Figure 4

Delivering the European manager

How will European business firms achieve these goals of greater international awareness and transnational competence in their organisations? How can they effectively form a European knowledge base to underpin operations in a marketplace of such diversity and complexity? How will they unite employees across a spectrum of countries into a shared vision and common identity? Current practice in several pioneering firms[11] points towards at least three avenues of approach:

- European recruitment of managers
- European career paths and management assignments
- European management development.

European recruitment of managers

Business organisations with a European strategy will need to recruit members of its management team across borders. Since they will need access to both well-educated young graduates and experienced business professionals, these companies will need to develop cross-border recruitment strategies, increasing their awareness and understanding of local national education systems and employment practices. This recruitment expertise will be a valuable asset to the European company and give it a competitive advantage over firms locked into national recruitment systems.

To succeed and be attractive to the pool of graduates and professionals in the employment market, European companies will also need a Europe-wide image and reputation. A number of leading companies in various countries in Europe have understood the importance of a strong corporate image at a European level, not only for the marketing of their products and services but for the recruitment of skilled employees as well.[12] These companies usually have strong links with *excellent* educational institutions in several countries and pursue an active campus recruitment policy. Medium-sized companies, however, are just beginning to realise the importance of corporate image for recruitment purposes. They will recognise that special links with educational institutions (e.g. campus recruitment, 'stages', joint projects) can be a valuable asset, especially with European schools (e.g. EAP European School of Management) or national schools linked in an international network (e.g. Community of European Management Schools which includes members in Belgium, Denmark, France, Germany, Italy, The Netherlands and Spain).

It is equally important that graduates and professionals have the requisite European education, expertise, exposure and experience to be able to integrate the transnational organisational structures and promote the cross-border development strategies critical to business success in Europe. At present there are few management education centres that provide a genuinely European response to corporate management requirements. Many national business schools claim to offer international programmes and graduates. These claims, however, cannot be substantiated in many cases.

More business schools and management development centres need to develop the potential to assist European companies in useful ways with educational services and well-trained graduates. They will need to restructure their educational resources to meet the demands and challenges of the emerging business environment in Europe.

There are at least six characteristics which an educational institution will need to develop in order to offer a genuinely European service to industry.

- The course and programme offerings must have a European/international orientation; European topics and issues form an integral part of all teaching and learning modules.
- The educational approach must be based on European/international materials and be supported by readings, case studies, project work, and international assignments to ensure awareness and understanding of cross-border business.
- The faculty must be European/international in composition to a very significant degree; a truly European business school will have as many as ten nationalities on the faculty with no single country representing more than 25 to 30% of the total.
- The course/programme participants must be international in origin; again one would expect at least ten nationalities to be represented in the student body with the largest national group weighing no more than 25 to 30% of the total.
- The institution will have multiple locations and operate as a transnational organisation; this structure must make sense in educational terms otherwise it is a recipe for resource dispersion; the aim is to lever one's educational expertise in different markets and learn from these local contexts to offer an educational perspective on European management.
- The institution's management team will be international and it will have a European/international advisory board to guide and support its development. Such boards will include recognised academic members and corporate representatives whose organisations have achieved European management excellence.

In short, for an educational institution to offer the products and services that will be of value to European organisations managing cross-border development and business operations, it must itself be transnational. With expertise in the design, development and delivery of international educational programmes for international audiences, the institution demonstrates that it fully understands the needs of European business.[13]

European career paths and management assignments

Knowledge is a firm's most valuable asset. Successful human resource management aims to secure that the company's expertise and human capital is not lost or squandered. To members of the European management team it is essential to offer cross-border management assignments and career paths. Through multinational project teams and task forces, managers at all levels gain valuable exposure and experience, enhancing their ability to operate across borders. European projects bring together managers from different cultures, increase the exchange of expertise, and expand the knowledge base of the corporation. Companies must also be able to offer an international career path involving long-term management assignments in different countries and job rotations across borders and functions. This will ensure that the members of the management team develop Europe-wide experience, exposure and expertise.

European management development

On-the-job experience and challenging assignments will sensitise management to the issues affecting individual and corporate performance in the context of day-to-day operations. In addition, management development programmes are necessary to reinforce and upgrade the core knowledge, technical skills and individual attitudes that guarantee a firm's competitiveness. These programmes need to provide high potential employees with both the hard and soft tools of management, from advanced functional knowledge and techniques to strategic awareness and leadership qualities. In the case of European organisations it is necessary to provide this training with an international perspective and to do so against the backdrop of transnational business operations. Therefore, European companies will offer on-the-job management training in a number of formats: in-company programmes, consortium programmes and open courses. As frequently as possible this training will take place in a foreign country setting and with international participants. In general, companies will need to encourage and support individual efforts to upgrade and update their 'human capital' in order to 'meet the new demands of the working environment.'[14] Management learning for Europe will challenge the individual to the extreme and he will need to know that the entire organisation supports his efforts to learn.

Conclusion

In this article we have looked at the need for European managers, the characteristics of European management as well as a profile of the Euromanager, and finally at educating and developing national managers for European business. In the future business organisations need to define their markets and products across many visible and invisible barriers. In the end it is the human capital of the organisation that guarantees its success. There is a considerable time-lag in recruiting and developing European managers. However if the European firm actively develops its knowledge of the new business environment and stimulates cross-border thinking and behaviour in its activity, it will have gone a long way to ensuring its international competitiveness.

Notes

1 With few exceptions (Germany and Ireland), European countries still import a higher percentage of high tech goods than they export. On the other hand, they export more medium tech goods than they import. Japan, in contrast, exports five times more high tech goods than it imports and four times more medium tech goods. The WCR (1991) report shows that R&D expenditure as a percentage of GDP is only 2.01% in Europe as compared with 2.79% in the USA and 2.91% in Japan. Germany, at 2.88%, maintains Europe above 2%.
2 cf, van Dijck (1990).
3 van Dijck (1990), *op. cit.*, p. 475.
4 *op. cit.*, p. 475.
5 *op. cit.*, p. 475.
6 van Dijck, *op. cit.*, p. 478.
7 cf, Keith Thurley and Hans Wirdenius' comment in a recent article (1991): 'Cultural assumptions, derived from previous education and the experience of managing in a particular society not only means that management practice is profoundly different in different societies, but that management theories, models and prescriptions are also considerably affected by the language and concepts used and the type of goals which are seen as important.'
8 The first stage in the development of a Euromanager is becoming aware and being uninhibited by the political, cultural and social diversities in Europe. The Euromanager will need to become aware of and be able to distinguish between distinct cultural clusters: the Anglo cluster (UK, NL, US), the Nordic cluster (DK, N, S), the Germanic cluster (D, A, CH) and the Latin cluster (B, F, I, E, P). cf. van Dijck.
9 cf. Hofstede, G. (1989): 'Culture is mental software which affects the way we think feel, perceive the world and behave.' p. 391. Culture manifests itself in several ways: through values and practices. Values are profound, often unconscious choices, and reflect broad personal feelings about others, situations, issues. Practices are more superficial and represent 'collective habits', the ways things are done (in a community or in an organisation). Thus culture is 'the collective

programming of the mind which distinguishes the members of one category of people from another.' p. 391. Thurley and Wirdenius (1989) argue: 'Cultural assumptions, derived from previous education and the experience of managing in a particular society not only means that management (ent practice is profoundly different in different societies, but that management theories, models and prescriptions are also considerably affected by the language and concepts used and the types of goals which are seen as important.' *op. cit.*, p. 128.

10 van Dijck (1990): 'Human resource management will have to play a strategic and critical role in the process of Internationalization and transnationalization of economic and social life in Europe,' *op. cit.*, p. 179.

11 See Barham (1991).

12 For the second straight year in 1991, Young & Rubicam and Le Point have published a ranking of leading companies as seen by 1000 graduates of top educational institutions in France, the UK, Germany, Italy and Spain who are interested in a European business career.

13 There are only a very few business schools in Europe today who can claim this expertise. Some examples include IMD, INSEAD, London Business School, and EAP.

14 van Dijck (1990), *op. cit.*, p. 478.

Bibliography

Barham, K., *The Quest for the International Manager: a Survey of Human Resource Strategies*. The Economist Intelligence Unit and Ashridge Management Guides, 1991.

Bartlett, C. and Ghoshal, S., *Managing across Borders*, 1989.

van Bockstaël, A., The Training of International Managers, *International Management Development*, no. 1, 1988, pp. 9–11.

Bials, J-M., Le Marché Unique des Cadres, *L'Express*, 6 October, 1989, pp. 45–251.

Bournois, F., Chauchat J-M., How to prepare Euromanagers for 1993, *European Management Journal*, 8/1, March 1990, pp. 3–18.

Commission of the European Communities, *Panorama of EC Industry, 1990*, 1990.

Davidson, S., *Building Pan-European Teams*, Eurobusiness, July 1989, pp. 28–35.

van Dijck, J. J. J., Transnational Management in an Evolving European Context, *European Management Journal*, 8/4, December 1990, pp. 474–479.

International Career Orientations of Young European Graduates, *European Management Development Journal*, no. 2, 1990, pp. 21–23.

Hofstede, G., Organising for Cultural Diversity, *European Management Journal*, 7/4, 1989.

Hofstede G., Bollinger, D., *Les Différences Culturelles dans le Management*, Editions d'Organisation, Paris, 1987.

IMD/World Economic Forum, *The World Competitiveness Report*, 1991.

Laurent, A., The Cultural Diversity of Western Conceptions of Management, In *Managing in Different Cultures*, Joynt P., Werner M., (eds), Oslo, 1985.

Handing, S., Philips, D., Fogerty, M., *Contemporary Values In Western Europe: Unity, Diversity and Change*, Macmillan, London, 1986.

Prahalad, C. K., Doz, Yves, L., *The Multinational Mission*, New York Free Press, 1987.

Saias, M., Compétitivité et Strategies des Entreprises face à l'Horizon – 92, *Revue Française de Gestion*, 3, 4, 5, 1989, pp. 114–122.

Van Schendelen, Business and Government Relations in Europe, *European Affairs*, 4/2, 1990, pp. 81–87.

Thèvenet, M., Une Gestion des Ressources Humaines Européenne, est-elle Possible? *Revue Française de Gestion*, 3, 4, 5, 1991, pp. 62–67.

Thurley, K., Wirdenius, H., *Towards European Management*, London, Pitman, 1989.

Thurley, K., Wirdenius, H., Will Managers become 'European'?: Strategic Choice for Organisations, *European Management Journal*, 9/2, June 1991, pp. 127–133.

Reproduced from Tijmstra, S. and Casler, K. (1992). Management learning for Europe. *European Management Journal*, **10** (1), 30–8, by permission of *European Management Journal*.

Index